International Patent Rights Harmonisation

With reference to China, this book examines the course of international patent rights harmonisation; its characteristics as well as impediments. It evaluates patent law development over the course of the last three decades by drawing on the most up-to-date Chinese language sources. In the process, the volume focuses on China's patent legislation, its achievements and weaknesses, as well as the intrinsic limitations, especially as far as enforcement is concerned. The author pays close attention to the unique societal background in China, a country that did not provide constitutional recognition to private property rights until 2004 and where a property law entered into force as late as 2013, 30 years after the first promulgation of the patent law.

Global trade policy makers, IP professionals and businesses will benefit from the insights presented by the chapters as they will help them to appreciate the achievements and the controversies pursuant to China's efforts in patent protection. While serving as a useful case study for countries seeking to leverage patent protection as a driver for economic development, the book will equally facilitate Chinese legislature to reflect on its patent legislation development, specifically on legislative policy choices.

An additional analytical strength of the volume is that it compares the Chinese patent legislation with the American Invents Act and the European Patent Convention. It discovers the differences between the three patent legislations by using the minimum patent protection standards set down by the TRIPS Agreement as the benchmark. The results of the comparisons suggest that China has successfully harmonised its patent legislation with the global patent protection system, and often opts for higher patent protection standards. The book also considers whether China could learn lessons from Japan and India in their respective patent legislation and policy choices.

With China undertaking a fourth patent law amendment, the provisions contained in the second draft of the Patent Law 2015, which was published in December 2015, are included in the analysis.

Weinian Hu is a research fellow at the Centre for Private and Economic Law, Vrije Universiteit Brussel, Belgium. A Chinese national from Shanghai, Dr Hu's career has bridged Asia and Europe at the intersection of academia, diplomacy and industry. In addition to her academic pursuits in international trade law in general, and patent law and intellectual property rights protection in particular, she acquired extensive international experience by working with a global bank in China, an inter-governmental organisation in Singapore, a non-governmental organisation in Malaysia and a global-leading public affairs agency in Belgium. She also served as consultant for the European Union for the Asia-Europe Meeting (ASEM), the multilateral political dialogue process between the Asian and the European regions. Dr Hu holds degrees from Chinese, British and Belgian universities.

'Weinian Hu's book offers an up-to-date introduction to Chinese patent law at the light of the global harmonisation process. The pan-Asian perspective and the insights on local features make the book a valuable source for those who want to understand Chinese patent law in a broader evolving context.'

Alain Strowel, *Professor UCLouvain, Université Saint-Louis, Munich Intellectual Property* Centre

International Patent Rights Harmonisation

The Case of China

Weinian Hu

to review in NOLO Patents Book + Patents Defns

— re-examination
— pre- + post-grant review
— supplemental exam / re-exam
— PCT, esp timeline
—

China questions
- time from application to grant + publish?
  from U.S. patent appl. date or beginning of China national phase?
- "Implementing Regulations of the Patent Law of China 2010"
  - is this the latest version?

Routledge
Taylor & Francis Group
LONDON AND NEW YORK

First published 2017 by Routledge

2 Park Square, Milton Park, Abingdon, Oxfordshire OX14 4RN
52 Vanderbilt Avenue, New York, NY 10017

Routledge is an imprint of the Taylor & Francis Group, an informa business

First issued in paperback 2018

British Library Cataloguing-in-Publication Data
A catalogue record for this book is available from the British Library

Library of Congress Cataloging-in-Publication Data
A catalog record for this book has been requested

ISBN: 978-1-4724-8138-2 (hbk)
ISBN: 978-0-367-19661-5 (pbk)

Typeset in Galliard
by Cenveo Publisher Services

Contents

Acknowledgements

I am indebted to many people who have, in their own capacity or out of pure kindness and friendship, spurred me on in my relentless pursuit of the subject of patent rights protection. I am grateful to Vivienne Feyen, Myra and Michael Somerton, Jens Schovsbo, Paul Vandoren and Johan Erauw for their immeasurable support – intellectually, physically or morally. Ambassador Vandoren first introduced me to the fascinating world of intellectual property rights protection more than ten years ago. Professor Schovsbo provided me with valuable insights in international patent rights harmonisation. Professor Erauw, my doctoral supervisor at the University of Gent (Belgium), to me epitomises the Chinese saying – 'He who taught you a day is your mentor for life'.

My thanks are due to Harold Tor, John Paul Van Keirsbilck, Deva Rangarajan, Wenliang Zhang, Tobias Rettig, Johanna Vrombaut and Erinda Mehmeti for helping to proofread the manuscript in the summer of 2016.

Delphine, my beautiful daughter, brought me many delightful moments amid the lonely and gruelling process of drafting. My deepest gratitude goes to my beloved parents who gave me the strength, the courage and the determination to overcome every hurdle life has thrown at me.

Abbreviations

AQSIQ	Administration for Quality Supervision, Inspection and Quarantine
ARIPO	African Regional Intellectual Property Office
ASEAN	Association of Southeast Asian Nations
ASPEC	ASEAN Patent Examination Co-operation Programme
CCOIC	China Chamber of International Commerce
CIETAC	China International Economic and Trade Arbitration Commission
CML	Chronic myeloid leukaemia
CRC	China Record Cooperation
DCGI	Drug Controller General of India
DSB	Dispute settlement body
DSM	Dispute settlement mechanism
DSU	Dispute settlement understanding
ECJ	European Court of Justice
EPC	European Patent Convention
EPO	European Patent Office
IP5	Five IP Offices
GAC	General Administration of Customs
GATT	General Agreement on Tariffs and Trade
GATS	The General Agreement on Trade in Services
GI	Geographical indications
ICJ	International Court of Justice
IPAB	Intellectual Property Appellate Board
IPR	Intellectual property rights
ISA	International Searching Authority
JPO	Japan Patent Office
KIPO	Korean Intellectual Property Office
LDC	Least developed country
MITI	Ministry of International Trade and Industry
MFN	Most-favoured-nation treatment
MoU	A memorandum of understanding
NCAC	National Copyright Administration of China
NPC	National People's Congress
OAPI	L'Organisation Africaine de la Propriété Intellectuelle
Paris Convention	Paris Convention on Industrial Property Protection
PCT	Patent Cooperation Treaty
PLT	Patent Law Treaty

PPH	Patent prosecution highway
PSB	Public Security Bureau
SAIC	State Administration for Industry and Commerce
SCP	Standing Committee on the Law of Patents
SHARE	Strategic Handling of Applications for Rapid Examination
SIPO	State Intellectual Property Office
SPC	Supreme People's Court
SPLT	Substantive Patent Law Treaty
SPP	Supreme People's Procuratorate
TDF	Tenofovir disoproxil fumarate
TRIPS	Agreement on Trade-Related Aspects of Intellectual Property Rights
UKIPO	United Kingdom Intellectual Property Office
USPTO	US Patent and Trademark Office
WIPO	World Intellectual Property Organization
WTO	World Trade Organization

Cases

Allen Archery Inc. v. *Browning Manufacturing Co.*
Assco Gerüste GmbH v. *Wilhelm Layher GmbH*
Bayer Corporation v. *Union of India*
Bishwanath Prasad v. *Hindustan Metal Industry*
Bocchi Food Trade International v. *Commission*
Canada – Patent Protection of Pharmaceutical Products
Centocor Ortho Biotech v. *Abbott Labs*
Chen v. *China Record Corporation*
China – Measures Affecting Financial Information Services and Foreign Financial Information Suppliers
China – Measures Affecting the Protection and Enforcement of Intellectual Property Rights
Chint v. *Schneider*
Cordis v. *Commission*
Cross Medical Products Inc. v. *Medtronics Sofamor Danek Inc.*
Darcy v. *Allein*
Denken KK v. *Yuai Shoji*
Diamond v. *Chakrabarty*
Diversitech Corp. v. *Century Steps Inc.*
Dowagiac Manufacturing Co. v. *Minnesota Moline Plow Co.*
Environmental Designs Ltd. v. *Union Oil Co. of California*
European Communities – Protection of Trademarks and Geographical Indications for Agricultural Products and Foodstuffs
F. Hoffmann-La Roche Ltd v. *Cipla Ltd*
Federal Republic of Germany v. *Council of the European Union*
Graham v. *John Deere Co.*
Haberman v. *Jackel Int'l Ltd*
Imperial Chem. Indus. Ltd v. *Controller General of Patents*
International Fruit Co. NY v. *Produktschap voor Groenten en Fruit*
Larson Manufacturing Company of South Dakota Inc. v. *Aluminart Products Limited*
Logan v. *Lehman*
Lucent Techs. Inc. v. *Gateway Inc.*
Meryem Demirel v. *Stadt Schwäbisch Gmünd*
Novartis AG v. *Adarsh Pharma*
Novartis AG v. *Union of India*
Parfums Christian Dior S.A. v. *Tuk Consultancy B.V.*

1 Introduction

I Background

I) *International patent rights harmonisation*

Patent rights protection is a key component of international trade. The expansion of international trade requires patent rights to be able to cross the national borders within which they are protected. This requirement can only be fulfilled when the relevant national patent systems are harmonised with regard to application and protection.

Concluded in 1883, the Paris Convention on Industrial Property Protection (Paris Convention) is the first attempt to harmonise patent protection at international level on procedural compatibility. In the last century a series of international patent harmonisation treaties succeeded in a few areas. For example, the Patent Cooperation Treaty (PCT) enables patent protection in multiple jurisdictions after a single international filing. Also, thanks to the Agreement on Trade-Related Aspects of Intellectual Property Rights (TRIPS), protection standards on substantive subject matters are harmonised at the minimum level among all the members of the World Trade Organization (WTO). Notwithstanding, no treaties on substantive patent harmonisation at the maximum level have ever been concluded. Notably, the negotiations for the Substantive Patent Law Treaty (SPLT) were suspended in 2006. When international patent rights harmonisation is not achieved at the substantive maximum level, the global patent system remains fragmented. Consequently, international trade will continue to be impeded and unable to realise its full potential.

Though in the past it was relevant only to a few economically advanced countries, international patent rights harmonisation has attracted global attention in recent years, mainly because more and more countries have acceded to the WTO. World Trade Organization accession means that all WTO members, including developing countries, transitional economies as well as the least-developed countries, must harmonise their respective patent legislation with the TRIPS Agreement in terms of protection and enforcement.

China's participation in the process of international patent rights harmonisation was prompted by the country's WTO accession negotiations, which started in the late 1970s in the aftermath of the Cultural Revolution. Although a latecomer to patent legislation, China is nowadays recognised as the force behind the world's growth in patent application and a major applicant of the multiple patent application systems, such as those established by the PCT and the European Patent Office. Up until July 2012, China has cumulatively granted more than one million invention patents, which made it the fastest growing country to achieve the number in merely 27 years.[1]

II) Patent rights protection in China

The evolution of China's patent legislation is itself a process of international patent rights harmonisation and it is characterised by achievements and controversies.

Within three decades of the enactment of the first patent law in 1984 China established a comprehensive framework of legislation for patent protection. It is not only in full compliance with the relevant international treaties to which China has acceded, but also often obliges higher protection standards *vis-à-vis*, for example, the minimum protection standards set down by the TRIPS Agreement. In recent years China has become one of the top patent applicant countries in the world. In 2015 Chinese applicants filed a total of 29,846 PCT applications, which ranked third in the world after the US and Japan. China's home-grown technology companies, such as ZTE Corporation and Huawei Technologies, have become the world's leaders in technology innovation. For example, since 2010, ZTE Corporation has been ranked among the world's Top three PCT applicants each year. As a global leader in telecommunications and information technology, ZTE Corporation has established 20 state-of-the-art R&D centres in Asia, North America and Europe, and employs over 30,000 research professionals in the development of next-generation technologies.

Despite the achievements, controversies over patent rights protection in China persist and are reflected mainly in two aspects. One concerns weaker enforcement and the other is in relation to the innovation policies that were implemented in more recent years. China's weaker enforcement in patent protection, or in intellectual property rights (IPR) protection at large, has as its root cause the judicial unpreparedness sustained prior to the promulgation of the country's first patent law. China's controversial innovation policies refer especially to the government's tactic of engaging patent application as a vehicle to nurture an innovative society, in order to transform its economy from an export-driven one to ultimately one driven by innovation. Some have cautioned that such a policy would cause market distortion and high patent application numbers may lead to compromised patent quality.

The issue of judicial unpreparedness may be examined in two forms: legislature and personnel. China's first Patent Law was promulgated before private property rights were recognised by the country's Constitution in 2004. China has been a Communist state since 1949 and therefore, by default, all properties, real and intellectual, are collectively owned by the State. In the absence of constitutional recognition, protection for patent rights, and for IPR at large, sought judicial justification from the general principles of civil law, which has established the principle of civil and property rights protection, including IPR protection, since 1986. Prior to that, in order to pave the way for providing private property protection, China declared that it would follow a socialist commodity economic development model. This being the case, rights of disposition over commodities were introduced to the society and IPR protection immediately found its logical place in legislation.

1 Available at http://english.sipo.gov.cn/specialtopic/number/index_4.html (last accessed 5 April 2016).

However, it is doubtful how much these efforts succeeded in influencing Chinese society concerning property and patent rights and their protection. With regard to personnel, China simply was not able to acquire adequate qualified staff for enforcement in the run up to reinstating the judiciary after the Cultural Revolution. As a consequence of the Cultural Revolution from 1966 to 1976, the country's higher education was completely abolished and resulted in the loss of a whole generation of legal professionals. In parallel, since at the time innocence and guilt were decided by social class and judged by the Communist Party, the legal profession became redundant in China and legal professionals were compelled to change their job to that of factory worker or peasant. As a quick solution to the personnel shortage, retired army officers ventured into the judiciary and were given the power of enforcement. Another solution to mitigate the lack of judicial capacity was to rely heavily upon administrative enforcement, for which personnel required less legal competence but, as a result, the enforcement outcomes could be compromised. In recent years, although China has taken concrete steps to enhance judicial enforcement, including in the area of patent rights, the legacy of personnel shortages has had a long-term effect on enforcement efficiency and effectiveness. Other causes resulting in weaker patent rights enforcement include institutional defects and local protectionism.

III) International patent rights harmonisation – the case of China

China has been at the forefront of patent protection ever since shortly after patent legislation was introduced in the country. It was, for example, one of the first countries in the world to extend the patent protection term to 20 years in 1992. Additionally, it may be surprising to many that China often opts for higher patent protection standards, if one makes a comparison between the substantive measures adopted by the Chinese patent legislation and those prescribed by the TRIPS Agreement. This policy choice nonetheless did not conform to China's cultural tradition and economic/social reality, especially at the beginning of its patent law development.

Once a technology-dependent country like China, Japan implemented patent legislation more than a century ago in order to facilitate technology transfer. Japanese patent legislation has been heavily influenced by industrial policies, which are, nonetheless, moulded on cultural traits and traditional values. Japan is now one of the world's most innovative countries. Looking at India, as one of the world's biggest developing countries, ever since independence it has been conscious of balancing international obligations to patent protection with domestic development objectives, such as the success of the generic pharmaceutical industry. Based on this premise and facilitated by the legislature, when public interest and patent protection are in conflict, the former shall always prevail. In comparison, China did not elect to have a moderate policy approach towards patent protection. Neither did China exploit the transitional measures offered by TRIPS in order to mitigate its adverse impact on the country's domestic industry and to allow the society to be better prepared for the transition from collective to private property ownership, including intellectual properties.

The contrast between China's more advanced legislation but weaker enforcement in patent protection results in much soul-searching. The controversies in patent policy also necessitate close examination. What methods did China use in order to harmonise its domestic patent legislation with international patent protection standards? Why is international patent harmonisation necessary? How has China's patent legislation been evolving in the last three decades? What measures did China undertake to strengthen its patent law enforcement mechanism? Why does weaker enforcement persist?

II Structure of the book

To reflect on these questions, the book will examine the process of international patent rights harmonisation and analyse China's patent protection legal framework from the point of view of international patent rights harmonisation. It will also evaluate China's patent legislation and policy choices by drawing on experiences from India and Japan in the same regard. The book will proceed in ten chapters.

Chapter 2 begins with a historical review of patent development throughout the world. Chapter 3 argues the rationales for establishing patent legislation and for international patent rights harmonisation. Chapter 4 presents China's judicial system and Chapter 5 examines the country's legal framework of IPR protection, including legislation and enforcement, as well as the jurisdiction of IP cases in China. Chapter 6 enquires into the evolution of patent legislation in China. Chapters 7 and 8 compare China's pursuit of patent legislation and policy with the cases of Japan and of India, respectively. The question of China's patent policy concerning the high number of patent applications will also be analysed. Chapter 9 evaluates how China harmonised its patent legislation with the TRIPS Agreement and investigates the strengths of China's substantive patent legislation by comparing it with American patent law and the European Patent Convention (EPC). The chapter will then provide an analysis of the challenges that China's patent protection is still facing and the achievements the country has amassed.

The book is as up-to-date as possible. The second draft text of China's Patent Law 2015, which was published in December 2015, is duly referred to in the book. Readers are welcome to suggest improvements or make other comments, and can email me at: weinian.hu@gmail.com. It goes without saying that all errors and omissions are the sole responsibility of the author.

2 The process of international patent rights harmonisation

I Overview

Patent rights are legal monopolies that the law recognises in their owners the privilege of exclusive use or exploitation of their creations, including inventions, utility models and industrial designs, for a limited time. Such privilege is obtained after the creation is publicly disclosed by the owner, based on the premise of encouraging industrial progress from which the community should profit. Once the period of the granted privilege lapses, the public will possess the creation.[1]

Patent legislation is usually drafted with the objective of incentivising innovation and developing and commercialising inventions.[2] What legislation aims to achieve in terms of protection is a balance between protecting the freedom of trade and avoiding the adverse effect of a monopoly harmful to the public. Patent legislation also defines formalities and obligations that a right-holder must follow including, for example, administrative procedures for obtaining the right, the duration of the privilege and the fees to be paid.

Initially, the remit of patent rights was confined to national territories so as to attract tradesmen to make new products and introduce new manufacturing processes; later, it went beyond national territories thanks to international trade,[3]of which patent is a component. Patent holders therefore started to look for efficient means to acquire, and subsequently to protect, their exclusive rights in new territories where trade reached, although the initial rights were awarded only in the locality where patent application was submitted. If protection in multiple locations succeeded, patent holders would, nonetheless, face challenges in enforcement while pursuing multiple actions against infringement in cross-border disputes.[4] Due to the characteristic of territoriality embedded in patent rights, successive litigations may trigger different applications of domestic and international patent protection standards

1 Ladas S., *Patents, Trademarks, and Related Rights, National and International Protection*, Vol. 1. (Cambridge, MA: Harvard University Press, 1975) pp. 2–3.

2 Mazzoleni R. and Nelson R., 'Economic theories about the benefits and costs of patents'. 32 *Journal of Economic Issues* 4 (1998) 1031, 1033.

3 Bouazzaoui A., *The Impact of the International Patent System on Developing Countries* (WIPO, A/39/13 ADD.2, 2003) Available at: www.wipo.int/meetings/en/doc_details.jsp?doc_id=17556 (last accessed 16 January 2016).

4 Bender G. A., 'Clash of the Titans: the territoriality of patent law v. the European Union'. 40 *The Journal of Law and Technology* 1 (2000) 49; also Berrier E. F. Jr., 'Global patent costs must be reduced'. 36 *The Journal of Law and Technology* 473 (1996) 476–477.

to the same set of facts. This may lead to conflicting judgments and sometimes irreconcilable outcomes.[5]

I) Introduction

When discussing harmonisation in general, one must look at four legal elements together, which are: 1) legislative texts and regulations containing rules of laws and procedures for their application; 2) judicial and administrative decisions construing and applying these texts; 3) traditional techniques and modes of handling legal materials, and finally; 4) philosophical, political and ethical ideas and ideals. Harmonising IPR laws will further involve two factors. First, the procedural mechanism of IPR application and, second, the amendment of existing laws, which reflects the challenges that law has always had to deal with. This process implies reconciliation of conflicting demands representing the need for stability and for change.[6] These two factors are interwoven; one cannot survive without the other.

Harmonising patent laws across a range of countries requires a quest for uniform solutions for specific problems transcending national territories and that are experienced universally by the countries involved. In this respect, attempts made at the international level so far aimed to remove the impediments and risks that foreign patent right-holders are exposed to by superimposing international protection standards on national patent laws. As the number of international patent applications has been increasing consistently over the years[7], and since a fragmented world patent system will damage effective and efficient protection worldwide, international patent rights harmonisation has been under deliberation for many years, in fact ever since the end of the Industrial Revolution when international trade began to boom.[8]

The Paris Convention on Industrial Property Protection (Paris Convention), concluded in 1883, is the first successful attempt to harmonise international patent rights, and the TRIPS Agreement is the most significant progress achieved in recent years in the same regard.

5 For example, International Association for the Protection of Intellectual Property, Question Q174–Jurisdiction and Applicable Law in the Case of Cross-border Infringement of Intellectual Property Rights, 2003/I Y.B. 827–28, Oct. 25–28, 2003 (recognising the need for a fairer and more efficient method of resolving cross-border controversies); European Max-Planck Group for Conflict of Laws in Intellectual Prop., 'Exclusive jurisdiction and cross-border IP (patent) infringement: suggestions for amendment of the Brussels I Regulation' 29(5) *European Intellectual Property Review* 195, 195–96 (2007), (suggesting the need to amend the Brussels Regulation on Jurisdiction and Enforcement of Judgments in Civil and Commercial Matters, EC Regulation No 44/2001, to improve the efficiency of transnational dispute resolution).

6 Professor Ladas further argued that, although many think about only the first element in law, the other three elements give law its living content which they constitute the law 'as is' rather than the illusion of law. Ladas S. *Patents, Trademarks, and Related Rights, National and International Protection* Vol. 1 (Cambridge, MA: Harvard University Press, 1975) pp. 10–11.

7 For example, in total, innovators filed some 2.7 million patent applications worldwide in 2014, up 4.5 per cent from 2013. Worldwide patent applications have grown in each year since 2003, with the exception of 2009. Press Release: *Global Patent Filings Rise in 2014 for Fifth Straight Year; China Driving Growth*, PR/2015/786. (Geneva: WIPO 14 December 2015). Available at www.wipo.int/pressroom/en/articles/2015/article_0016.html (last accessed 18 January 2016).

8 Reichman J. H. and Dreyfuss R. C., 'Harmonisation without consensus: critical reflections on drafting a substantive patent law treaty'. 57 *Duke Law Journal* 85 (2007).

II) Early history of patent development

The origin of the word 'patent' came from the Latin *litterae patentes*, which means 'open letter'. Therefore, essentially, patent means a public document conferring certain rights, privileges, titles, or offices.

Patent was founded in Europe. The German miners in the Alps seem to be the ones who first developed the notion of monopoly in their new processes back in the thirteenth century.[9]

Later, patent evolved to become a scheme of grace and favour granted only by the state or monarch.[10] This meant that patent protection, perhaps as a trade practice, was then offered as a reward for loyalty or a form of privilege when a patent, an 'open letter', was granted. The first recorded patent was granted to John of Ultynam by King Henry VI in England in 1449, for a method of making stained glass. The first patent legislation, the Statute of Monopolies, was enacted in 1623 in England following the landmark case *Darcy* v. *Allein*, which is most widely known as the Case of Monopolies. The case involved Edward Darcy, the plaintiff, who received from Queen Elizabeth a licence to import and to sell all playing cards that were to be marketed in England. This arrangement was partly motivated by the Queen's concern that card-playing had become a problematic pastime among her subjects and that having one person controlling the trade in cards would limit the activity. When the defendant, T. Allein, sought to make and to sell his own playing cards, Darcy sued him in order to defend his monopoly and prevent competition. The court eventually decided that the monopoly granted by the Queen was invalid. It was held that the monopoly restricted trade and was used only for the monopolist's private gains and not for public good although the Queen had intended it so. Later, Section 6 of the Statute of Monopolies stipulated that the 'true and first inventor' of 'any manner of new manufacture' could receive a 14-year-long privilege over the invention. The prerequisite for acquiring this privilege was that the monopoly should not be abusive or be abused in ways contrary to the law, state interests, trade and economic interests. In reflecting on contemporary patent legislation, finding a balance between monopolies and public good seems still to be what legislators aim to achieve nowadays. In addition, the Statute of Monopolies declared all monopolies void, except the monopoly of inventions. The Statute laid down the conditions for granting a patent and set the limit of the privileges that patent rights could confer. It stated that a patent grant might be conferred on any person, including foreigners, as long as they were 'the true and first inventor' for 'new manufactures within the realm' and 'which others at the time of making such letter patent and grant shall not use'.[11] This provision, which provided that no patent protection may be granted to an invention for manufactures which are already used abroad or are to be worked abroad, remains a valid principle to date.

Besides England's Statute of Monopolies, Venice established the world's first patent system in 1474.[12] At the time, a decree was promulgated in order to introduce the concept of novelty, registration of new device, term of exclusive rights, of infringement, as well as of compulsory licence.[13] Under the Venetian patent system, the term of market monopoly

9 Wegner H., *Patent Harmonisation* (London: Sweet and Maxwell) pp. 2–3.

10 MacQueen H. *et al.*, *Contemporary Intellectual Property: Law and Policy* (1st Ed.). (OUP, 2007) p. 360.

11 Section 6, the Statute of Monopolies (1624).

12 Anderson M. *et al.* (Eds), *The Modern Law of Patents.* (London: Butterworths, 2005) p. 3.

13 *Patent Teaching Kit.* (Munich: European Patent Office, 2009).

was ten years.[14] The patent system proved an effective instrument for encouraging innovation by offering incentives to inventors who then entered into social contract with the city state. It is said that about 600 patents, approximately five patents per year, were granted in Venice from 1474 to 1594. Galileo was awarded a patent on a water pump in 1594.[15] Records of patent protection in the early days also revealed that, although disputes always existed as far as contracts of patent grant were concerned, if a balance of interests was appropriately struck the court was always willing to award a monopoly.[16]

Following the English Statute of Monopolies and the Venetian patent system, the first patent legislation in the US came into force in 1790 and then the French Patents Act in 1791. Between 1800 and 1843 patent legislation was adopted by more countries. For example, Austria adopted patent legislation in 1810, Brazil in 1830, Mexico in 1832, Chile in 1840 and Paraguay in 1845.[17]

As is illustrated by the early patent history in Venice, over the centuries a patent system has served as an effective driver to stimulate a country's industrial development, although such a driver was sometimes construed with policy bias. For example, Germany did not grant product patents for substances manufactured by chemical processes at the end of the nineteenth century.[18] Similarly, Japan did not grant patents for chemical substances until 1976. India, after its independence, stopped granting patents for food and pharmaceutical products when the Patents Act was adopted in 1970, since the country wished to quickly develop a generic pharmaceutical industry.

Despite being territorial in nature, patent has, at the same time, an intrinsic international character. For example, one reason for the Venetian Republic to grant patents to tradesmen was to attract those from outside the Republic to bring new crafts and manufacturing methods to the city state. Nonetheless, restrained by territoriality, monopolies are only valid within the territories of the state where patent is granted and rights conferred. Inevitably, obstacles to patent protection will arise as soon as patent rights go abroad since the character of territoriality will be challenged after a border is crossed. Within this context, the obstacles are two-fold. Firstly, different countries have different patent laws and, therefore, the effect of protection and enforcement prescribed by national law stop at the national border. Once the border is crossed, patents will not be recognised, no protection will be provided and patent holders will not be able to enforce their rights as a result. Secondly, in order not to lose novelty of an invention, multiple applications of the same invention must be submitted almost simultaneously in all countries where protection is sought. This will be a strenuous task because, for example, patent applications must be submitted in the

14 In the Han Dynasty (206 BC–220 AD) in China, there was an occasional grant of patent-like privileges for certain industries for the exclusive use of new processes such as salt distilling or iron smelting, and for the exclusive sale of the products obtained there from. See Ganea P., 'Patents, utility models and designs' in C. Heath (Ed.) *Intellectual Property Law in China* (New York: Kluwer Law International, 2005) p.1.

15 Galileo nonetheless did not provide the details of his invention before the patent was granted – he only stated the prospective use and the performance of the water pump. He was given a privilege to use the invention exclusively, provided he made the device within a year. The requirement to actually make the invention in order not to lose the patent was common in the Venetian patent system. *Patent Teaching Kit*. (Munich: European Patent Office, 2009).

16 Therefore, in *Darcy* v. *Allein* the monopoly over trade in playing cards was struck down partly due to the fact that there was no discernible advantage to the public of allowing such a monopoly to continue. See MacQueen H. *et al.*, *Contemporary Intellectual Property: Law and Policy* (1st Ed.). (OUP, 2007) p. 360.

17 Available at www.encyclopedia.com/topic/Patents.aspx (last accessed 17 January 2016).

18 German Patent Law 1877.

official language of the country concerned and there are also different application formalities to follow.

At the end of the Industrial Revolution, following the expanding volume of cross-border trade, and in order to ensure that patent rights were recognised and mutually respected regardless of national frontiers, the need for international patent rights harmonisation became a compelling issue. Thus, in 1883, the Paris Convention was concluded in order to settle the conflict between the territorial nature of patent rights and the urgent need to extend recognition and protection for patent rights beyond territories and across borders.[19]

III) Characteristics of patent systems

While recognising the inherent diversities among the national patent systems, it is worth noting that they share certain characteristics at the same time.

1. Territoriality

Patent was born with the principle of territoriality,[20] which means that 'acts of foreign sovereigns should, when appropriate, give effect within another state's territory and that courts of all nations should indulge a presumption against the extraterritorial impact of law'.[21] Such a characteristic of territoriality limits the remit of patent rights within the jurisdiction where such rights are granted.[22] The territorial nature of patent rights is evident when considering the American patent law, as Professor Goldstein pointed out.[23] For example, 35 US Code 154(a)(1) states that every patent contains 'a grant to the patentee [...] of the right to exclude others from making, using, offering for sale, or selling the invention throughout the United States [...]' Also, 35 US Code 271(a) states that '[...] whoever without authority makes, uses or sells any patented invention, within the United States during the term of the patent therefore, infringes the patent'. The American case law consistently upholds the same principle. For example, in *Dowagiac Manufacturing Co.* v. *Minnesota Moline Plow Co.*, the Court decided that '[t]he right conferred by a patent under

19 Other similar international intellectual property conventions, such as the Berne Convention for the Protection of Literary and Artistic Works, were also enacted in the same context. The Berne Convention was concluded in September 1886 and came into force in December 1887. The Berne Convention is the first multilateral treaty for copyright protection and it sets out the national treatment. It provides a minimum standard for protection so that exclusive rights must be granted to an individual for his or her work over a duration of time. The Convention has 171 contracting parties as of August 2016.

20 Professor Ulrich Huber identified three precepts of the modern territoriality doctrine: (1) a state's laws have force within the state's boundaries; (2) anyone found within the state's boundaries is subject to the state's authority; (3) comity will discipline one sovereign's exercise of authority to respect the territorial competence of other sovereigns. Goldstein P., *International Intellectual Property Law: Case and Materials* (St Paul, MN: Fountain Press, 2008) p. 7.

21 Goldstein P., International Intellectual Property Law: Case and Materials (St Paul, MN: Fountain Press, 2008) p. 7.

22 Mühlendahl A. and Stauder D., 'Territorial intellectual property rights in a global economy – transit and other "Free Zones"' in M. J. Adelmann, *et al.* (Eds) *Patents and Technological Progress in a Globalised World* (London: Springer, 2009) pp. 653.

23 Goldstein P., *International Intellectual Property Law: Case and Materials* (St Paul, MN: Fountain Press, 2008) p. 183.

our law is confined to the United States and its territories [...] and infringement of this right cannot be predicated of acts wholly done in a foreign country.'[24]

2. *Policy tool for economic growth*

Assuming that there is a stable set of preferences within each jurisdiction, it is generally agreed that national laws are tailored to each jurisdiction and can better accommodate those individual preferences than a uniform set of laws imposed across all jurisdictions.[25] Therefore, a particular country will adopt policies that best fit its society and choose what intellectual assets to protect within its borders. Naturally, a government's patent policy will be fully tied to the nation's economic goals, its industries' technological potentials and to the types of innovation it wishes to foster. Certainly, religion and moral norms of a society also play a significant role in defining what should not be patented within the specific territory.

The development of China's patent law can provide a fitting example in this regard. The National Patent Development Strategy (2011–2020)[26] recognises that implementing the national patent strategy is to '[...] greatly improve China's level to create, utilise, protect and administer patent, actively serve market entities and make the patent system provide strong support in economic and social development as well as for the effort to make China an innovative country'. The Strategy Paper further reveals that the ultimate goal of the country's patent development is to elevate China into a powerful country on its merits of innovation. To elaborate on this point, a series of focuses and measures are listed, such as: further strengthening construction of the patent administration system and mechanism; vigorously enhancing the capacity to create and utilise patents; enhancing comprehensive capacity to examine patents. To implement this policy, for example under the Draft Patent Law 2015, employees' rights to service patents are defined for the first time and are better protected, and their additional rights are established as a means to encourage employment innovation. It's now made unequivocal that in the absence of an agreement concerning the ownership of a service patent, the inventor or designer shall have the right to apply for a patent grant even if the invention is accomplished by using the material and technical conditions of an employer.[27] In addition, a whole new chapter of 'exploitation and utilisation of patent' is added to the Draft Patent Law 2015 in order to encourage patent commercialisation, so as to bring about economic development.

3. *Reflecting a nation's social and economic reality*

Throughout history social influence is often found as a reason for economic outcomes. For example, Adam Smith viewed moral sentiments as an integral part of *The Wealth of Nations*, and John Stuart Mill regarded cultural constraints as sometimes more important than even

24 *Dowagiac Manufacturing Co.* v. *Minnesota Moline Plow Co.*, 235 US 641 (1915).

25 Goldstein P., *International Intellectual Property Law: Case and Materials* (St Paul, MN: Fountain Press, 2008) p.183.

26 Available at http://graphics8.nytimes.com/packages/pdf/business/SIPONatPatentDevStrategy.pdf (last accessed 18 January 2016).

27 Art.6, Draft Patent Law 2015.

the pursuits of personal interest.[28] A powerful example of how societal traits have affected the patent system may be seen in the contrasting comprehension of some countries of the notion of 'property'. Historically, property rights were emphasised by Western societies as one of the natural rights. John Locke believed that every man had an inherent property interest in his own person and asserted that 'life, liberty, and property' were the inalienable rights of a just society. As a result, intellectual property has long been included, in the eyes of law, under the general heading of 'property'.[29] Academics even argue that patents deserve as much of the same protection as real property.[30]

However, heavily influenced by Confucianism's humanistic way of life, of which altruism is an integral part, historically the Chinese conviction was laid upon sharing. Therefore, inventions and creative works were thought to belong to the community and they should be unconditionally shared for the public good. This assertion was further reinforced after communist China was established in 1949, when all property was held collectively in common and ownership was ascribed to the community or to the state. Consequently, protection of private property, real and intellectual, became redundant and therefore was not guaranteed by China's Constitution until 2004. Therefore, unsurprisingly, when China's first Patent Law was promulgated in 1984, the society's awareness of patent protection was next to none. The ideological formation of property rights, protection and enforcement only materialised in recent years after a socialist market economy has gradually come into being, when the ownership of real property, land, earnings and other personal assets were recognised by the Constitution. It was probably not until then that Chinese society began to accept that infringing IPR was like theft and that it must be dealt with by law. During the same period, Chinese IPR holders must also have become more conscious of protection and enforcement. In the past, many IPR infringers in China were most likely unaware of the offence they committed. Though the lack of IPR awareness is no excuse for infringement, it simply illustrates how its social background largely delayed China from implementing an effective IPR system and has rendered IPR enforcement weak to date. Under such circumstances, the real purpose behind China's patent legislation in the past was possibly more about awarding than protecting and enforcing patent rights. By the same token, China's social background restricted the country from imposing stricter IPR enforcement measures, especially at the beginning of the patent law evolution. For example, the precise amount of judicial fines for infringement was completely omitted in the first two patent laws enacted in 1984 and 1992 respectively, and the patent administrative

28 Also, often culture has a direct impact on expectations and preferences, which in turn will influence economic outcome. Within this context, culture can be defined as 'those customary beliefs and values that ethnic, religious, and social groups transmit fairly unchanged from generation to generation'. See Guiso L. *et al.*, 'Does culture affect economic outcomes?' 20 *Journal of Economic Perspectives* 2 (2006) 23.

29 The term 'intellectual property' first appeared in a patent case in 1845. The court observed that 'a liberal construction [...] given to a patent' will encourage 'ingenuity and perseverance' and 'only in this way can we protect intellectual property, the labours of the mind, productions and interests as much a man's own, and as much the fruit of his honest industry, as the wheat he cultivates, or the flocks he rears'. See Menell P. S., 'Intellectual property and the property rights movement'. 30 *Regulation* 3 (2007) 36, 38.

30 Among others, Professor Justin Hughes noted that 'the courts and legislatures had regularly discussed copyrighted works as 'property' throughout the seventeenth, eighteenth, and early nineteenth centuries, with the adjectival concepts of 'artistic,' 'literary,' and 'intellectual' orbiting around the property notion.' Cited by Menell P. S., 'The property rights movement's embrace of intellectual property: true love or doomed relationship'. 34 *Ecology Law Quarterly* 713 (2007).

authority was only empowered to order infringers to stop an infringement act if it was established beyond doubt.

Coming back to the characteristics of patent, a country's economic development stage decides the level of protection standard that a patent legislation institutes. During the period of economic take-off, legislators tend to impose patent protection for the purpose of facilitating technology transfer, and therefore enforcement measures often appear more lenient. Once a nation masters the concept of patent protection and is on track to become an innovative economy, its patent protection standards will be heightened in order to protect and further develop the economic gains that accrue from innovation. The evolution of China's patent law illustrates this route of development. So does the Japanese patent legislation, which will be analysed in detail in Chapter 7. In the more remote past, until 1908 the American patent law imposed the working requirement, which obliged patent holders to work with inventions or processes in the US where the patents were granted in order to promote technology transfer and diffusion of innovation. For the same reason, China's first Patent Law enacted in 1984 also imposed the working requirement. But it was scraped after the first patent law amendment took place in 1992.

III) Impediments to international patent harmonisation

With each country's individual patent legislation unique due to its national policy and social background, the world's largely fragmented patent system coped well until the eighteenth century when business and innovation activities were mostly restricted to domestic markets while cross-border trade was less frequent. However, since the beginning of the nineteenth century, with the increasing movement of economic resources beyond national borders and the explosion of international trade, governments and businesses increasingly recognised the value of IPR in order to pursue technological progress leading towards faster industrial development. Correspondingly, seeking effective patent protection in other countries to where trade had reached became imperative. This prompted international patent rights harmonisation, for which to proceed was to overcome the obstacles emanating from territoriality in relation to protection and multiple applications.

1. Patentability: patentable subject matters and novelty

The first impediment to securing patent protection in a foreign country is related to patentability, including patentable subject matters and the threshold for novelty, which have different meanings under each patent legislation. In terms of patentable subject matters, the divergence was very noticeable before the TRIPS Agreement came into force. For example, under the American patent legislation, the scope of patentable subject matters was so broad that 'anything under the sun that is made by man' was patentable;[31] while, for other countries, the scope of patentable subject matters was much more defined and considerably narrower. In 1988, among all 92 signatory countries of the Paris Convention, 49 countries did not award patents to pharmaceutical products, animal species were not patentable in 45 countries, and in as many as 44 countries patent protection was not granted to the treatment of the human or animal body. Plant varieties, food products,

31 *Diamond* v. *Chakrabarty*, 447 US 303 (1980).

chemical products and pharmaceutical processes, etc., were not patentable subject matters in many countries either.[32] After the TRIPS Agreement came into force, although the scope of patentable subject matters still varies among different patent offices, at least those non-patentable subject matters prescribed by Art.27 of the TRIPS Agreement are universally excluded from national patent legislation by all the members.

Similarly, the threshold for novelty differs among different patent offices. For example, 'absolute novelty' is a prerequisite under China's patent law while, for the European Patent Convention (EPC), 'non-obviousness' will suffice to pass the threshold test of novelty. Besides, filing a patent application in one country will often prevent the same invention from obtaining protection in other countries because of the loss of novelty as a result of the first patent application. This often happens in countries that apply a stricter rule of 'absolute novelty' when examining a patent application, meaning that any public disclosure of an invention, even by the inventor, will cause the loss of novelty and thereby a patent grant will be ruled out.[33]

Consequently, although a 'grace period' may mitigate the risks of 'loss of novelty', it is also applied differently among different patent offices. In certain countries, disclosure by publication in the form of a scientific article or a lecture or by public use is eligible to claim a 'grace period', which is also known as a 'general grace period', but it is not recognised by other patent jurisdictions, such as the EPC members. Also, most countries grant a six-month 'grace period', but America's grace period is 12 months. All these differences concerning patentability are impediments that stop right holders from obtaining protection in other patent offices.

2. *High costs for multiple patent applications*

A fragmented global patent system raises substantial application costs for multiple patent applications, while multinational corporations are the worst affected when they have to seek patent protection in every jurisdiction covered by their businesses. In some major economies, costs for obtaining and maintaining patent protection could easily reach hundreds of thousands of dollars. The World Intellectual Property Organization (WIPO) estimated that the patenting costs per application in the US and Japan, which are two of the world's biggest patent offices by application numbers, stayed approximately between 16,000 and 19,000 USD (14,397 to 17,096 EUR) in 2008.[34] As the estimate was applicable only to one single patent application, expenditure would be substantial for multinational companies

32 Straus J., 'Implications of the TRIPS Agreement in the field of patent law' in F. -K. Beier and G. Schricker (Ed.) *From GATT to TRIPS: the Agreement on Trade-Related Aspects of Intellectual Property Rights.* (Munich: Max Planck Institute for Foreign and International Patent, Copyright and Competition Law, 1996) pp. 160, 170–175.

33 Kilner C. B., *US Novelty v. International 'Absolute Novelty'.* (Roberts Abokhair & Mardula, LLC Vol.6, Issue 8, August 15, 2002). Available online at www.marburylaw.com/images/files/usnoveltyvsinternationalabsolutenovelty.pdf (last accessed 18 January 2016).

34 The patenting costs are based on estimates sourced from the Global IP Estimator, available at www.quantifyip.com/global-ip-estimator/overview.aspx (last accessed 3 July 2016). They include filing, examining, prosecution, granting costs and the costs for the international phase of the PCT applications. They do not include in-house and pre-filing costs. The costs are indicative only; actual costs will vary widely depending on the many options that are available to applicants and the many differences in costs and fees (including legal and translation costs) around the world. See: *World Patent Report: A Statistical Review* (Geneva: WIPO, 2008) pp. 51–58. Available at: www.wipo.int/ipstats/en/statistics/patents/wipo_pub_931.html (last accessed 18 January 2016).

to obtain and maintain thousands of patents. For example, pharmaceutical companies typically spend between 750,000 and 1,000,000 USD (674,882 to 900,864 EUR) to obtain comprehensive worldwide protection for a patent, and the figure is growing at a rate of 10 per cent each year.[35]

3. Patent backlogs and duplicated patent examination

As the number of non-resident patent applications has been high since the 1980s,[36] and because many applications are duplicated applications from the same patent families,[37] going through all the required procedures in each office where protection is sought, including search and examination, causes serious backlogs and depreciation of patent quality. For example, pending applications worldwide stood at 6.1 million in 2008, and at around 5.17 million in 2010. Although it fell to 4.9 million in 2014, this figure would have been higher if data from the State Intellectual Property Office (SIPO) in China had been available.[38] A study conducted by the United Kingdom Intellectual Property Office (UKIPO) shows that the cost to the global economy of the delays in processing patent applications may reach as much as 7.65 billion GBP (9.46 billion EUR) each year. Seeing a backlog of 750,000 applications in 2010, the US Department of Commerce also commented that the delay could ultimately cost the American economy billions of dollars annually in 'foregone innovation'.[39]

Ultimately, a fragmented global patent system with a huge number of patent applications as well as the potential delays in processing will lead to unpredictability with regard to patent validation or invalidation. If a patent office grants a patent that is subsequently invalidated or is subject to invalidation proceedings in another office, not only will the first patent office waste its own time and the applicant's time and money, but also that of the applicant's competitors. Delayed patent invalidation equally distorts the market[40] and may

35 Keating R. J., *Patent Reform: Protecting IP, Enabling Innovation and Bolstering Entrepreneurship.* (Oakton, VA: Small Business & Entrepreneurship Council) p. 18.

36 According to the statistics published by the WIPO, the applications of patent families grew sharply between 1983 and 1987, increasing from around 116,000 to 160,000. Between 1991 and 1994, the number of patent families fell, coinciding with the economic downturn in the early 1990s. The fastest growth occurred between 1994 and 2005, when the combined total grew by 85 per cent. Since peaking at 231,000 in 2005, the total has followed a downward trend, although it is still substantial. See: *World Intellectual Property Indicators 2015*, (Geneva: WIPO, 2015) p.9.*The World Intellectual Property Indicators 2015* used the term 'patent families' in an attempt to correct bias due to multiple counts of patent applications for the same invention and to provide better measurement of original/first inventions. A patent family is defined as 'a set of interrelated patent applications filed in one or more countries or jurisdictions to protect the same invention'. See: *World Intellectual Property Indicators 2015.* (Geneva: WIPO, 2015) p. 9.

37 The *World Intellectual Property Indicators 2015* reveals that, over the past seven years, the ratio of families to applications has remained more or less stable at around 0.5. This means that about half of all applications are initial filings and the other half are repetitive filings, mostly at foreign offices. See: *World Intellectual Property Indicators 2015.* (Geneva: WIPO, 2015) p. 9.

38 *World Intellectual Property Indicators* 2015. (Geneva: WIPO, 2015) p. 30.

39 Rai A. *et al.*, *Patent Reform: Unleashing Innovation, Promoting Economic Growth and Producing High-paying Jobs*, a White Paper from the US Department of Commerce (Washington, DC: US Department of Commerce, 13 April 2010).

40 *Cooperation Between Patent Offices: Prior Art Searching of Patent Applications*, prepared by the ICC Commission on Intellectual Property, document no. 450/1056 (Paris: ICC Commission on Intellectual Property, 28 June 2010) Available at: www.iccindiaonline.org/policy_state/ICCStatementPatentWorkSharing2010%5B1%5D.pdf (last accessed 7 April 2016).

cause a proliferation of litigation tactics, such as wasteful duplication, rising costs, delay and hold-up.[41]

Therefore, ever since the Paris Convention entered into force, the aim of international patent harmonisation has been to address the above-mentioned impediments.

II International patent harmonisation treaties concluded so far

After the Paris Convention was concluded, a few other landmark international patent harmonisation treaties have succeeded in tackling the challenges that foreign patent applicants are usually confronted with in respect of disparate standards of patentability, protection and enforcement, as well as the varied application procedures in which the different patent offices engage.

II) The Paris Convention and its main features

The Paris Convention, which provides protection for various industrial patents,[42] utility models and industrial designs, is the first successful attempt[43] to achieve harmonisation of procedural compatibility.[44] Concluded in Paris in March 1883, it superimposed a set of rules on national patent laws in each contracting state including, for example, the right of priority, the right to be mentioned, compulsory licence and independence of patent, which are still valid nowadays and are incorporated in the TRIPS Agreement.[45] The Convention,

41 Professor Harhoff pointed out three kinds of problems in a fragmented patent system: 1) wasteful duplication – whenever multiple litigation is undertaken, resources are wasted on duplication without generating concomitant benefits; 2) raising the cost for appropriating returns from patented inventions in Europe – leaving aside the cost of litigation, cross-border commerce is made more difficult and costly when diverging outcomes (patent protection in some, no patent protection in other EU Member States) prevail; 3) delay and hold-up – the system can be used to delay decisions in infringement cases or to raise the costs of entrants seeking access to the market, which may either reduce innovation incentives or the level of competition in a way that is welfare-reducing. Harhoff D., *Final Report on Economic Cost-Benefit Analysis of a Unified and Integrated European Patent Litigation System* (Munich: Max Planck Institute for Innovation Research, Technology Management and Entrepreneurship, 26 February 2009) pp. 14–18.

42 Under Art.1(4) of the Paris Convention, protection was rendered to industrial patents of various kinds which were recognised by the laws of the countries of the Union, including patents of importation, patents of improvement, patents and certificates of addition, etc.

43 According to Professor Ladas, international conventions are instruments meant to regulate interests, claims and demands paramount at national and international levels. Such instruments adopt a certain legal order that seeks to satisfy a greater number of schemes of interests involved with the least sacrifice to any. On the other hand, industrial evolution, economic growth and speedy availability of communication and transport created a unified world and no country could expect to satisfy the claims and protect the interests of its people in industrial property without securing protection at international level. Ultimately, law aims to protect the interests, claims and demands of the right-holders in order to encourage investment in new ideas and creative efforts for the advancement of human life and social and economic progress. See Ladas S., *Patents, Trademarks, and Related Rights, National and International Protection*, Vol.1. (Cambridge, MA: Harvard University Press, 1975), p.14.

44 The Paris Convention has presently 174 contracting members (as of April 2016). Although the Paris Convention was subsequently revised and its scope of cooperation has been extended since 1883, it is best seen as a facilitator for procedural compatibility among the patent systems of the contracting states. Torremans P., *Intellectual Property Law* (5th Ed.).(Oxford: OUP, 2008) p.43.

45 Under Art.2 of the TRIPS Agreement, members of the TRIPS Agreement are obliged to apply Arts.1–12 and 19 of the Paris Convention.

nonetheless, also left most areas of substantive patent protection open for national laws to decide, such as patentable subject matters, protection duration and rights conferred.[46]

1. *National treatment*

One of the innovative principles of patent rights harmonisation introduced by the Paris Convention is national treatment, which requires each Union member to offer, within its jurisdiction, the same treatment to all the nationals of the Union irrespective of nationalities.[47] Nationals of non-Union members may be equally entitled to national treatment thanks to Art.3 of the Convention, provided their domicile, or their 'real and effective industrial or commercial establishment', is within the territory of a contracting state.

2. *Right of priority*

Another innovative principle established by the Paris Convention is the right of priority. Art.4A(1) of the Paris Convention states that any applicant who files a patent application in one Union country shall enjoy the right of priority for 12 months[48] in other Union countries. Later applications will then be regarded as if they had been filed on the same day as the first application and, consequently, all the applications of the same invention that are filed after the date of the first application will enjoy the right of priority. Later applications will also enjoy a priority status with respect to all the acts accomplished after the first application date which would be otherwise sufficient to destroy the rights of the applicant or the patentability of the invention.[49]

3. *Independent national patents*

Art.4*bis* of the Paris Convention sets down the maxim extent to which national patents remain independent from each other. Therefore, granting a patent in one Union member does not oblige other members, as well as non-members, of the Union to grant a patent. In connection with the principle of the right of priority, patent applications submitted during the priority period are equally independent with regard to the grounds for nullity and forfeiture as well as to the duration for protection.[50]

46 Correa C., *An Agenda for Patent Reform and Harmonisation for Developing Countries*, a paper prepared for the Bellagio Dialogue on Intellectual Property and Sustainable Development: Revising the Agenda in a New Context, organised by International Centre for Trade and Sustainable Development (ICTSD), 24–28 September, Bellagio, Italy (Geneva: ICTSD, 2005).

47 Art.2, Paris Convention for the Protection of Industrial Property.

48 Art.4C(1), Paris Convention for the Protection of Industrial Property.

49 'International treaties and conventions on intellectual property' Chapter 5 in *The WIPO Intellectual Property Handbook: Policy, Law and Use* (Geneva: WIPO, 2004). Available at: http://www.wipo.int/about-ip/en/iprm/pdf/ch5.pdf (last accessed 20 January 2016).

50 The underlying reason for this principle is that national laws and administrative practices are different from country to country. Therefore, a decision not to grant or to invalidate an invention patent in one particular jurisdiction should not have any bearing in another jurisdiction.

4. *Right to be mentioned*

Art.4*ter* of the Paris Convention provides that the inventor shall have the right to be mentioned as such in the patent. In practice, some national legislation only offers an inventor the right for civil action against the patent applicant or the patent owner in order for the inventor's name to be included in the invention patent. Other countries allow the inventor's name to be mentioned when granting an invention patent, on an *ex officio* basis.

5. *Compulsory licence*

The Paris Convention lays down the requirements for granting a compulsory licence. Among these requirements, the local-working requirement, which was commonly applied by many countries during the time when the Paris Convention was concluded, was later abolished. Art.5A of the Paris Convention stipulates that each Union member may take necessary legislative measures to grant a compulsory licence, in order to prevent abuse that may result from exercising the exclusive rights conferred by a patent, such as failure to work or insufficient working on the patent concerned. The 'sufficient working' requirement is based on the premise that a patent should be used to introduce new technology to the country, and it should not be used to block the working of the invention (or the utility model) in the country or to monopolise the importation of the patented product by the patent holder.

Note that the Paris Convention provides national law the liberty to decide on other grounds upon which a compulsory licence may be granted. Such grounds may include excessive pricing or unreasonable terms for obtaining a contractual licence, or other restrictive measures that obstruct industrial development, etc. In line with the TRIPS Agreement, China's Patent Law 2008 provides five grounds upon which a compulsory licence may be granted. Under Art.48, a compulsory licence may be granted if: 1) a patent holder fails to exploit a patent sufficiently or; 2) a patent holder's behaviour is confirmed as monopolistic while exercising the patent rights. Equally, for the interest of public health, a compulsory licence may be granted to patented pharmaceutical products in order for them to be exported to countries that have insufficient or no manufacturing capacities based on the relevant international treaties to which China has acceded. Finally, a compulsory licence may be granted to an earlier patented technology if the later invention or utility model involves important technological progress of considerable economic significance and the exploitation of this requires the use of the earlier patented technology. Also, a national emergency may warrant a compulsory licence. The Draft Patent Law 2015 made no changes to the above-mentioned provisions concerning compulsory licence.

6. *Criticism*

Criticism of the Paris Convention focuses on two aspects. First, the Paris Convention does not provide any substantive standards for patent protection. As a consequence, Union members may legislate on patent protection measures at their discretion at any levels as long as the principles prescribed by the Convention, such as national treatment, are respected. Second, the Paris Convention lacks an enforcement mechanism. By virtue of Art.28(1) of the Paris Convention, disputes arising between the Union members should be settled by the International Court of Justice (ICJ), although its decision may be ignored by some members since they simply do not recognise the jurisdiction of the ICJ. Therefore, upon acceding to the Paris Convention, as a precaution, a member may very well declare that it does not consider itself to be bound by the provisions concerning dispute settlement before the ICJ. Moreover, rulings delivered by the ICJ are often ignored, even by members who recognise its jurisdiction – leaving injured members without any legal recourse in case of violation.[51]

II) WIPO Convention

Concluded in Stockholm on 14 July 1967, The Convention Establishing the World Intellectual Property Organization is administered by WIPO's International Bureau. With 188 contracting parties, WIPO currently oversees 26 IPR treaties, including the Paris Convention as well as the Berne Convention.[52] The WIPO aims to promote and facilitate efficient IPR protection worldwide through cooperation among states and with other international organisations.[53]

Just like the Paris Convention, the weaknesses of the WIPO Convention lie in enforcement. As Art.4 of the WIPO Convention reveals, WIPO relies on its members' voluntary cooperation in executing an unfavourable ruling out of a dispute resolution,[54] and as a consequence such rulings are often left unenforced. Although some contracting parties tried to equip the WIPO Convention with improved enforcement and a dispute settlement mechanism by proposing more specific provisions with legal effects, such as the power to impose sanctions,[55] such attempts had little success.[56]

III) Patent Cooperation Treaty and its main achievements

Concluded in 1970,[57] the PCT is a cooperation treaty that deals with international patent filing, search, examination and dissemination of the technological information contained therein.[58] The PCT created an Assembly of contracting states that only members of the Paris Convention may join.

51 Pechman, R. J., 'Seeking multilateral protection for intellectual property: the United States 'TRIPS' over special'. 301, 7 *Minnesota Journal of Global Trade* 179 (1998). See also: Hoekman, B., 'Services and intellectual property rights' in S. M. Collins and B. P. Bosworth (Eds), *The New GATT: Implications for the United States* (Washington, DC: The Brookings Institution, 1994).

52 Available at www.wipo.int/about-wipo/en/ and www.wipo.int/treaties/en/ (last accessed 20 January 2016).

53 Art.3, Convention Establishing the World Intellectual Property Organisation.

54 Su E., 'The winners and the losers: the Agreement on Trade-related Aspects of Intellectual Property Rights and its effects on developing countries'. 23 *Houston Journal of International Law* 169 (2000) 195.

55 Romano F., 'Global trademark and copyright 1998: protecting intellectual property rights in the international marketplace' in *International Conventions and Treaties.* (New York: Practising Law Institute, 1998).

56 Nonetheless, some other contracting parties argued that the WIPO had too much power in administering the Paris Convention as well as the Berne Convention. But, overall, the WIPO's ability to enforce the provisions set forth in the Conventions remains the same. See Su E., 'The winners and the losers: The Agreement on Trade-related Aspects of Intellectual Property Rights and its effects on developing countries' 23 *Houston Journal of International Law* 169 (2000) 195.

57 The PCT was subsequently amended in 1979 and modified in 1984 and 2001.

'International treaties and conventions on intellectual property' Chapter 5 in *The WIPO Intellectual Property Handbook: Policy, Law and Use* (Geneva: WIPO, 2004). Available at: http://www.wipo.int/about-ip/en/ m/pdf/ch5.pdf (last accessed 20 January 2016). On the other hand, it should be noted that the PCT does rant 'international patents'. Granting patents is a responsibility still reserved for the national offices where ion is sought.

1. *Streamlined application procedures with reduced application costs*

Under the Paris Convention, in order to claim the right of priority, a patent application must be filed in the foreign office where protection is sought within 12 months of the date of the first filing.[59] When filing an application in a few foreign offices, particular formality requirements imposed by each office must be duly complied with. Such requirements include, for example, the size of the paper used, as well as the arrangement of the description. Formality requirements usually vary from country to country, therefore applicants must prepare different application versions in order to meet the submission requirements imposed by a specific patent office. In addition, an application usually must be submitted in the official language of the country where protection is sought. Since most patent offices do not allow foreign applicants to represent themselves for patent prosecution, applicants must also engage a registered patent agent before approaching each foreign patent office. As a consequence, applying for a multiple patent application can indeed be an expensive endeavour since the application costs will include translation fees, patent agent's charges in multiple countries and registration fees payable to multiple patent offices. These expenses will be borne by an applicant regardless of whether or not the multiple patent application will succeed. The PCT was therefore negotiated in order to harmonise the forms, the contents and the procedural requirements of multiple patent filings so that the process conducted at the international level can become faster and cheaper.[60]

The patent-granting procedure under the PCT consists of two main phases, which are the international phase and the national phase. The international phase encompasses the steps of filing, search and international preliminary examination, and the national patent offices will manage the national phase before a patent is granted. Therefore, once the international phase is completed, within a specified timeframe and on the basis of the international application, an applicant must pay the required application fees to the national offices where patent protection is sought, furnish each of them with the requisite version of translation, and appoint a patent agent if required. Filing one single international application thus has the same effect as filing separate applications in each national office designated by the applicant, as long as the applicant is a national or a resident of a PCT-contracting state. An applicant may also choose to submit a PCT application in the International Bureau of the WIPO in Geneva. With such an application arrangement, the PCT materialised the objectives of simplifying the procedure for, and lowering the application costs of, multiple patent applications. Without the PCT, unless an application is submitted to a regional patent system such as the EPO, individual patent applications would have to be submitted separately in each national office where protection is sought. If this were the case, every single national patent office would have to examine the application it receives. The process of such examination typically involves a prior art search in order to determine the state of the art in the technical field of the invention as well as a thresholds test to determine the patentability of the invention.

2. *International search and international search report*

A PCT application is subject to an international search at the international phase, which is carried out by a national patent office acting as the International Searching Authority (ISA)

59 Art.4(C)(1), the Paris Convention.

60 Mossinghoff G. J., and Kuo V. S., 'World patent system circa 20xx, AD'. 80 *Journal of the Patent and Trademark Office Society* 523 (1998).

and appointed by the PCT Assembly. After a prior art search is completed, and in addition to a written opinion on patentability, the ISA will issue an international search report that should contain the classification of the invention, the technical fields searched, and a list of citations of such published documents that may affect the patentability of the invention concerned. The international search report as well as the written opinion will then be communicated to the patent applicant, who may wish to withdraw the application especially if the report or the opinion appears negative, making a patent grant unlikely. In the case that there is no withdrawal, together with the international search report, the international patent application will be published by the International Bureau of the WIPO. Note that in almost 80 per cent of all the PCT applications, applicants also request an International Preliminary Examination to be conducted for which, although non-binding, the result shall inform whether the invention is novel, involves an inventive step and is industrially applicable.[61]

Once the International Search Report and the result of the International Preliminary Examination are available, a patent application may be submitted to a few designated national patent offices where protection is sought. The international phase will only produce a standard national patent application with the same filing date among all contracting states. It is the national patent offices that will examine the application in light of the PCT reports but, nonetheless, either in granting or rejecting, the decision will be entirely based upon individual national patent legislation.

3. Advantages of the PCT

Under the PCT, accessing technological information contained in each application becomes more convenient because international applications are published 18 months after the priority date of the application, and all the applications are submitted in English or, if not, there must be an English abstract. Since the international search report, which is published together with the application, is also in English, evaluating the technology disclosed in the application becomes easier as well as earlier, considering that many important inventions are applied for via a PCT application these days.

Moreover, as all the PCT patents must first succeed in the international search and usually also the international preliminary examination, which suggests that the patent quality is assured, more and more applicants started to seek multiple patent protection by using the PCT system in order to earn 'credentials,' so as to be better prepared for technology transfer and licensing later on. National patent offices will be able to process more PCT patent applications in the meantime, since their qualities in terms of novelty and patentability have already been scrutinised by the ISA through 'international search', therefore the workload on examination could be considerably reduced. National patent offices may also be able to save part of the publishing cost for once an international application is published in the official language of one contracting state, it can forgo publication altogether in other PCT contracting states.

A PCT applicant spends much less on application fees because submitting an application at an ISA will give the same effect as submitting the application in all other designated PCT-contracting states. This means that no matter in how many PCT countries that patent protection is sought, an applicant is only required to submit one patent application, which is the international application within the priority year. Likewise, a national application may

61 Art.33(1), Patent Cooperation Treaty.

be submitted in the same language and form as the international application under the PCT. Although the cost of translation at the national phase has to be met eventually, it would not happen until eight or eighteen months later – when the national phase kicks in, and after the international search report and the international preliminary examination report are released. If an applicant declines to pursue patent application at the national phase, then all the subsequent costs can be avoided.

The PCT also brings advantages to national economies and industries. As an international application will be pursued at the national phase only if the applicant is totally convinced that there are adequate economic reasons for doing so, a PCT patent would generally provide a sound basis for investment and technology transfer appealing to an array of countries, including industrialised countries because they, too, need to stimulate domestic inventions and sometimes to import advanced technologies.

IV) Draft Patent Harmonisation Treaty 1991

The draft Treaty Supplementing the Paris Convention as far as Patents are Concerned (hereafter referred to as 'draft Patent Harmonisation Treaty 1991') was first negotiated in 1985, in a bid to harmonise national and regional patent laws. But it was never concluded.[62]

The North-South divergence, as well as some key disagreements sustained among the developed countries, was blamed for the ill-fated harmonisation treaty. It was said that, during the negotiations, while the developing countries were reluctant to compromise their freedom to pursue national patent regimes, the US, after failing to obtain a 'balanced package' that included, among other provisions, a grace period generally opposed by Europe, was not willing to give up its 'first-to-file' system since the US considered that the negotiating package offered little in exchange for abandoning the system.[63]

Nonetheless, some provisions of the failed draft Patent Harmonisation Treaty 1991 were later incorporated in the TRIPS Agreement. For example, the provisions regarding the patentable subject matters, the rights conferred, the term of protection and the reversal of the burden of proof for processing patent applications, etc., have all become components of the TRIPS Agreement, upon which uniform minimum standards for patent protection are drawn.[64]

V) Agreement on Trade-Related Aspects of Intellectual Property Rights

1. Introduction

The TRIPS Agreement was concluded on 15 April 1994, as part of the outcomes of the Uruguay Round of multilateral trade negotiations that established the WTO. In comparison with other international IP conventions, TRIPS is revolutionary as enforcement is

62 *Suggestions for the Further Development of International Patent Law*, by the WIPO Standing Committee on the Law of Patents, SCP/4/2. (Geneva: WIPO, 25 September 2000).

63 Correa C., An Agenda for Patent Reform and Harmonisation for Developing Countries, a paper prepared for the Bellagio Dialogue on Intellectual Property and Sustainable Development: Revising the Agenda in a New Context, organised by International Centre for Trade and Sustainable Development, September 24–28, Bellagio, Italy (ICTSD, 2005).

64 *Suggestions for the Further Development of International Patent Law*, by WIPO the Standing Committee on the Law of Patents, SCP/4/2, (Geneva: WIPO, 25 September 2000).

embedded in the Agreement and therefore a member who violates the Agreement will be subject to sanctions decided by the Dispute Settlement Body (DSB). Regarded as the most comprehensive multilateral IPR agreement to date, the TRIPS Agreement ensures that the basic principles, such as the national treatment and the most-favoured-nation treatment enshrined in the preceding international IPR treaties such as, for example, the Paris Convention and the Berne Convention, are upheld. TRIPS harmonises the minimum standards for IPR protection, including patent protection, while providing members with the liberty of imposing more extensive and stricter IPR protection measures, as long as the minimum standards are met. For example, members may define, under their respective national patent law, novelty, inventiveness and industrial applicability, for which TRIPS only provides a broad principle. Members are equally left free to determine appropriate methods to implement the TRIPS Agreement based on their own legal system and practice.[65]

2. *TRIPS characteristics vis-à-vis the Paris Convention*

A. 'PARIS PLUS' AND 'PARIS MINUS'

Not only does the TRIPS Agreement oblige its members to comply with Arts.1–19 of the Paris Convention (1967)[66], but it also adds new dimensions to the general principles established by the Paris Convention. For example, TRIPS prohibits discrimination *vis-à-vis* technology, it restricts exceptions to patentability, obliges judicial review against patent revoke or forfeit, and sets down the minimum term for protection.[67]

In parallel, TRIPS provides members with the possibility of providing a lesser degree of patent protection on certain aspects when compared with the Paris Convention. For example, Art.4*bis* of the Paris Convention states that parallel patent rights enjoyed by different Union members of the Paris Convention should not be subject to international exhaustion because those rights are independent. However, Art.6 of the TRIPS Agreement admits that international exhaustion, which provides a certain degree of protection for patent rights afforded under the Paris Convention, will not be addressed for the purpose of dispute settlement. Another example in this regard is illustrated by border measures on enforcement. Article 9(1) of the Paris Convention stipulates that all goods unlawfully bearing a trademark or a trade name shall be seized on importation into those countries of the Union where such a mark or trade name is entitled to legal protection. However, Art.51 of the TRIPS Agreement only requires the suspension of release of such infringing goods by customs authorities.

Having said that, by virtue of Art.2(2) of the TRIPS Agreement, members of the TRIPS Agreement must not derogate from the existing obligations to which they have already committed under the Paris Convention and a few other international IP treaties.

65 Art.1.1, TRIPS Agreement.

66 Art.2(1), TRIPS Agreement. To this end, Art.2(2) further specifies that 'Nothing in Parts I to IV of this Agreement shall derogate from existing obligations that Members may have to each other under the Paris Convention, the Berne Convention, the Rome Convention and the Treaty on Intellectual Property in Respect of Integrated Circuits'.

67 See Arts.27.1, 27.2, 32 and 33, TRIPS Agreement.

B. DIMINISHED POLICY CHOICES

By virtue of Art.2.1, the TRIPS Agreement provides members with lesser legislative options compared with the Paris Convention in relation to Arts.1 to 12 and Art.19 of the Paris Convention (1967). Specifically, for compulsory licence, Art.5(2) of the Paris Convention sets down the principle that Union members may issue a compulsory licence in order to prevent abusive behaviour, such as 'failure to work', as a result of the exclusive rights conferred to a patent holder. Within the remit of the Paris Convention, and since Art.5(1) prescribes that importing patented products manufactured in other Union countries by the patent holder into the country where the patent is granted shall not entail forfeiture of the patent, 'failure to work' may be understood as a requirement of local manufacturing and therefore importing patented products to the locality of the patent may not qualify as 'effective working'. In comparison, the legislative option of electing 'local manufacturing' is now dismissed outright by Art.27(1) of the TRIPS Agreement, which guarantees that patents shall be available and patent rights enjoyable without discrimination as to, for example, whether products are imported or locally produced.

Another example regarding diminished policy options that the TRIPS Agreement provides in comparison with the Paris Convention is that, by virtue of Art.31(c) of the TRIPS Agreement, it is only on two grounds that a compulsory licence may be granted to semi-conductor technology patents, which are either for public non-commercial use or for remedying an anti-competitive practice. In contrast, Art.5 of the Paris Convention does not set any boundaries concerning the technology field within which a compulsory licence may be issued. Similarly, while under the TRIPS Agreement, trademarks may be granted a compulsory licence and only the owner of a registered trademark shall have the right to assign the trademark.[68] The Paris Convention does not lay down any restrictions in this regard.

C. MORE POLICY CHOICES

The TRIPS Agreement provides its members with the possibility of electing between national and international exhaustion, while for the members of the Paris Convention the only possibility is national exhaustion. Under Art.6 of the TRIPS Agreement, members have the liberty to draft their respective national measures in order to address the issue of exhaustion, even if contrary to other provisions provided by the Agreement, as long as the principles of the national treatment and the most-favoured-nation treatment are respected; if not, such measures may be sanctioned by the DSB.[69]

3. *Three unique features of the TRIPS Agreement*

The TRIPS Agreement has three unique features, namely the minimum protection standards, the extended enforcement procedures as well as the dispute settlement mechanism.

68 Art.21 of the TRIPS Agreement.

69 Carvalho N. P. *The TRIPS Regime of Patent Rights* (3rd Ed.). (New York: Kluwer Law International, 2010), p.173.

A. MINIMUM PROTECTION STANDARDS

The TRIPS Agreement provides the minimum protection standards to each aspect of the IPR covered,[70] for which the national treatment and the most-favoured-nation treatment are the least requirements that members are obliged to meet in their respective IPR laws. Also, Arts.2.1 and 9.1 of the TRIPS Agreement require its members to comply with the substantive obligations set down by the Paris Convention and the Berne Convention in their most recent version.[71] Moreover, the TRIPS Agreement imposes on its members a number of additional obligations on matters where the previous IPR conventions are silent or have not provided adequate protection measures, for example in terms of protecting computer programmes, databases, sound recordings and pharmaceutical, agricultural and chemical products.[72]

B. EXTENDED ENFORCEMENT PROCEDURES

Unlike most international IP agreements that leave the matter of enforcement to national legislation, the TRIPS Agreement prescribes unambiguous principles with regard to procedures and remedies that members are obliged to implement in their respective national laws so that the minimum enforcement standards are harmonised among the members and, consequently, more legal certainty in enforcement is brought about at the national level overall.[73] Such principles include, for example: that remedies should be expeditious and effective as a deterrent to future IPR infringement; procedures should be fair and equitable and should not be unnecessarily complicated or costly, and should not entail unreasonable time limits or unwarranted delays; decisions should be reasoned, in writing, and taken on the weight of the evidence submitted on which both parties should have a right to be heard.[74] By virtue of Art.41.1, members are obliged to incorporate the enforcement provisions specified by the Agreement in their national law so as to enable effective enforcement against any IPR infringement act covered by the Agreement.

The TRIPS Agreement equally provides alleged IPR infringers with all the procedural instruments essential for obtaining a fair trial[75] and for guaranteeing damages when wronged.[76] At the same time, IPR holders must substantiate their infringement allegations with evidence, and demonstrate the merit of their complaints in court should provisional measures for protection be requested.[77]

70 For each aspect of the intellectual property rights, TRIPS defines the subject matter to be protected, the rights to be conferred and permissible exceptions to those rights, and the minimum duration of protection. Available at www.wto.org/english/tratop_e/trips_e/intel2_e.htm#generalprovisions (last accessed 21 January 2016).

71 With the exception of the provisions of the Berne Convention on moral rights, all the main substantive provisions of these conventions are incorporated under TRIPS between members. Available at www.wto.org/english/tratop_e/trips_e/intel2_e.htm#generalprovisions (last accessed 22 January 2016).

72 Available online at www.wto.org/english/tratop_e/trips_e/intel2_e.htm#generalprovisions (last accessed 22 January 2016).

73 Part III, Enforcement of Intellectual Property Rights of the TRIPS Agreement.

74 Sec.2, Part III of the TRIPS Agreement.

75 Art.42 of the TRIPS Agreement.

76 Art.48.1 of the TRIPS Agreement.

77 Art.43 of the TRIPS Agreement.

C. DISPUTE SETTLEMENT MECHANISM (DSM)

Article 64 of the TRIPS Agreement provides that disputes arising from the Agreement must be dealt with by the WTO dispute settlement mechanism (DSM), of which the procedures[78] are governed by the Dispute Settlement Understanding (DSU). As a result, WTO members are able to submit their complaints stemming from any of the multilateral trade agreements listed in the Annexes to the Agreement establishing the WTO. Under the DSU, the DSB[79] will exercise the authority of the General Council, the councils and the committees of the covered agreements.[80]

Article 3.2 of the DSU states that the objective of the DSM is to preserve members' rights and obligations under the covered WTO agreements, and to clarify the existing provisions of those agreements in accordance with the customary rules for interpreting public international law. Nonetheless, any recommendations and decisions pronounced by the DSB cannot add to, or diminish, the rights and the obligations provided by the covered agreements. Among all the 34 TRIPS-related dispute settlement cases brought before the DSB to date, 11 of them are patent dispute cases.[81]

The WTO DSM has three main features, which are the 'reversed' consensus, the streamlined procedures and the establishment of the Appellate Body.[82]

i) The 'reversed' consensus The 'reversed' consensus is a working method of the DSB. It means that a panel report, or a report issued by the Appellate Body, shall be automatically adopted by the DSB unless it is decided by a unanimous consensus, including the winning party itself, not to adopt it.[83] Thanks to the procedure of the 'reversed' consensus, decisions laid down by the DSB become fully enforceable which is contrary to the GATT, where decisions were often left unenforced since enforcing a decision laid down by the GATT DSB required a unanimous consensus including the offending party.

ii) Streamlined procedures Streamlined procedures ensure that disputes are dealt with swiftly so that injured parties can be compensated in a timely fashion. As a general rule, the DSU allows a panel, established by the DSB, a period of six months to decide on a dispute and issue a report. In case of urgency, the period for deliberation may be reduced to three

78 The procedure should not be seen as adversarial. Art.3.7 of the DSU declares that the aim of the dispute settlement mechanism is to secure a positive solution to a dispute. Art.3.10 further clarifies that the request for conciliation and the use of the dispute settlement procedures should not be intended or considered as contentious acts and that, if a dispute arises, concerned members will engage in these procedures in good faith in an effort to resolve the dispute. Also, complaints and counter-complaints in regard to distinct matters should not be linked.

79 Art.2.1 of the DSU stipulates that the DSB is established to administer the DSU rules and procedures and, except as otherwise provided in a covered agreement, the consultation and dispute settlement provisions of the covered agreements. Accordingly, the DSB shall have the authority to establish panels, adopt panel and Appellate Body reports, maintain surveillance of implementation of rulings and recommendations, and authorise suspension of concessions and other obligations under the covered agreements.

80 Available at: www.wto.org/english/docs_e/legal_e/ursum_e.htm#Understanding (last accessed 22 January 2016).

81 Available at: www.wto.org/english/tratop_e/dispu_e/dispu_agreements_index_e.htm?id=A26 (last accessed 22 January 2016).

82 Carvalho N. P. *The TRIPS Regime of Patent Rights* (3rd Ed.). (New York: Kluwer Law International, 2010), p.671.

83 Arts.16.3 and 17.4, DSU.

months.[84] Art.12.9 of the DSU further provides that in no circumstances should the procedures be delayed for more than three months.[85]

iii) Appellate Body As the DSM is meant to be non-adversarial in nature, three mandatory steps must be taken before a WTO member may request the DSB to establish a panel. In accordance with Art.3.7 of the DSU, a member must first make an assessment as to whether commencing the DSU procedures would yield any results before constituting a case by requesting consultation with the alleged offending member. In conjunction with Art.63.2 of the TRIPS Agreement, the second step is to clarify the relevant judicial decisions, administrative rulings or bilateral agreements with respect to IPR protection.[86] The aggrieved member may request access to detailed information about a specific judicial decision, administrative ruling or bilateral agreement in order to determine if its interests and rights under the TRIPS Agreement are infringed. If necessary, further clarification may be requested. The third mandatory step is consultation, by virtue of Art.4.3 of the DSU third parties may request to join the consultation.[87] If the consultation between the disputing parties fails, the aggrieved member is entitled to request the establishment of a panel in which time the procedures of good office, conciliation and mediation may commence if the disputing parties so agree.[88]

D. OUTCOMES OF THE DISPUTE SETTLEMENT MECHANISM

As far as TRIPS is concerned, violations usually occur when TRIPS-consistent measures are absent. Rarely does a violation take place because TRIPS-inconsistent measures are present. Thus, the first outcome of the DSM would be to adopt measures consistent with the TRIPS Agreement.[89] In case TRIPS-inconsistent measures are found, then withdrawal should be the first option and Art.3.7 of the DSU provides that if it's impracticable to withdraw such measures, compensation would be a solution – but only as a temporary step – pending the eventual withdrawal of the measures inconsistent with a covered agreement. Subject to the authorisation of the DSB, Art.3.7 of the DSU provides members with the possibility of invoking the dispute settlement procedures – as the last resort – to suspend the application of concessions or other obligations under the covered agreements on a discriminatory basis

84 Art.12.8 of the DSU states that the period in which the panel shall conduct its examination, from the date that the composition and terms of reference of the panel have been agreed upon until the date the final report is issued to the parties to the dispute, shall, as a general rule, not exceed six months. In cases of urgency, including those relating to perishable goods, the panel shall aim to issue its report to the parties to the dispute within three months.

85 As to the procedures of Appellate Review, see Art.17 of the DSU.

86 For the purpose of transparency, Art.63.2 of the TRIPS Agreement obliges members to notify the TRIPS Council of their respective laws and regulations, together with final judicial decisions and administrative rulings of general application, including the availability, scope, acquisition, enforcement and prevention of the abuse of IPR, in order to assist the Council to review the operation of the Agreement.

87 Art.4.3 of the DSU specifies that if a request for consultations is made pursuant to a covered agreement, the member to which the request is made shall, unless otherwise mutually agreed, reply to the request within 10 days of the date of its receipt and shall enter into consultations in good faith within a period of no more than 30 days of the date of receipt of the request, with a view to reaching a mutually satisfactory solution.

88 Art.5, DSU.

89 Carvalho N. P. *The TRIPS Regime of Patent Rights* (3rd Ed.). (New York: Kluwer Law International, 2010), p.673.

vis-à-vis the other member, subject to the authorisation of the DSB. The offending member's privilege of national treatment would be then suspended.

E. TWO OBSERVATIONS ON THE DISPUTE SETTLEMENT MECHANISM

The DSB obliges members to ensure certainty and predictability when incorporating the TRIPS Agreement into their respective national IPR laws. As is illustrated by the Panel Reports on India – Patent Protection for Pharmaceutical and Agricultural and Chemical Products (the mailbox case), administrative procedures will not be sufficient for the purpose of incorporating TRIPS into national legislation and the lack of legal security means that the objectives and purposes of the specific provisions will not be adequately achieved.[90] The mailbox case will be elaborated upon in greater detail in Chapter 8.

The same insistence on legal certainty and predictability was reiterated by the DSB Panel in the case of Canada – Terms of Patent Protection.[91] The US complained that Canada had failed to comply with Art.33 of the TRIPS Agreement by extending the patent protection term from 17 years to 20 years for patents granted before 1989, and therefore Art.70.2 of the Agreement was violated. The panel decided that patent applicants should not be compelled to take those artificial measures provided by Canada, such as abandonment, reinstatement, non-payment of fees and non-response to a patent examiner's report, in order to extend the life of a patent to 20 years. Instead, the 20-year mandatory protection term must be 'a readily discernible and specific right, and it must be clearly seen as such by the patent applicant when a patent application is filed'. Therefore, Canada was found in violation of the TRIPS Agreement. The Appellate Body later upheld the panel's findings.

The second observation is that the DSB will compel members to offer more IPR protection than otherwise is provided in their national legislation, by virtue of Art.13 of the TRIPS Agreement concerning limitations and exceptions. This is especially the case with regard to the scope of admissible exceptions, as is reflected by the panel's decision in Canada – Patent Protection of Pharmaceutical Products and in United States – Section 110(5) of the US Copyright Act.[92]

In relation to the case of Canada – Patent Protection of Pharmaceutical Products[93], the European Communities and their member states complained that the two provisions under Canada's patent law, which permitted the use and the manufacturing of generic pharmaceutical products for the purpose of obtaining approval for market entry in Canada and abroad as well as for stockpiling them (limited to the six-month period prior to the expiry of the patent) in order to sell them after the patent's expiry date, were in violation of Art.28 and were not within the exceptions sanctioned by Art.30 of the TRIPS Agreement. The findings delivered by the panel were that the regulatory exception imposed by Canada was TRIPS-consistent, justified by Art.30, while the stockpiling measure was not. The panel found that Canada did not set any limitations on the quantity of production for stockpiling, which resulted in a substantial curtailment of extended market exclusivity and, thus, was in violation of Art.30.

90 India – Patent Protection for Pharmaceutical and Agricultural and Chemical Products, WT/DS50/R, 5 September 1997 and WT/DS50/AB/R, 19 December 1997.

91 Canada – Terms of Patent Protection, Report of the Panel adopted on 12 October 2000, WT/DS170/R.

92 United States – Section 110(5) of the US Copyright Act, WT/DS160/R, 15 June 2000.

93 Canada – Patent Protection of Pharmaceutical Products, WT/DS114/R, 17 March 2000.

In the case of United States – Section 110(5) of the US Copyright Act, the European Communities and their member states complained that Section 110(5) of the US Copyright Act permitted, under certain conditions, playing radio and television music in public places, including in certain business establishments and in other public places with home-style equipment, but without the payment of a royalty fee, and this was in violation of Art.13 of the TRIPS Agreement. The panel decided that the 'home-style exemption' (for 'dramatic' musical works) sanctioned by the US did not violate Art.13, but the 'business exemption' (works other than 'dramatic' musical works) did. This was because, and echoing the three-step test, the 'business exemption' did not qualify as a 'certain special case' within the meaning of Art.13, and it was in contrast to a normal exploitation of the work as the exemption deprived rights holders of compensation for their musical works and, finally, the US did not show that the 'business exemption' did not unreasonably prejudice the legitimate interests of the right holder.[94]

The DSB's position of 'affording more protection than otherwise' was confirmed in the Panel Report of the European Communities – Protection of Trademarks and Geographical Indications for Agricultural Products and Foodstuffs, when the panel found that the EC Regulation 2081/92 was sufficiently constrained to qualify as a 'limited exception' to trademark rights.[95] In the case, the US complained that the EC Regulation 2081/92, as amended, did not provide national treatment with respect to geographical indications (GI) and did not provide sufficient protection to pre-existing trademarks that were similar or identical to a GI. The US alleged that this was inconsistent with the EC's obligations under the TRIPS Agreement, including but not necessarily limited to Arts.3, 16, 24, 63 and 65 of the TRIPS Agreement. The panel found that the EC Regulation 2081/92 failed to provide national treatment, but otherwise the substance of GI protection under the EC was consistent with the WTO obligations. The panel agreed with the EC that, although its GI protection measures allowed it to register GIs even when they conflicted with a prior trademark, the Regulation, as written, was sufficiently constrained to qualify as a 'limited exception' to trademark rights.

VI) Patent Law Treaty

Entering into force in April 2005, with presently 36 contracting parties including the EPO,[96] the Patent Law Treaty (PLT) incorporates requirements obliged by the PCT regarding forms and contents of international patent applications.[97] It also provides Model International Forms in order to procure streamlined procedures[98] in front of national patent offices.

94 United States – Section 110(5) of the US Copyright Act, WT/DS160/R, 15 June 2000.

95 European Communities – Protection of Trademarks and Geographical Indications for Agricultural Products and Foodstuffs, WT/DS174/R, 15 March 2005.

96 Available at: www.wipo.int/treaties/en/ShowResults.jsp?lang=enandtreaty_id=4 (last accessed 21 January 2016).

97 Such requirements include, for example, under Art.6(1)(2) of the PLT, the content of the PCT request form and the use of it with an indication that the application is to be treated as a national application. This will eliminate or reduce procedural gaps between national, regional and international patent systems.

98 Such procedures include the exceptions from mandatory representation, the restriction on requiring evidence on a systematic basis, the requirement for Offices to accept a single communication in certain cases (for example, power of attorney) or the restriction on the requirement to submit a copy of an earlier application and a translation thereof.

With the exception of the requirements concerning filing date,[99] the PLT establishes a set of maximum requirements that a Contracting Party may impose, while no additional requirements may be admissible within the remit of the PLT. Note that each Contracting Party remains free to prescribe any substantive patent registration requirements under its national or regional law, based on necessity or on policy grounds. The PLT sets down in the meantime procedures in order to avoid unintentional loss of substantive rights as a result of violating formality requirements or time limit, such as those requirements obliged by Art.8 of the PLT regarding notification and non-compliance with communication requirements,[100]Art.10 regarding revocation in the context of validity of patent[101] and Art.11 regarding relief in respect of time limits.[102] It was also expected that, under the PLT, administrative costs for national patent offices would become less, and the benefit of which would be passed on to applicants in the form of further lowered application fees.

The PLT ensures initially the juxtaposition of electronic and paper patent filings, but it was also envisaged that the latter would be phased out after 2 June 2005 by virtue of Rule 8 of the regulations under the PLT. To facilitate electronic patent filing, Art.8(1)(a) of the PLT provides that a Contracting Party should be entitled to use it as a form and a means of transmittal communication. At the same time, Art.8(1)(c) guarantees that no contracting party should be obliged to exclude paper filing and, by virtue of Art.8(1)(d), a contracting party should always accept paper filing especially if time permits.

For inventors, patent applicants and attorneys, standardised and simplified formality requirements promoted by the PLT have led to reduced risk of formality errors as far as patent application is concerned. As a result, loss of rights becomes less frequent and cost reduction can be achieved consequently. The set of patent formalities applicable to all PLT contracting parties may also be relied upon by a PCT patent applicant, since the PCT provisions regarding forms and contents of an international application are incorporated into the PLT as reference.

After the PLT entered into force, amendments to the regulations under the PLT were adopted in January 2006. The amendments were made in relation to application regarding indication[103] under Art.6(1-3), as well as payment terms (including late payment) under Art.6(7-8).

99 Art.5 (1)(a) of the PLT sets out three standardised and absolute requirements for obtaining a filing date. No additional elements may be required in order for a filing date to be accorded. The three requirements are: 1) an indication that the elements received by the Office of a Contracting Party are intended to be an application for a patent for an invention; 2) indications that would allow the Office to identify or to contact the applicant, however a Contracting Party is allowed to require indications on both; and 3) a part which appears to be a description of the invention.

100 Art.8(7)(8) of the PLT lays down the requirements related to notifications and non-compliance in the context of communications. For example, in case of non-compliance with the communication requirements stipulated by the same provision, the Contracting Party is obliged to notify and to give the opportunity to the applicant or other persons concerned in order for them to comply with any such requirements within the time limit prescribed in the regulations.

101 Art.10 of the PLT stipulates that non-compliance with certain formal requirements may not be a ground for revocation or invalidation of a patent.

102 Art.11 of the PLT provides that when the parties concerned fail to comply with the time limit fixed by the regulations, a Contracting Party may provide for an extension and continue processing the application or patent and, if necessary, reinstate the rights of application or patent.

103 For example, further requirements under Art.6(1)(iii)] (a) a Contracting Party may require that an applicant who wishes an application to be treated as a divisional application under Rule 2(6)(i) indicate: (i) that he wishes the application to be so treated; (ii) the number and filing date of the application from which the application is divided.

VII) Draft Substantive Patent Law Treaty

The draft Substantive Patent Law Treaty (SPLT) was intended to harmonise and streamline formal procedures with regard to national and regional patent applications and protection. To facilitate the negotiations of this substantive patent harmonisation treaty, the WIPO established the Standing Committee on the Law of Patents (SCP).

However, since November 2000, when the fourth session of the SCP took place and in its subsequent sessions until 2006, SPLT negotiations were much characterised by the divergences sustained among the various negotiating countries. Some countries advocated a limit to the scope of harmonisation to just the technical and legal aspects of patent protection; other countries lobbied for flexibility of national policies and of other issues, such as associating traditional knowledge with patent applications. Inserting provisions concerning limits of patentability and anti-competitive practices, as well as admitting exceptions to patent rights, were also raised as demands. Additionally, some countries submitted that the negotiations should not only address compulsory disclosure of the origin of genetic resources and prior informed consent together with a provision on benefit-sharing, but also examine effective procedures in order to challenge a patent's validity, its sufficiency for disclosure, potential for technology transfer and alternative models in order to promote innovation. On the other hand, other countries, mainly industrialised countries, wanted to restrict negotiations to the definition of prior art, as well as the questions concerning novelty, grace period and inventive step/non-obviousness.[104]

Note that during the negotiations divergences were also observed among the industrialised countries. For example, on the question of exceptions to patentability, the US did not want to prescribe national exceptions to patentability, while the EU wanted to follow the exceptions provided by Arts.27(2)(3) of the TRIPS Agreement on the grounds of morality and public order, as well as animals and plant varieties. Some countries also disagreed on whether an invention patent must have a technological character. The TRIPS Agreement provides that patents must be available 'in all fields of technology', but not for non-technological subject matters, while the American patent law does not set these boundaries, so therefore subject matters such as computer programmes and 'business methods' are patentable.[105]

Although SPLT was a momentous attempt to step up after the success of TRIPS for harmonising minimum patent protection standards, due to the wide divergences sustained among the negotiating countries the SCP decided that it was premature to establish a work programme as parties could not agree to the modalities and scope of the future work of the Committee.[106] The SPLT negotiations were thus suspended in 2006.

104 See proposal by the USA, Japan and the European Patent Office submitted to the 31st Session of the General Assembly of the WIPO in September 2004, WIPO document WO/GA/34/9.

105 For more details on the divergent positions among the negotiating countries, see GRAIN, *One Global Patent Law? WIPO's Substantive Patent Law Treaty.* (Barcelona: GRAIN, 4 August 2003). Available at: www.grain.org/article/entries/109-one-global-patent-system-wipo-s-substantive-patent-law-treaty (last accessed 22 January 2016).

106 Available at: www.wipo.int/patent-law/en/draft_splt.htm (last accessed 22 January 2016).

VIII) European Patent Convention

Apart from the patent harmonisation treaties concluded or negotiated at the international level, there are various harmonisation attempts taking place at the regional level as well. The EPC, which is a multilateral treaty that established the EPO,[107] is a case in point.

1. Introduction

For an applicant who wishes to apply for a European patent, the EPO provides the harmonised procedures, which consist of one application and one examination, while the resulting registration and protection will be as effective in any EPC contracting states that the applicant may have sought as if the patent were granted by the national patent office.[108] A single EPC patent application means applying for a patent in one language and submitting it either at the EPO in Munich, or at its branches in the Hague or Berlin, or at a national patent office of a contracting state, if applicable.

An important feature of the European patent system is the opposition procedure,[109] which allows any party to object to a patent grant[110] and to notify the EPO in accordance with the Implementing Regulations within nine months after the grant is published.[111] The opposition procedure has been increasingly used in recent years, particularly in the field of biotechnological inventions because the subject matter often causes controversies and therefore attracts much attention from various groups that may have legitimate genuine concerns.[112] The post-grant opposition procedure may be divided in two types of unified procedures, namely 1) the time-limited opposition procedure and 2) the limitation and revocation procedure. The former can be instituted by any person except a patent holder while the latter is a process only reserved for patent holders.

A European patent may be acquired from the EPO by two means.[113] An applicant may file and prosecute an invention patent application in each of the EPC countries where

107 The European Patent Organisation is an intergovernmental organisation that was set up on 7 October 1977 on the basis of the European Patent Convention (EPC) signed in Munich in 1973. It has two bodies, the European Patent Office and the Administrative Council, which supervises the Office's activities. There are presently 38 contracting member states. Available at: www.epo.org/about-us/organisation.html (last accessed 22 January 2016).

108 MacQueen H. *et al.*, *Contemporary Intellectual Property: Law and Policy* (1st Ed.). (Oxford: OUP, 2007).

109 Part V, Limitation and Opposition Procedure, EPC 2010.

110 Art.100 of the EPC 2010 provides grounds for opposition, which are: a) the subject-matter of the European patent is not patentable under Arts.52 to 57; b) the European patent does not disclose the invention in a manner sufficiently clear and complete for it to be carried out by a person skilled in the art; c) the subject-matter of the European patent extends beyond the content of the relevant application.

111 Art.99, EPC 2010.

112 Harmon S., 'The rules of re-engagement: the use of patent proceedings to influence the regulation of science (what the science does when the salmon comes back downstream)'. 4 *Intellectual Property Quarterly* (2006), 378–403.

113 When compared with PCT applications, a PCT application does not mature into a patent unless the applicant takes the necessary steps for the application to enter the national stage in each of the countries or regional offices where protection is sought. See World Intellectual Property Organisation, PCT Applicant's Guide – National Phase (2010).

protection for the invention is sought. This procedure is also known as 'national patent application' and may be elected as a favoured application option if an applicant is seeking patent protection in only one or a few EPC countries. Alternatively, a European invention patent application may be simply submitted at the EPO. If this is the case, the application may be drafted in one of the three official languages of the EPO, which are English, French and German, a single application fee will be charged and the application will be examined by a single patent office. This application choice provides patent applicants the advantage of single filing and multiple protection in a few EPC countries where protection is sought.

2. *Problems of European patent*

Note that European patent issued by the EPO is not a unitary right, but a bundle of essentially national patents which are independent, nationally-enforceable, nationally-revocable, and subject to central revocation.[114] Since a European patent may be challenged under the opposition procedure within nine months after it is granted, if a challenge is successful the patent would not be enforceable in any EPC country. In the meantime, even if the EPO upholds the validity of a European patent pursuant to a challenge, the validity will not shield the patent holder from further challenges which may be lodged subsequently in other EPC countries. Additionally, a decision pronounced by one national court regarding patent validity or invalidity will be binding only within the jurisdiction where litigation takes place.[115]

In order to become enforceable 'EPC-wide', after examination a European patent application must be further validated in each of the EPC countries where protection is sought. For this purpose, the majority of the EPC countries require patent applications to be fully translated into their respective official languages. Moreover, since each EPC country maintains its sovereignty over patent matters following the issuance of an European patent, the power of patent enforcement therefore rests with each EPC country and enforcement in Europe is thus fragmented, inaccessible to inventors and businesses, and engenders legal uncertainties and high costs,[116] putting Europe at a disadvantage globally. A study conducted by the European Commission in 2009 revealed that the high costs involved in

114 A patent holder must sue an alleged infringer in the national court of each country where the alleged infringement takes place. Accordingly, and subsequently, only the national court is competent in handling actions such as patent revocation and counterclaims. This causes divergent, sometimes conflicting, decisions and provoking uneven levels of protection among the EPC countries.

115 Therefore, the same patent issued by the EPO may be held valid in one EPC country, requested for modification in another, and found invalid in yet another EPC country. See: Assessment of the Impact of the European Patent Litigation Agreement, by the European Patent Office acting as secretariat of the Working Party on Litigation, February 2006. Available at: http://eplaw.org/wp-content/uploads/2015/12/EPLA_Impact_Assessment_2006_.pdf (last accessed 31 December 2016).

116 The main issues identified in the European patent system were: 1) high costs related to securing a patent in multiple European countries, including translation, publication and renewal; 2) differences in patent maintenance in the EU member states; 3) administrative complexity of registering transfers, licences and other rights related to patents; and 4) the likelihood of infringement and revocation proceedings in a number of national courts where patent protection is sought. For example, the translation cost is always huge, not to mention that each patent application would be usually more than 20 pages long. As for patent maintenance, presently annual renewal fees must be paid in each country where the patent is held valid. See: European Commission, *Proposal for a Regulation of the European Parliament and of the Council*, COM(2011) 215 final (Brussels: European Commission, 2011).

European patent application are fifteen times greater than the amount required for obtaining a patent grant in America.[117]

3. EU unitary patent and the EU Unified Patent Court

In order to make the 'patent system attractive for promoting innovation in Europe',[118] negotiations have been undertaken since the 1970s in order to create a unitary patent together with a specialised European patent court so that patent applicants would be afforded an efficient and cost-effective way to obtain patent protection as well as enforcement throughout Europe. In December 2012, the EU member states (except Spain and Italy) and the European Parliament finally agreed on the 'patent package', consisting of two regulations and one agreement,[119] for the creation of unitary patent protection in the EU.

Following the adoption of the two regulations in December 2012, the 26 contracting states are presently in the process of ratifying the Agreement on a Unified Patent Court in order to materialise a single and specialised patent jurisdiction. Once the agreement and the regulations enter into force, it will be possible to obtain a European patent with unitary effect, which is meant to be supranational. It is envisaged that the legal title of a unitary patent would ensure uniform protection for an invention across 26 contracting states on a one-stop-shop basis, providing huge cost advantages and reducing administrative burdens.[120]

With regard to the EU unified patent court, taking into account the opinion expressed by the European Court of Justice (ECJ) that creating a unified patent court would have created an international court outside of the institutional and the judicial framework of the EU,[121] the modified draft agreement of the European Unified Patent Litigation System

117 Pottelsberghe B. V. and Danguy J., *Economic Cost-Benefits Analysis of the Community Patent*, Working Paper 336 (Brussels: Bruegel.org, 2009). The Impact Assessment Report released by the EC in 2011 states that the total cost of validating a typical European patent in France, Germany and the United Kingdom is 680 Euros. If the patent is validated in 13 European countries the total cost increases to 12,500 Euros, and if the patent is validated in all 27 countries of the EU the total cost is 32,000 Euros.

118 *Promoting Innovation through Patents*, the follow-up to the Green Paper on the Community Patent and the Patent System in Europe, Communication from the Commission to the Council, the European Parliament and the Economic and Social Committee. Available at: http://ec.europa.eu/internal_market/indprop/docs/patent/docs/8682_en.pdf (last accessed 22 January 2016).

119 The two regulations and one agreement are: 1) Regulation (EU) No 1257/2012 of the European Parliament and of the Council of 17 December 2012 implementing enhanced cooperation in the area of the creation of unitary patent protection; 2) Council regulation (EU) No 1260/2012 of 17 December 2012 implementing enhanced cooperation in the area of the creation of unitary patent protection with regard to the applicable translation arrangements; 3) the draft agreement on the Unified Patent Court.

120 Available at: http://ec.europa.eu/growth/industry/intellectual-property/patents/unitary-patent/index_en.htm (last accessed 10 April 2016).

121 The ECJ ruled on 8 March 2011 that the proposed draft agreement on the European and Community Patents Court (renamed the Unified Patent Court) was not compatible with the European Community Treaties. The court based its decision on the findings that the proposed agreement would have conferred on an 'international court which is outside of the institutional and judicial framework of the EU, exclusive jurisdiction to hear a significant number of actions brought by individuals in the field of patent and would have altered the essential character of the powers which the EU treaties confer on the institutions of the EU and on the Member States'. Mahne K. P., 'Unitary patent and Unified Patent Court for the European Union: an analysis of Europe's long-standing attempt to create a supranational patent system'. 94 *Journal of the Patent and Trademark Office Society* 162 (2012).

thus ensures that the Unified Patent Court is to be a court common to the EU member states only, and will be subject to the EU law, and will have jurisdiction over litigation involving current and future European patents and future EU unitary patents.[122] The Unified Patent Court will have exclusive jurisdiction to decide actual and potential infringement, declare non-infringement, provide provisional and protective measures, issue injunctions, revoke patents, award damages and compensation, determine prior use, and award compensation for licenses. National courts will retain jurisdiction over all other patent matters not specifically set forth in the Unified Patent Court (Draft) Agreement. Decisions of the Unified Patent Court will have effect within the territories of all contracting states, whereas decisions regarding European patents will have effect only in the contracting states where a patent has been previously validated.[123] The Central Division of the Court of First Instance will be based in Paris, with two specialised sections in both London and Munich. The office of the Patent Court's President will be based in Paris.[124]

It is anticipated that the Unified Patent Court Agreement will enter into force following the ratification of the agreement by at least 13 EU member states, which is not yet a *fait accompli*. As of August 2016, ten contracting states have ratified the agreement.[125] It is yet to be seen if some EU countries are able to obtain the political support necessary to ratify the agreement because of the sweeping changes the agreement would bring to the *status quo vis-à-vis* national patent legislation. Under the Unified Patent Court Agreement, contracting states will have to relinquish nearly all sovereignty over European patents and future EU unitary patents to the Unified Patent Court.

122 Arts.1, 2, 14a, 14b, Draft Agreement on a Unified Patent Court and Draft Statute – 11 November 2011. The proposed Patent Court will consist of a Court of First Instance, a Court of Appeal and a Registry. The Court of First Instance will include a central division as well as local and regional divisions and the Court of Appeal will consist of a 'multinational composition of five judges'.

123 Arts.4, 5, 7, 15, 16, Draft Agreement on a Unified Patent Court and Draft Statute – 11 November 2011.

124 EU Unitary Patent - A Historic Breakthrough, European Council - EU Unitary Patent, 29 June 2012.

125 Available at: www.consilium.europa.eu/en/documents-publications/agreements-conventions/agreement/?aid=2013001 (last accessed 29 August 2016).

3 Assessing the progress of international patent rights harmonisation

I Introduction

Reflecting on the international patent treaties concluded so far, it is observed that minimum protection requirements as well as standardised procedures and formalities for multiple patent applications are the two successful means through which international patent rights protection has gained its success. What has failed to be achieved so far is substantive patent law harmonisation epitomised by the suspension of the SPLT negotiations.

I) Overview

Harmonisation is a slow and gradual process of seeking approximation of laws amidst constant reconciliation of conflicting demands for stability and for changes.[1] It is a very cumbersome process since IP law-making has always been a domestic matter because national legislation is a culmination of a country's level of wealth, economic structure, technological capability, political system and cultural tradition. Coupled with the fact that each country's traditional legal practice is distinctive, differences in substantive IP protection measures are therefore naturally expected among national legislations. For patent legislation, history can also reveal that many countries drew experience and knowledge from other countries that pioneered legislation on industrial property rights. Moreover, countries tend to adopt principles as well as measures from their counterparts whose general law and legal phraseology are more akin to theirs.[2] Therefore, a country's national patent law may very well be a blend with various origins.

In China's case, while the founding patent legislation was influenced by the German *Bürgerliches Gesetzbuch*, in the course of development the legislation has been motivated by the government's prevailing development needs and is shaped by the obligations derived from international patent treaties to which China has acceded. As a result, aside from complying with the TRIPS Agreement, China's patent legislation retains its unique features

1 Ladas S., *Patents, Trademarks and Related Rights: National and International Protection*, Vol.1 (Cambridge, MA: Harvard University Press, 1975), p. 15.

2 Thus, according to Professor Ladas, there are three general groups among the various countries with regard to principles and administrative regulations: the English-speaking countries, the Latin countries (France, Italy, Spain, Latin American countries and the Near East), and the Germanic or Northern European countries (Germany, Austria, Hungary, the Netherlands and the Scandinavian countries). See: Ladas S., *Patents, Trademarks, and Related Rights: National and International Protection*, Vol. 1 (Cambridge, MA: Harvard University Press, 1975), p. 10.

such as awarding patent rights to utility models after simplified examination, with a short protection term of ten years. The purpose of encouraging utility model patent applications is to popularise innovation activities in the society at large. After that, the government hopes that an innovative society will be nurtured and China's manufacturing-led economy will be transformed to become innovation-driven for sustainable development.

In terms of enforcement measures, while incorporating international treaties into domestic law, the same international provisions may lead to different outcomes in practice in each country. This is because domestic enforcement measures are typically determined by national market conditions, social contexts and local practices.[3] The outcomes of legal harmonisation, which is the process of incorporating international treaties into national law, are therefore determined by the socio-economic and cultural situation of the countries participating in the harmonisation process.[4] In this regard, India's patent law may stand out as a powerful example.

Although the Indian patent legislation has been in full compliance with the TRIPS Agreement since 2005, in order to continue to defend its citizens' constitutional rights to health, India's Patent (Amendment) Acts 2005 as well as its judiciary have been applying extremely stringent standards with regard to, for example, patentability in order to mitigate the impact of pharmaceutical products patenting, which might curtail the right to health. As a result, patenting pharmaceutical products can be a very tough undertaking in India, despite the legislation reversal illustrated in Chapter 8. In any case, while being incorporated into the Patent Law 2005, the relevant provisions of the TRIPS Agreement are augmented to such higher protection standards by the Indian legislature that certain pharmaceutical product patent applications are doomed to fail. Indian citizens are therefore able to continue benefitting from generic pharmaceutical products and the growth of the domestic industry is less affected by pharmaceutical products patenting in the wake of the entry into force of the TRIPS Agreement in India.

Therefore, in the course of international patent rights harmonisation, national patent legislation may be equally influenced by local interest groups so that favourable provisions could be maintained in order to enable the continued growth of such groups.[5]

II) Options for international patent rights harmonisation

Taking into account the above factors, a few options are available for undertaking international patent rights harmonisation.

3 Dinwoodie G.B., 'International intellectual property litigation: a vehicle for resurgent comparativist thought'. 49 *American Journal of Comparative Law* 429 (2001) 436.

4 Yu P.Y., 'The harmonisation game: what basketball can teach about intellectual property and international trade'. 26 *Fordham International Law Journal* 218 (2003). See also Ladas S., *Patents, Trademarks and Related Rights: National and International Protection*, Vol. 1 (Harvard University Press, 1975), p. 14.

5 The power of interest groups is also evident at the international level in terms of treaty negotiations. For example, GI protection for wines and spirits is guaranteed by Art.23 of the TRIPS Agreement thanks to the industry's successful lobby. By the same token, the plant breeding industry succeeded in inserting specific protection measures and therefore, by virtue of Art. 27, the TRIPS signatory countries must 'provide for the protection of plant varieties either by patent or by an effective *sui generis* system or by any combination thereof'. Moreover, the semiconductor industry managed to include certain provisions contained in the Treaty on Intellectual Property in Respect of Integrated Circuits (the IPIC Treaty) in the TRIPS Agreement, by virtue of Art.35, for additional protection.

The first option is legal transplant. Defined by Paul Geller, it is a process by which 'any legal notion or rule which, after being developed in a "source" body of law, is ... introduced into another "host" body of law'. China's initial patent legislation is a result of legal transplant, with the German *Bürgerliches Gesetzbuch* as a source of law. In Japan's case, some legal features from the French and the American patent laws were transplanted into the Patent Monopoly Ordinance, which was Japan's first enforced patent legislation promulgated on 18 April 1885.

Second, there is the option for diversification in order to achieve international patent rights harmonisation, meaning that a group of countries agree to disagree on certain provisions and, based on this, eventually reach an agreement nonetheless. A case in point in this regard is the provision of exhaustion contained in the TRIPS Agreement, which provides that 'nothing in this Agreement shall be used to address the issue of the exhaustion of intellectual property rights'. Such wording preserves the need for diversification while recognising the negotiation impasse among the contracting parties.

Third, there is full-fledged harmonisation, in which case countries or regions approximate laws of different countries. Such a process is often witnessed in the legislation process of the European Union when national laws of different member states are harmonised by the Union's directives.

Fourth, countries may adopt the legal standards imposed by other countries, engaging therefore in a hybrid harmonisation process of legal transplant and diversification. For example, under the TRIPS Agreement, while extending patent protection to all 'fields of technology', each member of the TRIPS Agreement is entitled to decide itself on the thresholds of patentability.

Finally, compromised harmonisation may also be an option. For example, when some contracting parties were not ready for a change, the Rome Act of the Berne Convention 1928 established the optional term for copyright protection which was life of the author plus 50 years.

II Modes of international patent rights harmonisation

I) Introduction

International patent rights harmonisation may be achieved by incorporating international patent treaties, which usually only provide the minimum protection standards, into national legislation. Consequently, a signatory country is at liberty to tailor the national provisions based on its economic priorities, legal practice and social background as long as the minimum protection standards are met. Therefore, as is reflected by India's case as mentioned above, provisions derived from the same international treaty may appear differently in practice after incorporation, in terms of scope and degree. The patentability thresholds test, which varies in different TRIPS members, serves a good illustration. Article 27 of the TRIPS Agreement sets down the principle that patents are available for any inventions, products or processes in all fields of technology as long as they are new, involve an inventive step and are capable of industrial application. While implementing the principle, concerning 'novelty' for example, the Chinese patent legislation imposed a higher threshold requiring an 'absolute novelty' test to be passed as far as invention and utility-model patent applications are concerned. Under the American patent law and the EPC, a 'non-obviousness' test, which is of a lower threshold in comparison with the 'absolute novelty' test, will suffice to qualify for 'being new'. Since the TRIPS Agreement is an international treaty that provides minimum IPR protection standards, when incorporating the TRIPS Agreement the signatory countries are not required to draft uniform provisions as long as the minimum protection standards prescribed by the Agreement are met by national legislation. In the process, the principle of flexibility may be called into play and that is how China legislates in its Patent Law, although China usually opts for a higher degree of patent protection.

Contrary to international treaties of 'minimum standards', in theory international treaties of 'maximum standards' specify the maximum protection standards and, in which case, signatory countries may not provide any protection measures of a lesser degree at the national level. So far, no international agreement on substantive patent protection measures at the maximum level has been reached.

II) Minimum harmonisation

Since the TRIPS Agreement provides the minimum IPR protection standards, the substantive patent protection measures are harmonised internationally at the same minimum level among the signatory countries.

Note that some of the minimum protection standards prescribed by TRIPS are built on the principles previously established by the Paris Convention such as, for example, the principle of priority right which is established by Art.4A(1) of the Paris Convention. Signatory countries may delay the implementation of the TRIPS Agreement if they are eligible to benefit from the transitional arrangements, either as a 'developing country', a 'transitional economy' or a 'least-developed country'. By virtue of Art.65 of the TRIPS Agreement, developing countries and transitional economies may delay implementing product patent protection requirements obliged by the Agreement for up to ten years if areas of technology were previously not protected by domestic patent laws. As to least-developed countries, Art.66 states that the ten-year grace period may be further extended upon a duly motivated request. Nonetheless, all TRIPS signatories must respect the national and the most-favoured-nation treatment from the date that they accede to the WTO Agreement. Being a developing country, a transitional economy or a least-developed country is irrelevant in this case, and the transitional arrangements provided by TRIPS are inapplicable.[6]

1. Eligibility

The TRIPS Agreement sets down the minimum standards for patent protection with regard to the eligibility of patentable subject matters that all signatory countries must obey. Article 27(1) of the agreement stipulates that members may not exclude any fields of technology from patentability, and no discrimination is admissible against the place of invention as far as patent application is concerned.[7] This provision prompted the US to amend its

6 On the other hand, Art.65(5) of the TRIPS Agreement states that countries eligible for the transitional period should not backslide. They must make sure that any changes in their laws, regulations and practices made during the transitional period do not result in a lesser degree of consistency with the provisions of the Agreement.

7 Note, however, that Art.27(2) of the agreement provides exceptions to patentability at the same time. For example, members may exclude subject matters such as 'diagnostic, therapeutic and surgical methods for the treatment of humans or animals' from patentable subjects.

patent law as, contrary to Art.27, at the time the US discriminated against the country of invention, which also affected the date of invention as it was dependent on the place of invention. On the other hand, until the America Invents Act came into force in March 2013, 'first-to-invent' was in practice in order to establish the right to a patent grant in the US. This was in fact in conflict with Art.27 of the TRIPS Agreement since Art.27 requires that patent rights must be available without discrimination in relation to the place of invention.

2. *Protection term*

Article 33 of the TRIPS Agreement stipulates that domestic patent laws must provide the same protection term of 20 years, counting from the date of application, and such protection can only be granted if the requirements concerning patentability are met after scrutiny. In order to comply with the protection standard, the US amended its law by extending the patent protection term from 17 years, counting from the time when the patent was granted, to 20 years, counting from the date when the application is filed.

3. *Thresholds test*

With regard to the thresholds test for patentability, Art.27(1) stipulates that an invention must be new, involve an inventive step and be capable of industrial application. While implementing the minimum protection standard, for example by virtue of Section 3(d) of the Patents (Amendment) Act 2005, India's legislature sets a much higher test for inventiveness that states that 'the mere discovery of a new form of a known substance' will not suffice to qualify as inventiveness. Section 3(d) further sets the limit that '… derivatives of known substance shall be considered to be the same substance, unless they differ significantly in properties with regard to efficacy […]'. Due to the higher threshold test of inventiveness, multinational pharmaceutical companies are often defeated in their pharmaceutical product patent applications in India, especially when 'evergreening' tactics are allegedly involved.[8]

4. *Exceptions to rights conferred*

Article 30 of the TRIPS Agreement provides that members may provide limited exceptions to the exclusive rights conferred by Art.28. However, exceptions to the exclusive rights conferred are only admissible if they: 1) involve public health and nutrition and public interest in sectors of vital importance to socio-economic and technology development; 2) prevent IPR holders' abusive behaviour or remedy unreasonable trade restraints that adversely affect international transfer of technology. Additionally, Art.7 of the TRIPS Agreement may be invoked to limit the scope of exclusive rights when it comes to promoting technological innovation and transferring and disseminating technology for maintaining social and economic welfare.

8 In this context, 'evergreening' takes place when pharmaceutical companies artificially extend the period of patent protection by patenting trivial secondary elements of their patented drug when the patent is about to expire. Basheer S. and Prashant R., '"Ducking" TRIPS in India: a saga involving Novartis and the legality of Section 3(D)'. 20 *National Law School of India Review* 131 (2008), 135–36.

5. *Compulsory licence*

Subject to Art.31 of the TRIPS Agreement, and building on Art.5A of the Paris Convention, under Art.8 of the TRIPS Agreement compulsory licence may be granted when public interest is at risk or if abusive behaviour takes place. As to what kind of behaviour will constitute an abuse of rights, members are at liberty to decide by taking either a TRIPS-comparable or a TRIPS-plus approach. For example, the US regards anti-competitive practices as 'abusive behaviour',[9] but, to some other countries, abusive behaviour will begin to surface when a patent holder fails to work the patent locally in due course or refuses to grant a license on reasonable terms that consequentially slows down industrial development. Abusive behaviour may also become apparent when a patent holder does not supply the national market with a sufficient quantity of the patented products, or demands an excessive price for such products.[10] As far as the TRIPS Agreement is concerned, Art.31 details a broad list of conditions restricting the proliferation of compulsory licences.

Art.48 of China's Patent Law 2008 acknowledges two scenarios in which any eligible entity or individual may apply for a compulsory licence for an invention or a utility model patent. In general, a compulsory licence may be granted in China when: 1) the patent holder fails to exploit or to fully exploit his patent without justification after the mandatory timeframe has lapsed[11]; 2) the patent holder's behaviour is deemed monopolistic. The Draft Patent Law 2015 upholds the same positions.

6. *Scope of patent protection*

The TRIPS Agreement also sets down the minimum standards with regard to the scope of IPR protection. In this regard, members are granted the privilege of flexibility while legislating, as long as the minimum protection standards are met and for which non-violatory state actions and changing circumstances may nullify and impair benefits otherwise conferred.[12] Additionally, Art.71 of the TRIPS Agreement establishes that the Council for TRIPS is authorised to review any relevant new modification or amendment of members' legislation.

III) Maximum harmonisation

Negotiating the SPLT was an attempt to harmonise the substantive patent protection measures at the maximum level. Although the negotiations were suspended in 2006 due to the divergent positions seen between the developing and the developed countries, as well as among the developed countries themselves, it is useful to list the divergence in detail in order to reflect on the distance between the minimum and the maximum patent protection standards, as well as the challenges that international patent rights harmonisation has yet to tackle.

9 Raskind L., 'Licensing under United States Antitrust Law'. 20 *Brook Journal of International Law* 49 (1994).

10 Bodenhausen G., *Guide to the Application of the Paris Convention for the Protection of Industrial Property as Revised at Stockholm in 1967.* (Geneva: WIPO, 1968) p. 71.

11 That is after the lapse of three full years from the date when a patent is granted and after the lapse of four full years from the date when a patent application is filed. See: Art.48, Patent Law 2008.

12 Hudec R., *Enforcing International Trade Law: The Evolution of the Modern GATT Legal System.* (London: Butterworth, 1993) p. 131.

1. *First-to-file vs. first-to-invent*

At the time of the SPLT negotiations, the US was the only country in the world that still followed the first-to-invent system, while the rest of the world followed the first-to-file system. Both systems were juxtaposed for a long time in the history of patent protection, until the first-to-invent system ceased to exist in the US in 2013, when the America Invents Act came into force. For the sake of completeness, a comparison is nonetheless made below to highlight the different philosophies that lie behind the two systems.

Under the first-to-file rule, a patent and its rights are granted to the first invention patent applicant when other patentability requirements are met. As to the first-to-invent rule, rights were granted to the first inventor who conceived and reduced the technology or invention to practice – i.e., to a working prototype or a well-written description. The first-to-file system provides the legal certainty regarding the right to a patent grant because the first applicant is always easy to identify in order for a patent office to decide and award a patent. Under the first-to-invent system, however, an 'interference proceeding'[13] was required in order to identify who was actually the first inventor to create the claimed invention.[14] As for the first-to-file system, if there is more than one patent application that claims the same invention, the priority right to patent would be based on the earlier-filed application. Also, under the first-to-file system, prior art is defined as public disclosure made available before the filing date. In the case of the first-to-invent system, the cut-off date of a priority art was the date of invention, which was often decided by the interference proceeding. Although interference proceedings rarely took place, it was regarded as the only apparent disadvantage of the first-to-invent system.

The first-to-file system is formulated on the premise of the contract theory of a patent. Under this theory, a patent is a contract between an inventor and the public, which grants the inventor a public franchise, a patent monopoly, in exchange for public disclosure of the invention. When a patent is a *quid pro quo* for public disclosure of the invention, it is not unreasonable to reward the first inventor with a patent monopoly for disclosing the invention to the public.[15] Therefore, compared with the first-to-invent rule, the practical advantage of the first-to-file system is its simplicity, in that whoever files the application first shall be entitled to a patent grant, if other requirements are met. Having said that, the first-to-file rule would become unfair in a country, such as the US, which spans multiple time zones and where the working hours of the patent offices follow the local times. The first-to-file rule would always give the advantage to applicants in the east and the disadvantage in the west. There were examples of near-simultaneous application submissions where the time zone made the decisive difference between succeeding, and missing out, on a patent grant.

13 Under the first-to-invent system, when two inventors filed the same invention patent application, an interference hearing would take place before the Board of Appeals and Interferences at the US Patent Office to determine who conceived the invention first, and whether the inventors were diligent in reducing the invention to practice. Available at: www.generalpatent.com/first-file-vs-first-invent-who-really-benefits-changing-u-s-patent-system (last accessed 23 February 2016).

14 Jenei S., 'Patent reform: what does first-to-file mean to me?' (*Patent Baristas*, 17 January 2008), available online at: www.patentbaristas.com/archives/2008/01/17/patent-reform-what-does-first-to-file-mean-to-me/ (last accessed 23 February 2016).

15 General Patent Corporation, 'First-to-file *vs.* first-to-invent: who really benefits from changing the US patent system?' *Wealth of Ideas* Newsletter (October 2007). Available at: www.generalpatent.com/first-file-vs-first-invent-who-really-benefits-changing-u-s-patent-system (last accessed 23 February 2016).

Note that one advantage that the first-to-invent system could offer was that it rewarded a patent to the first inventor, not the champion of the race to the Patent Office, when other requirements are met. Under the first-to-invent system, a grace period of 12 months, counting from the date of invention to the date of submitting the patent application, allowed inventors to work further on the invention for modification or improvement and to find the best mode to carry it out before submitting a patent application. Moreover, during the grace period, an inventor could disclose the invention for technical and financial negotiations without losing the right to patent.[16]

2. *Grace period*

Within the context of patent application, a grace period offers a specific period of time, usually six or twelve months, during which an inventor or the successor in title may file a patent application in spite of previous disclosure, orally or in writing, by use or on exhibition. Under the circumstances, novelty is not destroyed despite the disclosure, which means a prior date will not be established and therefore a patent may still be granted, provided all other requirements concerning patentability[17] and formalities are fulfilled.

A grace period may be awarded under three circumstances by national patent legislation. First, non-prejudicial disclosure at an exhibition, which means an invention is disclosed when it is being displayed at an exhibition by the inventor or by a third party with the agreement of the inventor. This scenario falls under the remit of Art.11(1) of the Paris Convention. Second, disclosure in consequence of an abuse, which means an invention was unlawfully disclosed by a third party because of lawfully or unlawfully acquired information. Examples in this case include the theft of objects containing information on an invention or violation of a promise to keep an invention secret. Third, lawful non-prejudicial disclosure other than at an exhibition, which means an invention is disclosed by the inventor or lawfully disclosed by a third party of a kind unrelated to the first two scenarios. Such disclosure takes place when an invention is disclosed by publication in the form of a scientific article or a lecture or by public use (in particular, use made in order to test the invention). A grace period awarded in the third circumstance is often referred to as 'the general grace period'.[18]

The Paris Convention grants temporary protection to disclosures that take place under the first scenario. Article 11(1) of the Paris Convention protects patentable inventions, utility models, industrial designs and trademarks when they are exhibited at official or officially recognised international exhibitions held in the territory of the Union members.

Awarding a 'grace period' is a patent protection measure applied in many countries, such as the US, Japan, China,[19] the Russian Federation, Brazil, Australia and Spain, which

16 Jenei S., 'Patent reform: what does first-to-file mean to me? (*Patent Baristas*, 17 January 2008). available at: www.patentbaristas.com/archives/2008/01/17/patent-reform-what-does-first-to-file-mean-to-me/ (last accessed 23 February 2016).

17 See *Grace Period and Invention Law in Europe and Selected States* (from IPR Helpdesk – a project of the European Commission DG Enterprise).

18 Straus J. and Galama J., *Introduction of a Grace Period into European Patent Law – Submission of Expert Opinions*, Doc. CA/41/00, 26 May. (Munich: European Patent Office, 2000) pp.1–23 at 11.

19 Art.24 of the Chinese Patent Law 2008 provides a grace period of six months for inventions that have been exhibited for the first time at an international exhibition sponsored or recognised by the Chinese government, or disclosed without the applicant's consent, or disclosed for the first time at a prescribed academic or technical conference. The Draft Patent Law 2015 upholds this application.

typically grant inventors a period of six or 12 months from the date the invention is disclosed to the public until the date when the patent application is submitted. It is closely linked to the 'first-to-invent' system that the US undertook at the time,[20] thanks to which an inventor may publish the invention during the grace period and the publication would not destroy the novelty of the invention as a consequence. In Europe, however, Art.55 of the EPC provides a grace period of six months only in the first two scenarios as mentioned above, which are 'non-prejudicial disclosure at an exhibition' and 'disclosure in consequence of an abuse',[21] but not in the third scenario of 'general grace period'.[22] This omission has attracted considerable controversy, especially between the EPC signatory countries and the US. In the course of international patent harmonisation in the mid-1980s, the EPC's resistance to recognising the general grace period was said to be one of the main reasons for the US withdrawing its support for the process, and it was equally a key trade-off sought by the US for changing its 'first to invent' rule.[23]

3. *Prior art*

Prior art, also known as 'the state of the art', constitutes all information that has been made available to the public in any form before a given date that might be relevant to a patent's originality claim. If an invention is already described in a prior art, the invention loses its novelty and will not be patentable. Prior art was defined differently under the first-to-file and first-to-invent systems. Under the first-to-file system, prior art refers to the knowledge that has been made available to the public in any form before the filing date of a patent application, which is also called the priority date. As for the first-to-invent system, prior art referred to the knowledge made available to the public preceding the moment that the invention came into being.

Different countries apply different standards as far as prior art is concerned. Some countries apply an absolute standard, in which case disclosure that takes place anywhere in any form before the patent filing date will be considered as prior art. The EPO and Japan follow the 'absolute standard' application method. Article 29 of the Japanese Patent Act defines 'prior' as the period of time that precedes the moment of filing a patent application. The US, China, India and some other countries follow the 'relative standard' approach, thereby only disclosure made in writing within the territory of the country concerned will be seen as prior art. Oral or other forms of disclosure won't qualify as prior art. This being the case, traditional/indigenous knowledge is not recognised as prior art in these countries.

20 Roucounas E., 'The debate regarding the grace period in international patent law: a reminder' in *All European Academies Biennial Yearbook: New Perspectives in Academia* (Amsterdam: ALLEA, 2006), p. 31.

21 Art.55(1)(a)(b), European Patent Convention.

22 Nonetheless, Art.7(c) of the Spanish Patent Law 1998 provides a six-month grace period for tests carried out by the patent applicant or by his legal predecessor, provided that they do not imply working the invention or offering it for sale and that the tests were carried out during the six months preceding the filing of the application. Note that this provision is enforceable only within the Spanish patent jurisdiction. Applicants enjoying this privilege are not able to extend it to other EPO national patent offices, which do not offer a comparable grace period.

23 Correa C., *An Agenda for Patent Reform and Harmonisation for Developing Countries*, a paper prepared for the Bellagio Dialogue on Intellectual Property and Sustainable Development: Revising the Agenda in a New Context, organised by International Centre for Trade and Sustainable Development, September 24–28, Bellagio, Italy (ICTSD, 2005).

'Prior art' is a much debated issue during the process of international patent rights harmonisation, with debate on, for example, whether secret disclosure of a pending application should be seen as prior art as far as an inventive step is concerned. Secret prior art or conflicting application is seen as an 'inventive step' in the eyes of the American patent law. Also, while examining novelty, the US, the EPO and Japan consider the content of a prior application as a whole, and other countries, for example India, only compare later and earlier claims in order to check if the claims are coterminous.

There are also discussions concerning whether to include prior secret commercial use or offer for sale without disclosing the invention by the patent applicant as prior art. The American patent law qualifies both as prior art, in order to prevent an inventor from extending rights by not disclosing the invention.[24] Whether to include the prior art admitted in the application submitted on the filing date as prior art remains equally an issue among different countries. Also, there is a question concerning whether information disclosed on digital media, such as internet, should disqualify novelty. Article 29(1)(iii) of the Japanese Patent Act states that an invention made publicly available by an electric telecommunication in Japan or in a foreign country will lose its novelty, and thus not be qualified for patent grant.

4. *Novelty*

Novelty is directly linked to patentability. It sits between the existing prior art at the date of filing, or the date of priority, and the claimed invention. An invention is not patentable if the claimed subject matter was disclosed before the filing date of the application, or before the date of priority if the priority of an earlier patent application is already claimed.

'Novelty' is not defined by the TRIPS Agreement, so therefore members are able to take advantage of the instrument of flexibility to set their respective threshold. The US maintains its 'relative novelty' standard with regard to the place where disclosure takes place. Japan and the EPO impose a 'universal novelty' threshold, while New Zealand requires 'local novelty'. In practice, novelty is defined very narrowly by most patent offices. In some cases, 'photographic' disclosure in a single prior document is required in order to discount a novelty claim. Controversies thus arise, especially when the so-called 'selection inventions' take place, which means an invention is not found *expressis verbis* in a document but may be derived therefrom, and where the invention is selected from a family of products that are already disclosed.[25]

The timeline as to when a patent document is published is decisive when assessing if an invention has lost its novelty. Rule 34.1(c)(i) of the Regulations under the PCT states that national patent documents are those documents of patent applications published from 1920 onwards by a number of countries, such as Japan, the UK and the US, and which are at the disposal of each international patent search authority. The implication of this rule is

24 Available at: www.law.cornell.edu/uscode/text/35/102?quicktabs_8=1#quicktabs-8 (last accessed 23 February 2016).

25 Correa C., *An Agenda for Patent Reform and Harmonisation for Developing Countries*, a paper prepared for the Bellagio Dialogue on Intellectual Property and Sustainable Development: Revising the Agenda in a New Context, organised by International Centre for Trade and Sustainable Development, September 24–28, Bellagio, Italy (ICTSD, 2005).

that certain traditional knowledge would be denied novelty and thus disqualified from being a patentable subject matter.

Within the context of the first-to-file system, the issue of novelty kicks in when two or more applications for the same invention are filed on the same day. Under Art.39(2) of the Japanese Patent Act, when two or more patent applications claiming an identical invention are filed on the same date, only one applicant selected after consulting all the applicants concerned may be entitled to obtain a patent grant for the invention claimed. In case no agreement could be reached after consultation or if consultation is unable to take place, none of the applicants would be entitled to a patent grant for the claimed invention. Moreover, Art.39(1) of the Japanese Patent Act states that if two or more patent applications claiming an identical invention are filed on different dates, only the applicant who file the patent application on the earliest date may be entitled to a patent grant for the invention claimed.

5. *Inventive step*

Also known as 'non-obviousness', an inventive step is a step not obvious to a person skilled in the art, having regard to any matter that forms part of the state of the art comprising all matters and has, at any time before the priority date of that invention, been made available to the public by written or oral description, by use or in any other way. In order to pass the threshold test of inventive step, it is necessary to ask whether the invention in question is at an adequate distance beyond or above the state of the art.[26] The purpose of imposing the threshold of 'inventive step' is to avoid granting patent protection to inventions which only follow 'normal product design and development', and consequently the balance between the social costs incurred and the incentives created by the patent system would be in jeopardy.

As 'inventive step' is, nonetheless, not defined by the TRIPS Agreement, it is thus of no surprise to find that divergent standards divide the EPC and American patent law, although both standards meet the minimum requirement set down by Art.27(1) of the TRIPS Agreement. The EPC adopts a 'problem-solution approach', which consists of three steps, namely: 1) identifying the closest prior art, which is the most relevant prior art; 2) determining the objective technical problem, which means to determine the technical problem that the claimed invention addresses and successfully solves; and 3) examining whether or not the claimed solution to the objective technical problem is obvious to a skilled person in view of the state of the art in general. Under the jurisdiction of the EPC, the examining process will be conducted with a 'could-would approach', which means not asking whether the skilled person could have carried out the invention, but whether he would have done so in the hope of solving the underlying technical problem or in the expectation of some improvement or advantage.[27] If a skilled person would have been prompted to modify the closest prior art in such a way as to arrive at something falling within the terms of

26 Professor Barton wrote that 'only research beyond that done as part of normal product design and development should be rewarded with a patent. Routine redesign should not be enough, for there is no need for monopolies as an incentive for such research'. See Barton, J. H., 'Non-obviousness'. 43 *The Intellectual Property Law Review* 3 (2003), 475–506.

27 Available at: www.epo.org/law-practice/legal-texts/html/caselaw/2013/e/clr_i_d_5.htm (last accessed 15 August 2016).

the claims, then the invention does not involve an inventive step. Under the American patent law, by virtue of 35 US Code 103, to pass the 'inventive step' test is to see if a person 'having ordinary skill in the art' would not know how to solve the problem at which the invention is directed by using exactly the same mechanism. To determine 'inventive step', American courts adopted the Graham Factors[28] test in order to investigate: 1) the scope and the content of the prior art; 2) the level of ordinary skill in the art; 3) the differences between the claimed invention and the prior art; and 4) the objective evidence of non-obviousness, which must denote a) commercial success, b) long-felt but unsolved needs, and c) failure of others.

Just as with the novelty test, the test of inventive step is of great importance in patent examination. On the one hand, patent should only be granted to inventions that satisfy the legal prerequisites so that monopoly rights would be justifiably conferred in exchange for efforts paid in innovation. On the other hand, if, however, a patent is granted to an invention that only involves a little non-obviousness and trivial technological development, a proliferation of patent grants will increase research costs and obstruct competition, innovation would therefore be impeded rather than being motivated by the monopoly rights derived therefrom. Certainly, a higher threshold for inventive step is indispensable in order to curb patent malpractices aimed at blocking competition and follow-on innovation.

6. *Industrial applicability*

The TRIPS Agreement did not define 'industrial application' and, in the context of patentability, different countries provide different meanings to the test, mainly due to the language divide. Initially, 'industrial application' was understood as 'an application in the automated production of material goods'. In the English language, 'industry' also has a broader meaning of 'type of work' that may refer to, for example, the software industry, the patent industry, the pharmaceutical industry. In French, however, the word '*industrie*' is still restricted to mean '*ensemble des activités économiques qui produisent des biens matériels par la transformation et la mise en oeuvre de matières premières*'[29] which is close to the initial meaning of 'industrial application' as is given above. This definition has been upheld by courts in various judgments. For example, in the Schlumberger case,[30] software is not regarded as a patentable subject matter since it does not constitute an inventive part of an industrial production process.

Article 12(4) of the draft SPLT provided 'inventive step' with three alternative definitions that epitomised the disparate opinions on 'industrial applicability' that different countries advocated at the time.[31] The draft text states that an invention shall be considered industrially

28 *Graham* v. *John Deere Co.* 383 US 1 (1966). Courts in other cases also considered the following as an indicator of non-obviousness: 1) scepticism or disbelief before an invention (*Environmental Designs, Ltd. v. Union Oil Co. of California*); 2) copying, praise, unexpected results, and industry acceptance (*Allen Archery, Inc.* v. *Browning Mfg. Co.*; *Diversitech Corp.* v. *Century Steps Inc.*).

29 See Larousse.

30 *Schlumberger Canada Ltd.* v. *Canada (Commissioner of Patents)* concerns the patentability of a software invention within the context of the Patent Act (Canada). At issue was the patentability of a method of combining and analysing borehole measurements for oil and gas exploration using a computer programme according to mathematical formulas.

31 See the Draft Substantive Patent Law Treaty, prepared by the International Bureau, for the Standing Committee on the Law of Patents, Tenth Session, Geneva, May 10 to 14, 2004, SCP/10/2.

applicable if it: a) can be made or used for exploitation in any field of [commercial] [economic] activity; b) can be made or used in any kind of industry – 'Industry' shall be understood in its broadest sense and shall not be limited to industry and commerce proper, but include agricultural and extractive industries as in the Paris Convention; c) has a specific, substantial and credible utility. To reflect on China's patent legislation, Art.22 of China's Patent Law 2008 defines 'practical applicability' as 'the invention or utility model can be made or used and can produce effective results', which is maintained by the Draft Patent Law 2015. The EPC does not seem to go much further than what Art.27 of the TRIPS Agreement provides. Article 57 of the EPC simply defines 'industrial application' as an invention which 'can be made or used in any kind of industry, including agriculture'.

7. Enabling disclosure

Article 29(1) of the TRIPS Agreement requires an invention to be disclosed in a manner sufficiently clear and complete so that a person skilled in the art can carry it out. A patent applicant may be also required to indicate in the application the best mode for carrying out the invention known to the inventor at the date of application or, where priority is claimed, at the priority date of the application. Provisions concerning 'disclosure' laid down by different legislations are similar, although in some countries a higher degree of disclosure is required, especially when applicants are compelled to disclose 'the best mode' for carrying out the invention concerned. For example, Art.36(4) of the Japan Patent Act stipulates that an invention must be explained in detail and be described in a manner sufficiently clear and complete in order for the invention to be carried out by a person having ordinary skill in the art to which the invention pertains. China's Patent Law 2008 sets down in Art.26 that an invention must be described in a manner sufficiently clear and complete that a person skilled in the relevant field of technology can accurately produce it; where necessary, drawings should be appended. The Chinese patent legislation equally requires that the abstract of an application must describe briefly the technical essentials of an invention or a utility model, and a patent claim must, on the basis of the specifications, state the requested scope of patent protection. The provisions are maintained by the Draft Patent Law 2015. The American patent legislation imposes the same requirements. 35 US Code 112 provides that specifications of a patent application

> shall contain a written description of the invention, and of the manner and process of making and using it, in such full, clear, concise, and exact terms as to enable any person skilled in the art to which it pertains, or with which it is most nearly connected, to make and use the same, and shall set forth the best mode contemplated by the inventor or joint inventor of carrying out the invention.

8. Exceptions to patentability

Articles 27(2)(3) of the TRIPS Agreement set down the exceptions to patentable subject matters. In the first place, Art.27(2) stipulates that patentable inventions must not harm *ordre public* or morality. This requirement has long been in existence in some countries. For example, Schering AG (now Bayer Schering Healthcare) was not able to apply for a patent for Anovlar in Belgium because the oral contraceptive pill was considered as an invention against morality in the 1960s and therefore it was not a patentable subject matter. Ferdinand Peeters, the Belgian inventor of the pill, did not apply for patent on his invention. As a devout Catholic, Dr Peeters in fact never came to terms with his invention as it clashed with the view of the Church. Equally, under Art.27(3) of the TRIPS Agreement, treatment of humans or animals, plants and animals other than micro-organisms, and essential biological processes for the production of plants or animals other than non-biological and microbiological processes, may be excluded from patentability. In addition, though not mentioned by the TRIPS Agreement, inventions of military importance or of national (military) interest, such as the atomic bomb, will not be patentable. Therefore, national security also plays a crucial role in deciding patentability of an invention.

Owing to the principle of flexibility, while incorporating the provisions of 'exceptions to patentability' into national legislation, varied positions appear. For example, businesses from the developed countries have urged the developing countries to grant patent protection to biotechnological inventions, while the developing countries are often convinced that this would harm their pharmaceutical industry, which is usually in its infancy. For the developing countries, patenting biotechnological inventions may only become appropriate after a country gains sufficient development in the industry.

The issue of business method is yet another area where divergence exists in terms of exceptions to patentability. Patent laws in Japan and the US do not prohibit patenting business methods while the EPC does.[32] In the US, the current case law requires a business method to be tied to a particular machine (for example, computer) or to a transformation of objects before it may become patentable. The Court of Appeal for the Federal Circuit reiterated the machine-or-transformation test in the case *In re Bilski*[33] as the applicable test for patentable subject matters (and therefore affirmed the decision of rejecting the patent claim that involved the business method of hedging risks in commodities trading). In June 2010, on appeal, the US Supreme Court rejected the machine-or-transformation test as the sole test for examining patent eligibility. In any event, business methods continue to be patentable in the US

9. *Exhaustion of rights*

The concept of exhaustion of rights, which may also be referred to as 'first sale', limits the exclusive rights that a patent holder may continue to enjoy after an authorised sale of a patented product. The concept is based on the principle that a patent holder should not be allowed to profit twice from the exclusive rights by re-selling the same patented product, after already being awarded for disclosing the invention when a patent is granted. Therefore, under the concept of exhaustion of rights, once an authorised sale of a patented product takes place, the patent holder's exclusive rights to control the use and the sale of that patented product will be exhausted, and the authorised purchaser is free to use or resell that patented product without further restraints.[34] The concept of exhaustion of rights protects authorised purchasers from infringement claims with respect to the use or the sale of a patented product after the patent holder authorised its sale. Thus, pursuant to the first sale, a patent holder can no longer control or oppose subsequent acts of resale, rental, lending or other forms of commercial use by third parties.

32 Art.52 (2)(c) and (3), EPC.

33 545 F.3d 943, 88 USP.Q.2d 1385 (Fed. Cir. 2008).

34 Note, however, the patent owner retains the right to exclude purchasers of the articles from making the patented invention anew, unless it is specifically authorised by the patentee.

There is, nonetheless, a disagreement regarding the extent to which the sale of a patented product abroad may exhaust the exclusive rights that cover the patented product in the context of domestic law. Questions will arise when parallel importation takes place, referring to importing goods outside of the distribution channels that are contractually negotiated by the patent holder. A patent holder may thus try to object to importation in order to separate markets. If marketing a patented product abroad is undertaken by the patent holder or with his/her consent, it will lead to the exhaustion of the domestic patent rights and the rights of importation will also be exhausted and, subsequently, they can no longer be invoked against such parallel importation.[35]

There are three types of exhaustion: national, regional and international exhaustion. National exhaustion does not allow a patent holder to control the commercial exploitation of the patented products that are sold in the domestic market by the patent holder or with his/her consent. However, the patent holder, or an authorised licensee, may still oppose the importation of the originally patented products marketed abroad based on the right of importation. As for regional exhaustion, the first sale of the patented product by the patent holder or with his/her consent exhausts any patent rights over the given products not only domestically but within the whole region. As a result, parallel imports within the region can no longer be opposed based on the patent right. If international exhaustion is applied, the patent rights are exhausted once the product is sold by the patent holder or with his/her consent in any part of the world.

In summary, as is illustrated above, when the minimum protection standards and the principle of flexibility are applied together in the course of international patent rights harmonisation, a series of divergent protection measures emerge in patent legislation in different TRIPS members. Among them, some undertake a 'TRIPS-plus' approach while incorporating the TRIPS Agreement into national legislation, and others a 'TRIPS-compliance' or 'TRIPS-minus' approach by taking advantage of the principle of limitations and exceptions which is offered by Art.13 of the TRIPS Agreement. In the case of the 'TRIPS-minus' approach, to determine whether the rights of a patent holder are eroded during the exercise, the three-step test may be called in for verification.

III Three-step test

The three-step test is defined by Art.13 of the TRIPS Agreement, and it may be best explained by the WTO dispute settlement case United States – Section 110(5) of the US Copyright Act (hereunder the US Copyright case).[36]

I) Introduction

First introduced by Art.9(2) of the Berne Convention for the exclusive right of reproduction, the three-step test aims to safeguard copyright holders' interests by placing restraints on the limitations and exceptions that a signatory member may exploit while incorporating the Convention into its national legislation, so that the interests of the right holder will not erode. Since then, the concept was embodied in a few international IPR treaties and, among them,

35 Available at: www.wipo.int/sme/en/ip_business/export/international_exhaustion.htm (last accessed 23 February 2016).

36 United States – Section 110(5) of the US Copyright Act, WT/DS160/R, of 15 June 2000.

the TRIPS Agreement in relation to Arts.2(2),[37] 7,[38] 9(1)[39] and 13, as well as the WIPO Copyright Treaty (Art.10) and the WIPO Performances and Phonograms Treaty.[40]

The three-step test requires that any exceptions to IPR protection must 1) be a special case, 2) not unreasonably interfere with normal commercial exploitation, and 3) not unreasonably prejudice the legitimate interests of an IPR-holder. The test aims to achieve two objectives. First, the test canvasses the areas where an IPR-holder does not need such rights to maximise their income. Second, the test provides a compensation scheme for exceptions that are considered desirable from a public interest point of view but nonetheless could affect the material interests of an IPR-holder.[41]

So far, three cases that concern the three-step test were brought in front of the WTO DSB, namely Canada – Patent Protection of Pharmaceutical Products, the US Copyright case and European Communities – Protection of Trademarks and Geographical Indications for Agricultural Products and Foodstuffs.

II) An analysis of the three-step test

1. 'certain special cases'

The requirement of 'certain special cases' obliges that an exception be clearly delineated and is only applied to a specifically defined area either with or without specific public policy objectives.[42] In the US Copyright case,[43] the panel of the WTO DSB precluded from the outset exceptions of broad general application. The panel then clarified that the term

37 Art.2(2) of the TRIPS Agreement stipulates that members shall not relinquish their existing obligations under the Paris Convention, the Berne Convention, the Rome Convention and the Treaty on Intellectual Property in Respect of Integrated Circuits.

38 Under Art.7 of the TRIPS Agreement, among others, the protection of IPR should contribute to the mutual advantage of producers and users and in a manner conducive to a balance of rights and obligations.

39 Art.9(1) of the TRIPS Agreement stipulates that members shall comply with Arts.1 through 21 of the Berne Convention (1971) and the Appendix, except Art.6*bis* (moral rights).

40 Art.13 of the TRIPS Agreement first of all requires members to confine limitations or exceptions to exclusive rights to certain special cases only. Such special cases must not be in conflict with a normal exploitation of the work and do not unreasonably prejudice the legitimate interests of the right holder. Art.13 of the TRIPS Agreement concurs with Art.10 of the WIPO Copyright Treaty which provides that Contracting Parties may provide limitations or exceptions to authors in certain special cases when it does not conflict with a normal exploitation of the work and does not unreasonably prejudice the legitimate interest of the author (by virtue of Agreed Statement Concerning Art.10, the limitations and exceptions may extend to the digital environment). Similarly, Art.16 of the WIPO Performances and Phonograms Treaty states the same possibility of providing exceptions to certain special cases in the Contracting Parties' national legislation with regard to the protection of performers and producers of phonograms in connection with the protection of copyright in literary and artistic works. The remit of the limitations and exceptions is also applicable to industrial designs and patent rights protection which are provided by Art.26(2) and Art.30 of the TRIPS Agreement, respectively.

41 Gervais D., 'Intellectual property and human rights: learning to live together' in P. Torremans (Ed.) ***Intellectual Property and Human Rights – Enhanced Edition of Copyright and Human Rights*** (New York: Kluwer Law International BV, 2008), p. 8.

42 Gervais D., 'Towards a new core international copyright norm: the reverse Three-Step Test'. 9 *Marquette Intellectual Property Law Review* 1 (2005), 1.

43 In January 1999 the EC alleged that Section 110(5) of the US Copyright Act, which permitted, under certain conditions, the playing of radio and television music in public places without the payment of a royalty fee to the performing rights societies, was inconsistent with US obligations under Art.9(1) of the TRIPS Agreement, which requires members to comply with Arts.1–21 of the Berne Convention.

'certain special cases' required that 'limitation or exception' must be clearly defined in national legislation and be narrow in scope and reach. The panel further stated that 'limitation or exception must be limited in its field of application or exceptional in its scope. In other words, an exception or limitation should be narrow in quantitative as well as a qualitative sense'.[44]

2. *'do not unreasonably interfere with normal commercial exploitation'*

Within the context of the three-step test, 'exploitation' suggests that by working the IPR concerned, an IPR-holder could achieve a maximised profit.

With regard to the term 'normal', as noted by Professor Gervais, the question is particularly relevant to new forms of, and emerging, business models that have not been common or 'normal' in an empirical sense thus far. As the purpose of the second step is to 'fortify authors' interests in their accustomed markets against local legislative inroads',[45] being 'normal' seems to refer to an exception that is not allowed if it were to cover any form of exploitation, which has, or is likely to acquire, considerable importance. This means that if an exception is used to limit a commercially significant market or, more so, to enter into competition with an IPR holder, the exception will be prohibited.[46]

3. *'unreasonable prejudice to legitimate interests of rights holders'*

The panel for the US Copyright case observed that the third step of the three-step test requires an analysis with regard to the qualities of 'interests', 'legitimate'[47] and 'unreasonable'. The panel noted that 'interests' need not be 'limited to actual or potential economic advantage or detriment'.[48] The need to balance the rights of IPR holders and the interests of users may be also taken into account.[49] As to 'legitimate interests', the Records of the Stockholm Conference revising the Berne Convention 1967 noted that some

44 United States – Section 110(5) of the US Copyright Act, WT/DS160/R, para 6.109.

45 Professor Paul Goldstein, Stanford Law School.

46 In the US Copyright case, the panel of the WTO DSB first addressed the question as to whether the term 'normal' meant 'empirical' or 'normative' in order to examine if the term implied ways with which the work was in fact exploited or if the nature of exploitation was potential, admissible or desirable. The panel ruled that both connotations were appropriate. Moreover, after having consulted the drafting documents of Art.9.2 of the Berne Convention which were submitted at the Stockholm Revision Conference in 1967, the panel decided that 'all forms of exploitation which have, or are likely to acquire, considerable economic or practical importance must be reserved to the authors'. The panel then concluded that 'in addition to those forms of exploitation that generate significant or tangible revenue, one way of measuring normative connotation of normal exploitation is to consider if those forms of exploitation which, with a certain degree of likelihood and plausibility, could acquire considerable economic or practical importance'. United States – Section 110(5) of the US Copyright Act, WT/DS160/R, paras 6.179, 180.

47 For 'legitimate', the panel adduced both a 'legal positivist' perspective which authorised or protected by law and 'a more normative perspective in the context of calling for the protection of interests that are justifiable in the light of objectives that underlie the protection of exclusive rights'. See United States – Section 110(5) of the US Copyright Act, WT/DS160/R, para 6.224.

48 United States – Section 110(5) of the US Copyright Act, WT/DS160/R, para 6.223.

49 Gervais D., 'Intellectual property and human rights: learning to live together' in P. Torremans (Ed.) *Intellectual Property and Human Rights – Enhanced Edition of Copyright and Human Rights* (New York: Kluwer Law International BV, 2008), p. 9.

contracting parties took the view that 'legitimate interests' meant 'justifiable interests' in the sense that they are supported by social norms and relevant public policies.

In relation to 'prejudice', the panel concluded in the US Copyright case that 'not unreasonably prejudice' connotes 'a slightly stricter standard' than 'reasonable'.[50] While acknowledging that the treaty text accepts in case a copyrights holder's interests suffer some prejudice, the panel took the view that the prejudice would reach an 'unreasonable' level 'if an exception or limitation causes, or has the potential to cause, an unreasonable loss of income to the copyrights owner'.[51] Nonetheless, the panel also noted that prejudice might be brought back to a tolerable level should compensation be provided.[52] The panel further decided that the combination of the notion of 'prejudice' with that of 'interests' would point at a legal-normative approach, which implies that 'legitimate interests' are those that are protected by law and those interests are almost, by definition, legal interests.

As to 'unreasonable prejudice', it is noted that in the French version of the Berne Convention the expression '*préjudice injustifié*' is used in order to include a reasonableness/justifiability criterion which would, in return, allow the establishment of a balance between the rights of authors and other copyrights holders as well as the needs and interests of users. In other words, to a certain level, prejudice may be warranted when the justification of a public interest is present in order to limit the remit of copyrights. In line with this analysis, the panel for the US Copyright case decided that 'prejudice to the legitimate interests of rights holders reaches an unreasonable level if an exception or limitation causes or has the potential to cause an unreasonable loss of income to the copyright owner'. Moreover, a public interest imperative may lead a government to apply an exception to a particular copyright that may result in a loss of revenue for the copyrights holder, but nonetheless may be 'justified'.

To sum up the above explanations, and following the panel decision on the US Copyright case, to determine if an IPR-holder's rights are eroded when the flexibility of 'exceptions and limitations' is applied by a national legislation is to see if the exception in question: 1) is limited to a narrow scope and confined to a specifically defined area, although local policies that underline the exception do not need justification; 2) competes with the actual or the potential source of economic gains in the same ways that a right-holder would usually exercise under copyrights; and, finally, 3) unreasonably harms a right-holder's interests that may be justified in light of the general objectives of copyrights, although the unreasonableness may be mitigated if some compensation is provided, for example in the form of a compulsory licence.[53]

The implication of the test is that any exceptions without compensation must be measured against an IPR-holder's demonstrable loss of income. To translate this principle into commercial terms, it is to see if an exception would significantly limit a right-holder's existing sales or licensing income, or prevent a right-holder from trying to sell or license. If yes,

50 United States – Section 110(5) of the US Copyright Act, WT/DS160/R, para 6.225.

51 United States – Section 110(5) of the US Copyright Act, WT/DS160/R, para 6.229.

52 Ginsburg J. C., 'Toward supranational copyright law? The WTO Panel decision and the "Three-Step Test" for copyright exceptions'. *Revue Internationale du Droit d'Auteurs*, January 2001. See also: United States – Section 110(5) of the US Copyright Act, WT/DS160/R, para 6.229, that the panel noted that 'in case where there would be a serious loss of profit for the copyright owner, the law should provide him with some compensation (a system of compulsory licensing with equitable remuneration'.

53 Ginsburg J. C., 'Toward supranational copyright law? The WTO Panel decision and the "Three-Step Test" for copyright exceptions'. *Revue Internationale du Droit d'Auteurs*, January 2001.

the exception is almost certainly incompatible with the second, and probably also the third, step of the test.[54]

IV National treatment

The national treatment is another method by which patent rights may be harmonised.

I) Introduction

The principle of national treatment is regarded as a benchmark for IPR protection after it was introduced by the Paris Convention in 1883. Although certain exceptions may still apply, Art.3 of the TRIPS Agreement states that each member shall accord the nationals of other members a treatment no less favourable than that it accords to its own nationals with regard to IPR protection.[55] Additionally, under Art.27.1 of the TRIPS Agreement, the national treatment must be available and patent rights enjoyable without discrimination as to the place of invention, the field of technology and the location of production. Article 3.2 of the TRIPS Agreement lays down certain conditions that must be met when applying exceptions to the national treatment. It provides that: 1) exceptions may be applied only if it is for the necessity of securing compliance with laws and regulations; 2) these laws and regulations must not be inconsistent with the provisions of the TRIPS Agreement; and finally 3) such exceptions must not be applied in a manner which would constitute a disguised restriction on trade.

II) An analysis of the national treatment

The principle of 'necessity' is established by the TRIPS Agreement as a *sine qua non* for admitting judicial and administrative procedures that would limit the scope of IPR protection in national legislation. Based on the dictionary definition[56] and the jurisdiction of the WTO case law,[57] within the remit of Art.3.2, a 'necessary measure' is a measure without which compliance with laws and regulations cannot be guaranteed.

Art.2(1) of the Paris Convention provides that nationals of one Union country shall enjoy the same level of advantages, protection and legal remedy that nationals from all other Union countries may enjoy. However, the Paris Convention did not establish the minimum standards for patent protection, but only those for industrial designs, trade names, unfair competition

54 Gervais D., *The TRIPS Agreement: Drafting History and Analysis* (3rd Ed.). (London: Sweet and Maxwell, 2008), pp. 239–243.

55 See: Art.3.1 of the TRIPS Agreement. Exceptions are referred to as those provided by the Paris Convention (1967), the Berne Convention (1971), the Rome Convention or the Treaty on Intellectual Property in Respect of Integrated Circuits.

56 According to the Cambridge Dictionary Online, 'necessary' means being needed in order to achieve a particular result. Available at: http://dictionary.cambridge.org/dictionary/british/necessary?q=necessary (last accessed 26 June 2016).

57 In the case of European Communities – Protection of Trademarks and Geographical Indications for Agricultural Products and Foodstuffs, the panel report wrote that 'necessary' is very close to meaning 'indispensable'. As to whether a measure is not 'indispensable' but is, nevertheless, 'necessary', the panel decided that it is to see if a WTO-consistent alternative measure which the Member concerned could 'reasonably be expected to employ' is available or if a less WTO-inconsistent measure is 'reasonably available'. See WT/DS174/R, 15 March 2005.

and the direct or the indirect use of a false indication of the source of goods.[58] It has therefore become legitimate for a Union country not to grant patent protection to other Union nationals as long as the particular Union country does not grant the same patent protection to its own nationals. Consequently, countries are at liberty to grant patent protection of varied standards, or to grant no protection at all. This created barriers to export of goods and services of which IP is a component.

To remedy this situation, the members of the TRIPS Agreement are compelled to provide the minimum standards for patent protection so that they may not grant less favourable protection measures to nationals of other members than to their own nationals. By doing so, where the standards for patent protection provided by one member conform to what TRIPS prescribes, nationals from other members will be eligible to enjoy the same standards of protection. If, however, the standards set down by a member are higher than what the TRIPS sets down, the same higher standards will also be extended to other nationals. Ultimately, standards of patent protection are harmonised among the members of the TRIPS Agreement, thereby their national patent legislation can no longer be completely based on national interests.

While applying the principle of national treatment within the context of the TRIPS Agreement, each WTO member must ensure that nationals of other members are afforded a protection level that at least meets the minimum obligations established by the Agreement. To compare with the national treatment stipulated by the Paris Convention, the advance that the TRIPS Agreement has made is that it provides foreign nationals with a treatment no less favourable than the treatment that national citizens may enjoy. This implies that even when a WTO member fails to protect the IPR of its own nationals, the IPR of the nationals from other WTO members must nevertheless be protected – at least to the minimum level imposed by the Agreement.[59] Reflecting on the Paris Convention, if a country does not grant certain patent protection to its own nationals it would not be obliged to provide such protection to other nationals. It is therefore acknowledged that the TRIPS Agreement provides a traditional trade-based form of national treatment which allows more favourable treatment to foreigners than to nationals,[60] and the Paris Convention[61] and the Berne Convention[62] afford only the 'same treatment'.

The national treatment under both the Paris Convention and the TRIPS Agreement does not imply any reciprocal remedies. Under the Paris Convention, when one member denies its own nationals as well as the nationals of other Union members certain rights, those members may not resort to any reciprocal measures as retaliation against nationals of that member. At the same time, other members may not deny the nationals of that member those protection measures that are granted to their own nationals, as well as to the nationals of other members of the Paris Convention.[63]

The footnote of Art.3 of the TRIPS Agreement defines the term of 'protection' and offers a broad coverage of such protection for the purposes of the national and the

58 The Paris Convention provides the minimum mandatory standards for protection for industrial designs (Art.5*quinquies*), trade names (Art.8), and unfair competition (Art.10*bis*) and the direct or indirect use of a false indication of the source of goods (Art.10).

59 Carvalho N. P. *The TRIPS Regime of Patent Rights* (3rd Ed.). (New York: Kluwer Law International, 2010), p. 144.

60 Gervais D., *The TRIPS Agreement: Drafting History and Analysis* (3rd Ed.). (London: Sweet and Maxwell, 2008), pp. 179–183.

61 Art.2, the Paris Convention.

62 Art.5(1), the Berne Convention.

63 Carvalho N. P. *The TRIPS Regime of Patent Rights* (3rd Ed.). (New York: Kluwer Law International, 2010), p. 145.

most-favoured-nation treatment. The notion of 'protection' falls within a very wide remit indeed, including matters affecting availability, acquisition, scope, maintenance and enforcement of IPR, as well as those matters affecting the use of IPR specifically addressed in the TRIPS Agreement.

V Most-favoured-nation treatment

International patent rights harmonisation may be achieved by applying the most-favoured-nation treatment (MFN), which is considered of fundamental importance to the TRIPS Agreement and the world trading system.[64]

I) Introduction

The MFN treatment embedded in the TRIPS Agreement is built on the principle provided by the General Agreement on Tariffs and Trade (GATT), although IPR matters are not covered by GATT. With a few exemptions, by virtue of Art.4 of the TRIPS Agreement, any advantages, favours, privileges or immunities granted by a member to the nationals of any other member[65] shall be accorded immediately and unconditionally to the nationals of all other members. Note, however, Art.4 does not oblige members to grant their own nationals the same treatment as they grant nationals of all other members.[66]

II) Exemptions to the MFN treatment

When applying the MFN treatment, one must take note that certain exemptions may be admitted by national legislation under the auspices of Arts.4(a)(b)(c) of the TRIPS Agreement. Nonetheless, by virtue of Art.4(d), such exemptions are confined to those derived from international agreements related to IPR protection, which were concluded prior to the entry into force of the WTO Agreement, and they must be, at the same time, notified to the Council for TRIPS and must not constitute arbitrary or unjustifiable discrimination against nationals of other members. Consequently, when judging if an exemption is legitimately applied, the following requirements must be satisfied. The first requirement concerning 'IPR-related international agreements' sets a virtually unlimited boundary, and the applicable agreements will consist of 1) those of a general nature but include specific provisions on IPR, and 2) those that do not include specific provisions on IPR but nonetheless may have an impact on IPR.[67] Regarding what does not constitute

64 See para 297, United States – Section 211 Omnibus Appropriations Act of 1998, WT/DS176/AB/R, 2 January 2002.

65 'any other country' must refer to its literal meaning which is 'any other country', regardless of whether this country is a WTO Member or not.

66 Carvalho N. P. *The TRIPS Regime of Patent Rights* (3rd Ed.). (New York: Kluwer Law International, 2010), p. 163.

67 Professor Carvalho raised a few queries as far as the application of Art.4(d) of the TRIPS Agreement is concerned. For example, it's unclear whether the exemption is applicable to amendments to the treaties that came into force before the WTO Agreement. Secondly, it's not clear if a mere notification to the TRIPS Council about the IPR-related agreement would suffice to qualify for the exemption. It is equally not clear whether the existing agreements as well as their possible ensuing regulations should both be notified to the TRIPS Council. Finally, it was not clear from which time onwards the notification would be effective, whether from the date on which the notification was made or if there is a retroactive effect. See Carvalho N. P. *The TRIPS Regime of Patent Rights* (3rd Ed.). (New York: Kluwer Law International, 2010), p. 163.

arbitrary or unjustifiable discrimination, it is suggested that, as a general rule, measures that discriminate against nationals of other members but are based on sound trade-related reasons would not be deemed arbitrary and unjustified. This being the case, no exemptions to the MFN treatment would actually be permissible no matter which international agreement falls within the remit of Art.4(d). In other words, the MFN treatment must be duly accorded to all the applicable international agreements as far as Art.4(d) is concerned.

VI Principle of flexibility

International patent rights harmonisation may be achieved by applying the principle of flexibility, in which case national interests are accommodated and yet provisions and principles under the TRIPS Agreement are complied with at the same time.[68] The principle of flexibility is derived from the national treatment.

I) Introduction

To apply the principle of flexibility, two rules must be respected. First, 'flexibility' must be applied in consistency with the relevant obligations imposed by the TRIPS Agreement. Second, to conform to Art.7 of the TRIPS Agreement regarding the objectives of IPR protection and enforcement, measures derived from the principle of flexibility must aim to mitigate the social cost that IPR protection may induce and to attain a balance of rights and obligations in order to achieve overall social and economic welfare. In essence, 'flexibility' must not reduce the positive impact of IPR for promoting invention and enhancing competitive business environment.[69]

II) Four approaches to apply the principle of flexibility

There are four approaches that TRIPS members may engage in applying the principle of flexibility when incorporating the Agreement into their respective national legislation.[70]

1. Flexibility as a method of implementing TRIPS obligations

Article 1.1 of the TRIPS Agreement provides that members are free to determine how they wish to implement the principles set down by the Agreement within their own legal system and practice. Therefore, for example, a TRIPS member may apply this approach when defining patent protection measures concerning novelty and inventive step since TRIPS only sets down principles without any definition. Another substantive protection measure with which a TRIPS member may exploit the principle of flexibility under this approach concerns compulsory licence. Under Art.31(b) of the TRIPS Agreement, members may exploit the conditions of 'national emergency' or 'extreme urgency' in order to set aside the requirement of 'a failure to obtain authorisation from a right-holder despite reasonable commercial terms'.

68 Carvalho N. P. *The TRIPS Regime of Patent Rights* (3rd Ed.). (New York: Kluwer Law International, 2010), p. 168.
69 Carvalho N. P. *The TRIPS Regime of Patent Rights* (3rd Ed.). (New York: Kluwer Law International, 2010), p. 67.
70 See: www.wipo.int/ip-development/en/legislative_assistance/advice_trips.html (last accessed 25 February 2016).

By the same token, in accordance with Art.66(1) of the TRIPS Agreement, the least developed country (LDC) members enjoy the flexibility to delay the implementation of the Agreement for ten years, which may be further extended upon request. Note that the transitional arrangement is in conformity with the Preamble of the TRIPS Agreement, which particularly recognises the LDC members' special needs for maximum flexibility in implementing laws and regulations due to the economic, financial and administrative constraints that they are confronted with.

2. *Flexibility as a substantive standard for protection*

This approach may be divided into 'TRIPS-plus' and 'TRIPS-minus' flexibilities.

A. 'TRIPS-PLUS' FLEXIBILITY

The 'TRIPS-plus' flexibility becomes available thanks to Art.1.1 of the TRIPS Agreement, which states that members may, but shall not be obliged to, implement in their legislation more extensive protection measures than is required by the Agreement, provided that such measures do not contravene the provisions of the Agreement. Consequently, members have the liberty to prescribe increased standards for IPR protection in their respective national laws, usually in order to pursue social or policy objectives, as long as such higher standards conform to the provisions derived from the TRIPS Agreement.

The higher thresholds test for patentability that India's patent law requires is a typical example of exploiting the 'TRIPS-plus' flexibility in order to defend the national interests of the 'right to health', which will be explained in detail in Chapter 8. Sometimes, the 'TRIPS-plus' flexibility is also pursued by countries in their bilateral trade negotiations when specific IPR protection measures are drafted.[71] This is especially the case with regard to the free trade agreements concluded between the EU and the third countries.[72]

There are a few provisions under the TRIPS Agreement that offer members the possibility of pursuing the 'TRIPS-plus' flexibility such as, for example, Art.30 concerning the 'exceptions to rights conferred'.[73] Also known as Bolar exemption, thanks to Art.30 members may provide limited exceptions to the exclusive rights conferred by a patent, and subsequently researchers may use a patented invention for research in order to be able to understand the invention more fully, as long as it is for the purpose of advancing science and technology or for promoting public interest. As a result, Bolar exemption may be relied upon by manufacturers of generic drugs in order to conduct research on the patented invention, without the patent holder's permission and before the patent protection term expires, for obtaining marketing approval so that the generic version of the patented drug can be launched as soon as the original patent expires.[74]

71 Carvalho N. P. *The TRIPS Regime of Patent Rights* (3rd Ed.). (New York: Kluwer Law International, 2010), p. 63.

72 Pelkmans J. and Hu W. *et al.*, *Tomorrow's Silk Road, Assessing an EU-China Free Trade Agreement* (Brussels: Centre for European Policy Studies, 2016), pp. 201–210.

73 Other examples of 'TRIPS-plus' are extending the term of patents in order to compensate for delays in granting the marketing approval for products, or extending the scope of patentability and/or registrability of trademarks beyond the minimum standards established, which are based on Arts.27 and 15 of the TRIPS Agreement, respectively.

74 This *modus operandi* was recognised by the panel report on Canada — Patent Protection for Pharmaceutical Products, which was adopted on 7 April 2000. See: www.wto.org/english/tratop_e/trips_e/factsheet_pharm02_e.htm (last accessed 25 December 2015).

Providing temporary protection before a patent is granted is another substantive patent protection area where members may apply the principle of 'TRIPS-plus' flexibility. So is the area of extending the term of patent protection in order to compensate for the delays that occur while granting marketing approval of the patented product.

B. 'TRIPS-MINUS' FLEXIBILITY

The 'TRIPS-minus' flexibility is also referred to as exceptions and limitations. Exceptions are factors that reduce the enforceability of rights against certain acts of infringement, while limitations are factors that affect the integrity of rights and therefore their enforceability in general against all acts of infringement.[75] The 'TRIPS-minus' flexibility may apply to rights themselves but also to the use of rights. For the former, examples can be found under Art.6 of the TRIPS Agreement concerning 'exceptions to rights conferred' (as mentioned above) and Art.31 for 'other use without authorisation of the right holder'. Article 31 provides a series of prerequisites upon which government-authorised use may take place. For example, 'limitations' may be applied as far as Arts.33 and 38(3) of the TRIPS Agreement are concerned. Article 33 provides that the term of protection for invention patents shall not be less than 20 years counting from the date of filing and, for lay-out design patents, Art.38(3) provides that the term of protection should be no more than 15 years after the lay-out design is created. On the other hand, since 'exceptions and limitations' of the use of the rights do not affect the rights themselves, the rule of 'TRIPS-minus' is not subject to any special restrictions.

3. *Flexibility as a means for enforcement*

Part III of the TRIPS Agreement provides the possibility for members to exercise the principle of flexibility in enforcement. For this purpose, members (i) may identify and then adopt enforcement means for IPR protection; and (ii) are not obliged to adopt stricter measures against alleged IPR offenders than those that are already established. This being the case, TRIPS members may only be able to apply the principle of flexibility as a means for enforcement when they can resort to their own legal system and practices in order to implement the obligations concerning enforcement laid down by TRIPS, including the flexibility of determining patent protection standards. Thanks to Art.41(5) of the TRIPS Agreement, which stipulates that members may follow any form of judicial system for IPR enforcement, they are, at the same time, free to maintain their existing judicial system while exploiting the principle of flexibility for IPR enforcement. As a result, for example, pursuant to its legal practices and based on the present judicial enforcement arrangement, IPR enforcement in China is undertaken by the administrative and judicial dual-track mechanism, in which both tracks are of equal importance.

4. *Flexibility is applied to areas not covered by the TRIPS Agreement*

The TRIPS Agreement does not provide protection to each and every IPR subject matter, such as, for example, traditional knowledge and handicrafts. This being the case, members have full flexibility to pursue their policy objectives in patent legislation based on national

75 Carvalho N. P. *The TRIPS Regime of Patent Rights* (3rd Ed.). (New York: Kluwer Law International, 2010), p. 63.

interests. Consequently, members may provide protection to traditional knowledge and may extend it to foreign nationals on the basis of the national treatment.

III) Another way of looking at the principle of flexibility

The principle of flexibility may be examined from the point of view of IPR lifespan, which may be divided in three stages, namely: 1) acquiring; 2) framing and dimensioning; and 3) enforcing rights.[76]

1. Acquiring rights

While acquiring IPR, the title of the right must be adequate and proper for the purpose of legal certainty. In this regard, the principle of flexibility may be applied in relation to conditions that must be met before rights can be acquired. For example, members may apply the principle of flexibility when setting down the conditions as far as disclosure is concerned. By virtue of Art.29.1 of the TRIPS Agreement, 'members shall require that an applicant for a patent shall disclose the invention in a manner sufficiently clear and complete for the invention to be carried out by a person skilled in the art and may require the applicant to indicate the best mode for carrying out the invention…' Owing to the principle of flexibility, which may be exploited as a means to acquire rights, the mandatory requirement for disclosure prescribed by the Agreement may be extended to include, for example, technical specifications or other ancillary information. Accordingly, although the requirement of 'the best mode for carrying out the invention' is omitted, Art.26 of China's Patent Law 2008 obliges that, when applying for invention and utility model patents, disclosure submitted by applicants must include the main technical points of the invention or the utility model; drawings must be provided when necessary.[77] The same requirements are maintained by the Draft Patent Law 2015.

The principle of flexibility may also apply to substantive patentability requirements for acquiring rights for invention patents. To this end, in relation to Art.27 of the TRIPS Agreement, as mentioned before, India's patent legislation lays down a much higher threshold test concerning 'inventive step' in order to curb attempts to patent incremental technological improvements, especially as far as pharmaceutical products are concerned.

2. Framing and dimensioning rights

After rights are acquired, the principle of flexibility may be applied in order to ensure that the rights are adequately framed and dimensioned for better protection, as is the aim of Art.7 of the TRIPS Agreement for IPR protection as a whole. Within this context, and for the purpose of patent protection, members may, for example, extend the lifespan of a patent in order to compensate for the unreasonable delays occurred during the patenting process or while granting marketing approval. Likewise, members may grant IPR-holders the privilege of seeking retrospective damages when infringement takes place before patent protection is granted. Also, members may legislate to award compulsory licence in order to

76 Carvalho N. P. *The TRIPS Regime of Patent Rights* (3rd Ed.). (New York: Kluwer Law International, 2010), p. 65.

77 Art.26 of China's Patent Law (2008) also requests, where applicable, disclosure of generic resources in the application document. The requirement is maintained by Art.26 of the Draft Patent Law 2015.

achieve economic advantages for the sake of public interests. For example, China's Patent Law 2008 prescribes that if, while exercising the patent rights, a patent holder's behaviour amounts to anti-competition, a compulsory licence may be granted.[78] If public health is at risk, under Art.50 of the Patent Law 2008 a compulsory licence may be granted to a patented medicine in order to produce and export it to the countries or the regions in need. The Draft Patent Law 2015 upholds the same positions.

3. Enforcing rights

Finally, after rights are properly framed and dimensioned, the principle of flexibility may be applied in order to ensure that rights are properly used and enforced, while abusive and anti-competitive practices are dealt with. To this end, Art.48(2) of China's Patent Law 2008 sets down the same grounds as the TRIPS Agreement prescribes, and therefore a compulsory licence may be issued if a patent holder's behaviour is confirmed as monopolistic with a negative impact on competition. For the same purpose of enforcing rights, members may grant injunction orders based on equity by exploiting the principle of flexibility while private and public interests may be taken into account. Article 66 of China's Patent Law 2008 provides that the court may grant an injunction order within 48 hours upon request but, if error occurs, the injunction applicant must compensate the party against whom the application is filed. The same provisions are maintained by the Draft Patent Law 2015. Also, for the purpose of enforcement, TRIPS permits members to directly involve public agencies in order to solicit their assistance in patent rights enforcement. China has included this principle in its legislation as far as IPR criminal enforcement is concerned.

VII Categorisations of harmonisation

International patent rights harmonisation may be achieved by procedural or substantive means. Procedural harmonisation deals with forms and procedures as far as multiple applications are concerned, and substantive harmonisation aims to harmonise measures and standards with regard to patent grant and enforcement. Therefore, the PCT is a treaty for procedural harmonisation and the TRIPS Agreement is an agreement that focuses on harmonising substantive protection measures.

I) Procedural harmonisation – the PCT

Epitomised by the PCT, procedural harmonisation is a filing tool with which multiple patent applications may be processed more effectively by the PCT contracting members willing to exploit the work done by others.[79] The purpose of this exercise is to save time and work as well as costs, both for patent applicants and for the national offices where patent protection for the same invention is sought. Thanks to the PCT, the likelihood of granting wider patent protection has become higher, specifically because national offices with lesser capacity for prior art search and examination could exploit the work done by the

78 Art.48(2), China's Patent Law 2008.

79 See: *The Need for Improving the Functioning of the PCT System*, a study prepared by the International Bureau of the WIPO (PCT/WG/3/2), Patent Cooperation Treaty (PCT) Working Group, Third Session. (Geneva: WIPO, June 14–18, 2010), p. 19.

ISA and, consequently, they would be able to grant patent protection to eligible inventions.[80]

The PCT provides an alternative route for multiple patent applications and, ultimately, it is the national patent offices that determine if a patent should be granted. Since it was concluded in Washington in June 1970, more and more countries have acceded to the PCT and the number of contracting states reached 148 as of March 2016.[81] The number of PCT applications is also on the increase on a yearly basis. The total number of filings submitted under the PCT system amounted to 218,000 applications in 2015, registering a 1.7 per cent increase on the previous year.[82]

However, it is noted that the economic benefits accrued from patent procedural harmonisation are not significant because a PCT patent, issued after the examination conducted at the international and the national stages, consists of a set of individual national patents that remain separately enforceable under national patent legislation.[83] The application costs incurred by using the PCT route are high, especially if an application seeks multiple protection in a few national offices. The contributing factors for high costs are, for example, the high charges for conducting international preliminary examination, and the fact that often elected Offices do not give significant attention to the international search reports and therefore examination may have to be conducted anew. According to the survey conducted among PCT offices by the WIPO in 2012, the automation, formatting and media for PCT documents, the range of PCT tools for filing and processing international applications made available to Offices and applicants, and the availability of international application documents in additional languages were identified as areas for improvement.[84] The ISA is equally blamed for causing delays, since it is often not able to begin search and examination in a timely manner because it takes a long time to receive information, documents or fees from the applicant or the receiving Offices. Any delays will reduce the lifespan of a patent grant since lifespan is calculated from the date of its first filing. For example, it was revealed that, in 2009, 26 per cent of the total international applications were published without an attached ISR because of delayed search. In the same year, over 6 per cent of the ISRs were delivered more than 30 months after the priority date. Sometimes, delays also occur due to the time expended in processing applications within an Office and communications between receiving Offices and the ISA may also cause delays.[85]

Therefore, procedural harmonisation alone will not solve problems such as delays and higher costs that are derived from the world's fragmented patent system. After all, as procedural harmonisation only deals with forms and procedures as far as multiple patent applications are concerned, one has to examine if substantive harmonisation could be an effective

80 Another principle aim of the PCT is to disseminate knowledge and organise technical assistance, particularly for the developing countries. See: *The Need for Improving the Functioning of the PCT System*, a study prepared by the International Bureau of the WIPO (PCT/WG/3/2), Patent Cooperation Treaty (PCT) Working Group, Third Session. (Geneva: WIPO, June 14–18, 2010), p. 8.

81 Available at: www.wipo.int/pct/en/pct_contracting_states.html (last accessed 15 March 2016).

82 Available at: www.wipo.int/pressroom/en/articles/2016/article_0002.html (last accessed 27 June 2016).

83 Reichman J. H. and Dreyfuss R. C., 'Harmonisation without consensus: critical reflections on drafting a substantive patent law treaty'. 57 *Duke Law Journal* 85 (2007) 90.

84 WIPO, *PCT Office Feedback Survey 2012: Report of Results.* (Geneva: WIPO, 2012).

85 WIPO, *The Need for Improving the Functioning of the PCT System*, study prepared by the International Bureau, WIPO, PCT/WG/3/2, May 5 (Geneva: WIPO, 2010), pp. 29–30.

instrument for international patent harmonisation while resolving the conflict between cross-border patent protection and the fragmented global patent system.[86]

II) Substantive harmonisation

Substantive harmonisation addresses the residual issues pursuant to procedural harmonisation as far as patent grant and enforcement are concerned. There are two directions in which substantive harmonisation may be pursued: legal harmonisation and administrative harmonisation.

Also known as 'deep harmonisation', substantive legal harmonisation focuses on standards of patentability as well as drafting, filing and examination of a patent application. It aims to adopt identical rules with regard to: the amount of information revealed by patent disclosure; the criteria for determining a novel and useful invention when a technological advance meets the requirement for an 'inventive step'; the priority of inventorship; and whether an inventor will be entitled to a grace period permitting publication prior to filing.[87]

1. Introduction

The Paris Convention and the TRIPS Agreement are agreements of substantive legal harmonisation. The Paris Convention sets down the basic principles, such as the national treatment, and the common rules that the contracting parties must incorporate into their respective national legislation. For example, derived from the national treatment, inventors from any contracting party are eligible to claim priority in other contracting parties based on the filing date of its first application.[88] Nonetheless, the Paris Convention lacks an enforcement mechanism for IPR protection in general, despite the various amendments that have taken place since it was enacted. In comparison, the TRIPS Agreement was concluded with the dispute settlement mechanism for effective enforcement, which is a major achievement in substantive legal patent harmonisation.

Building on the national and the MFN treatment, the TRIPS Agreement establishes, among others, the minimum IPR protection standards that each member must provide to the right holders of fellow WTO members. Additionally, the TRIPS Agreement equips its members with the principle of flexibility so that members are free to determine how they wish to incorporate the Agreement into national legislation depending on their own legal system and practice.[89] Moreover, thanks to Art.27(2) of the Agreement, members are eligible to offer exceptions to patentability when it is necessary to protect '*ordre public* or morality' if certain conditions are met.

86 Many provisions in the PCT emphasise this point. For example, Art.27(5) states 'nothing in this Treaty and the Regulations is intended to be construed as prescribing anything that would limit the freedom of each Contracting State to prescribe such substantive conditions of patentability as it desires …'.

87 Reichman J. H. and Dreyfuss R. C., 'Harmonisation without consensus: critical reflections on drafting a substantive patent law treaty'. 57 *Duke Law Journal* 85 (2007) 90. See also: Hauda K. M., 'The role of the United States in world-wide protection of industrial property' in F. Gotzen (Ed.) *The Future of Intellectual Property in the Global Market of the Informational Society, Who Is Going to Shape the IPR System in the New Millennium?* (Brussels: Les Éditions Bruylant, 2003) pp. 89, 97.

88 Art.4A(2) of the Paris Convention.

89 Art.1.1 of the TRIPS Agreement.

2. *Impediments to substantive patent harmonisation*

Having said the above, substantive legal harmonisation commonly involves high financial and social costs while domestic patent laws also have to be amended. Implementing provisions of substantive legal harmonisation, amending existing legislation, enhancing patent administration and developing compatible enforcement capacity, etc., will potentially incur extra costs and efforts. As a result country may become less keen to pursue the idea of substantive legal harmonisation, especially if its patent system was established not long ago. Moreover, national interests that different countries are keen to pursue compel international harmonisation efforts to accommodate conflicting initiatives. This being the case, harmonisation efforts would often be watered down, if not thwarted. For example, the US priority rule of first-to-invent hampered the process of international harmonisation and caused US inventors to pay higher costs but, nonetheless, legal change was in vain for almost 50 years until 2013 when the America Invents Act came into force.[90] Some countries may be equally suspicious about substantive legal harmonisation because of worries about compromised sovereignty during the national patent legislative change.

Certainly, the level of importance that a country would attach to international patent rights harmonisation depends on the country's industrial development stage. A country that only has a modest patent application number with few innovative industries will naturally have minimum concerns for clearing patent application backlogs; its interest in international patent rights harmonisation would be likely to be limited too. Therefore, flexible patent harmonisation policies that accommodate countries' distinctive industrial progress and favour economic development would be preferred.[91] In this regard, some scholars have argued that standards potentially imposed by substantive legal harmonisation would challenge the technological catch-up strategies that certain developing countries contemplate and, instead, saddle them with social costs that they would be struggling to absorb.[92] As a result, although international harmonisation of patent protection is necessary and urgent due to trade globalisation and the mounting application volumes, it is a very intricate process because of countries' varied perceptions, economic development levels, laws, cultures and practices, etc. In the same breath, continuing to harmonise the fragmented global patent system appears, nonetheless, to be inevitable in order to overcome the obstacles to cross-border patent protection and enforcement, etc., and to mitigate the economic loss as a result thereof.

Some scholars have thus recommended only harmonising patentability requirements and suggested that this may be an effective means for increased cooperation between national offices in order for expediting the examination process. This approach is based on the

90 Efforts to replace the first-to-invent rule with a first-to-file rule dated back to February 1967, as seen from the Report of the President's Commission on the Patent System, *To Promote the Progress of Useful Arts in an Age of Exploding Technology*. Committee on the Judiciary, United States Senate, Subcommittee on Patents, Trademarks, and Copyrights, 90th Congress, 1st Session, Document No.5.

91 Mohanty N. K., *The Advantage/Disadvantage of the Harmonisation of the Patent System*. (Japan Patent Office, October 2007–March 2008), p. 60. Also, WIPO reported that the TRIPS Agreement restricts developing countries from fine-tuning their patent systems in line with their level of techno-economic development. See: Mengistie G., *The Impact of the International Patent System on Developing Countries: a Study by Getachew Mengistie*, 16, A/39/13 Add.1, 15 August (Geneva: WIPO, 2003).

92 See: CIPR, *Integrating Intellectual Property Rights and Development Policy*. (London: Commission on Intellectual Property Rights, September 2002), pp. 159–62 and Correa C. M., *Intellectual Property Rights, The WTO and Developing Countries: the TRIPS Agreement and Policy Options* (London: Zed Books, 2000).

premise that the growing delays in multiple patent examinations confronted by national patent offices is equally one compelling reason that prompted international patent harmonisation. Note that the number of patent applications worldwide has been growing rapidly every year, and among them are a considerable number of cross-border as well as multiple applications for which examination will involve a few jurisdictions. Reflecting on the growth in patent applications in China alone, until February 2016 the yearly foreign invention patent applications that the SIPO received reached 19,820, which registered a year-on-year increase of 3 per cent. In the same month, the SIPO received 40,721 domestic invention patent applications, as opposed to the 8,813 foreign applications that accounted for 22 per cent of China's monthly total invention patent applications. Among them, American applicants submitted 2,309 patent applications, which was the highest application number among all foreign applicants in China.[93]

In parallel, because prior art search has become more and more complex, and since examining patentability requires every national office where protection is sought to carry out the same procedure individually, the time limit for granting a multiple patent application has become longer. For example, the average time limit from filing to granting a patent in Japan is currently 31.6 months, while the same proceedings take 45.3 months to complete in Europe. In both the US and China, the proceedings take around two years. If such a trend continues, not only will the backlog of multiple patent applications increase, but the ensuing legal uncertainty will also grow and adversely affect all industries concerned. This is because, before a patent is granted, no binding business plans may be possible. Also, as a new invention is often based on earlier inventions, the long time limit may result in lost investment in innovation for follow-up inventions.

Accelerated development of new technologies also increases appeals for harmonised examination procedures. In recent years, many patent applications have been submitted for inventions that involve new technologies, such as information technology and biotechnology. Since highly specialised knowledge is indispensable when examining such patent applications, substantive harmonisation in examination procedures will become a necessity so that highly specialised knowledge can be pooled together for examination purposes and examination results may be shared in order to help mitigate the risk of disparate examination decisions. Moreover, as the patentability requirements for inventions involving high-technologies such as, for example, the patentability of DNA fragments, often can't be duly determined under the existing examination guidelines, central patent offices are now compelled to issue respective patentability criteria at the appropriate time and have them harmonised internationally.[94]

This being the case, if big patent offices could forge cooperation in (prior art) search and examination, especially as far as multiple patent applications are concerned, examination speed may be accelerated since information would be shared, duplicate work avoided, examination costs lowered and the backlogs at the national patent offices also reduced as a result. The process of patent application would become less onerous and cheaper. Ultimately, applicants and national offices would both benefit. Also, uniform standards for

93 Available at: http://english.sipo.gov.cn/statistics/2016/2/201603/t20160318_1252648.html (last accessed 20 March 2016).

94 See: interview with Shinjiro Ono, Deputy Commissioner of Japan Patent Office, available at: http://documents.epo.org/projects/babylon/eponet.nsf/0/31F44F2D53252ECEC12572D80039EAE4/$File/Interview_Ono.pdf (last accessed 20 March 2016).

patentability requirements may help to mitigate the risk of falling examination standards and contrasting examination results, which are likely to be the consequences of increased volume and the ever more complicated technical features of patent applications.

As in recent years more countries have started to focus on innovation and, although some of them are technologically less advanced, international patent harmonisation, or the lack of it, has attracted global attention.

VIII Finding a solution

I) Introduction

When discussing international patent rights harmonisation, a practical question is on what level and in which order a workable harmonisation might be achievable.[95] A few initiatives have emerged in the course of this pursuit. For example, the European Community succeeded in formulating a European patent system and the English-speaking African countries work in the same manner in order to pool together the financial and the human resources of its member countries to avoid duplicating examination procedural work as far as (regional) multiple patent applications are concerned. The African Regional Intellectual Property Organisation (ARIPO) was thus established to promote harmonisation and the development of the industrial property laws existing among its members whose number reached 19 in March 2016.[96]

1. The European Patent Office

The EPC was concluded in 1973 in order to provide an autonomous legal system for granting European patents via a single and harmonised procedure before the EPO, with which inventors are able to seek patent protection in up to 40 countries in the region at the moment.[97] As is discussed in Chapter 2, a European patent is not a unitary right, but a group of independent, nationally-enforceable and nationally-revocable patents.

However, once the European unitary patent system comes into being, the EPO will be competent to grant unitary patents whereby the unitary effect within the territories of the 26 participating states will be guaranteed at a patent holder's request.[98] Applying the EU unitary patent will become an alternative option for patent protection in the European region, in addition to the national patent system and the classical European patent system.

2. The African Regional Intellectual Property Office

The ARIPO was set up by the Lusaka Agreement, which was adopted in 1976 by the English-speaking African countries. The rationale for setting up the ARIPO was that, at the time, the majority of the countries concerned had only 'dependent industrial property legislations' that did not authorise for registration or award original grant but

95 Reichman J. H. and Dreyfuss R. C., 'Harmonisation without consensus: critical reflections on drafting a substantive patent law treaty'. 57 *Duke Law Journal* 85 (2007), 126.

96 Available at: http://aripo.org/about-aripo/membership-member-states (last accessed 20 March 2016).

97 Available at: www.epo.org/about-us/office.html (last accessed 20 March 2016).

98 Available at: www.epo.org/law-practice/unitary/unitary-patent.html (last accessed 20 March 2016).

could only extend to their territories the effects of the industrial property rights obtained in a foreign country, in most cases the UK. Also, the whole procedure was normally governed by the British patent law. To change the situation, the ARIPO was set up to, for example, establish common services or organs for coordination, harmonisation and the development of industrial property activities.[99] Under the ARIPO procedures, once a patent application is received, the Regional Office will first carry out a substantive examination to ensure that the invention is patentable and, second, it is to see if the application complies with the substantive patentability requirements. Once examination is completed, copies of the examination result will be sent to each designated ARIPO Contracting State which may, within six months, indicate to the ARIPO that the grant *per se* will not have effect in its territory in case the ARIPO awards patent protection to the claim.[100]

Inventions, utility models and industrial designs under the ARIPO system are equivalent to a bundle of national registrations and their management is all centralised. This means that only one filing, one grant and one agent is required for application purposes. All the procedures, such as renewal, amendment and representation, etc., are consolidated under the ARIPO. Besides, the ARIPO is the Receiving Office for all ARIPO Contracting States[101] who are parties to the PCT. The duties that ARIPO will discharge in this regard include, for example: 1) specifying ISA and international examining authorities for PCT applications in the international phase; 2) prescribing the languages in which PCT applications must be employed at the ARIPO; 3) fixing the amount of transmittal fee; 4) undertaking formality checks and prescribing filing dates, etc.[102] For each PCT application filed at the ARIPO, after formality checks are completed the ARIPO will accord an international filing date, assign an international application number and undertake correspondence for the applicant, the international bureau of the WIPO and the ISA, and receive fees on their behalf. An applicant who is not a resident in any ARIPO Contracting State will be required to appoint an agent to manage patent-related matters.

The advantages of filing a PCT patent by exploiting the ARIPO route are: uniform rights protection of 20 years in all states concerned; a single application but multiple protection; and centralised renewal and single representation. Nonetheless, the ARIPO also faces some challenges that are chiefly centred on inadequate resources for IP services and the lack of national IP strategies among the Contracting States.[103]

99 Available at: www.aripo.org/index.php/about-aripo (last accessed 20 March 2016).

100 For details see: www.aripo.org/about-aripo (last accessed 20 March 2016).

101 Except Somalia, which is a member of the ARIPO but not a member of the PCT.

102 The preliminary formality checks include: applicant's residence; a request form must be properly completed; applicants and inventors must be identified; specification must have a description and at least one claim; three copies must be lodged; fees or undertaking to lodge fees and the ARIPO will also help applicants to correct defects. See: WIPO, *African Regional Patent Systems and the PCT: Brief Overview of the ARIPO Patent System*, a presentation delivered at WIPO Regional Forum on the Role of Patents and the Patent Cooperation Treaty (PCT) in Research in Developing Countries, 30 March to 1 April 2009, Nairobi, Kenya. (Geneva: WIPO, 2009).

103 See: WIPO, *African Regional Patent Systems and the PCT: Brief Overview of the ARIPO Patent System*, a presentation delivered at WIPO Regional Forum on the Role of Patents and the Patent Cooperation Treaty (PCT) in Research in Developing Countries, 30 March to 1 April 2009, Nairobi, Kenya. (Geneva: WIPO, 2009).

II) Substantive administrative harmonisation

Patent conventions such as the EPC, the Lusaka Agreement and its subsequent protocols do not yield true harmonisation because patents awarded under these legal frameworks are typically a set of individual national patents that remain separately enforceable under the local laws.[104] On the other hand, since substantive legal harmonisation involves such impediments as mentioned earlier, including the issue of sovereignty, one may reflect on substantive administrative harmonisation, the second direction of substantive harmonisation, for furthering international patent rights harmonisation. Substantive administrative harmonisation focuses on patent prosecution but foregoes harmonising enforcement or infringement procedures in which case a legal basis is a prerequisite.

Substantive administrative harmonisation is often referred to as work-sharing, which reflects the purpose of this harmonisation modality.[105] Work-sharing does not require the change of laws nor ratification in order to reduce examination pendency and improve patent quality.[106] By participating in work-sharing, countries would gradually harmonise their respective patent management systems, especially with regard to rule-making, adjudication and enforcement. Once relevant rules are harmonised among the group of offices, such rules may be effectively exported to third countries by means of, for example, capacity-building. By doing so, substantive administrative harmonisation would be achieved at working level among a broader range of countries. Therefore, perhaps as a compromise to substantive legal harmonisation, work-sharing, or substantive administrative harmonisation, could be a direction for furthering international patent rights harmonisation for the time being.

1. Trilateral Offices – as an example

The Trilateral Offices project is a pioneer project of 'work-sharing' that was established by the EPO, the JPO and the USPTO in 1983. The objectives of the project were, among others, to improve the quality of examination, reduce processing time and harmonise practices of the three offices.[107] The initial cooperation of the Trilateral Offices was confined within the remit of exchanging know-how and establishing standards for exchanging data files. Later, the cooperation areas were extended to producing new databases and subsequently new systems for exploitation. New tools, such as the *Catalogue of Differing Practices*, have been made available for public libraries and the general public in recent years.[108] *The Catalogue* identifies the differences in patent examination practice in the three offices, as well as in the KIPO and the SIPO. *The Catalogue* equally provides readers with

104 Reichman J. H. and Dreyfuss R. C., 'Harmonisation without consensus: critical reflections on drafting a substantive patent law treaty'. 57 *Duke Law Journal* 85 (2007), 88.

105 Korea Intellectual Property Office (KIPO), *A Study on Mutual Recognition of Patent Examination* (Korea: KIPO, 2008).

106 David Kappos once commented that 'harmonisation allows us to maximise the vital tool for reducing pendency and improving quality and that is with work-sharing'. Quinn G., 'Kappos talks patent reform and gene patents at BIO Convention', 4 May (*IPWatchdog*, 2010). Available at: www.ipwatchdog.com/2010/05/04/kappos-talks-patent-reform-and-gene-patents-at-bio-convention/id=10382/ (last accessed 20 March 2016).

107 Available at: www.trilateral.net/about/objectives.html (last accessed 20 March 2016).

108 More detailed description is available at: www.trilateral.net/about/history.html (last accessed 20 March 2016).

quick access to patent examination procedures undertaken in the world's other offices without requiring a detailed knowledge of the underlying legislative systems.[109]

The influence of the Trilateral Offices in global patent harmonisation is strong. Its power over rule-interpretation is most evident, for example, concerning new claim formats for specific areas of technology that require eradication of statutory limitations on the scope of patentable subject matter.[110] To achieve this goal, the Trilateral Offices have been trying to harmonise patent rules worldwide through cooperation, capacity-building, technical assistance and examiner-to-examiner exchange. For example, the EPO provided examination manuals to a few patent offices, especially those in the developing countries, and trained their examiners on the use and the set-up of a technical system for tracking down the examination decisions delivered by the EPO. The EPO-edited manual functions as an 'installation manual' and, as a result, its technical specifications are naturally followed, or referred to, by these patent offices. One such technical assistance programme is the EC-ASEAN Patents Programme. As a component of the Programme, the EPO assisted the Philippines in compiling the patent examination manual of 2004 where the clauses of the Swiss-style second-use claims for pharmaceutical products were found. This inclusion was somehow controversial because, despite the EPO prohibiting the patenting of second medical indications by strict interpretation, based on Decision G 5/83 of 1984, the Enlarged Board of Appeal (EBoA) of the EPO allowed Swiss-style claims to be employed to apply patents for substance or composition meant for manufacturing a pharmaceutical product of a specified new and inventive therapeutic application. As a result, it is possible that the EPO may still grant patent protection for the second use of a known compound in a method of medical treatment if a Swiss-style claim is drafted by referring to the use of substance X in the manufacturing of a pharmaceutical product for the treatment of disease Y. Within the same framework of the EC-ASEAN Patents Programme, the Swiss-style second-use claim for pharmaceutical products is also found in Indonesia's patent examination manual, as well as in that of Vietnam.[111]

The long-standing technical assistance programmes existing between members of the Trilateral Offices and the countries-in-need have promoted a relationship of concrete trust among each other, especially on issues concerning technicalities. It is undeniable that, with different cooperation and capacity-building programmes, substantive patent rules tend to be harmonised much more subtly but also effectively through a networking of influences, without tedious harmonisation treaty negotiations.

2. *Work-sharing*

Work-sharing aims 'to eliminate unnecessary duplication of work among the offices, and to enhance patent examination efficiency and quality'.[112] It is a long-term viable solution to

109 Available at: www.trilateral.net/catalogue.html (last accessed 20 March 2016).

110 Drahos P., 'book review on Evans G.E., *The Global Governance of Knowledge: Patent Offices and Their Clients*'. 33 *European Intellectual Property Review* 1 (2011), 63–66.

111 Evans G. E., *The Global Governance of Knowledge: Patent Offices and Their Clients.* (Cambridge: Cambridge University Press, 2010), p.128, on capacity-building as a means of globalising regulation.

112 Kazenske E. R., *Patent Offices: Strategies for Work Sharing 'Need for a Pragmatic Outcome'*, Microsoft Corporation, Fordham IP Conference, 15–16 April (Microsoft Corporation, 2009). Available at: http://fordhamipconference.com/wp-content/uploads/2010/08/Kaz_Kazenske_Patent_Offices_Strategy_for_Work_Sharing.pdf (last accessed 20 March 2016).

the escalating workloads as far as multiple patent applications are concerned. When an applicant files a patent application in a patent office, the application will be examined through the procedures of filing, prior art search, office action and patent grant decision. If a multiple patent application is filed, the same procedures will be repeated by the offices concerned and followed by their respective patent law procedures and administrative rules in order to independently determine patentability. Time and resources are duplicated and spent, since patent authorities conduct virtually the same work on hundreds of thousands of patent applications each year, and many of them are filed in multiple countries for protection.[113] Therefore, to save time and resources, and in order to guarantee reliable patent examination results, it would be ideal if search strategies, search results and examination results for multiple patent applications could be shared among the offices concerned.[114]

Depending on the specific information that is shared between the first and second office, there are three forms of work-sharing.[115]

A. SEARCH-SHARING

Search-sharing refers to patent offices in different jurisdictions mutually exploiting the same search strategy and search result. In practice, this means that the second filing office shall fully recognise the search result published by the first filing office or refer to the search result concluded by the first filing office in its own search report on prior art. Note that search-sharing is only relevant with regard to prior art search and each patent office retains its ultimate responsibility and discretion to decide if a patent should be awarded.[116]

In order to obtain a patent award the quality of novelty must be guaranteed. Presently, when an application is submitted in a few countries, the patent office in each jurisdiction will have to perform independent and separate prior art searches on the same invention. This means that each patent office will search all available documents before the latest filing date in order not to miss any of them, whether published at home and abroad. In reality, subject to a few exceptions, prior art that defeats novelty in one jurisdiction will also defeat novelty in other jurisdictions, which means that each of the patent offices will search approximately the same body of documents for prior art and comparing it to the same invention for the novelty test. The mechanism of search-sharing therefore comes into play in order to mitigate the deficiency concerning documentation search when novelty is being determined by a few patent offices repeatedly and separately.

An advantage of search-sharing is that it does not require patent examiners to possess considerable technical skills and experiences, while also accelerating the process of multiple patent applications. Although language barriers may still exist, patent examiners could rely

113 Quinn G., 'Kappos talks patent reform and gene patents at BIO Convention', 4 May (IPWatchdog, 2010). Available at: www.ipwatchdog.com/2010/05/04/kappos-talks-patent-reform-and-gene-patents-at-bio-convention/id=10382/ (last accessed 6 December 2012).

114 ICC Commission on Intellectual Property, *Cooperation Between Patent Offices: Prior Art Searching of Patent Applications*, prepared by the ICC Commission on Intellectual Property, document no. 450/1056 – 28 June (2010).

115 Korea Intellectual Property Office (KIPO), *A Study on Mutual Recognition of Patent Examination* (Korea: KIPO, 2008).

116 ICC Commission on Intellectual Property, *Cooperation Between Patent Offices: Prior Art Searching of Patent Applications*, prepared by the ICC Commission on Intellectual Property, document no. 450/1056 – 28 June (2010).

on drawings, pictures, and math formula, etc., in order to discover the prior art rather than reading full description of publications. Also, with the mechanism of search-sharing, costs for applying for multiple patent applications are effectively reduced since conducting comprehensive prior art search by one patent office will incur less cost than doing the same by two or more offices. Furthermore, search-sharing could cut down the risks of patent invalidation caused by different prior art search results.

Search-sharing is also a component of the PCT system. By virtue of Art.15(5) of the PCT, after an application is submitted, as is explained in Chapter 2, an ISA will conduct an international search and a search report will be issued, while a written opinion on patentability may also be produced upon request. As a consequence, national offices will be able to make considerable savings since the system already performs all or most of the work involved in a search, while the examination report issued at the end of the process may be safely referred to by national offices.[117] However, an opinion shared by some national patent offices is that the international search process does not guarantee high quality and, therefore, prior art search will be conducted again when a multiple patent application enters the national phase.[118] Consequently, to improve on the content of a international search report for increased usefulness for national offices, there were proposals to develop model clauses for written opinions as well as for an international preliminary examination report in a limited area with identified general principles, which may be used in the formulation of further clauses at the national level.[119]

Search-sharing has been widely supported. In the international business community, the International Chamber of Commerce fully endorsed the necessity and viability of search-sharing.[120] Among the world's biggest patent offices, one senior official from the JPO commented that 'the first stage [toward global patent] is to get agreement on the sharing and mutual recognition of prior art search results'.[121]

Many patent offices have taken initiatives to implement the search-sharing procedure. For example, since 2005, the UK Intellectual Property Office has been in

117 World Intellectual Property Organization, *The Need for Improving The Functioning of the PCT System*, Patent Cooperation Treaty (PCT) Working Group, third session, 14 to 18 June. (Geneva: WIPO, 2010).

118 United Kingdom Intellectual Property Office (UKIPO), *Informal Consultation on Reform of the Patent Cooperation Treaty (PCT)*. (UKIPO, November 2009). Available at: www.ipo.gov.uk/consult-pct.pdf (last accessed 1 January 2013).

119 World Intellectual Property Organization, *Implementation of Recommendations to Improve the Functioning of the PCT*, by Patent Cooperation Treaty (PCT) Working Group, Fifth Session, Geneva, 29 May to 1 June, 2012, PCT/WG/5/3, (WIPO, 8 May, 2012).

120 The International Chamber of Commerce wrote that 'continued and improved cooperation between patent offices of an early coordinated comprehensive search would create efficiencies for patent offices'. See: ICC Commission on Intellectual Property, *Cooperation Between Patent Offices: Prior Art Searching of Patent Applications*, prepared by the ICC Commission on Intellectual Property, document no. 450/1056 – 28 June (2010).

121 Arai H., *WIPO Intellectual Property Handbook: Policy, Law and Use* (Geneva: WIPO Publication No.489(E), 2004). Available at: www.wipo.int/about-ip/en/iprm/ (last accessed 27 June 2016). Explaining the necessity of search-sharing among the three countries, Arai wrote that 'there is, for example, an application pending in the US for a patent on a DNA sequence. This is a single patent, but it is expected that it will cost the patent office about 9,100 dollars to ascertain whether or not the same basic application has already been filed, or the information is already commonly known. It would be very wasteful to have to duplicate this effort in Japan and Europe. If one patent office has conducted a prior-art search, it would make sense for the other jurisdictions to recognise those search results. An ordinary filing in Japan currently costs 191 dollars, and it is impossible for the JPO to hope to break even if it has to spend about 9,100 dollars just for ascertaining patentability. Likewise, business would prefer not to spend the time and money filing the same application in three different regions'.

collaboration with the Danish Patent and Trade Mark Office as well as the Netherlands Intellectual Property Office for mutual exploitation of search results.[122] Equally, within the framework of the Triway Pilot project, search-sharing was promoted among the EPO, the JPO and the USPTO as a means to leverage the expertise of prior art search of each of the three Offices, for the benefit of both the applicants and the offices. Within the context of the project, each Office conducted prior art search on corresponding applications filed under the Paris Convention in a sufficiently earlier time period. The search result issued by each Office was then shared among all the three Offices so that the workload for search and examination in each Office was reduced, and the applicant and the offices were able to consider the search results delivered by all three Offices in a timely manner. This exercise helped to improve the quality of any patent issued on the corresponding applications by each Office.[123] At the end of the 'Triway' project (2008–2009),[124] and because Korea and China have gained leverage in patent protection and have become the biggest patent offices in the world, the five major patent offices established the 'IP5' cooperation project. Since October 2008, the Five IP Offices (IP5) Cooperation has been engaging in ten collaborative projects known as the Foundation Projects, including projects of 'Common Access to Search and Examination Results (One Portal Dossier)'.[125]

Decision-sharing and action-sharing are two other forms of work-sharing that are developed upon search-sharing.

B. DECISION-SHARING

Decision-sharing means sharing the final decision on prior art search delivered by the first filing office with the second office, and the decision will then be used by the second offices as a basis for concluding whether to grant a patent.[126] Or, the decision of the first filing office may be served as reference material for the second offices. Thus, decision-sharing reduces a considerable amount of examination workload as far as the second filing offices are concerned. However, the final decision on patentability will remain in the hands of the second offices and the decision issued by the first office is only for reference purposes, since the substantive patent law of each national office can be quite different.

122 United Kingdom Intellectual Property Office, *The Patent Office Cooperation Plan 2005*. (UKIPO, 2005).

123 See: Trilateral Cooperation, the Objective of Trilateral Cooperation. The objective of the cooperation was to, for example: 1) improve the quality of examination processes and reduce the processing time of patent applications; 2) develop common infrastructure and compatible data for electronic business systems and search tools; 3) harmonise the practices of the three offices; and 4) exploit the full potential of work performed by the other Trilateral Offices in search, examination, documentation and electronic tools. Available at: www.trilateral.net/about/objectives.html (last accessed 21 March 2016).

124 Established on 28 July 2008, the 'Triway' project was scheduled to run for a year or to cease to operate when the acceptance of 100 requests submitted to the USPTO as the Office of First Filing (OFF) was reached, whichever occurred first. For more details of the Triway project, see: www.uspto.gov/patents/int_protect/triway/triwaypilot.jsp (last accessed 21 March 2016).

125 Other projects conducted by the IP5 Offices are, for example: common documentation; common application format; mutual machine translation; common examination practice rules and quality management; a common approach to sharing and documenting search strategies; and common search and examination support tools. Available at: www.fiveipoffices.org/about.html (last accessed 21 March 2016).

126 Korea Intellectual Property Office (KIPO), *A Study on Mutual Recognition of Patent Examination* (Korea: KIPO, 2008).

The patent prosecution highway (PPH) project is an example of 'decision-sharing'. The PPH consists of a set of initiatives that provides accelerated patent prosecution procedures in order for the second patent offices to share decisions with regard to patentability.[127] Under the scheme, when a patent applicant receives a decision issued by the first filing office, and if it states that at least one claim in the application is patentable, the applicant will be able to request the second offices to conduct fast-track examination of the corresponding claims contained in the application filed in the second offices.[128] By doing this, redundant and duplicated work may be avoided and pendency reduced, and the process of decision-sharing would eventually involve fewer patent claims and narrow down the scope of such claims.[129] The PPH therefore benefits applicants with quicker and more consistent decisions on patentability in multiple jurisdictions within the PPH framework. Also, costs for a patent application to 'enter the highway' is approximately only 20–30 per cent of the costs that would incur if examination is pursued without the PPH procedure.

Note, however, that within the context of decision-sharing, multiple patent applications will not be examined in the second offices until the examination in the first filing office is entirely completed and, therefore, examination is not conducted in parallel, but in sequence. As a result, the total lead time required for obtaining multiple patents may become longer. Moreover, in order to benefit from the scheme, the scope of a patent claim must be strictly identical in all the applications submitted at the PPH offices, meaning that the scope of a claim submitted in the second filing offices must be limited to the same scope of the claim lodged in the first filing office. This requirement under the PPH may potentially result in narrower patent claims than if an application were to be prosecuted separately in each national office.[130]

In any case, decision-sharing could significantly reduce the workload of the second filing offices as far as further examination is concerned if the second offices and the first office share similar examination rules and standards. For example, applicants who file patent applications in Korea and Japan may greatly benefit from the PPH scheme since the substantive patent laws in both countries are similar. It is reported that in one case an applicant in Japan

127 For example, the USPTO has concluded a PPH agreement with countries such as Australia, Austria, Canada, Denmark, EU, Finland, Germany, Hungary, Japan, South Korea, Singapore, Spain and the United Kingdom; the JPO has concluded a PPH agreement with countries like the United States, South Korea, the United Kingdom, Germany, Denmark, Finland, Russia, Austria, Singapore, Hungary, Canada, the EU and Spain; the UK IPO has also concluded a PPH agreement with the United States, Japan and Korea.

128 PPH will leverage fast-track examination procedures already available in the OSF to allow applicants under the OSF to obtain corresponding patents faster and more efficiently. See: United States Patent and Trademark Office (USPOT), Patent Prosecution Highway (PPH) - Fast Track Examination of Applications, available at: www.uspto.gov/patents/init_events/pph/index.jsp (last accessed 21 March 2016).

129 For example, the statistics provided by Microsoft for its use of PPH in Japan as the second filing office showed that the acceptance rate for PPH requests was 73 per cent. On average, it took 1.9 months for the first filing office to take action after a PPH request was submitted, and 8.7 months for a PPH request or an examination request to be accepted. IBM had a similar experience in Japan. The acceptance rate for PPH requests was 86.7 per cent. On average, it took 49 days for the first filing office to take action after a PPH request was submitted. The JPO noted that PPH applications in the JPO, as the Office of second filing, averaged a 1.9-month pendency for first action, compared with a 29.3-month pendency for non-PPH applications. From first to final action, Nüdome reported an average timeline of 6.9 months, compared with 10.5 months for non-PPH applications. See: Chun D., 'Patent law harmonisation in the age of globalisation: the necessity and strategy for a pragmatic outcome'. 93 *Journal of the Patent and Trademark Office Society* 2 (2011), 127.

130 Pitts A. and Kim J., 'The patent prosecution highway: is life in the "fast lane" worth the cost?' 1 *Hastings Science and Technology Law Journal* 127 (2009), 141.

obtained a patent decision from Korea in only 28 days by taking advantage of the PPH scheme.

On the other hand, exploiting the decision-sharing mechanism requires trust and confidence among the participating patent offices. Once a country decides to join the decision-sharing process, it must hold conviction of the quality of the patents granted by other countries although they may have differences in their substantive provisions of patent protection. One of the most practical and fundamental hurdles in relation to decision-sharing is language inaccessibility. Countries naturally require patent applications to be submitted in their official languages, in which actions and decisions will be issued consequently. To share information on decisions, examiners must be able to understand patent applications written in highly technical and specialised terms, as well as examiners' opinions which define the legal rights and the scope of patent protection. Otherwise, decision-sharing will be rendered impossible. This being the case, to facilitate decision-sharing among countries using different languages, quality translation must be guaranteed.

In summary, whether a particular decision-sharing scheme will succeed depends on how deep those practical factors, such as substantive examination standards, reliability of examination results, and language accessibility are shared among the participating offices.

C. ACTION-SHARING

Action-sharing is a process whereby offices share information on prior art search results and office actions. The mechanism could be very helpful in synchronising examination results delivered by two patent offices when, for example, the examination speed of the two offices is so different that it is difficult for them to use the information in a timely way to share the workload between them. In the process of action-sharing, the first filing office has the responsibility to conduct the first action in prior art search, and the result of this exercise shall be given precedence.

Statistics from the USPTO revealed that, for the cross-filings between the USPTO and the JPO, the USPTO produced the results of the first action before the JPO publication in about 90 per cent of the applications submitted, whereas the JPO produced the results of the first action before the USPTO publication in only about 10 per cent of the applications submitted.[131] Since the availability of the results published by the first office for the second offices is far from optimal, the USPTO proposed a programme called SHARE, or Strategic Handling of Applications for Rapid Examination, to address the problem.[132]

By exploiting information provided by the first office as a basis for the second offices to formulate opinions or to contemplate decisions on patent award, action-sharing synchronises timings for efficient examination and improves examination quality in the second offices. Therefore, action-sharing may be an additional instrument for work-sharing when

131 Fowler P. N., *International Policies and Norms to Address Emerging IP Challenges*, at WIPO High Level Forum on the Global Intellectual Property Infrastructure for Promotion of Innovation, 1–2 March. (WIPO, 2010).

132 Within the framework of SHARE, the second offices are able to use the search and examination results delivered by the first office 'to the maximum extent practicable' to eliminate timing imbalances that may affect the availability of the search and examination results that other offices deliver and, in turn, to reduce redundancy. Available at: www.trilateral.net/projects/worksharing/share.html (last accessed 21 March 2016).

different timings of search and examination prevent efficient cooperation among multiple national offices.

D. SUMMARY

Work-sharing is a powerful instrument for reducing backlogs of multiple patent applications and for accelerating the search process among participating patent offices, without obliging them to amend their national laws while cooperating on the scheme. Possibilities for a group of countries to export their patent examination methods to other countries through technical assistance programmes are equally real, thereby bringing about substantive administrative patent harmonisation.[133]

Among the three work-sharing methods, search-sharing appears the most viable and practical instrument when information and resources are shared in order to determine patentability. During the exercise, patent offices retain their discretion and authority in prosecuting examination. To succeed, cooperation on search-sharing, trust and confidence must be present when sharing search results presented by fellow patent offices. Decision-sharing, on the other hand, is built on the foundation of search-sharing. Although decision-sharing means sharing reference data and records that are produced by other patent offices, in reality the available information for sharing may be very limited as decision-sharing depends rather on the similarity of national patent laws, the understanding of the records as well as the confidence in the examination results. Adversely, decision-sharing may result in delays due to the lengthy examining process that the first filing office requires. As to action-sharing, it may be an additional instrument complementing the other two work-sharing methods when, for example, different lead timings occur while patent claims are examined by two patent offices.

3. *Conclusion*

A. OVERVIEW

The process of international patent rights harmonisation is presently driven by the world's biggest patent offices in the direction of work-sharing. Exemplified by the Trilateral Cooperation and the IP5 Project, the US, the EU, Japan, China and Korea are in the lead in the process of work-sharing. These five patent offices file the world's highest numbers of patent applications and are the worst affected by the adverse consequences of the fragmented global patent system: patent backlogs, waste of resources and high application costs as far as multiplied patent applications are concerned. Naturally, once a good level of substantive administrative harmonisation, epitomised by work-sharing, is materialised among the five patent offices, the impact on global patent harmonisation will be substantial.

133 Former Commissioner of the Japan Patent Office Hisamitsu Arai introduced a four-stage-approach to true harmonisation and global patents: the first stage consists of countries agreeing on the sharing and mutual recognition of prior art search results; the second stage is to recognise each other's patents; the third stage is to implement trilateral patents between the US, Europe and Japan; and the fourth stage is to extend trilateral patents worldwide in order to provide a truly global patent system. See: Arai H., *WIPO Intellectual Property Handbook: Policy, Law and Use* (Geneva: WIPO Publication No.489(E), 2004).

Joining the process of work-sharing is convenient because no legislation changes are required and therefore more patent offices may participate in the process in future. As substantive legal harmonisation is suspended at the moment, substantive administrative harmonisation, which is based on work-sharing, may indeed be one way to bring forward international patent rights harmonisation.

Alternatively, the work-sharing mechanism may be pursued through the following means.

B. LANGUAGE-BASED COOPERATION

Language inaccessibility is one of the most frequently quoted obstacles for achieving international patent rights harmonisation, and it also contributes to a substantial part of the patent application costs. For example, when applying a patent in America or Japan, the translation cost may amount to as much as 36 per cent of the total application costs.[134] Also, while undergoing work-sharing, it is assumed that the shared information is written in a language that is understandable to all the participating patent offices. If a common written language does not exist, the work-sharing mechanism would then only work with compromised efficiency and provided good translation is available. Presently, there are three official languages within the EPO (English, French and German), and six languages under the IP5 cooperation (English, Japanese, French, German, Korean and Chinese). In these circumstances, a few initiatives were launched in recent years as an attempt to facilitate cooperation through linguistic diversity. For example, the patent offices of the IP5 Cooperation have developed a system of 'mutual machine translation' to enable access to patent information shared among the offices. In 2010 the EPO and Google also signed a memorandum of understanding to improve access to patent translation in multiple languages. Notwithstanding this, as patent applications and decisions are usually highly technical and the nuance of expression may result in varied conclusions with regard to inventive steps and scope of claim, which are both decisive factors to a patent award, machine translation is hardly a sophisticated tool for translating patent applications. Legal repercussions may occur if the errors in translation concern the scope of patent claim.[135] This being the case, work-sharing undertaken by countries sharing the same language may yield better results in substantive administrative harmonisation since countries that share the same language often share the same cultural background and legal heritage for the purpose of legislation, and therefore it may be easier to identify mutually agreed areas for cooperation. To this end, the two patent harmonisation groups in Africa were established according to the divide of languages. *L'Organisation Africaine de la Propriété Intellectuelle* (OAPI) consists of 17[136] African countries that use French as their official language, while the ARIPO groups the English-speaking African countries, whose number has reached 19 as of March 2016.[137] Also, thanks to the shared legal heritage and the long-standing

134 World Intellectual Property Organization, *World Patent Report: A Statistical Review*. (WIPO, 2008).

135 Chisum D. S. and Farmer S. J., '"Lost in translation": the legal impact of patent translation errors on claim scope' in T. Takenaka (Ed.) *Patent Law and Theory: A Handbook of Contemporary Research* (Cheltenham, UK: Edward Elgar, 2008).

136 Available at: www.oapi.int/index.php/en/aipo/etats-membres (last accessed 21 March 2016).

137 Available at: http://aripo.org/about-aripo/membership-member-states (last accessed 21 March 2016).

tradition of cooperation, the UK, Canada and Australia formed the 'Vancouver Group' and have been pursuing mutual exploitation of patents since 2008.[138]

C. OFFSHORE-OUTSOURCING PATENT EXAMINATION

Offshore-outsourcing patent examination is a new form of cooperation that is built on the premise of search-sharing. As offshore-outsourcing is undertaken for commercial activities where companies can engage external suppliers for certain business functions because of expertise and lowered cost, so patent examination could benefit from offshore-outsourcing too, based on the same operational model.[139] Note, however, that only patent examination may be outsourced since prior art search is a very technical function. Patent examination does not involve legal interpretation but provides only preliminary information for formulating examination decisions. Thus, if there is an external source that could conduct prior art search, participating patent offices may benefit from its efficiency and expertise for the benefit of an expedited examination process and lowered cost, as well as more consistent examination quality.

The UK intellectual property office has been outsourcing some of its patent examination functions to India since the beginning of 2011. The outsourcing services include answering telephone inquiries, search and examination. Also, the Danish Patent Office is one of the world's leading patent offices that provide search information for patent examiners. The Danish Patent Office offers expeditious opinions on patentability of inventive ideas and the availability of existing patents to which a patent holder's competitors, or other Patent Offices, may refer when deciding whether to challenge a patent award. Only ten working days are usually required in order to complete the said services. The Danish Patent Office also prides itself on providing this set of services, which combines its patent search competencies with knowledge of the different practices within the areas of rights and legislation.[140] Operating as if it is a private law firm, and in order to encourage potential clients to engage its services, the Danish Patent Office has advertised itself as an authority with one hundred experts who charge hourly rates for prior art search services.

Thanks to the ever faster-developing IT technologies, offshore-outsourcing for patent examination has been made easier, speedier, more economical, and therefore leads towards more efficiency in processing patent applications.

D. REGIONAL PATENT SYSTEMS

In the absence of global patent harmonisation, regional patent harmonisation, under which patents are designated for mutual recognition by all the participating members in the region concerned, has taken shape in recent years. Both the EU and the Association of South East Asian Nations (ASEAN) have established their respective regional patent

138 Vancouver Group, ***Mutual Exploitation: Work Sharing for Improved International Collaboration on Search and Examination***, presentation delivered at the Meeting of the Directive Committee of the South American Regional Cooperation System on IP, Washington DC, April 2013.

139 Chun D., 'Patent law harmonisation in the age of globalisation: the necessity and strategy for a pragmatic outcome'. 93 *Journal of the Patent and Trademark Office Society* 2 (2011), 127.

140 Abramowicz M. and Duffy J. F., 'Ending the patenting monopoly'. 157 *University of Pennsylvania Law Review* 1570 (2009).

system. Note, however, that a regional patent system is not a mutual recognition system, but a multilateral form of unilateral recognition,[141] and the system may be introduced only after the following prerequisite conditions are met.

First of all, regional patent is usually derived from regional economic integration. A common market or a free trade area usually serves as an enabling environment in which a regional patent system can embed itself. This is because IP protection has long been recognised as one of the most important features in a common market agreement since differences among national IP laws may distort competition and constitute protectionist barriers to the free movement of goods and services and thus undermine an integrated single market. Conversely, as regional economic integration promotes regionalisation, countries participating in the integration process most likely will also have an interest in establishing a common patent system, for the simple reason that patent is an important component of international trade.

A second prerequisite for establishing a regional patent system is the existence of a common patentability denominator, which should be mutually accepted and is compatible with the relevant thresholds prescribed by the national patent law in the countries concerned. Ultimately, a regional patent award should be fully recognised by all the participating countries in the region. Identifying a common working language is also an important step as far as establishing a regional patent system is concerned so that information-sharing is able to proceed with fewer language hurdles. Presently, although there are 24 official working languages in the European Union, only English, French and German are prescribed as official languages for patent application purposes, therefore applications submitted under the EPO all over Europe are able to proceed with the desired speed.

The EPC provides an excellent example of regional patent harmonisation, which was launched in the early stage of the European economic integration out of fear that national IPR might be abused, resulting in restricted trade within the Community.[142]

The EPC system consists of a preliminary search and a complete examination procedure (in accordance with the Implementing Regulations) for all invention patent applications submitted at the EPO.[143] Once the examination procedure is completed and the question of patentability is determined, a copy of the patent application will be forwarded to the national patent offices that are designated for patent protection in the application. The application will be translated (if required) and a decision will then be taken by the national offices. Therefore, although an applicant files a single patent application at the EPO, the application will result in as many individual patents as is designated in the original application.

The economic integration process launched by the ASEAN has also brought about a regional patent system. In 1995, seven ASEAN member states decided to establish the ASEAN Framework Agreement on Intellectual Property Cooperation. By virtue of Art.1(4) of the Agreement, and in order to promote region-wide patent protection and to develop

141 Chun D., 'Patent law harmonisation in the age of globalisation: the necessity and strategy for a pragmatic outcome'. 93 *Journal of the Patent and Trademark Office Society* 2 (2011).

142 Weiler J. and Kocjan C., *Intellectual Property in The Law of European Union*, NYU School of Law Teaching Material (Academy of European Law at the EUI in Florence and the Jean Monnet Center at NYU School of Law, 2004/05).

143 Goldstein P., *International Intellectual Property Law: Cases and Materials*. (St Paul, MN: Foundation Press, 2008). See also: Benson R. B., 'The impact of the Patent Cooperation Treaty (PCT) and the European Patent Convention (EPC) on US practitioners'. 60 *Journal of the Patent and Trademark Office Society* 118 (1978), 128.

a system thereof, the ASEAN Patent Examination Co-operation Programme (ASPEC) was established in June 2009. The purpose of the ASPEC, which is a work-sharing programme, is to share search and examination results among the offices in order to allow applicants from participating countries to obtain corresponding patents faster and more efficiently. Presently, there are nine ASEAN member countries that participate in the scheme, including Brunei Darussalam, Cambodia, Indonesia, Laos PDR, Malaysia, the Philippines, Singapore, Thailand and Vietnam. As described above concerning work-sharing, ASPEC aims to reduce duplication on the search and examination work done, thereby saving time and effort. Additionally, search and examination work done on a corresponding application serves as a useful reference in producing quality reports. The English language is identified as the ASPEC working language. The ASPEC services involve no costs to applicants from the participating ASEAN countries, although local fees incurred at the ASPEC national offices will still apply.[144]

E. WORK-SHARING AND THE PCT COMBINED

Since 1970, the PCT has served as an effective instrument for procedural harmonisation by simplifying procedures for multiple patent applications and affording cost efficiency. In the meantime, although within the PCT framework some form of work-sharing cooperation does exist among, for example, the five biggest IP offices in the world, substantive cooperation has yet to materialise. On the other hand, as to work-sharing, it operates practically without the necessity of treaty negotiations among the participating offices. Therefore, it may be viable to combine the PCT with work-sharing so that the PCT could help extend the network of, and obtain a more recognised structure for, work-sharing and to enhance the sense of trust among the work-sharing partners. In the meantime, work-sharing could bring about more substantive administrative cooperation among the PCT contracting members.

To this end, a few proposals emerged in recent years in order to reform the PCT by: 1) combining it with search-sharing in order to make search reports and preliminary examination more compliant and consistent; and 2) combining it with the decision-sharing mechanism to make international examination more complete, relevant and useful.[145]

4. *Decision-sharing – enhanced cooperation with mutual recognition*

As mentioned before, the ultimate goal of work-sharing, especially in terms of decision-sharing, is to establish mutual recognition of patents granted by fellow offices,[146] which denotes accepting each other's examination methodology and procedures and acknowledging patents granted by each other. More than just sharing information, the decision-sharing mechanism is an enhanced form of cooperation based on institutional agreements for which mutual trust among the group of patent offices is earnestly required. Therefore, the

144 Available at: www.ipos.gov.sg/AboutIP/TypesofIPWhatisIntellectualProperty/Whatisapatent/Applyingforapatent/ASEANPatentExaminationCo-operationASPEC.aspx (last accessed 22 March 2016).

145 United Kingdom Intellectual Property Office (UKIPO), *Informal Consultation on Reform of the Patent Cooperation Treaty (PCT)*, available at: www.ipo.gov.uk/consult-pct.pdf (last accessed 1 January 2013).

146 Chun D., 'Patent law harmonisation in the age of globalisation: the necessity and strategy for a pragmatic outcome'. 93 *Journal of the Patent and Trademark Office Society* 2 (2011), 127.

decision-sharing procedure combines the strengths of substantive legal and administrative patent harmonisation, but foregoes substantive national legislation change, which is one of the impediments to furthering substantive legal harmonisation. The combined framework will equally lead to more certainty in substantive administrative harmonisation. This is because the substance of mutual recognition of patent rights is commonly well defined and concluded as a bilateral or a multilateral agreement among participating countries. In addition, should 'mutual recognition' materialise, streamlined examination procedures will naturally take place resulting in reduced costs, a shortened application process and enhanced predictability concerning prior art search and novelty examination – since, once mutually recognised, participating patent offices will not conduct any further examination if the same claims were already previously examined by another patent office.[147]

147 London Economics, *Economic Study on Patent Backlogs and a System of Mutual Recognition – Final Report to the Intellectual Property Office*. (London: London Economics, 2010). The UKIPO further estimated that the mutual recognition system reduces the amount of time spent on duplicate applications by 25 per cent, which will reduce the backlog by nine backlog months (19 per cent) after 5 years. As a result, it is expected that mutual recognition could achieve savings between 6 and 23 GBP billion (6.92 and 26.57 EUR billion) per annum.

4 The judicial system in China

Before unveiling China's IPR legal framework, it is necessary to explain the country's overall judicial system so that the structure of its IPR legal framework can be better understood in context. Therefore, Chapter 4 will proceed with an overview of China's judicial system, followed by an analysis of the country's legal reform in the post-WTO era. The WTO accession in 2001 marks a watershed in the country's overall judicial transformation. Due to the WTO accession, not only was China obliged to enact new legislation that should be in conformity with the order of the trading system, but also was China required to instil new spirit in its overall judicial system, such as checks and balances. It is as part of this process that the IPR legislation was established from scratch in the country.

I Overview

China's judicial system is described as a 'socialist legal framework with Chinese characteristics'.[1] Uniform yet multi-tiered, it is divided into seven branches and three levels. With the Constitution at the top of the hierarchy, other branches of law include the Constitution-related laws, civil and commercial laws, administrative laws, economic laws, laws on society, criminal laws and litigation and non-litigation procedural laws. The three levels of laws are: laws, administrative regulations and local regulations, including autonomous and separate regulations.

China's judicial system may be looked at from two aspects. First, the institutional structure together with the legislative process and, secondly, the process of internationalisation, especially in the run up to the WTO accession when China started to amend and to promulgate a series of laws in order to comply with the order of the WTO trading system.[2] China's second Patent Law amendment (2000) and the promulgation of the Government Procurement Law (2002) were the consequence of this transformation. The process of judicial internationalisation has persisted ever since. China has successfully integrated into the world trading system and the country rose to become a world-leading economy in recent years.

1 See the White paper: *China's Efforts and Achievements in Promoting the Rule of Law*. Beijing: The State Council, February 2008.

2 According to its WTO Accession Protocol, China pledged to amend its IP laws in order to bring in full compliance with and full application of the TRIPS Agreement. Moreover, in terms of IPR protection, China pledged to enhance its IPR enforcement efforts through the application of more effective administrative sanctions. See Accession of the People's Republic of China, WT/L/432, 23 November 2001.

II Institutional structure

The legislative power in China is exercised by the National People's Congress (NPC) and its permanent body, the Standing Committee.[3] The NPC enacts and amends criminal, civil and other elementary laws[4] and so does the Standing Committee, except for those that fall under the jurisdiction of the NPC.[5] Both the central and the local governments are also endowed with legislative power because the social and economic development in the different regions in China can be highly diverse so, therefore, tailored laws, including rules and regulations, may be required in order to better accommodate the different development needs in the region concerned. According to the Chinese Constitution, the legislature and the judiciary are interrelated. The local people's congress at and above the county level may elect and shall have the power to recall the president of the people's court and the chief procurator of the people's procuratorate at the corresponding level.[6] Likewise, the standing committee of a local people's congress at and above the county level supervises the work of the people's court at the corresponding level.[7]

III Legislative process

China's legislative process is prescribed by the Legislation Law. Under Art.8 of the Legislation Law, matters concerning economic system, finance, taxation, foreign trade and banking, etc. must be governed by law.[8] For other matters that are not yet governed by law, by virtue of Art.9 of the Legislation Law the NPC or its Standing Committee may authorise the State Council to issue administrative regulations before the relevant legislation is enacted by the NPC.

The local people's congress and local government have the authority to issue local regulations and rules until such regulations and rules are superseded by the same legislation at the national level.[9] Provinces, autonomous regions, municipalities which are directly under

3 The NPC is composed of deputies from provinces, autonomous regions, municipalities directly under the central government, the special administrative regions and from the armed forces. Each NPC has a term of five years, meets in session once a year and is convened by its standing committee.

4 The elementary laws include, for example, the Organic Law of the State Council, and the Organic Law of the Local People's Congresses and Local People's Governments.

5 Art.88 of the Legislation Law stipulates that the NPC has the power to alter or annul laws formulated by its Standing Committee; the Standing Committee of the NPC has the power to annul administrative regulations that contradict the Constitution and laws or local regulations that contradict the Constitution, laws and administrative regulations; the State Council has the power to annul departmental rules and local government rules that are inconsistent with the Constitution and laws.

6 Art.101, Constitution of the People's Republic of China, 2004.

7 Art.104, Constitution of the People's Republic of China, 2004.

8 By virtue of Article 8 of the Legislation Law, other matters that must be governed by law are, for example, the system of regional national autonomy, the system of special administrative regions, the system of self-government among people at the grassroots level, criminal offences and their punishment, mandatory measures and penalties involving deprivation of citizens of their political rights or restriction of the freedom of their person, and requisition of non-state-owned property.

9 Art.88 of the Legislation Law stipulates that rules and regulations enacted at lower legislative levels may be annulled by a higher legislative level should such rules and regulations become contradictory with the Constitution and laws.

the central government and certain large cities may announce local rules and regulations.[10] Interim provisions concerning the country's economic reforms and policies are also defined as law in China and may be issued by the State Council.[11]

Additionally, ministries, commissions and other departments of the State Council may issue departmental rules within their respective departmental competence prescribed by the relevant laws or the administrative regulations.

On the other hand, the State Council is empowered to issue 'interim provisions', which are equally a source of law in China. These interim provisions mainly relate to economic and tax reforms and may be transformed to become specific legislation if they are tested fit and when the relevant authorities believe it appropriate. Aside from the overall hierarchy of legislation, there are also 'regulatory trials' which are actually implementing rules.

Indeed, in China, 'law' has a very broad meaning while the boundary between law and policy has become increasingly blurred over the years. In hierarchical order, China's legislative framework consists of the Constitution, which is the highest law, followed by national laws, administrative regulations and local regulations, autonomous regulations and separate regulations (see below, Figure 4.1). Such legislative arrangement contributes to a staggering number of laws. For example, there are currently over 7,000 local regulations that are enacted by the local people's congresses and their standing committees at various administrative levels. These local regulations are in addition to the 229 laws enacted by the NPC and its Standing Committee. Moreover, the State Council has enacted nearly 600 administrative regulations and the various people's congresses of the ethnic autonomous areas have enacted an equally great number of autonomous and separate regulations. All these laws are currently in force. In parallel, many rules were enacted in past years by the various departments under the State Council, the people's governments of the provinces, autonomous regions, municipalities directly under the central government and the larger cities.[12] Keeping up with such an astounding number of rules and regulations is no doubt a tough undertaking, let alone identifying one of them for enforcement. The aforesaid legislative

10 Such government bodies may formulate regulations on matters requiring specific provisions due to conditions in the locality concerned. They may also formulate rules to implement provisions of laws, administrative regulations and local regulations, and rules on specific administrative matters pertaining to the respective administrative areas. These local regulations are issued by the local people's congress and its standing committee, provided that they do not contradict the Constitution, laws and administrative regulations. Local regulations of comparatively larger cities must be submitted to and obtain approval from the standing committee of the province or the autonomous region concerned. Autonomous regulations and separate regulations are issued by people's congress in the autonomous areas. Local rules are formulated by the local government in the provinces, autonomous regions, municipalities and comparatively larger cities, in accordance with the relevant laws, administrative regulations or local regulations. 'Comparatively larger cities' refers to a city where the provincial or the autonomous regional people's government is located or where a special economic zone is located, or a city approved as such by the State Council (Art.63 of the Legislation Law). These local regulations may govern the following matters: those requiring the formulation of specific provisions to implement laws or administrative regulations; those of a local character; and those subjects for which the State has not yet formulated any laws or administrative regulations. For the latter, once the State has enacted laws or administrative regulations, local regulations that contradict State laws or administrative regulations become null and void, unless promptly amended.

11 See the Decision of the Third Session of the Sixth National People's Congress on Authorising the State Council to Formulate Interim Provisions or Regulations Concerning the Reform of the Economic Structure and the Open Policy (1985).

12 See the White Paper: *China's Efforts and Achievements in Promoting the Rule of Law*. Beijing: the State Council, February 2008.

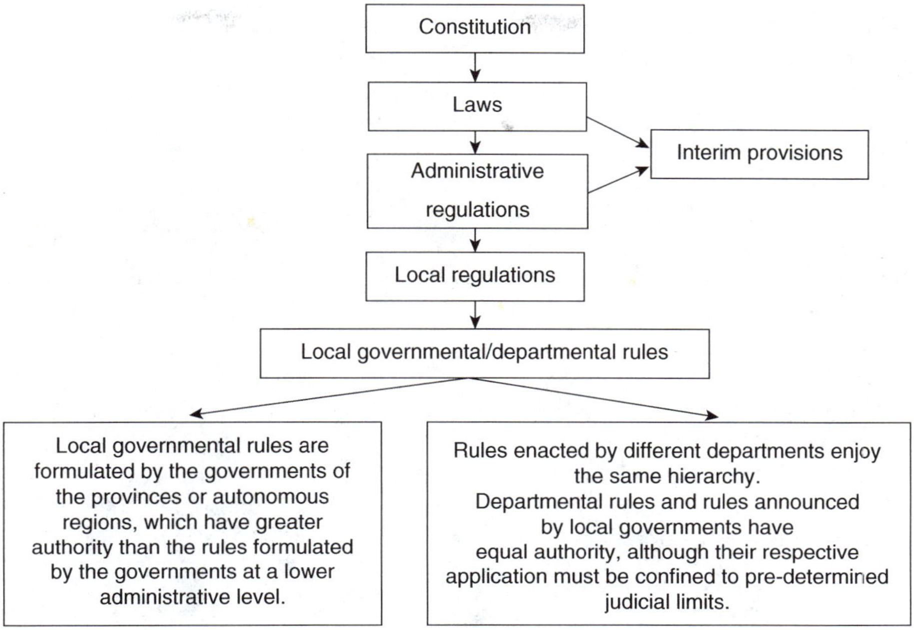

Figure 4.1 China's legislative framework

arrangement is criticised for causing the country's judicial system to be complex and opaque, and it results in judicial loopholes, weaker enforcement, breeds local protectionism and engenders corruption.

I) Judiciary

China's judicial system consists of the Supreme People's Court (SPC), the local people's courts at different levels,[13] and the military and other special courts (for example, railway and maritime courts). The SPC comprises the Judicial Committee, the No. 1 Criminal Tribunal, the No. 2 Criminal Tribunal, the Civil Tribunal, the Economic Tribunal, the Administrative Tribunal, the Complaint and Appeal Tribunal and the Communication and Transportation Tribunal.

Decisions issued by the lower courts may be appealed at the higher courts. Judgments and orders delivered by the people's courts of the second instance are final except for cases involving the death penalty which will be reviewed by the SPC.[14] For criminal cases, the procuratorate may file a protest against a judgment issued by the people's court at the same hierarchy level if errors in the judgment are found. A retrial will be then conducted.[15]

13 Local people's courts are divided into basic people's courts, intermediate people's courts and higher people's courts.

14 All the decisions and judgments issued by the SPC for cases of the first instance are final.

15 Arts.203–207, the Criminal Procedure Law.

The Supreme People's Court (SPC) is China's highest judicial body. It is composed of a Chief Justice, Grand Justices and other judges. The functions of the SPC include: trying cases within its original jurisdiction, hearing appeals against the legal decisions delivered by the higher courts, supervising the work of the local courts and the special courts, issuing judicial interpretations for the specific utilisation of laws.

Each province, autonomous region and municipality has a Higher People's Court, but there are two higher courts in the Xinjiang Uygur Autonomous Region. The intermediate people's courts are established in the cities at the prefecture-level. Counties have the basic people's courts.

According to the Judges Law, the president of a local court is appointed or removed by the people's congress at the corresponding hierarchy level and judges of a local court are appointed or removed by the standing committee of a corresponding local people's congress.

The SPC supervises the administration of the local people's courts at the different hierarchy levels and also of the special people's courts. People's courts at higher levels supervise the administration of those at lower levels.

Source: http://www.court.gov.cn

Figure 4.2 The court structure in China

II) Enforcement: administrative and judicial enforcement

Judicial enforcement in China is undertaken by an administrative–judicial dual-track system. An administrative enforcement action is instituted by filing a complaint at a local administrative office. If the judicial enforcement route is elected, litigation will start in court. Both enforcement tracks are of equal importance.

Administrative enforcement proceeds with mediation, which is formally recognised as part of the civil law procedure in China. On a voluntary basis, and in the spirit of legitimacy and democracy, while carrying out administrative enforcement the principle of 'doing all it can to mediate first, adjudicating when so doing is proper, and combining mediation with adjudication to close the case' must be upheld.[16]

Administrative enforcement has the advantage of being affordable in its costs and fast in its procedure. But the drawback is that, since the structure is less formal, disputing parties tend to treat the procedure with less respect, leaving settlement unenforced or only partially executed as a result. To remedy this, in recent years, the administrative enforcement mechanism has been granted more judicial powers for better enforceability. Using patent rights protection as an example, through each patent law amendment the administrative enforcement mechanism is provided with new judicial powers, such as those powers provided by the Patent Law 2008 with regard to the powers of on-site inspection, issuing injunction orders and detaining suspected infringing goods. The Draft Patent Law 2015 continues to empower the administrative enforcement mechanism when, for example, the newly added

16 See the White Paper: *China's Efforts and Achievements in Promoting the Rule of Law*. Beijing: The State Council, February 2008.

Art.61 states that the Patent Administration Department may mediate in the damages resulting from patent infringement. In order to render more enforceability towards an agreement reached via mediation, Art.61 prescribes that failing to execute a mediation agreement or when such an agreement is not faithfully executed, the court may step in for enforcement.

In the context of administrative enforcement, and in order to consolidate the power that the local governments at the different administrative levels exercise and to clarify the responsibilities that they discharge, the Chinese legislature has also enacted a series of administrative laws. For example, the Administrative Supervision Law was enacted to strengthen the supervision function of administration and to guarantee the effective implementation of government decrees, etc.

The procedure of administrative reconsideration was established amid the process of strengthening the overall administrative enforcement mechanism. The Administrative Reconsideration Law aims to protect the lawful rights and the interests of citizens, legal persons and organisations, and to ensure that the government's functions are duly performed and its power is discharged lawfully. Article 3 of the Administrative Reconsideration Law lists seven functions and responsibilities that an administrative reconsideration body must discharge when a specific matter is brought for administrative reconsideration. Article 4 also stipulates that, under the process of administrative reconsideration, the principles of legality, impartiality, openness, promptness and convenience to the people must be upheld. By the same token, in order to ensure effective administration, the Administrative Permission Law 2003[17] standardises the procedures for granting administrative permission while protecting the legitimate rights and interests of citizens, legal persons and organisations.[18] The Administrative Permission Law defines the coercive power of the government and specifies which government bodies can exercise them.

In parallel with administrative enforcement, there are always the avenues for transferring cases from the administrative to the judicial enforcement mechanism, whereby the enforcement procedure is governed by the Civil Procedure Law.[19] It is observed that, in recent years, although the number of cases settled through administrative enforcement remains high, judicial enforcement has grown in its importance. The number of cases dealt with by the people's courts has been increasing fast. With regard to IPR enforcement, for example, cases dealt with by the civil courts are on the rise on a yearly basis. In 2014, local people's courts nationwide accepted 95,522 new IP civil cases in the first instance and 13,760 in the second instance, registering a year-on-year increase of 7.83 per cent and 15.08 per cent respectively.[20]

17 In accordance with Art.2 of the Administrative Permission Law, administrative permission means approval given to citizens, legal persons and other organisations for engaging in special activities by administrative departments on the basis, and upon the examination, of their applications.

18 Art.1, Administrative Permission Law 2003.

19 In terms of IPR enforcement, in 2006 four regulations were issued to facilitate transferring cases from administrative to judicial enforcement. The four regulations are the Provisional Regulation on Better Connection in the Fight Against Crimes Involving Infringement on the Exclusive Use of Trademarks (13 January 2006); the Opinion on Speedy Referral of Suspected Criminal Cases by Administrative Law Enforcement Authorities (26 January 2006); the Provisional Regulation on Better Coordination in IPR Law Enforcement (24 March 2006) and the Provisional Regulation on Better Connection in the Fight Against Crimes Involving Infringement on Copyrights (26 March 2006). They were jointly promulgated by the Supreme People's Procuratorate, the Ministry of Public Security, the National Copyright Administration, the SAIC and the Customs.

20 *Intellectual Property Rights Protection in China*. SIPO, 2014, p.11.

IV Legal reforms in the post-WTO era

The WTO accession is a milestone in China's legal history, while the sweeping changes that it has brought to the country are two-fold. First, in terms of legislation and in the process of accession negotiations which lasted 15 years (1986–2001), China started to enact and amend many laws in order to comply with the order of the trading system as well as to materialise the commitments it pledged at the accession. Second, China was obliged to instil new legal principles and methods, such as transparency, impartiality, predictability, enforceability, public consultation, checks and balances, etc. into legislation and its overall judicial process. This exercise was conducted against the legacy of the feudalism that had lasted for more than 3,000 years, whereby society was divided into those who ruled and those who were ruled, who were always strictly on the receiving end. Therefore, acceding to the WTO trading system not only meant incorporating the WTO agreements into China's national laws, but also meant conducting international trade in a manner corresponding with the WTO spirit as is prescribed.

In order to become ready to materialise the commitments that China pledged at its WTO accession, the SPC abolished around 20 legal interpretations that were not consistent with the relevant provisions of the WTO Agreement. In 2002, the SPC further issued a series of judicial interpretations to clarify the Court's jurisdiction over international trade-related 'administrative litigations'.[21] As a result, from then on it has become possible to apply uniformly the various provisions in relation to trade in goods and services, the TRIPS Agreement and the control of foreign exchange in the country's entire customs territory in a manner that conforms with the WTO rules. For the purpose of checks and balances, private parties, including individuals and enterprises, have been guaranteed the right to be informed, via the government's publication, of the above-mentioned provisions and empowered to bring any non-conformity to the attention of the relevant national authorities.

In a similar vein, China installed the procedure of judicial review in its overall legal proceedings. Tribunals were established in order to review all the administrative actions relating to the implementation of the laws, regulations, judicial decisions and administrative rulings of general application that are referred to in Art.X:1 of the GATT 1994 (publication and administration of trade regulations), Art.VI of the GATS (domestic regulation) and in the relevant provisions of the TRIPS Agreement. Such tribunals are meant to be impartial and independent of the agencies that are entrusted with the power of administrative enforcement, and they should not have any substantial interest in the outcome of the matter. In addition, as part of the process of judicial review, the procedure of appeal was established. The right to appeal, without penalty, has become available to aggrieved private parties who unwarrantedly suffer from the government's administrative actions. In this context, in case an appeal is instituted against an administrative body, the appellant will have the privilege to lodge an appeal before a judicial body.[22] For the purpose of transparency,

21 Such judicial interpretations are: Rules of the Supreme People's Court on Certain Issues on Handling of International Trade-related Administrative Cases, Rules of the Supreme People's Court on the Legal Application of Anti-Subsidy Administrative Cases, and Rules of the Supreme People's Court on the Legal Application of Anti-Dumping Administrative Cases.

22 This being the case, notice concerning a decision on appeal must be delivered to the appellant and the reasons for such a decision must be provided in writing. The appellant must also be informed about any rights for further appeal.

public consultation has become a component of legislation in China. This being the case, all laws, regulations and other measures relating to trade in goods and services, the TRIPS Agreement or the control of foreign exchange must be published first, followed by a public consultation exercise, before they may be announced.[23]

Private parties in China, including individuals and enterprises as well as WTO Members, are guaranteed the right to access information of laws, regulations and other measures relating to trade in goods and services, the TRIPS Agreement or the control of foreign exchange.[24] Additionally, China promised to make available to WTO Members, upon request, those legal provisions concerning the above-mentioned subject matters before they are enforced, while only in an 'emergency' can laws and regulations be announced at the time when they are enforced.

Although all the above-mentioned judicial mechanisms may be taken for granted as a *sine qua non* by the world's democracies, the overall judicial reforms have proven to be challenging, especially in terms of implementation and enforcement in China due to the legacy of feudalism as mentioned above. The difficulties that China has encountered are, however, not about the legislation itself, but in instilling the spirit of impartiality, fairness and transparency in its judicial system. It is a huge undertaking that will not be completed overnight, perhaps not even in a couple of decades due to both the historical reasons and the present institutional arrangements where the government stands supreme above the legislature and the judiciary, and with the legislature overpowering the judiciary. This melange of powers results in weaker judicial implementation and enforcement in general, and engenders local protectionism and corruption. This being the case, the judicial reforms in China in the post-WTO era cannot claim to be a true and full success as yet.

23 This commitment does not apply to those laws, regulations and other measures involving national security, specific measures setting foreign exchange rates or monetary policy and those measures that the publication of which may impede enforcement.

24 There is a 30-day timeframe for providing a reply to a request for information. In exceptional cases, the government may take up to 45 days. If this is the case, a notice of the delay and an explanation for the reasons causing the delay must be communicated.

5 Intellectual property rights protection in China

Legislation and enforcement

I Introduction

Intellectual property rights protection is an essential component of China's open-door policy and of its socialist legal reform.[1] With the aim of stimulating the country's economic development after the Cultural Revolution, in 1978 China launched the campaign of the Four Modernisations namely: agriculture, industry, national defence, and science and technology modernisations. Consequently, a series of laws on IPR protection and related laws were enacted in the early 1980s. For example, Criminal Law was enacted in 1979, Trademark Law in 1982 and Patent Law in 1984. Intellectual property rights were recognised as a civil right by the General Principles of Civil Law in 1986, when citizen's rights and protection in relation to copyrights and trademarks, as well as discoveries, inventions and other achievements in scientific and technological research were guaranteed.[2] Note that IPR was only granted constitutional protection in 2004 on the occasion of the fourth amendment of the Constitution, whereby citizen's rights to private property was acknowledged and confirmed as inviolable.[3] China promulgated the Law on the Laws Applicable to Foreign-related Civil Relations in 2010, in which Chapter 7 sets down the rules for the resolution of choice of law specifically in the area of intellectual property.

II Legislation

China's IPR legislation includes the main IP laws (such as Patent Law) and IP-related laws (such as the Law of the People's Republic of China on the Laws Applicable to Foreign-related Civil Relations), implementing rules (such as Decision of the State Intellectual Property Office Amending the Guidelines for Patent Examination) and IPR jurisprudence (such as Regulations of the Supreme People's Court on the Jurisdiction over cases of the Intellectual Property Courts in Beijing, Shanghai and Guangzhou). Intellectual property laws and IP-related laws are enacted by the legislature and IPR jurisprudence is issued by the SPC. Intellectual property rights enforcement departments and governments at different administrative levels are competent to issue IPR implementing rules.

China's IPR laws are updated regularly in order to reflect the prevailing domestic needs and to comply with international obligations, as will be illustrated in Chapter 6. Because

1 Report of the Working Party on the Accession of China, WT/ACC/CHN/49, 1 October 2001.
2 Arts. 94–97, General Principles of Civil Law.
3 Art.13, Constitution of the People's Republic of China, adopted in March 2004.

weaker enforcement is a persistent issue in IPR protection in China, enhancing enforcement is therefore one of the objectives that each IP law amendment aims to achieve. The result of this endeavour is that the administrative enforcement mechanism is granted with increased judicial powers for enforceability after each amendment, while the judicial enforcement mechanism imposes higher penalties for deterring future IP infringers. At the same time, transferring cases from administrative to judicial enforcement has become easier thanks to the series of judicial interpretations that the SPC has issued over the years.

After having promulgated a few main IP laws in the 1980s, the 1990s witnessed more IP legislation coming in to force in order to complete China's overall IP protection framework. The Regulations on Customs Protection of Intellectual Property Rights (1995) and the Law against Unfair Competition of the PRC (1993) were promulgated during this period. The latter prohibits trademark passing off, trade secrets infringement, misrepresentation and other deceptive conduct, and the illegal use of well-known goods or names of other people. The Advertising Law was enacted in 1994 to prohibit unfair, misleading and deceptive conduct involving patent advertising and other advertising activities in general.

After acceding to the WTO in the new millennium, and especially in the past few years, China enacted and amended more rules and regulations at a faster pace to further improve its IPR legislation. In 2014 alone, across the IP spectrum of copyright, trademark and patent protection, many legislation amendment activities took place. For example, the SIPO amended the Guidelines for Patent Examination by including the 'graphic user interface' in the scope of design patent protection. The revised Draft on Measures for Reduction of Patent-related Fees was also published,[4] so were a few judicial interpretations issued by the SPC in order to update the guidance on trials on IP cases. For example, the SPC issued the Interpretation on Issues Concerning the Scope of Jurisdiction and Applicable Laws in the Trial of Trademark Cases, and revised the Regulations on Issues Concerning Applicable Laws to the Trial of Patent Disputes.

III Enforcement

As mentioned previously, IPR enforcement in China adopts an administrative-judicial dual-track system. Under the administrative enforcement track, to start an enforcement procedure one is required to file a complaint at a local administrative office. If the judicial enforcement route is elected, the IPR dispute will be dealt with in court based on tort. If this is the case, a lawsuit may be instituted, not only at the place where the infringement act takes place but also at the place of the defendant's domicile.

The overall competence of administrative enforcement is shared by a number of government agencies and each is responsible for one particular type of IPR protection. An administrative enforcement action can be brought upon on the request of an IPR-holder, a third party, or on the initiative of an administrative enforcement authority. When mediation does not produce satisfactory results, the administrative enforcement authority may refer the dispute to the people's court whereby the enforcement procedure will be governed by the civil procedural law. To facilitate case transfer from the administrative to the judicial enforcement route for greater predictability and enforceability, the SPC issued a series of

4 For other IP amendments enacted in 2014, see: State Intellectual Property Office of the People's Republic of China (SIPO), *Intellectual Property Rights Protection in China*. (SIPO, 2014).

judicial interpretations. Additional avenues for transferring cases from administrative to judicial enforcement are provided by Art.60 of the Patent Law 2008, in cases where the disputing parties are not willing to mediate or mediation fails. Also, if the acts of infringement are established but the infringer is dissatisfied with the patent administration department's decision, the infringer may institute a lawsuit in court within 15 days after receiving the notification of the decision. These provisions are maintained by the Draft Patent Law 2015. As a result of the facilitated case transferring route, more and more case transfers have taken place in recent years. For example, in 2014, local people's courts accepted 9,918 new IPR administrative cases of the first instance, registering a year-on-year increase of 243.66 per cent. For infringement cases tried at the second instance, in the same year, local people's courts nationwide accepted 2,435 new IPR administrative cases, seeing a year-on-year rise of 63.42 per cent. In addition, the SPC accepted 145 IPR administrative cases.[5]

In general, though the administrative enforcement mechanism remains a favourite choice for enforcement among Chinese IPR holders, IP cases dealt with by judicial enforcement are constantly on the rise. In 2014, local people's courts nationwide accepted 95,522 new IPR civil cases of the first instance, registering a year-on-year increase of 7.83 per cent.[6] Compared with 42,931 civil IP cases accepted by court in 2010, in four years' time IP civil cases dealt with by the judicial enforcement mechanism more than doubled. In fact, since 2005, China has become the world's most IP litigious country.

Intellectual property-specialised chambers were established in Chinese courts as early as in 1993. Currently, there are about 560 IP chambers and 3,000 IP judges at four levels of people's court, namely basic, intermediate, higher and supreme levels. However, decisions laid down by the IP chambers are often criticised for lacking consistency and some insist that the chambers require more competence, especially when handling cases that involve technologically challenging matters. In November 2014, three IP-specialised courts were established in Beijing, Shanghai and Guangzhou as a three-year experiment to adjudicate technologically complex cases of the first and the second instance for both civil and administrative litigation. With the status of intermediate court, at the IP-specialised courts technology experts serve as assistants to judges.

Patent administration authorities may impose fines on the infringing party and/or confiscate/destroy the infringing products, components, tools, modules, equipment and so on that are exclusively used for manufacturing infringing products or for applying infringing methods. The Draft Patent Law 2015 further empowers the patent administration authorities to deal with acts of group infringement, repeated infringement and other acts of intentional patent infringement that disturb the market order.

Remedies available for judicial enforcement include monetary compensation based on either the value or the volume of the counterfeit goods, or both. Criminal prosecutions may be instituted under certain circumstances, in accordance with the Criminal Law. The public security body is in charge of criminal investigation against IPR infringement, and the General Administration of Customs (GAC) is responsible for enforcing IPR at the border.

5 State Intellectual Property Office of the People's Republic of China (SIPO), *Intellectual Property Rights Protection in China*. (SIPO, 2014), p. 12.

6 State Intellectual Property Office of the People's Republic of China (SIPO), *Intellectual Property Rights Protection in China*. (SIPO, 2014), pp. 10–11.

I) Administrative enforcement: actors, procedures and remedies

1. Actors

There are two levels of administrative enforcement authority in China, namely the central and the local administrative enforcement departments. The administrative enforcement department at the central governmental level under the State Council enjoys ministerial status. It is competent to enact laws on IPR protection, responsible for examining, granting and registering IPR, and supervises the work undertaken by the local administrative enforcement departments. For example, the SIPO, which is directly under the charge of the State Council, is at the ministerial level as an IP administration body in China.[7] In addition to issuing IPR laws, such as the Decision amending the Measures on the Executive Enforcement of Patents, which was issued on 29 May 2015, the SIPO is responsible for examining foreign and domestic patent applications, coordinating domestic and foreign-related IPR issues involving copyrights, trademarks and patents, supervising the local SIPO bureaus and registering semiconductor layout designs.[8] The SIPO represents China in the international fora on IPR cooperation and takes charge of improving local patent authorities' competence in enforcement. The local SIPO offices generally handle patent disputes as a patent administrative enforcement authority.

In addition to the SIPO and its local SIPO offices,[9] the other main IPR administrative enforcement agencies are as follows (also see below, Figure 5.1):[10]

- **Administration for Quality Supervision, Inspection and Quarantine (AQSIQ).** As an agency for standardisation, the AQSIQ's primary tasks include ensuring the quality and standards of Chinese products and handling infringement of registered trademarks. The AQSIQ also issues administrative regulations to protect geographical indications that are registered in China.
- **State Administration on Industry and Commerce (SAIC).** The Trademark Office under the SAIC has the authority over trademark registration, administrative recognition of well-known marks and trademark enforcement. The Fair Trade Bureau, which is also under the SAIC, manages disputes arising from the Law on Anti-Unfair Competition, including matters concerning trade secrets. The SAIC is competent to investigate trademark infringement cases. If an infringement act is

7 China's Patent Office (CPO), which was set up in 1980, was a subordinate office under the Ministry of Science and Technology. The State Intellectual Property Office was established in 1998 and CPO was renamed SIPO.

8 A Chinese-English bilingual web portal on IPR protection was launched by SIPO in 2006.

9 The administrative authority under the SIPO is responsible for solving patent infringement disputes, investigating and handling acts of passing off and counterfeit, mediation, etc. See Arts.1-4 Measures of Patent Administrative Enforcement, 2015.

10 Other agencies are: the State Drug Administration, which deals with pharmaceutical counterfeit; the Ministry of Culture copyright materials and markets; the Ministry of Commerce agriculture-related chemicals; the Ministry of Agriculture new plant varieties, and the Ministry of Information Industry is responsible for protecting the layout designs of integrated circuits, etc. Some IPR is enforced by several agencies. For example, protection of geographical indications is jointly undertaken by the State Trademark Office, the General Administration of Quality Supervision, Inspection and Quarantine and the Ministry of Agriculture.
At the local level, in order to establish more coordinated enforcement efforts, some provinces and municipalities established joint IPR bureaus or IPR committees to coordinate public awareness campaigns and, to a more limited extent, enforcement.

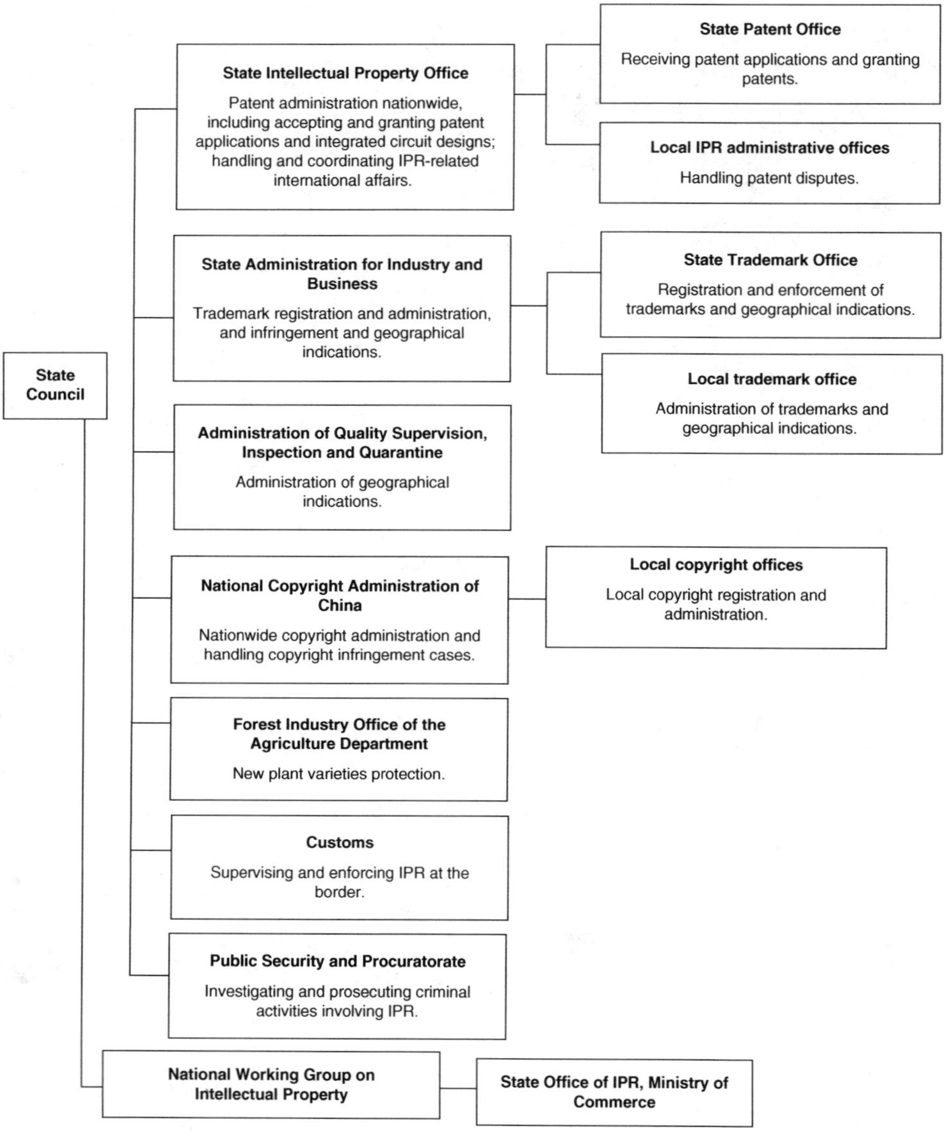

Figure 5.1 IPR administration and enforcement agencies in China

established, SAIC has the power to impose fines and order the infringer to cease the infringement act, and the power to confiscate and destroy the infringing goods and tools used in producing such infringing goods or forging logos of the registered trademark.

- **National Copyright Administration of China (NCAC)**. The NCAC is responsible for copyright administration and enforcement. The NCAC at the national level is responsible for nationwide copyright issues, including promulgating and implementing copyright laws and regulations, investigating copyright infringement cases, administering foreign-related copyright issues, developing foreign-related arbitration rules and supervising the local copyright administration authorities.

- **General Administration of Customs (GAC)**. The GAC is responsible for enforcing IPR at the border and the enforcement procedure may be launched only if the IPR in question is recorded at Customs through a central filing system. The GAC has the authority to seize IP-infringing goods, and to investigate and deal with alleged infringing goods. Note that although the TRIPS Agreement does not oblige its members to apply border measures in case of export of IPR-infringing goods, China deals with both import and export of IPR-infringing goods. Clothing, handbags, watches, cosmetics, pharmaceutical products, food, electronics and home appliances destined for Africa, the US, Europe, Hong Kong and Southeast Asia are the focus of regular inspections.

2. *Procedures*

The administrative enforcement procedure has the advantage of being less formal and relatively simple, although certain rules must still be followed. For example, for patent infringement cases, the Measures for the Executive Enforcement of Patents[11] sets down detailed administrative enforcement rules in relation to requirements, procedures and remedies, which supplement the Patent Law and the Implementing Rules of the Patent Law.

Reflecting on the latest amendment on patent rights enforcement, the following is observed with regard to the administrative enforcement procedure.

A patent holder or any interested third party may submit a complaint to the patent administration department in a patent infringement dispute. If the dispute is already undergoing the judicial enforcement procedure, then the patent administration department will not accept the complaint. When all submission requirements are met, the patent administration department will register the complaint within five working days and appoint three officers or more, always an odd number, in order to proceed with the complaint.[12] A dispute may be settled by mediation should the disputing parties elect to do so.

Within five days,[13] which is two days less than what was prescribed by the previous version of the Measures, the patent administration department will inform the complainant if it will proceed to deal with the complaint. Subsequently, depending on the complaint in question, the patent administration department may start the investigation by conducting an oral hearing, in which case the hearing notice would be delivered to the disputing parties at least three days in advance.[14] In case the disputing parties opt not to settle the case by mediation, and if the complainant decides not to withdraw the infringement complaint, the patent administration department will issue a resolution after an investigation based on the relevant provisions contained in the Patent Law. Note that the respective scope for protection for invention and utility model patents is clarified by Art.18 of the Measures for the Executive Enforcement of Patent 2015. Article18 specifies that a scope for protection is not only confined to what is claimed – by virtue of Art.59 of the Patent Law 2008 – but also includes 'similar technological characteristics to what is claimed'. In this regard, 'similar

11 The Measures for the Executive Enforcement of Patents was first enacted in December 2001. The latest amendment was announced on 29 May 2015.

12 Arts.10–14, Measures for the Executive Enforcement of Patent, 2015.

13 Art.13, Measures for the Executive Enforcement of Patent, 2015.

14 Art.16, Measures for the Executive Enforcement of Patent, 2015.

technological characteristics' refer to using similar means in order to perform similar functions and that are able to achieve a similar effect while an ordinary technician from the same professional domain may envisage such characteristics without spending innovative labour. The patent administration department will issue a resolution in order to inform the parties of the avenues for administrative appeal as well as the time-limit if parties are not satisfied with the decision.[15]

As far as the procedure against repeated infringement is concerned, Art.20 of the Measures for the Executive Enforcement of Patent 2015 specifies that if a respondent commits again the same infringement act concerning the same patent, the patent administration department may, upon the request of the patent holder or of any interested party, order the infringing act to be ceased with immediate effect. Note that Art.60 of the Draft Patent Law 2015 provides the patent administration department with the power to deal with wilful acts of patent infringement suspected of disrupting the market order such as group infringement and repeated infringement. If such infringement is established, the patent administration department may order the infringer to cease the infringement act immediately, confiscate the infringing products and the parts, tools, modules and equipment that are particularly used for manufacturing the infringing products or carrying out the infringement method. When the illegal gains exceed 50,000 RMB (6,850 EUR), a fine of one to five times the illegal gains may be imposed. If there are no illegal gains or the illegal gains do not exceed 50,000 RMB (6,850 EUR), a fine not more than 250,000 RMB (34,235 EUR) may be imposed.

A patent infringement dispute submitted for administrative enforcement must be concluded within three months. The deadline may be extended for one more month if the dispute is very complicated and an approval is obtained beforehand.[16] Dispute cases concerning patent passing off should be concluded within one month, excluding the days spent on communication and hearing, while a maximum extension of 15 days may be granted.[17] This being the case, administrative enforcement is indeed a very swift process.

Investigation and collection of evidence are under the jurisdiction of the patent administration department at the locality where the infringing act took place[18] and should be conducted by following the relevant provisions prescribed by the Patent Law.

After a patent infringement act is established, the patent administration department must inform the infringer about the facts, the reasons and the decision for sanction, as well as the infringer's rights, before a decision is issued. In case the amount of administrative fine is large, and once the decision is communicated, the infringer is entitled to apply for a hearing in order to institute an appeal and to present counter-arguments.[19] If a dispute involves complicated facts, or when heavy punishment measures are likely to be laid down, a meeting must be convened among the administrative department heads in order to discuss the matter before a decision may be finalised and handed down.[20]

Article 44 of the Measures for the Executive Enforcement of Patent 2015 states that after a decision against an infringement act is laid down, and if the infringer does not stop

15 Art.19, Measures for the Executive Enforcement of Patent, 2015.
16 Art.21, Measures for the Executive Enforcement of Patent, 2015.
17 Art.36, Measures for the Executive Enforcement of Patent 2015.
18 Art.29, Measures for the Executive Enforcement of Patent 2015.
19 Art.33, Measures for the Executive Enforcement of Patent 2015.
20 Art.34, Measures for the Executive Enforcement of Patent 2015.

the infringement act nor appeals against the decision, the patent administration department may apply at people's court for compulsory enforcement. In a case where the infringer appeals the decision laid down by the patent administration department, the decision will be nonetheless executed and must not be suspended during the court proceedings.[21]

Under the Measures for the Executive Enforcement of Patent, patent infringement is defined as those acts of manufacturing patent-infringing products, exploiting a process patent, selling or promising to sell and import patent-infringing products or products obtained directly by exploiting a process patent. If infringement acts are established, the patent administration department has the power to order the patent infringer to immediately cease the infringing acts and to destroy the equipment used for infringement or for exploiting the process patent. Destruction may be ordered if the infringing products are difficult to keep.[22] Patent counterfeiting refers to acts of: falsifying patent marking on a product or on its packaging; continuing to use a patent marking that is no longer valid or has already expired; marking another's patent number on a product or on its packaging without permission; misrepresentation; falsifying a patent certificate and documents or application documents. Once a counterfeiting act is established, the patent administration department may order the patent counterfeiting party to cease the sale and the distribution and to stop the counterfeiting act with immediate effect; remove the counterfeiting markings; destroy the counterfeiting products or packaging and the relevant materials, such as product manuals; and eliminate ill effect.[23]

It is observed that two additional infringement acts are included in the patent enforcement measures amended in 2015, which are: displaying infringing/counterfeiting exhibits at exposition and committing infringement/counterfeiting acts on an e-commerce platform. For the former, if facts are established by virtue of Arts.43.6 and 45.6 of the Measures for the Executive Enforcement of Patent 2015, the patent administration department may order the exhibitor to withdraw the infringement/counterfeiting exhibits, to destroy and seal off related promotional materials, and to replace or conceal related exposition panels. As to patent infringement and counterfeit that takes place on an e-commerce platform, Arts.43.7 and 45.7 of the Measures stipulate that, once a decision is issued by the patent administration department, the e-commerce platform provider must be notified by the decision and should remove the relevant web-page content as well as the web link related to the products that are obtained by infringing a patent or a patented process, or by counterfeiting.

3. *Remedies*

After acts of patent infringement or counterfeiting are established, the patent administration department should publish its decision for punishment within 20 days.[24] Illicit gains resulting from patent counterfeit will be confiscated and may be determined by the sales price of the counterfeiting products multiplied by the quantity of the products sold. In the

21 Art.44, Measures for the Executive Enforcement of Patent, 2015.

22 Art.43.1–5, Measures for the Executive Enforcement of Patent, 2015.

23 Art.45.1–5, Measures for the Executive Enforcement of Patent, 2015.

24 Art.46, Measures for the Executive Enforcement of Patent 2015.

event that there is a contract which is concluded for patent passing off, the fees collected subsequently shall be calculated as the illicit gains.[25]

Finally, if refusing or obstructing the patent administration department to discharge its duty, a penalty may be imposed according to the Rules by the Social Security Authority on Penalty for the Purpose of Administration of Social Security, and criminal liability may be imposed depending on the circumstances.[26]

II) Judicial enforcement: courts and judges, procedures and remedies

The Chinese courts operate with the principle of 'justice and efficiency'. Enhancing the courts' adjudication capacity has been a priority for the judiciary ever since it was reinstated in the wake of the Cultural Revolution. Because nowadays more and more competent judges are ready to adjudicate, the Chinese legislature is able to promote judicial enforcement as an effective parallel means for enforcement alongside administrative enforcement, and the courts have been able to accept an increasing number of IPR infringement cases in recent years.[27] As a result, for example, while in the past only the intermediate people's courts in the capitals of the provinces, autonomous regions and municipalities and those specially designated by the SPC had jurisdiction over patent infringement cases, today more intermediate people's courts are competent to adjudicate patent disputes. In 2014, the number of Chinese courts eligible for IP adjudication reached 87. In the same year, three IP-specialised courts were also established, as was mentioned previously.

1. Courts and judges

Based on the Constitution and the Law on the Organisation of People's Courts, China's court system consists of local courts, special courts and the SPC which undertakes a supervisory function over other courts and is responsible for unifying trial procedures in order to ensure judicial predictability.

In China, local courts are established by the government body in a different administrative hierarchy, and they are accountable to the government which established them.[28]

25 Art.47, Measures for the Executive Enforcement of Patent 2015.

26 Art.50, Measures for the Executive Enforcement of Patent 2015.

27 In 2014, local people's courts nationwide accepted 95,522 new IPR civil cases of the first instance and concluded 94,501 cases, seeing a year-on-year increase of 7.83 per cent and 7.04 per cent respectively. Among them, there were 9,648 patent cases, up by 4.93 per cent compared with 2013. For civil cases of the second instance, in 2014 there were 13,760 new cases and 13,708 of them were concluded, seeing a year-on-year increase of 15.08 per cent and 18.65 respectively. In addition, the SPC accepted 336 IPR civil cases and concluded all of them (in addition to three cases that were brought over from previous years). See: State Intellectual Property Office of the People's Republic of China (SIPO), *Intellectual Property Rights Protection in China*. (SIPO, 2014), p. 11.

28 Art.128, Constitution of the People's Republic of China. Moreover, Art.104 of the Constitution stipulates that the work of people's courts is scrutinised by the standing committee of a local people's congress at and above the county level. Also, among other functions, Art.67 of the Constitution stipulates that the standing committee of the NPC has the authority to appoint and remove vice-presidents and judges of the SPC, members of its judicial committee and the president of the military court at the suggestion of the president of the SPC.

The courts are under the supervision of the corresponding people's congress and its standing committee at the national, provincial, municipal or local levels.[29]

Local courts are divided into three levels: the basic, the intermediate as well as the higher people's courts.

The basic people's courts[30] deal with criminal, civil and administrative cases of the first hearing, except otherwise provided by law. To facilitate the administration of justice, the basic people's courts may set up tribunals, which shall have the competence to, for example, hear general civil misdemeanours, publicise laws and regulations, and handle petitions. Intellectual property cases may be heard by the basic people's courts as far as copyright and trademark disputes are concerned, but not patent dispute cases.

The intermediate people's courts[31] deal with cases of the first instance. According to the Law on Civil Procedures, civil cases heard by the intermediate people's courts are major foreign-related cases and cases that are instructed to be heard by the SPC. Additionally, according to the Law on Administrative Procedures, the intermediate people's courts are authorised to hear cases regarding verification of patent rights and other IPR matters involving foreigners, though nowadays trademark and copyright infringement cases involving foreign elements may also be heard by the basic people's courts. Only the intermediate people's courts in the capital of the provinces, autonomous regions and municipalities directly under the central government and those specially designated by the SPC have the jurisdiction over patent infringement cases. However, for trademark and copyright cases, judicial actions may be brought to any intermediate people's court if the case concerned involves territorial jurisdiction.

Among other judicial competences, the higher people's courts[32] hear IPR disputes of the second instance, supervise trials conducted by the lower courts and approve their decisions, as long as enforcement of a foreign arbitration award is not involved.[33]

The SPC[34] is the highest judicial organ in China and is accountable to the NPC and its Standing Committee. Presided over by one president and a number of vice presidents, chief justices and justices[35], the SPC supervises trials conducted by the lower courts and the special courts, and may act *ex officio* and delegate itself to hear a particular case.[36] The Law

29 Art.16, Organic Law of the People's Courts of the People's Republic of China.

30 The basic people's courts are established in counties/autonomous counties, cities without administrative districts or administrative districts of cities.

31 The intermediate people's courts are set up in prefectures, cities directly under the authority of provinces, which are autonomous regions and the four municipalities directly under the central government, namely: Beijing, Shanghai, Tianjing and Chongqing, and the districts in the four municipalities.

32 The higher people's courts are set up in provinces, including autonomous regions and municipalities directly under the central government.

33 Decisions concerning such awards require no approval. In case of doubt, the final decision must be delivered by the SPC. See: The Notice Concerning the Handling of Foreign and Foreign-Related Arbitration, issued on 28 August 1995 by the SPC.

34 The SPC consists of a judicial committee, which is China's highest judicial organisation, the No.1 and No.2 Criminal Tribunal, the Civil Tribunal, the Economic Tribunal, the Administrative Tribunal, the Complaint and Appeal Tribunal and the Communication and Transportation Tribunal.

35 The president of the SPC is elected by the NPC and remains in office for no more than two successive terms with each term lasting for five years. The deputy presidents of the SPC, members of the judicial committee, presiding judges of affiliated courts and their deputies, and judicial officers are appointed and recalled by the Standing Committee of the NPC.

36 By virtue of Art.21 of the Civil Procedure Code, the SPC shall act as the court of the first instance over the following civil cases: (1) cases that have major impact on the whole country; and (2) cases that the SPC deems it should try.

on Administrative Procedure equally provides the SPC with the jurisdiction of the first-hearing over administrative cases of a material and complicated nature. Additionally, the SPC has the judicial power to interpret laws and writs, and issue implementing rules, clarifications, notices, opinions or circulars, which are sources of law in China and enforceable nationwide.

The SPC is instrumental in strengthening IPR enforcement in China and one of its major contributions in this regard is to facilitate case transfer from the administrative to the judicial enforcement track as has been highlighted previously.

In China, the rules of selecting and appointing judges are governed by the Judge's Act, which came into force on 28 February 1995. There are 12 grades[37] of judges, including president, vice president, judicial committee member, chief judge and associate chief judge of divisions, as well as judge and assistant judge at the SPC, the local people's courts and the special people's courts, such as the military court.[38] Except for assistant judges at people's courts, all appointments of judges and their dismissals are determined by the standing committees of the NPC at the different administrative levels.[39]

2. *Procedures*

By virtue of Art.7 of the Chinese Organic Law of the People's Courts, all cases tried at people's courts shall be heard in public, except for those cases that involve state secrets, individual privacy and minors.

Procedures of judicial enforcement concerning, for example, preparation, pre-trial hearing, court hearing and evidence examination are provided by the Civil Procedure Law and the subsequent judicial interpretations issued by the SPC.[40] The latest interpretation, Interpretation of the Supreme People's Court Concerning the Application of the Civil Procedure Law, which came into force in February 2015, provides the guidelines on, and has updated, jurisdiction, third party participation,[41] the timeframe for adducing evidence and the withdrawal of a lawsuit, and enforcement, etc. It is worth noting that, with regard to adducing evidence, Art.166 of the Interpretation provides that electronic data[42] will be admissible from now on as evidence in civil cases.

37 Art.16, Judge's Law.

38 Art.2, Judge's Law.

39 Assistant judges of a people's court may be appointed and removed by the president of the court where they work. See: Art.11, Judge's Law.

40 In February 2015 the latest Interpretation of the Supreme People's Court Concerning the Application of the Civil Procedure Law came into force. The latest Interpretation consists of 552 articles, which is the most lengthy judicial interpretation containing the largest number of articles in the history of China's judicial interpretations. Two previous interpretations were issued by the SPC in 1992 (Opinion of the Supreme People's Court on Several Issues Concerning the Application of the Civil Procedure Law) and in 2002 (Several Provisions of the Supreme People's Court on Evidence in Civil Procedures) respectively.

41 From now on, a third party who does not participate in the first instance trial has the right to apply to participate in the second instance proceedings. See: Art. 81, Interpretation of the Supreme People's Court Concerning the Application of the Civil Procedure Law 2010.

42 Based on the said article, emails, electronic data exchange, online chat records, blogs, microblogs, short messages on phones, electronic signatures or domain names that are formed or stored in electronic media are within the remit of electronic data. Likewise, audio-visual data stored in electronic media may be subject to electronic data requirements and become admissible evidence in civil cases.

In accordance with Art.8 of the Several Provisions of the Supreme People's Court on Issues Relating to Application of Law to Adjudication of Cases of Patent Disputes, when instituting a lawsuit against a utility patent infringement, the plaintiff must provide a search report issued by the patent administration department. Additionally, when an infringement case involves a utility model or a design patent, the defendant must file a request to invalidate the plaintiff's patent grant when defence is being conducted. Article 10 of the same Provisions further stipulates that, in case the invalidation application is submitted after the time-limit expires, the people's court will not suspend the proceedings unless it is found necessary upon due consideration.

As far as utility model and design patents are concerned, a request for suspending the judicial proceedings may be granted if the application is submitted within the prescribed time-limit. However, suspension will not be granted if: 1) no technical documentation is found in the search report provided by the plaintiff that leads to the loss of novelty or inventiveness; 2) the defendant's evidence is sufficient to prove that the technology used has been known to the public; 3) the evidence that the defendant furnished for invalidation is ostensibly insufficient; or 4) other circumstances that justify a non-suspension.[43] Additionally, when a design or a utility model patent is upheld by the Patent Re-examination Board upon re-examination, a people's court may not suspend the judicial proceedings.[44] In a case where a court suspends the judicial proceedings upon application, the court may simultaneously issue a provisional injunction to order the defendant to desist from the infringing act.[45]

Article 64 of the Civil Procedure Law prescribes that parties must bear their own burden of proof in order to substantiate their claim or to rebut the claim of the opposite party. However, people's courts may collect evidence on behalf of the plaintiff when evidence is preserved by a state authority which may not be accessible without a court's intervention, or when state secrets, trade secrets or private information are involved, or if the plaintiff is unable to obtain proof because of objective reasons. In a case where it is impossible to decide which party should bear the burden of proof, the court shall exercise its discretion to decide this, based on fairness, honesty and good faith.

If ever an infringement dispute concerns an invention patent for the method of manufacturing a new product, the unit or the individual manufacturing the same product shall prove that the manufacturing method of their own product is different from the patented method. If a dispute concerns a utility model or a design patent, the court or the patent administration department may request the patent holder or the interested party to present a patent rights assessment report as evidence.[46] An expert's evaluation may also be admitted as evidence.[47]

The time limit for adducing evidence must not be less than 15 days for cases of the first instance, and the precise term will be determined by the court during the pre-trial preparatory stage, which counts from the expiration of the answering period (within 15 days upon

43 Art.9, Amendments to the Several Provisions of the Supreme People's Court on Issues in Relation to Application of Law to Adjudication of Cases of Patent Disputes 2015.

44 Art.11, Amendments to the Several Provisions of the Supreme People's Court on Issues in Relation to Application of Law to Adjudication of Cases of Patent Disputes 2015.

45 Art.12, Amendments to the Several Provisions of the Supreme People's Court on Issues in Relation to Application of Law to Adjudication of Cases of Patent Disputes 2015.

46 Art.61, Patent Law 2008. The same requirement is maintained by the Draft Patent Law 2015.

47 Art.79, Civil Procedure Law 2012.

receipt of a copy of the complaint) to the commencement of the hearing.[48] Evidence must be obtained by legal means, of course. Evidence obtained unlawfully or by prejudicing the legitimate rights and interests of others may not be admitted in court. Evidence originating from abroad must be notarised and legalised by the Chinese embassy in the locality concerned before becoming admissible as evidence. All documents in a foreign language must be translated into Chinese.

Parties in proceedings may apply for evidence preservation if such evidence may soon cease to exist, or become lost or difficult to obtain later on.[49] This being the case, and before the litigation starts, a bond must be placed when submitting an application for assets or property preservation. The amount of the bond must be equivalent to the assets under preservation; otherwise, the court shall decide on the amount in a case where the preserved evidence is property. When evidence preservation takes place amidst litigation, the court shall decide if a bond is required from either party, as well as the amount of the bond, depending on the circumstances.[50] In a case where the court wishes to institute the preservation of a property derived from a patent, it may send the patent administration department a request for assistance. A further notice may be dispatched if ever an extension for property preservation is required. Usually, property preservation should not last for more than six months and it's not possible to re-preserve what is already preserved.[51]

Withdrawing a lawsuit during the trial of the first instance, the second instance and retrial is possible if an application is submitted. But, if a withdrawal application is submitted after cross-examination takes place, the defendant's consent must be obtained before the application may be granted.[52] During a retrial, in order for a withdrawal application to be granted, the plaintiff must also obtain the consent of the other parties involved.[53] Once a withdrawal takes effect, the complaint will be seen as if it were never submitted. During a trial of the second instance or a retrial, a complaint that was withdrawn during the trial of the first instance must not be filed again for a second time.

Courts must now ascertain the information concerning the identity and the property of the parties who are subject to enforcement, while organisations and individuals who control the relevant information are obliged to follow the instructions imposed by the enforcement facilitation notice. In general, the period for property seizure is extended under the Interpretation 2015. Compared with the previous measures, the maximum seizure period is extended from six months to one year in case of a bank deposit, from one year to two years for personal property, and from two years to three years for immovable property. The period for the continued seizure must be kept the same as that of the first seizure.[54]

48 Art.99, Interpretation of the Supreme People's Court Concerning the Application of the Civil Procedure Law 2015.

49 Art.81, Civil Procedure Law 2012.

50 Art.152, Interpretation of the Supreme People's Court Concerning the Application of the Civil Procedure Law 2015.

51 Art.13, Several Provisions of the Supreme People's Court on Issues in Relation to Application of Law to Adjudication of Cases of Patent Disputes 2015.

52 Art.238, Interpretation of the Supreme People's Court Concerning the Application of the Civil Procedure Law 2015.

53 Art.410, Interpretation of the Supreme People's Court Concerning the Application of the Civil Procedure Law 2015.

54 Arts.485, 487, Interpretation of the Supreme People's Court Concerning the Application of the Civil Procedure Law 2015.

The court proceedings will last approximately six months in total for a trial of the first instance[55] and three months for the second instance,[56] if no foreign elements are involved.[57] In comparison, judicial proceedings require twice the time as that required by the administrative proceedings as far as patent enforcement is concerned, which partly contributes to the popularity of administrative enforcement in China.

Chinese courts adopt a collegial system in the administration of justice. Cases of the first instance are tried by a panel of three to seven judges.[58] Appeals and contested cases will be decided by a collegial panel of three to five judges.[59]

Decisions of IP litigation will first be deliberated by a collegial panel of three to five judges, with one serving as a chief judge who is responsible for reporting on the case closure and for completing a judgment. It usually takes one to two months for a judgment to be delivered, and it may require up to three months if a case is of a complicated nature. Once a judgment is served, either party may appeal the judgment to the next higher court for IP matters or to the Higher People's Court.

Judgments of the first instance delivered by a local people's court may be appealed at the court at the next higher level by a party to the case or by the people's procuratorate. Judgments of the second instance announced by the intermediate courts, the higher courts or by the SPC, as well as judgments decided by the SPC of the first instance, are final.[60] If the SPC finds some definite errors in a judgment of the last instance, or if a court at a higher level finds such errors in a judgment delivered by a lower court, the SPC shall have the authority to review the case itself or to direct a lower court to conduct a retrial.[61]

3. *Remedies*

The right for remedies as far as IPR infringement is concerned is provided by Art.118 of the General Principles of the Civil Law. Article 118 stipulates that if the right to authorship (copyrights), patent and the exclusive use of trademarks are infringed by such means as plagiarism, alteration or imitation, the right holder is entitled to demand the infringement act to be stopped, the ill effects to be eliminated and the damages to be compensated for. By virtue of Art.134 of the same law, the main remedies afforded by civil litigation are, among others, cessation of infringements, removal of obstacles, elimination of dangers, return of property, restoration of original condition, repair, reworking or replacement, compensation for loss, payment for damages for breach of contract, elimination of ill effects and rehabilitation of reputation, and extension of apology.

In addition to the General Principles of the Civil Law, China's Tort Law provides compensation as a remedy for serious mental distress if liability to IPR infringement is established with regard to copyright, patent right, exclusive right to use a trademark and

55 By virtue of Art.135 of the Civil Procedure Law, if an extension is necessary for special circumstances, a further extension of six months may be granted, subject to the approval of the president of the said court. Any further extension must be reported to the people's court at a higher level for approval.

56 Art.159, Civil Procedure Law. Any further extension due to special circumstances shall be subject to the approval of the president of the said court.

57 Art.250, Civil Procedure Law.

58 Simple civil cases, petty criminal cases and cases otherwise provided for by the law may be tried by a single judge.

59 Art.9, Organic Law of the People's Courts of the People's Republic of China.

60 Art.11, Organic Law of the People's Courts of the People's Republic of China.

61 Art.13, Organic Law of the People's Courts of the People's Republic of China.

right to discovery.[62] The Tort Law addresses contributory infringement[63] and consequential liabilities too, which complement the enforcement measures provided by the IP laws and the relevant implementing regulations. Before the Tort Law was adopted, contributory IPR infringement was seen as civil rights violation, while the sources of jurisprudence were only found in a few judicial interpretations issued by the SPC.[64]

It is for the first time that the Tort Law acknowledges the right for compensation as an individual right, as far as serious mental distress is concerned, which is an additional right for compensation on top of the right for compensation for material loss.[65] In the past, the right for compensation due to moral damage was a concurrent right while remedies were provided only by the civil law principles; IP laws did not provide any remedies in this respect.[66]

Additionally, the Tort Law provides remedies for IPR infringement committed via the internet by a network user or a service provider.[67]

4. *Executing a judgement*

Article 224 of the Civil Procedure Law states that judgments and arbitral decisions laid down under both civil law and criminal law concerning property must be enforced by the court of the first instance or by a court at the same level as the court of the first instance in

62 Art.2, Tort Law.

63 By virtue of Art.9 of the Tort Law, a person who abets or assists another person in committing a tort shall be jointly and severally liable with the tortfeasor.

64 For example, the Implementing Regulations of the Trademark Law of the People's Republic of China (2002) provides a non-exhaustive list of contributory infringement of trademark rights that, by virtue of Para 2, Art.50 'the act of intentionally facilitating any other person's acts of infringing upon the exclusive right to use a registered trademark, such as storage, transportation, postage, and concealing, is recognized as an infringing act upon the exclusive registered trademark right'.
Also, the Opinions on Patent Infringement Issues issued by the Beijing Higher People's Court in 2001 offers a few references in order to determine contributory infringement of patent rights applicable at trials in a local court. The Interpretation of the Supreme People's Court on Issues Relating to Application of Law in the Trial of Copyright Disputes over Computer Networks (2000, 2003, 2006) and the Regulations on the Protection of the Right to Network Dissemination of Information (2006) set down the rules concerning contributory infringement acts committed on internet copyright infringement.

65 Art.22 of the Tort Law provides that if serious mental distress results from an act of tort, compensation may be awarded.

66 For example, the Interpretation of the Supreme People's Court on Issues Regarding the Determination of Compensation Liability for Moral Damages in Civil Torts (2001) provided guidelines to determine liability for tort for moral damage under general civil right. In the Reply of Supreme People's Court on Copyright Infringement Dispute between *WU Guanzhong* v. *Shanghai Duoyunxuan Art House and Hong Kong Yongcheng Auction Company Ltd.*, the SPC stated that 'the range and the amount of compensation shall be determined based on the plaintiff's total loss, including both material loss and spiritual sufferings, and overall circumstances of the case'. Also, under Art.21 of the Guiding Opinions on Damages Determination for Compensation Liabilities Relating to the Copyright Infringement (Beijing Higher People's Court, 2005), when serious copyright infringement took place, compensation for moral damage may be awarded concurrently if compensation in other forms were not sufficient to recover the moral injuries suffered by the copyright holder in the case.
However, decisions in the above cases may only serve as reference since in China case decision is not a source of law. As a result, courts remain cautious when awarding compensation for moral damage. Before the Tort Law came into force in July 2010, *Zhuang Yu* v. *Guo Jingming* was the only copyright infringement case where the plaintiff successfully claimed compensation for moral damage for copyright plagiarism, and the defendant and his publisher were ordered to pay damages to the plaintiff of 200,000 RMB (26,958 EUR) for economic loss and 10,000 RMB (1,348 EUR) for moral damage.

67 Art.36, Tort Law.

which location the property subject to enforcement is situated.[68] The people's procuratorate shall exercise its role of supervision during the course of enforcement.[69]

Disputing parties, or any interested party, may oppose in writing in order to lodge an appeal at the enforcing court if an enforcing act is seen as unlawful. The court must subsequently conduct an investigation, and then either rectify or uphold the enforcement decision. If still unsatisfied with the decision, the parties concerned may apply at a higher court for reconsideration.[70]

An enforcement order must be executed within six months. Otherwise, the applicant for enforcement may apply for execution at a higher court.[71]

5. *Preservation and injunction*

In the course of civil litigation, disputing or interested parties may apply for property preservation and injunction at a people's court. Since 2000, in the light of the Civil Procedure Law, IP laws explicitly afford IPR holders a course of action when, if action is not taken, potential irreparable damages would become immediate.

In case the behaviour of a disputing party becomes destructive to enforcement or poses a threat to the opposite party, in accordance with Art.100 of the Civil Procedure Law 2012, the people's court may order a property preservation should the party concerned make such a request or upon the court's own initiative. In both cases, a bond is prerequisite. An order for property preservation may be issued within 48 hours, with immediate effect.[72] Though an order for property preservation may be subject to reconsideration, once the execution begins no suspension may be envisaged.[73]

In accordance with the Civil Procedure Law, IP laws provide the same course of action regarding property preservation in order to provide better protection to IPR holders and to mitigate their potential loss. For example, for patent infringement cases, after the second patent law amendment came into force in 2000, it has become possible for patent holders or any interested party to rely on the Patent Law to seek property preservation.[74] Article 50 of the Copyright Law (2010) and Art.66 of the Trademark Law (2013) provide the same recourse.

In the course of property preservation, upon the request of a disputing party, a people's court may also decide to impose an order of injunction before legal proceedings are ever instituted, by virtue of Art.107 of the Civil Procedure Law.[75] Under these circumstances, although a bond is equally a prerequisite, if the applicant loses the lawsuit, the person

68 Enforcing civil law judgments involving foreign elements within the territory of China is governed by Part Four of the Civil Procedure Law. Article 265 of the same law states that when contractual or disputes of other kinds occur, and if one disputing party has no domicile within the territory in China, parties may elect the court of the location in which there are connections with the dispute as the court of jurisdiction.

69 Art.235, Civil Procedure Law 2012.

70 Art.225, Civil Procedure Law 2012.

71 Art.226, Civil Procedure Law 2012.

72 Art.100, Civil Procedure Law 2012.

73 Art.108, Civil Procedure Law 2012.

74 In 2001 the SPC also issued an interpretation to clarify the question of bond and property preservation. See: Arts.6 and 16, Several Provisions of the Supreme People's Court for the Application of Law to Pre-trial Cessation of Infringement of Patent Right.

75 The prerequisites for applying an injunction order are: a definite relationship of rights and obligations between the parties; serious impairement of life and business affecting the applicant if a preliminary execution is denied; capability of fulfillment by the party against whom the application is made, etc. See Art.107, Civil Procedure Law 2012.

against whom the application is applied shall be entitled for compensation for any loss of property incurred as a result of the injunction order.[76]

In 2001 the SPC issued the Several Provisions of the Supreme People's Court for the Application of Law to Pre-trial Cessation of Infringement of Patent Right in order to clarify the procedures of injunction application as far as patent infringement cases are concerned. In addition to the mandatory administrative requirements[77] that are also applicable to other litigation cases, an injunction application concerning a patent infringement case must be submitted together with the documents that prove the authenticity and the validity of the patent in question, including a valid patent certificate, claim, description, receipts of payment for the annual patent fee and a search report issued by the SIPO if a utility model patent is involved.[78] The interested parties may submit a relevant patent licensing contract and the proof that the contract is already submitted to the SIPO.[79] Additionally, while applying for an injunction order, the applicant must submit evidence to prove that the party against whom the application is filed is committing or will commit an act to infringe the applicant's patent rights. As a result, the alleged infringing product, the technical features of the patented technology and the comparison between the two must also be submitted as evidence.[80]

In the context of injunction order application, and in accordance with Art.107 of the Civil Procedure Law, the above-mentioned Provisions issued by the SPC stipulate the means by which the amount of the bond must be calculated.[81] Also, in the course of executing an injunction order, a people's court may request an additional bond and if this request is not satisfied in due time the interim injunction order may be dissolved.[82]

An injunction order may be appealed, unless the order is already under execution under the proceedings of reconsideration.[83] Additionally, when an applicant institutes legal

76 Art.107, Civil Procedure Law 2012.

77 For example, when applying an injunction order in patent infringement cases, an application must be submitted in writing and must indicate the interested parties and the basic information regarding the claims and the extent of, and the reasons for, the application. Reasons for the application must include the specific statement that irremediable damages will incur, and the legitimate rights and the interests of the applicant will suffer, if the infringing act is not promptly stopped. See Art.3, Several Provisions of the Supreme People's Court for the Application of Law to Pre-trial Cessation of Infringement of Patent Right 2001.

78 Art.4(1), Several Provisions of the Supreme People's Court for the Application of Law to Pre-trial Cessation of Infringement of Patent Right 2001.

79 Art.4(2), Several Provisions of the Supreme People's Court for the Application of Law to Pre-trial Cessation of Infringement of Patent Right 2001.

80 Art.4(3), Several Provisions of the Supreme People's Court for the Application of Law to Pre-trial Cessation of Infringement of Patent Right 2001.

81 The amount of a bond must be determined by a people's court, taking into account the sales of the product, the reasonable costs of storage and stock-keeping, the loss that may be caused by stopping the relevant act of the party against whom the application is filed and other reasonable costs, such as the wages or salaries and any other factor involved. See Art.6, Several Provisions of the Supreme People's Court for the Application of Law to Pre-trial Cessation of Infringement of Patent Right 2001.

82 Art.7, Several Provisions of the Supreme People's Court for the Application of Law to Pre-trial Cessation of Infringement of Patent Right 2001.

83 Art.10, Several Provisions of the Supreme People's Court for the Application of Law to Pre-trial Cessation of Infringement of Patent Right 2001. On the other hand, an application for reconsideration must be examined based upon the facts, i.e., whether: 1) the alleged infringing act does constitute a patent infringement act; 2) failing to adopt any interim injunction measures would cause irremediable damage to the rights and interests of the applicant; 3) the contents of the information is related to the applicant's provisions of the bond; and finally 4) failing to adopt the interim injunction measures would impair the public interest, etc. See Art.11, Several Provisions of the Supreme People's Court for the Application of Law to Pre-trial Cessation of Infringement of Patent Right 2001.

proceedings against a patent infringement and simultaneously applies an injunction order, the court may first decide on the injunction request in order to prevent the tactics of delaying proceedings.[84]

Once an injunction order is issued by a court, the applicant must commence the legal proceedings within 15 days, failing which the injunction order may be recalled.[85] An injunction order remains effective in principle until the entry into force of the court's final decision. The court may also set a specific timeframe during which period the injunction measures may be applied according to the circumstances of the case. Nonetheless, even after the timeframe expires, the court may still order to reinstate the injunction measures on the request of an interested party.[86]

III) Criminal law enforcement: actors, principles and punishment

By virtue of Chapter III Section 7 of the Criminal Law 1997, criminal prosecution may be pursued, against an individual or an entity, for IPR infringement cases if 'a crime is constituted'.[87] The threshold test for a criminal act is set down by Arts.69–72 of the Provisions (II) of the Supreme People's Procuratorate as well as by the Ministry of Public Security on the Standards for Filing Criminal Cases under the Jurisdiction of the Public Security Organs for Investigation and Prosecution (May 2010). In accordance with Art.72 of the said Provisions, for patent infringement cases criminal liability may be pursued if: 1) the illegal turnover exceeds 200,000 RMB (27,187 EUR) or the illegal gain is more than 100,000 RMB (13,592 EUR); 2) the direct monetary loss caused to a patent holder exceeds 500,000 RMB (67,958 EUR); 3) counterfeiting more than two patents while the illegal turnover exceeds 100,000 RMB (13,592 EUR) or the illegal gain is more than 50,000 RMB (6,796 EUR).

Note that in 2007, when China was brought to the WTO Dispute Settlement Body for the case China – Measures affecting the Protection and Enforcement of Intellectual Property Rights (DS362), the allegedly high numerical criminal thresholds with regard to copyright and trademark infringement, which, as the US claimed, to some extent appeared to protect infringers from being prosecuted under China's IPR criminal enforcement system, was one of the disputes between the US and China. In the end, though China's criminal thresholds were not endorsed, the panel avoided ruling on the issue but concluded that the factual evidence presented by the US was inadequate to establish the case. Note that, on the other hand, Art.61 of the TRIPS Agreement does not require members to criminalise all copyright and trademark infringement.[88]

The IPR administrative enforcement authorities and the Public Security Bureau (PSB), which is responsible for conducting criminal investigation, are IPR criminal enforcement bodies. Criminal investigation may be launched in two instances, either when a petition is

84 Art.17, Several Provisions of the Supreme People's Court for the Application of Law to Pre-trial Cessation of Infringement of Patent Right 2001.

85 Art.12, Several Provisions of the Supreme People's Court for the Application of Law to Pre-trial Cessation of Infringement of Patent Right 2001.

86 Art.14, Several Provisions of the Supreme People's Court for the Application of Law to Pre-trial Cessation of Infringement of Patent Right 2001.

87 For example, Art.63 of the Patent Law 2008 and Art.60 of the Draft Patent Law 2015 provide that criminal liability may be pursued if patent infringement takes place.

88 Available at: www.wto.org/english/tratop_e/dispu_e/cases_e/1pagesum_e/ds362sum_e.pdf (last accessed 18 September 2015).

filed directly at the PSB by an IPR holder or when a case is transferred to the PSB by an IPR administrative enforcement authority. Petty criminal cases concerning IPR infringement may be heard directly by a people's court of the first instance. Cases that are likely to 'gravely endanger public order and national interests' will be dealt with through the procuratoral system for criminal investigation.[89] Articles 213–220 of the Criminal Law 2011 detail criminal punishment against IPR infringement.

1. Basic principles of prosecution

Under the Criminal Procedure Law, though public and private prosecutions are both viable, the latter may be instituted for minor criminal cases only.[90] If public prosecution is the case,[91] then the SPP is responsible for examining and for deciding on the case[92] and the PSB is responsible for investigation, detention, execution of arrests and preliminary inquiry.[93] On the other hand, by virtue of Art.170(3) of the Criminal Procedure Law 2012, an individual may apply for private prosecution when it can be proven that the defendant should be investigated for criminal liability because the infringing act violated the party's personal or property rights. This being the case, the PSB or the SPP will not investigate criminal liability of the accused.[94]

In general, before instituting a criminal enforcement action against IPR infringement, certain circumstances stipulated by Art.15 of the Criminal Procedure Law 2012 must be examined in order to see if they are applicable to the complaint.[95] If so, the investigation for criminal liability will not commence.

The content of a petition must be treated as confidential. Moreover, while lodging an application for criminal investigation, certificates and evidence of the alleged infringement such as original and fake trademarks, materials such as photographs, samples, promotional materials, invoices, and written and oral statements of witnesses, must be included. Evidence obtained secretly may also be admitted. However, if evidence is found lacking, the private prosecution may be ordered to withdraw or the prosecution may be rejected altogether.[96] During the proceedings of a trial, a court may step in to investigate cases

89 In 2014, local people's courts nationwide concluded 10,803 IPR criminal cases of the first instance, registering a 17.27 per cent increase on a year-on-year basis. See State Intellectual Property Office of the People's Republic of China (SIPO), ***Intellectual Property Rights Protection in China***. (SIPO, 2014), p.12.

90 Art.170(2), Criminal Procedure Law 2012.

91 Art.83, Criminal Procedure Law 2012.

92 Art.136, Criminal Procedure Law 2012.

93 Art.3, Criminal Procedure Law 2012.

94 Should the People's Procuratorate decide not to initiate a prosecution, within seven days the victim may appeal against the decision to the authority of the next highest level to request that the latter initiate a public prosecution. Alternatively, the victim may bring a lawsuit directly at a people's court without presenting an appeal. In the event that the case is accepted by the people's court, the People's Procuratorate shall transfer the case file to the court concerned. Article 145, Criminal Procedure Law 2012.

95 Such circumstances include: (1) if an act is obviously minor, causing no serious harm, and is therefore not deemed a crime; (2) if the limitation period for criminal prosecution has expired; (3) if an exemption of criminal punishment has been granted in a special amnesty decree; (4) if the crime is to be handled only upon complaint according to the Criminal Law, but there has been no complaint or the complaint has been withdrawn; (5) if the criminal suspect or defendant is deceased; or (6) if other laws provide an exemption from investigation of criminal responsibility. If one of the circumstances is applicable, no criminal liability shall be investigated.

96 Art.171(2), Criminal Procedure Law 2012.

launched by private prosecution if evidence is held to be doubtful and therefore verification is required.[97] If this is the case, an adjournment will be announced.[98]

Mediation may also be an option under criminal enforcement proceedings, although this procedure is not available to criminal violations against personal or property rights when evidence is indisputable.[99] By virtue of Art.172 of the Criminal Procedure Law 2012, the court may conduct mediation for a case instituted by private prosecution and, in these circumstances, it is possible that a settlement may be reached before a case launched by private prosecution is decided.

2. *Punishment*

The types of punishment available under the Criminal Law are divided into principal and supplementary punishment. Principal punishment includes a restraint order, criminal detention, fixed-term and life imprisonment and the death penalty, and supplementary punishment includes fines, deprivation of political rights and confiscation of property. Note that supplementary punishment may be imposed independently.[100] Chapter III Section 7 of the Criminal Law 1997 provides the terms of imprisonment when IPR is infringed. For example, Art.216 stipulates that for any patent infringement case that is committed under serious circumstances, the infringer may be handed down a sentence of up to three years' imprisonment, criminal detention and/or a fine. A monetary fine is calculated on the entirety of illegal gains and turnover, loss caused to the right holder and harm caused to society. As a principle, when IPR infringement is established, a fine of less than five times the illegal gains or not more than the same amount of the illegal turnover will be imposed.[101]

IV) Border enforcement

Intellectual property rights border enforcement in China is governed by the Customs Law 2000, Regulations on Customs Protection of Intellectual Property Rights 2010 (hereafter 'Customs Regulations') and its implementation rules.[102] Under the jurisdiction of the Customs Regulations, IPR refers to trademark, copyrights and related rights, as well as patent rights.[103]

Chapter VI of China's Customs Law 2000 provides grounds for dealing with the criminal act of smuggling. Article 47(2) specifies that transporting, importing or exporting prohibited articles, other than narcotic drugs, weapons or counterfeit currencies and pornography (which are dealt with by Art.47(1)), in large quantities or of a high value for

97 Art.171(2), Criminal Procedure Law 2012.

98 Art.158, Criminal Procedure Law 2012.

99 Art.170(3), Criminal Procedure Law 2012.

100 Arts.33and 34, Criminal Law 1997.

101 Art.4, The Interpretation II of the Supreme People's Court and Supreme People's Procuratorate of the Issues concerning the Specific Application of Law in Handling Criminal Cases of Infringement of Intellectual Property Rights 2007.

102 Rules of the General Administration of Customs of the People's Republic of China for the Implementation of the Regulations of the People's Republic of China on Customs Protection of Intellectual Property Rights. The latest amendment came into force in April 2010.

103 Art.2, Regulations on Customs Protection of Intellectual Property Rights 2010.

the purpose of making a profit, will constitute the crime of smuggling and be prosecuted.

1. Competent authorities and procedures

The GAC is the authority for border enforcement against IPR infringement, and it has the authority to detain infringing goods. It is important to note that such action may be instituted by either the right holder or *ex officio*; in either case the IPR in question must already be verified by, and recorded at, the GAC upon the right holder's prior application for recordation.[104] In case a recordation is absent, while requesting the GAC to detain an alleged IPR-infringing consignment, the right holder must provide the relevant documents and evidence as required by a recordation application.[105]

When applying for detention of alleged infringing goods at the GAC, a right holder should provide information concerning, for example, the name of the consignee and the consignor, the specifications of the suspected consignment and its possible embarking and disembarking port and time, as well as the transporting vehicle.[106] The application must be accompanied by a bond of no more than the value of the alleged infringing goods, which is determined on their transaction value.[107] A bond, either in the form of a cash deposit or of a letter of guarantee provided by a financial institution,[108] will be held for two purposes. First, a bond will be held as possible compensation to the consignee and the consignor in case a loss occurs when the allegation proves unfounded. Second, a bond will be held to pay for expenses incurred in the course of goods detention for warehousing, storage and disposal.[109] In the meantime, the consignee or the consignor may present the relevant evidence to the GAC in order to prove that the goods in question are not IPR-infringing and make a request for their release, provided that a bond equivalent to the value of the goods is handed over to the GAC.[110]

IPR-infringing goods may be detained *ex officio*. When such is the case, the GAC shall inform the right holder once it detects that the importing or exporting goods are likely to be IPR-infringing. Under these circumstances, the right holder shall apply to the GAC for their detention and an investigation will be undertaken by the GAC subsequently in order to ascertain, within 30 working days, whether the goods in question are indeed infringing goods.[111] In the meantime, if the consignee or the consignor is convinced that the consignment in question is not IPR-infringing, a declaration of status must be submitted to the GAC together with evidence, followed by an application for release after providing a bond equivalent to the value of the consignment. The bond will be returned if, subsequently, no legal action is undertaken by the right holder at a people's court

104 Chapter II, Regulations on Customs Protection of Intellectual Property Rights 2010. Once approved, a recordation will be valid for ten years and so will a renewed recordation. See: Arts.9 and 10, Implementing Rules of Regulations on Customs Protection of Intellectual Property Rights 2009.

105 Art.14, Implementing Rules of Regulations on Customs Protection of Intellectual Property Rights 2009.

106 Art.13, Regulations on Customs Protection of Intellectual Property Rights 2010.

107 Art.39, Implementing Rules of Regulations on Customs Protection of Intellectual Property Rights 2009.

108 Art.38, Implementing Rules of Regulations on Customs Protection of Intellectual Property Rights 2009.

109 Art.14, Regulations on Customs Protection of Intellectual Property Rights 2010.

110 Arts.18 and 19, Regulations on Customs Protection of Intellectual Property Rights 2010.

111 Art.20, Regulations on Customs Protection of Intellectual Property Rights 2010.

within the specified time limit.[112] In the course of an investigation, the GAC may solicit assistance from the relevant authorities for IPR matters, as well as from the right holder, the consignee and the consignor, for which cooperation must be provided.[113] In a case where the GAC fails to determine whether the detained goods are IPR-infringing, the right holder may apply for an injunction order in order to cease the infringing act or for property preservation.[114] The bond that is put down by the consignee or the consignor will be forfeited if a people's court agrees to deal with the detained goods on the allegation of IPR infringement raised by the IPR holder. Otherwise, the GAC will refund the consignee or the consignor, who may apply for property preservation at a people's court against the bond provided by the right holder. When this happens, a notice to this effect must be dispatched from the people's court to the GAC. If not, after 20 working days counting from the date of the forfeiture of the bond provided by the consignee or the consignor, the GAC will refund the bond to the right holder.[115]

Article 23 of the Customs Regulation 2010 states that, after applying for goods detention at the GAC, the right holder shall nonetheless commence an action of litigation at a people's court, including applying for property preservation. In the event that a criminal act of IPR infringement is established by the GAC, the PSB will step in to investigate the case for criminal liability.[116]

Article 27 of the Implementing Rules of the Customs Regulation foresees the possibility that the IPR holder, the consignee or the consignor may reach an agreement concerning the detained goods. In this case, the parties shall apply to the GAC for releasing the goods and the GAC may therefore terminate the investigation for IPR infringement, unless a criminal offence is already constituted.

Note that a foreign IPR holder may engage an agent established in China in order to apply for IPR border enforcement or recordation.[117] On the other hand, in the course of investigating an alleged IPR-infringing consignment, the GAC is under the obligation to keep any business secret involved in the consignment confidential unless such information is required to be made public as is prescribed by law.[118]

2. *Disposal of IPR-infringing goods and legal liability*

The detained goods will be confiscated by the GAC once it is confirmed upon investigation that they are IPR-infringing goods, and the right holder will be duly informed in writing. Subsequently, the infringing goods may be handed over to charities for social welfare undertakings if such goods are deemed fit for the purpose, in which case the GAC may be required to exercise its supervision duty in the process.[119] The GAC may also transfer the infringing goods to the right holder for a fee if the latter wishes to buy them back. When both options are ruled out, the infringing goods may be auctioned off by the GAC after removing the infringing features from the goods. However, the GAC must first seek the

112 Arts.18 and 19, Regulations on Customs Protection of Intellectual Property Rights 2010.
113 Arts.21 and 22, Regulations on Customs Protection of Intellectual Property Rights 2010.
114 Art.29, Implementing Rules of Regulations on Customs Protection of Intellectual Property Rights 2009.
115 Art.36, Implementing Rules of Regulations on Customs Protection of Intellectual Property Rights 2009.
116 Art.26, Regulations on Customs Protection of Intellectual Property Rights 2010.
117 Art.2, Implementing Rules of Regulations on Customs Protection of Intellectual Property Rights 2009.
118 Art.5, Implementing Rules of Regulations on Customs Protection of Intellectual Property Rights 2009.
119 Art.33, Implementing Rules of Regulations on Customs Protection of Intellectual Property Rights 2009.

opinion of the IPR holder before proceeding with this option.[120] This disposal measure is nonetheless not applicable to trademark-infringing goods. Except for extraordinary reasons, infringing goods must not be allowed to return to the commercial channels by merely removing an infringing trademark while other infringing features remain intact. The GAC must destroy such infringing goods outright.[121] This measure was adopted in order to comply with the decision laid down by the WTO Appellate Body pursuant to the case China – Measures Affecting the Protection and Enforcement of Intellectual Property Rights (DS362).

In any event, when IPR-infringing goods are confiscated by the GAC, the responsibility lies with the right holder to pay the expenses for warehousing, storage and disposal of the detained goods. The right holder may be exempt from these expenses if the GAC fails to dispose of the detained IPR-infringing goods within three months, counting from the date when the decision of confiscation is served on the consignee or the consignor. By the same token, when the GAC assists a people's court in detaining goods suspected of infringement or in releasing detained goods, the right holder will be liable for the expenses of warehousing, storage and disposal, etc. incurred during the detention period imposed by the GAC.[122]

When goods are detained after an allegation is lodged by a right holder, if it is impossible to ascertain whether the goods are indeed IPR-infringing, or if a people's court decides that the detained goods are not IPR-infringing, the right holder shall be liable for compensation.[123] However, once it's determined that the detained consignment is indeed IPR-infringing, the right holder may include the expenses of warehousing, storage and disposal as reasonable expenditure incurred for ceasing the IPR-infringing act,[124] in which case it may be claimed for compensation by virtue of Art.65, Patent Law 2008. The same measures are maintained by the Draft Patent Law 2015.

Nevertheless, what is still absent concerning the disposal of IPR-infringing goods is how charities may handle donated IPR-infringing goods since these goods, which still include the infringing features and marks, often reappear in the market. Article 33 of the Implementing Rules requires the GAC to exercise necessary supervision in this respect, but the effectiveness of this is not clear. Moreover, despite the amendment, at this moment IPR holders do not have the right to demand the destruction of the infringing goods nor to instruct the Customs as to how to dispose of the infringing goods.

V) Arbitration

Arbitration in China is governed by Chapter 26 of the Civil Procedure Law 2012 and the Arbitration Law 1994. Article 271 of the Civil Procedure Law stipulates that contractual disputes arising from Sino-foreign economic activities concerning trade, transport or maritime matters, if the contractual clauses on arbitration are specified by the parties or if a written agreement on arbitration is subsequently reached after a dispute arises, should

120 Art.33, Implementing Rules of Regulations on Customs Protection of Intellectual Property Rights 2009.
121 Art.27, Regulations on Customs Protection of Intellectual Property Rights 2010.
122 Art.34, Implementing Rules of Regulations on Customs Protection of Intellectual Property Rights 2009.
123 Art.28, Regulations on Customs Protection of Intellectual Property Rights 2010.
124 Art.25, Regulations on Customs Protection of Intellectual Property Rights 2010.

only be settled by arbitration by a Chinese arbitration body for foreign-related disputes, but not for litigation at people's court.[125] Litigation may be an option only when arbitration clauses are missing in the contract or when disputing parties do not subsequently reach a written agreement on arbitration. Parties to an arbitration agreement may elect the applicable laws as well as the procedural rules, which may be seen as independent and separate from other clauses of a contract.[126] However, an arbitration agreement may be challenged either before an arbitration commission or before a people's court and, in any case, such a challenge must be brought up before the first hearing takes place at an arbitration tribunal.[127]

The Chinese arbitration body responsible for dealing with economic and trade disputes arising from contractual or non-contractual transactions is the China International Economic and Trade Arbitration Commission (CIETAC).[128] Also known as the Arbitration Court of the China Chamber of International Commerce (CCOIC), CIETAC

125 Such an arbitration clause or agreement shall contain, based on the requirements set down by the Arbitration Law, for example, an expression of intention to apply for arbitration, matters for arbitration and a designated arbitration commission, etc. See: Art.16, Arbitration Law 1994. For other requirements concerning an arbitration agreement, see Chapter III, Arbitration Requirements, Arbitration Law 1994.

126 Art.5.3, Arbitration Agreement, China International Economic and Trade Arbitration Commission (CIETAC) Arbitration Rules (2012). It is worth noting that the former Shanghai and Shenzhen sub-commissions rejected the Arbitration Rules 2012 with regard to, in particular, Art.2.6 whereby the sub-commissions could potentially lose a substantial number of cases. Article 2.6 of the Arbitration Rules (2012) stipulates that, *inter alia*, 'where the agreement is ambiguous, the Secretariat of CIETAC shall accept the arbitration application and administer the case. In the event of any dispute, a decision shall be made by CIETAC'. Under Arbitration Rules 2005, the model arbitration clause reads as follows: 'any dispute arising from or in connection with this Contract shall be submitted to China International Economic and Trade Arbitration Commission for arbitration, which shall be conducted in accordance with the Commission's arbitration rules in effect at the time of applying for arbitration. The arbitral award is final and binding upon both parties'. In accordance with the 2012 Rules, arbitration agreements reached between the parties who adopted the 2005 model clause may be interpreted as ambiguous and subject to the administration of CIETAC, resulting therefore in a substantial number of potential cases for arbitration of which only CIETAC Beijing would have the jurisdiction.
Also, Article 47.4 of the 2012 Rules provides that the seal of CIETAC shall be affixed on an arbitral award before issuance. Prior to this, the seals of CIETAC Shanghai or CIETAC South China were sufficient for them to issue arbitral awards. As a result, the 2012 provision effectively removed the powers of CIETAC Shanghai and CIETAC South China (Shenzhen) to issue an arbitral award in their own names.

127 Art.20, Arbitration Law 1994.

128 CIETAC was formerly known as the Foreign Trade Arbitration Commission, which was set up in April 1956 under the China Council for the Promotion of International Trade (CCPIT). After the 'reform and opening-up' policy was adopted in the late 1970s, the said Commission was first renamed as the Foreign Economic and Trade Arbitration Commission in 1980, and then as CIETAC in 1988. With its headquarters in Beijing, CIETAC had four sub-commissions in Shanghai, Shenzhen, Tianjin and Chongqing. Available at: http://www.cietac.org/index.cms (last accessed 17 September 2015).
However, in the course of 2012, CIATEC modified its Arbitration Rules, which has brought some criticism and disapproval within its branches. A fierce and raw battle was waged between CIETAC's affiliates and Beijing. Shanghai and Shenzhen refused to adopt the Rules and declared themselves as independent arbitral institutions, and Tianjin also refused to adopt the new Rules although it did not declare its independence. CIETAC Beijing did not recognise Shanghai and Shenzhen as legitimate arbitral forums and revoked the authorisation to accept and administrate arbitration cases. CIETAC Beijing further forbade the former CIETAC Shanghai and Shenzhen from continuing to use the name, brand, or logo of 'CIETAC', either in Chinese or in English, and to conduct any further arbitration activities in the names of CIETAC Shanghai Sub-Commission and CIETAC South China Sub-Commission. Since 11 April 2013, CIETAC Shanghai was renamed as Shanghai International Arbitration Centre, or SHIAC, while Shenzhen CIETAC, in the meantime, changed its name to Shenzhen Court of International Arbitration, or SCIA.

is one of the major permanent arbitration institutions in the world. Parties to arbitration may select an arbitration commission through agreement because, in arbitration, jurisdiction is not differentiated based on judicial hierarchy levels and territorial jurisdiction is not involved.[129]

In the course of an arbitration proceeding, a party may institute an application for property preservation measures and such an application must be submitted to an intermediate people's court. By virtue of Art.272 of the Civil Procedure Law, the rule of domicile will apply while recognition and enforcement will be subject to the same principle. Should an application for property preservation be wrongly submitted, the applicant will be liable for compensation for any loss incurred to the party against whom the application was submitted.[130]

The formation of an arbitration tribunal may be negotiated with regard to the number of arbitrators and their qualifications as well as their fitness for the role as an arbitrator, which may be challenged.[131] Article 39 of the Arbitration Law 1994 stipulates that, under usual circumstances, arbitration is conducted by means of oral hearings, although it is also possible for an arbitration tribunal to hand down an award on the basis of the written materials submitted by the disputing parties. Arbitration must be conducted *in camera*, unless the parties agree to conduct the hearings in public, in which case state secrets must not be involved.[132]

If the claimant in the dispute fails to appear before an arbitration tribunal without handing in valid reasons or leaves the hearing without permission prior to its conclusion, the application for arbitration may be deemed withdrawn. On the other hand, if the respondent behaves in such ways as just mentioned, a default award may be handed down.[133]

A party may apply for evidence preservation if the evidence would be destroyed or lost or difficult to obtain at a later time. After such an application is submitted to the arbitration commission, the arbitration commission shall forward it to the basic people's court in the locality where the evidence is based.[134]

An arbitration award may be handed down without going through a hearing. It is viable for the parties to reach an agreement to settle their dispute and subsequently submit the agreement to the tribunal and request a corresponding award. Alternatively, the parties may withdraw their application for arbitration altogether if an agreement is reached between them.[135]

Conciliation is possible pursuant to a voluntary request submitted by both parties. When conciliation fails, an arbitration award must be handed down promptly. If not, the arbitration tribunal will issue a conciliation statement or an arbitration award based on the settlement agreement, of which the statement as well as the agreement will take equal and immediate effect[136] upon the signatures of the parties.[137] Also, under Art.54 of the Arbitration Law, parties may opt to omit the facts of the dispute as well as the reasons for

129 Art.6, Arbitration Law 1994.
130 Art.28, Arbitration Law 1994.
131 Arts.30–38, Arbitration Law 1994.
132 Art.40, Arbitration Law 1994.
133 Art.42, Arbitration Law 1994.
134 Art.46, Arbitration Law 1994.
135 Art.49, Arbitration Law 1994.
136 Art.51, Arbitration Law 1994.
137 Art.52, Arbitration Law 1994.

the decision from the arbitration award. At the same time, an arbitrator with the dissenting opinion may refrain from signing the award. Otherwise, an arbitration award must specify the arbitration claim, the facts of the dispute, the reasons for the decision, the results of the award, the allocation of arbitration fees, as well as the date of the award that will serve as the effective date of the settlement agreement.[138] In case a panel of arbitrators is unable to reach a majority opinion, the opinion of the presiding arbitrator shall constitute the arbitration award.[139]

Article 58 of the Arbitration Law specifies the conditions upon which an arbitration award may be set aside by an intermediate people's court in the locality where the arbitration commission is located. However, such possibility is only available within six months from the date of the receipt of the award.[140]

The principle of 'single and final award' is applied in arbitration in China. This means that, although subject to legal challenge,[141] after an arbitration award is handed down, no further arbitration or litigation may be instituted unless the award is subsequently set aside or its enforcement is quashed by a people's court in accordance with the relevant laws.[142] An arbitration award may be enforced by a people's court in accordance with the Civil Procedure Law, but the court may also decide to suspend the enforcement procedures should one party apply for setting aside the arbitration award.[143]

For disputes arising from economic, trade, transportation and maritime activities involving a foreign element, a foreign-related arbitration commission must be appointed by the China Chamber of International Commerce, which must formulate the arbitration rules, while foreign experts with the required skills may be appointed as arbitrator. Procedures applicable to both foreign-related and domestic arbitrations are similar except that, for the former, if an award will be enforced overseas, the party enforcing the award must directly apply to a competent foreign court for recognition and enforcement of the award.[144]

As far as IPR is concerned, Arts.48–50 of the Law on the Application of Law in Foreign-related Civil Relations governs the question of jurisdiction when a dispute concerning ownership, content, transfer, licensing and infringement involving a foreign element takes place. In a case where the disputing parties did not elect any applicable laws, then the relevant provisions on the contract that are set down by the Law on the Laws Applicable to Foreign-related Civil Relations 2010 shall apply.[145]

138 Art.57, Arbitration Law 1994.

139 Art.53, Arbitration Law 1994.

140 Art.59, Arbitration Law 1994.

141 When challenging the validity of an arbitration agreement, the party concerned may request that the arbitration commission make a decision or apply to a people's court for a ruling. If one party requests that the arbitration commission make a decision and the other party applies to a people's court for a ruling, the people's court shall choose to deliver a ruling. Such a challenge must be raised prior to the arbitration tribunal's first hearing. Art.20, Arbitration Law 1994.

142 Art.9, Arbitration Law 1994.

143 Chapter VI on Enforcement, Arbitration Law 1994.

144 Chapter VII Special Provisions for Arbitration Involving Foreign Elements, Arbitration Law 1994.

145 Art.49, Law on the Laws Applicable to Foreign-related Civil Relations 2010.

IV Jurisdiction of IPR cases

The issue of IPR jurisdiction in China will be discussed in two contexts, first domestic disputes and second disputes involving a foreign element. The former is governed by Chapter II of the Civil Procedure Law, while the latter by Chapter XXV of the same law.

I) Jurisdiction over domestic disputes

By virtue of Art.39 of the Civil Procedure Law, a higher court may retry those civil cases over which a lower court has the jurisdiction as the court of the first instance. A higher court may also transfer the civil cases over which it has the jurisdiction as the court of the first instance to a lower court. In the meantime, a lower court may also request a higher court to try a case in its place if necessary.

For those cases administered by the administrative enforcement mechanism, their jurisdiction falls upon the court in the locality where the initial administrative enforcement action takes place.[146] When a lawsuit involves two or more courts, the plaintiff shall have the option to bring the lawsuit to either one of the courts, while jurisdiction shall fall upon the first court that receives the lawsuit.[147]

By virtue of Art.15 of the Administrative Procedure Law 2014, an intermediate people's court shall have the jurisdiction as the court of the first instance over: 1) cases concerning legal proceedings derived from administrative enforcement actions and that are undertaken by the departments of the State Council or by the local people's governments at or above the county level; 2) cases dealt with by the GAC; 3) grave and complicated cases within the same jurisdiction; and 4) other cases that are designated for trial by the intermediate people's courts.

1. Jurisdiction of IPR infringement cases

The IP-specialised courts in Beijing, Shanghai and Shenzhen sit at the same level as the intermediate people's courts in China's judicial hierarchy and hear: 1) both civil and administrative cases of the first instance over patents, new varieties of plants, layout design of integrated circuits, know-how and computer software; 2) administrative enforcement cases of the first instance in respect of copyright, trademark and unfair competition, which are decided by the departments of the State Council or by the local people's governments at and above the county level; 3) civil cases that involve the identification of well-known trademarks.[148]

After the IP-specialised courts were established, the intermediate people's courts in Beijing, Shanghai and Guangzhou no longer hear IPR-related civil and administrative cases, while other intermediate people's courts in the Guangdong Province (where Guangzhou is its capital city) only hear administrative enforcement cases of the first

146 Art.17, Administrative Procedure Law. Article 17 further provides that, for a reconsidered case, if an administrative body which conducted the reconsideration procedure and subsequently amended the original specific administrative act, the reconsidered case may be placed under the jurisdiction of the people's court in the locality of the administrative body concerned.

147 Art.20, Administrative Procedure Law.

148 Art.1, Regulations of the Supreme People's Court on the Jurisdiction over cases of the Intellectual Property Courts in Beijing, Shanghai and Guangzhou, October 2014.

instance concerning copyright, trademark and unfair competition decided by the departments of the State Council or by the local people's governments at and above the county level. The basic people's courts in Beijing, Shanghai and Guangdong Province have the same jurisdiction.[149] The Beijing IP Court has the privilege of hearing appeal cases against the decisions laid down by the departments of the State Council concerning: 1) licencing agreements with respect to patent, trademark, new varieties of plants, layout design; 2) compulsory licencing fees and remuneration with respect to patent, trademark, new varieties of plants, layout design; and 3) authorisation and validation.[150] In the past, the aforesaid cases were heard by the Intermediate Beijing People's Court for the first instance and the Higher Beijing People's Court for the second instance. Patent disputes may be heard by other courts, but the SPC must first grant its approval.[151]

Cases of the first instance concerning trademark infringement are heard by the intermediate or the higher people's courts. The higher people's courts can, based on their jurisdiction and with an approval issued by the SPC, designate one or two basic people's courts in large cities to hear trademark cases of the first instance.[152] When a party appeals against a decision laid down by a basic people's court of the first instance, which is derived from a judicial or an administrative enforcement action concerning copyright, trademark, technology contract or unfair competition, an application must be lodged at a specific IP court in the city in which the concerned basic people's court is located.[153]

Although the IP courts have the jurisdiction over a lower people's court's decision derived from civil and administrative actions and appeal cases, when parties appeal against a decision of the first instance laid down by an IP court or apply for reconsideration at a higher court, the higher people's court at the locality where the specific IP court is based shall have the jurisdiction to hear the case.[154] According to the white paper released by the Shanghai Intellectual Property Court on 14 April 2016, the Court received altogether 285 cases in 2015 involving parties from Hong Kong, Macao, Taiwan and other foreign origins, accounting for 16.13 per cent of the total cases that the Court handled in the same year. The foreign parties involved came from a total of 15 countries and regions, and include General Electric, Hewlett-Packard, BASF, Microsoft and other Fortune 500 companies as well as international brands, such as Burberry, BMW, BOSS, LV, Rafi and Gucci.

2. *Territorial jurisdiction*

Concerning territorial jurisdiction in civil litigation, and in accordance with Art.34 of the Civil Procedure Law 2012, IPR infringement cases must be heard by the court in the locality of the domicile of the defendant/respondent or in another place where its direct relation

149 Art.3, Regulations of the Supreme People's Court on the Jurisdiction over cases of the Intellectual Property Courts in Beijing, Shanghai and Guangzhou, October 2014.

150 Art.5, Regulations of the Supreme People's Court on the Jurisdiction over cases of the Intellectual Property Courts in Beijing, Shanghai and Guangzhou, October 2014.

151 Art.1, Circular on Several Problems in Patent Trial Work, 1985.

152 As of August 2005, the High Court had designated 14 elementary courts to hear cases of the first instance concerning trademark disputes.

153 Art.6, Regulations of the Supreme People's Court on the Jurisdiction over cases of the Intellectual Property Courts in Beijing, Shanghai and Guangzhou, October 2014.

154 Art.7, Regulations of the Supreme People's Court on the Jurisdiction over cases of the Intellectual Property Courts in Beijing, Shanghai and Guangzhou, October 2014.

with the dispute prevails, as long as the requirements concerning the judicial levels and the exclusive jurisdiction determined by the same Law are complied with.

For patent infringement cases, territorial jurisdiction lies in the locality where an infringement act takes place. Such locality refers to: 1) manufacturing, using, offering for sale, selling or importing products alleged to infringe an invention or a utility model patent; 2) using a patented process and where acts of using, offering for sale, selling or importing products acquired directly from the patented process take place; 3) manufacturing, selling or importing products of patented designs; 4) counterfeiting; and 5) where the consequences of the preceding infringing acts arise.[155]

If only the manufacturer of an infringing product is sued in court, and when the places of manufacturing and selling are different, the court of the locality of manufacturing shall have the jurisdiction. In a case where the manufacturer and the seller are co-defendants, the court of the locality where the infringing product is sold shall have the jurisdiction. Additionally, when the seller is a subsidiary of the manufacturer and in a case where the plaintiff takes action against the manufacturer for manufacturing and selling the infringing product, the court of the locality where the product is sold shall have the jurisdiction.[156]

If several IPR holders bring a single action against one defendant, the court of the locality where the infringing act takes place shall have the jurisdiction over the case.

II) Jurisdiction over disputes involve a foreign element

Before discussing disputes that involve a foreign element, the question of conflict of laws must be explained for two reasons. First, due to patent's intrinsic characteristic of territoriality, successive litigations may trigger different applications of domestic and international norms of patent protection to the same set of facts. This may lead to conflicting judgments and sometimes irreconcilable outcomes,[157] in which case the question of conflict of laws must be addressed. Second, concerning IPR protection, against the backdrop of global exploitation, challenges emerge when searching for an appropriate national court for jurisdiction over a dispute involving a foreign element and when determining the prerequisites in order to ascertain applicable national laws to make clear the legal relationships concerned.[158] With regard to patent rights, as ever more patent applications are submitted in multiple countries, patent disputes often involve multiple jurisdictions as well as a result. This being the case, the rules of conflict of laws must be called into play.

155 Art.5, Several Provisions of the Supreme People's Court on Issues Relating to Application of Law to Adjudication of Cases of Patent Disputes, 2001.

156 Art.6, Several Provisions of the Supreme People's Court on Issues Relating to Application of Law to Adjudication of Cases of Patent Disputes, 2001.

157 See, for example: International Association for the Protection of Intellectual Property, Question Q174 – Jurisdiction and Applicable Law in the Case of Cross-border Infringement of Intellectual Property Rights, 2003/I Y.B. 827–28, Oct. 25–28, 2003 (concerning recognising the need for a fairer and more efficient method of resolving cross-border controversies); 'European Max-Planck Group for Conflict of Laws in Intellectual Prop., Exclusive jurisdiction and Cross-Border IP (Patent) Infringement: Suggestions for Amendment of the Brussels I Regulation' in 29(5*) European Intellectual Property Review* 195 (2007) 195–96 (suggesting the need for amending the Brussels Regulation on Jurisdiction and Enforcement of Judgments in Civil and Commercial Matters, EC Regulation No 44/2001, to improve the efficiency of transnational dispute resolution).

158 Rotstein F., 'Is there an international intellectual property system? Is there an agreement between states as to what the objectives of intellectual property should be? 33 *European Intellectual Property Review* 1 (2011) 1–4.

Furthermore, in recent decades due to trade globalisation, more and more domestic laws are amended in order to comply with international treaties to which a country has acceded. While solving the above-mentioned questions with regard to disputes involving a foreign element, the issue of how international treaty provisions are incorporated in domestic laws must also be addressed since it affects how a private citizen may invoke such provisions for protection. For example, the WTO Agreement obliges its members to conform their laws with the provisions of the Agreement while, at the same time, members are not required to provide that the Agreement has direct effect in their domestic laws.[159] As a result, members are at liberty to determine how to meet the obligations. Coupled with the different approaches exercised by monist and dualist countries concerning the question of direct effect of international law,[160] before trying to rely on a right derived from an international treaty for protection, one must first ascertain that the right in question is rectified and is directly applicable in a domestic context in the country concerned.

As a party to the United Nations Convention on the Recognition and Enforcement of Foreign Arbitral Awards (for commercial disputes only), both China's Civil Procedure Law and the relevant judicial interpretations adopt the principle that, when an international treaty that is concluded or acceded to by China contains provisions that differ from the provisions of the Civil Procedure Law, the provisions of the international treaty shall prevail, except for cases in which China has made reservations.[161] Further, under China's Constitution and the Law on the Procedures of the Conclusion of Treaties (1990), the WTO Agreement, including the TRIPS Agreement, falls within the category of 'important international agreements', which means that the Agreement shall be subject to ratification by the Standing Committee of the NPC. As a result, the WTO Agreement and China's Protocol of Accession are implemented domestically through enabling legislation – in this case, Art.142 of China's General Principles of Civil Law – and consequently the provisions of the TRIPS Agreement are directly applicable in China's domestic courts.[162]

159 Art.XVI:4, Agreement Establishing the World Trade Organisation.

160 Countries, such as most of the continental countries and Japan, Korea, etc., with a civil law tradition operate a code-based legal system and generally follow the monist approach. They consider international law as part of the land, therefore individual citizens may invoke this directly. However, most of the WTO members from the Commonwealth, including Australia, Canada, India, Singapore, etc., operate the common law system and follow the dualist approach. They do not see that all international law can be relied upon by individuals, but only those laws that are given direct effect.

161 Art.260, Civil Procedure Law 2012.

162 However, this is not the position held by the European Court of Justice (ECJ). The ECJ decided that the WTO Agreements are not capable of having direct effect and do not in principle form part of the European courts' legality review. In the eyes of the EU legal system, WTO Agreements are 'mixed agreements' since 'the subject-matter of an agreement or contract falls in part within the competence of the Community and in part with that of the Member States'. (Opinion 1/91, 1993 E.C.R. I-1061, para 36.)

Four cases decided by the ECJ confirm that the WTO Agreement has no direct effect in the EC courts: *International Fruit Co. NY* v. *Produktschap voor Groenten en Fruit* (Joined Cases 21–24/72, 1972 E.C.R. 1219), *Federal Republic of Germany* v. *Council of the European Union* (C-280/93, 1991 I E.C.R. 2069), *Portugal* v. *Council of the European Union* (C-149/96, 1999 E.C.R. I-8395) and the EC-Bananas cases which is a collective name for four cases: *Cordis* v. *Commission*, *Bocchi Food Trade International* v. *Commission*, *T Port* v. *Commission* (the Quota Damages Cases) and the ECJ judgment in OGT Fruchthandelsgesellschaft (OGT). For the TRIPS Agreement, the Community and the member states have shared competence, which means the Agreement is jointly implemented by the Community at the EC level and by the member states at the national level. (Opinion 1/94, 1994 E.C.R. I-5276, para 105.) Therefore, the Community adopted the implementing legislation in December 1994 in order to implement the TRIPS Agreement. On the level of member states,

III) Apply the choice of law rules in IPR cases in China

Article 142 of China's General Principles of Civil Law governs the application of law in civil relations with foreign elements[163] and provides international treaties, which are ratified or acceded to by China, an overriding power above the choice of law rules applied in China.[164] Although this overriding power may not necessarily give international treaties the status of applicable law, they nonetheless have gained access to and become a source of law in the Chinese legal system. As a result, and as a generally accepted international practice, Chinese courts do not examine in the first place if there is a Chinese domestic law applicable to the dispute concerned based on the Chinese choice of law rules.[165] This

---

for those monism members, such as Belgium, France and the Netherlands, the Agreement automatically becomes part of the domestic law after ratification; as to dualism members, such as the UK and Denmark, the Agreement became part of the domestic legislation after an act of transformation.

As to the question of whether international treaties may be applied by private parties before national courts within the Community, the ECJ reiterated in *Meryem Demirel* v. *Stadt Schwäbisch Gmünd* (Case 12/86, 1987 E.C.R. 3719) that when relying on a provision of an international agreement, regard will be given to its wording, the purpose and the nature of the agreement itself, the provision must contain a clear and precise obligation which is not subject to the adoption of any subsequent measure in its implementation or effects. In other words, the agreement itself must be capable of being directly invokable.

With regard to the possibility of directly invoking the provisions of the TRIPS Agreement, in *Parfums Christian Dior S.A.* v. *Tuk Consultancy B.V.* and *Assco Gerüste GmbH* v. *Wilhelm Layher GmbH* (joined case C-300/98 and C-392/98 2000 E.C.R.), the ECJ concluded that the provisions of the TRIPS Agreement are not as such to create rights upon which individuals may rely directly before courts by virtue of the Community law. As a result, there are two scenarios concerning the direct invokability of the TRIPS Agreement. First, when the Community legislation is present, the Community law will govern and the private parties are not able to directly invoke the TRIPS Agreement before national courts. Second, when the Community legislation is absent while the competence of the member states prevails, the member states shall have the liberty of providing individuals with the right to reply on the provisions of the TRIPS Agreement. In other words, the private parties may directly invoke provisions of the TRIPS Agreement in front of national courts.

163 Art.142 of the General Principles of Civil Law 1986 provides that 'if any international treaty concluded or acceded to by the People's Republic of China contains provisions differing from those in the civil laws of the People's Republic of China, the provisions of the international treaty shall apply, unless the provisions are ones on which the People's Republic of China has announced reservations. International practice may be applied to matters for which neither the law of the People's Republic of China nor any international treaty concluded or acceded to by the People's Republic of China has any provisions'.

164 For issues that fall neither into the scope of Chinese laws nor any international treaty, Art.142 provides that international custom may apply, for which two judicial approaches may be adopted by a Chinese court. First, international custom may apply as part of the Chinese judicial system pursuant to China's choice of law rule whereby a relevant Chinese national law should apply as the governing law. In case there are no Chinese laws that address the dispute, then international custom would be invoked, which means it is not applied as an independent body of law, but a part of the Chinese legal system. The second approach is that international custom may be invoked as a directly applicable law. There are also cases where Chinese courts regard contract clauses designating international treaties that are not ratified or acceded to by China as an effective act of incorporating such treaties into the contract concerned. Tang Z., 'International treaties in Chinese private law'. 42 *Hong Kong Law Journal* 597 (2012).

165 It is suggested that such approach has its root in public international law, by which accepting international treaties, that are acceded to by China and have become part of the Chinese legal system, does not require ratification by statutes. On the other hand, China's Constitution does not specify whether it is the monism or the dualism position that the country pursues. Therefore, if a Chinese court directly applies international treaties as if part of the Chinese legal system, and permits international treaty provisions to override rules prescribed by the Chinese domestic legal system, this may be regarded as legitimate based on the premise of China's public international law. Xue H. Q. and Qian J., 'International treaties in the Chinese domestic legal system'. *8 Chinese Journal of International Law* 299 (2009).

approach was confirmed by the Notice of Issuance of the Guiding Opinions on Several Issues in Foreign-related Commercial Trials, which was issued by the Higher People's Court in Guangdong Province in 2006.[166] In essence, if a dispute falls within the remit of a particular international treaty, the treaty shall apply; otherwise, Chinese courts will elect an applicable domestic law based on China's choice of law rules. As to the question of whether an international treaty can be applied as a governing law *vis-à-vis* cross-border relationships, by virtue of Art.142 of the General Principle of Civil Law, arguably it may be applied directly as a governing law to a dispute as if it were a piece of Chinese substantive legislation.[167]

The issue of protecting IPR in the context of a conflict of laws only became relevant in China in 1991 when some Chinese academics called for the development of such a body of law,[168] although IPR's characteristic of territoriality has prompted such law-making at the international level for a long time. In general, while deciding an IPR case involving a foreign element, local courts in different countries apply the territoriality-based choice of law rules, such as *lex loci protectionis*, *lex fori*, or *lex loci delicti*.[169] At the international level, and while recognising *lex loci protectionis* as a universal principle for adjudicating IPR

166 It is stipulated that Art.142 of the General Principle of Civil Law provides the important principle of 'priority of international treaties' so, therefore, when a dispute falls within the scope of an international treaty that was ratified, or acceded to, by China, the treaty should apply outright unless the treaty permits the disputing parties to exclude its application by an explicit agreement. See: Art.3(24), Notice of Issuance of the Guiding Opinions on Several Issues in Foreign-related Commercial Trials, Higher People's Court, Guangdong Province, 2006 (no.32).

167 However, some scholars argue the opposite. See Cao J., the WTO and Speech: and the Rule of Law in China. 16 *Temple International and Comparative Law Journal* 379 (2002). For example, the SPC, in its Notice on Several Questions that Deserve Attentions Concerning Trial and Handling of Foreign Civil and Commercial Cases (17 April 2000), instructed the lower courts to grant the choice of law clause drafted by the contracting parties and to give priority to the application of international treaty as well as international custom. Moreover, in its Notice of the Meeting Minutes of the Trial Work in Coastal Areas on Economic Cases Involving Foreign, Hong Kong and Macau Elements (1989), the SPC directed the lower courts to apply the provisions of the CISG in contracts, since the treaty has come into force in China. With regard to the contracts involving CISG-contracting members and the disputes arising therefrom, the provisions of the CISG shall automatically and directly apply unless the contract stipulates otherwise. In *Shanghai Dong Da Import and Export Co., Inc.* v. *Laubholz-Meyer Company*, Shanghai Yangpu People's Court held that, since the parties did not choose the governing law for the contract in time of dispute, and as both the disputing parties are citizens of contracting members of the CISG, the contract fell into the scope of the CISG, therefore the Convention should apply. The case (including its decision), which was later published by the Shanghai Higher People's Court as a model case, indicates that: 1) an international treaty may be applied directly to a contractual dispute involving foreign elements; 2) parties may be subject to international treaty provisions without the necessity of referring to any domestic legislation; 3) people's courts may elect an applicable treaty in the absence of the disputing parties' choice of law clause. See Shanghai Higher People's Court, The 2003 Selected Cases Tried by People's Courts in Shanghai (Shanghai: Shanghai People's Publishing House, 2004), pp. 166–170.

168 Professor Dinwoodie noted that a leading Chinese scholar in 1991 called for the development of such a body of law in order to respond to the decision of the UK courts in *Tyburn Productions* v. *Conan Doyle*. See Dinwoodie G. B., 'Developing private international intellectual property law: the demise of territoriality?' 51 *William and Mary Law Review* 713 (2009).

169 Zhang M., 'Codified choice of law in China: rules, processes and theoretic underpinnings'. 37 *North Carolina Journal of International Law and Commercial Regulations* 1 (2011) 83. Also: Fentiman R., 'Choice of law and intellectual property' in J. Drexl and A. Kur (Eds) *24 Studies in Industrial Property and Copyright Law, Intellectual Property and Private International Law – Heading for the Future* (Oxford: Hart Publishing, 2005) pp. 147–148.

infringement cases,[170] the Rome II Regulation (EC) No 864/2007 adopted the choice of law rules for governing IPR protection. Set out in Art.8 and Art.8(1) of the Rome II Regulation, it stipulates that the law applicable to a non-contractual obligation arising from an IPR-infringing act shall be the law of the country where IPR protection is claimed. If, however, a unitary community IPR is infringed, the applicable law shall be the law of the country where the infringement act takes place in a case where the question involved is 'not governed by the relevant Community instrument'.[171]

In the context of China's conflict of law rules, disputes arising from IPR protection are decided first by international treaties/conventions on IPR protection, which are, in general, categorised as substantive law,[172] and second by an elected domestic law. This opinion is in line with the above discussion on Art.142 of China's General Principles of Civil Law.[173]

Reflecting on China's conflict of law rules in disputes concerning IPR infringement, the Law on the Laws Applicable to Foreign-related Civil Relations provides two rules concerning applicable laws when IPR infringement act occurs.[174] The first rule is the rule of *lex loci protectionis*. Article 48 stipulates that 'the ownership and contents of intellectual property rights' shall be governed by the law of the place where protection is claimed. Article 50 then further states that the rule of *lex loci protectionis* shall also apply to determine liability for tort when IPR infringement occurs. The second rule is the rule of party autonomy, which may be applied in two instances. The first instance is when IPR

170 Art.14(2), Rome II Regulation, states that 'where all the elements relevant to the situation at the time when the event giving rise to the damage occurs are located in a country other than the country whose law has been chosen, the choice of the parties shall not prejudice the application of provisions of the law of that other country which cannot be derogated from by agreement'.

171 Art.8(2), Rome II Regulation.

172 Huang J., *Private International Law* (Beijing: Law Press, 1999) at 527.

173 For example, in *Chen* v. *China Record Corporation* (Beijing Municipal No.1 Intermediate People's Court (2005) No. 12783), Chen, the successor of a famous Beijing Opera artist, sued China Record Corporation for infringing the artist's copyright. Since the right-holder was a resident in Hong Kong, the court in Beijing treated the dispute as a dispute with a foreign element. By virtue of Art.142, the court further made its decision based on the relevant provisions of the TRIPS Agreement, of which both mainland China and Hong Kong are contracting parties. Note that the court extended the same approach to other cases concerning IPR infringement, such as *Star TV Film Entertainment (HK) Ltd.* v. *China Record Corporation* (Beijing Municipal No.1 Intermediate People's Court (2005) No. 9337). In *Tsuburaya Prod.* v. *Yuyuan Shopping Centre*, the Shanghai No.1 Intermediate People's Court held that since both Japan and China were contracting parties of the Berne Convention for the Protection of Literary and Artistic Works, the Convention should apply by virtue of Art.142 of the General Principle of Civil Law. As Art.5(1) of the Berne Convention provides authors equal protection of their work by the relevant laws of any member other than the one from the country of origin, the matter was therefore brought back to be governed by China's domestic copyright law. Subsequently, the court in Shanghai applied China's Copyright Law, together with the Berne Convention, and decided the rights and obligations of the dispute (Shanghai Higher Court (2000) No. 43, 11 September 2000). See: Tang Z., 'International treaties in Chinese private international law'. 42 *Hong Kong Law Journal* 597 (2012).

174 Before the Law on the Laws Applicable to Foreign-related Civil Relations was enacted on 28 October 2010, only the Model Law of Private International Law 2000 provided the choice of law rules for IPR protection. Section Seven of the Model Law, which is entitled 'Intellectual Property', contains eight articles and provides the choice of law rules governing IPR issues such as scope, related rights, contracts and torts, etc. For example, Art.99 provides that 'the legal remedy for torts in intellectual property is governed by the law of the place where the protection is sought'.

infringement takes place while parties agree to make a choice of applicable laws.[175] However, there are two restrictions while applying this rule. First, parties must choose the law of the forum when electing applicable laws. Second, choice may only be made after an infringement act actually occurs.[176] In the second instance, the rule of party autonomy may apply when IPR transfer or licensing takes place, in which case parties may elect the applicable law. In the absence of parties' choice, the relevant rules concerning the choice of law contained in the Law shall apply.[177]

175 Art.49, Law on the Laws Applicable to Foreign-related Civil Relations 2010.
176 Art.50, Law on the Laws Applicable to Foreign-related Civil Relations 2010.
177 Art.49, Law on the Laws Applicable to Foreign-related Civil Relations 2010.

6 The evolution of patent legislation in China

Patent legislation in China includes patent and patent-related laws, implementing regulations, judicial interpretations and other patent protection regulations. The legislature, the SPC, departments of the central government such as the SIPO and local governments at different administrative levels are all competent to issue patent legislation. The SIPO is in charge of patent administration nationwide, managing IPR-related international affairs, as well as representing China on IPR matters at the international level. The State Patent Office under the SIPO is in charge of patent application, examination and patent grant, while the local patent administrative department is responsible for handling patent disputes at the locality concerned.

I Introduction

An invention patent may be granted if the invention is new, involves an inventive step and is capable of industrial application. Patent applications must be submitted to the SIPO for examination and grant. If an application is found in conformity with the requirements laid down by the Patent Law upon preliminary examination, the SIPO will publish it within 18 months counting from the date of filing, although the applicant may request the SIPO to publish it at an earlier date. Subsequently, the applicant must submit a request for substantive examination within three years counting from the date of filing, otherwise the application will be deemed withdrawn. The SIPO will conduct substantive patent examination as soon as possible after receiving a request for substantive examination, which may only be delayed for two reasons. Firstly, when the SIPO wishes to provide some time space for an applicant to consider withdrawing the application and, secondly, when the SIPO considers that an examination may be unnecessary. In any case, a patent is provisionally protected from the time of its publication until it is granted. In 2014, the average pendency for patent examination was 21.8 months as far as invention patent applications are concerned.[1]

Once a decision for patent grant is issued, the applicant must complete the registration formalities within two months, including paying for registration, printing and annual fees. If not, it will be assumed that the applicant wishes to relinquish the patent rights. A patent grant may be revoked upon re-examination. Along with the surge of patent applications in China in recent years, more and more re-examination requests are submitted at the same

1 State Intellectual Property Office of the People's Republic of China (SIPO), *Intellectual Property Rights Protection in China*. (SIPO, 2014), p. 6.

time. For example, there were 24,452 requests for re-examination in 2014, which registered a year-on-year increase of 29.9 per cent.[2]

II Evolution of patent legislation in China

The history of patent protection in China may have commenced during the Han Dynasty (206 BC–220 AD), when evidence shows occasional grants of patent-like privileges for the exclusive use of new processes such as salt distilling or iron smelting, and for the exclusive sales of products obtained therefrom.[3]

I) Prior to 1984

China's first patent legislation Regulations to Promote Industrial Technology is said to be enacted in 1889,[4] while the country's first patent office was established in Shanghai in 1903 in the reign of the Qing Dynasty.[5] After the Republic of China (1911–1949) toppled the Dynasty, a number of patent legislations were promulgated, including the Interim Regulation on Awards for Devices (Creations) which offered protection to both Chinese and foreign patents on a reciprocal basis.[6]

After the People's Republic of China was established in 1949, despite the country's ideological principle of collective property ownership, a series of patent regulations were promulgated but the number of patents awarded was meagre. Patent regulations were continuously updated[7] until all were abolished before 1963, when the Cultural Revolution began and patent protection measures were struck off and patent rights stopped being recognised. Inventive activities were still permissible then, but the ownership of all inventions belonged to the State.[8]

2 State Intellectual Property Office of the People's Republic of China (SIPO), *Intellectual Property Rights Protection in China*. (SIPO, 2014), p. 6.

3 Ganea P., 'Patents, utility models and designs' in C. Heath C. (Ed.) *Intellectual Property Law in China* (New York: Kluwer Law International, 2005), pp. 2–3.

4 Available at: http://beijing.usembassy-china.org.cn/iprpatent.html (last accessed 10 August 2015).

5 The Treaty between the United States and China for the Extension of the Commercial Relations between Them, which was concluded in 1903 in Shanghai, provided that China would establish a patent office. After that, when special laws with regard to inventions were enacted, the patent office would issue certificates of patent protection for a limited term of years to 'citizens of the United States on all their patents issued by the United States, in respect of articles the sale of which is lawful in China, which do not infringe on previous inventions of Chinese subjects, in the same manner as patents are to be issued to subjects of China'. See: Art.10, the Treaty between the United States and China for the Extension of the Commercial Relations between Them (Shanghai, 1903).

6 Other patent legislations enacted during this period were, for example, the Provisional Regulation of Rewards for Manufactured Products (1912 and 1923, respectively), Provisional Regulation of Rewards for Handicrafts (1928) and Provisional Regulation of Rewards for Industrial Technique (1932), see Zheng H. R., 'The patent system of the People's Republic of China'. 21 *University of San Francisco Law Review* (1987) 345–392, and Liu D., 'Now the wolf has indeed come! Perspective on the patent protection of biotechnology invention in China'. 53 Winter *American Journal of Comparative Law* 207 (2005).

7 For example, the Provisional Regulations on the Protection of Invention Rights and Patent Rights were enacted in 1950. It was supplemented by a set of Provisional Regulations on Awards for Inventions, Technical Improvements and Rationalisation Proposals Concerning Production which were issued in 1954.

8 Patent protection measures were struck off by Regulations to Encourage Inventions and Regulations to Encourage Improvements in Technology, which were both enacted in 1963. By virtue of Art.23 of the Regulations to Encourage Inventions, 'all inventions are the property of the State: all enterprises (both state-owned and collectives) are free to make use of them when they think fit.'

In the wake of the Cultural Revolution, China launched the campaign of the Four Modernisations, including the modernisation of industry, science and technology[9], since the country was determined to catch up with the world's advanced technologies. In fact, for one hundred years until the end of 1970s when the Cultural Revolution came to an end, Cathay, the giant in the East, was embroiled endlessly in rebellions, revolutions, wars and various campaigns without interruption. Once the country woke up from all the nightmares, especially the devastating Cultural Revolution, the world was already advancing with an accelerating speed and left China with a broken economy lagging far behind. In 1976, amidst the political and natural disasters,[10] and although China tried to cut imports due to the sluggish economy and financial difficulties,[11] the country bought several large plants in the spring, including the Krupp-Koppers Chemical Plant and the Toray polyester polymerisation factory. China also purchased compressor technology from Italy and helicopters from West Germany. But the most innovative deals were three large computers from Hitachi and a Japanese iron ore pelletising plant. It should be noted that importing foreign technology was very much a taboo in the political climate in China at the time when the Communist dogma was reigning over every corner of the society. Contacting the West could be condemned as treason. This general atmosphere of fear was aggravated at the end of the Cultural Revolution by the political struggle between the radicals and the moderates when the later were accused of being subservient to the Western capitalists. Against this historical backdrop, China's desire to acquire new technologies originated from a certain faction of the leadership that was nonetheless adamant that it took the risk of departing from its Communist dogma.

Since then, the abolished regulations on patent protection were gradually reinstated, leading eventually to the promulgation of the Patent Law in 1984.[12]

II) Patent Law 1984 and the three patent law amendments

1. Patent Law 1984

In 1984, China promulgated its first modern-day patent law to provide protection to inventions, utility models and designs. The huge efforts made to create the first patent legislation were evident. For example, the full patent laws of 35 jurisdictions were translated

9 The campaign of the Four Modernisations was launched after China pledged its ambition to achieve world-class strength in agriculture, industry, science, technology and national defence by the end of the twentieth century.

10 In January 1976 the then Premier Zhou Enlai passed away, followed by Chairman Mao Zedong's death in September. The intensified power struggle between the radicals and the moderates culminated when the Gang of Four were captured and charged with a series of treasonous crimes in October. On 27 July, the deadly Tangshan earthquake took place. A death toll as high as 650,000 was reported, in what is believed to be the largest earthquake of the twentieth century.

11 In 1976, based on estimates, China had a hard currency surplus of a few hundred million dollars at most. Imports were down 15 per cent below those of 1975. At the end of 1976, China shipped 80 tons of gold (worth about 350 million USD) to London, only some of which was sold right away. In the same year, due to a poor harvest, China spent about 550 million USD (489 million EUR) on grain imports for delivery in 1977. MacDougall C., 'The Chinese economy in 1976'. No. 77 *The China Quarterly* (June 1977), pp. 366–367.

12 The Patent Law was promulgated to '… protect patent rights for invention-creations, encourage invention-creations and facilitate their popularisation and application, promote the development of science and technology and meet the needs of the socialist modernisation'. See: Art.1, Patent Law 1984.

and those of more than 100 other nations were summarised for reference purposes. The legislation and the practice of the Nationalist Chinese, both on the mainland prior to 1949 and in Taiwan, were equally scrutinised as was the experience of Hong Kong. In the meantime, China sent envoys with varied backgrounds to foreign patent offices and international organisations, such as the WIPO, to study and conduct research on their practice on patent management.[13]

The Patent Law 1984 was nonetheless promulgated without the legal and theoretical foundation that it ought to have. As a Communist country, China's Constitution did not recognise, and therefore no protection was offered to, private property ownership. Rights and protection of private property ownership became constitutional only in 2004 when the country's Constitution was amended for the fourth time.[14] At that time, the country's patent law had already completed its second amendment, which took place in 2000. Patent, and IPR at large, is in essence a form of private property rights. It is certainly the opposite of the collective property ownership that is the cornerstone of communism, upon which China has been built since 1949. Nonetheless, patent protection found its strong foothold in China's then newly established development model of 'socialist commodity economy', which was proclaimed by the Decision of the Central Committee of the Communist Party of China on Reform of the Economic Structure and adopted by the Third Plenary Meeting of the Central Committee of the Communist Party on 20 October 1984. The fundamentals of the new economic model were that central state supervision was to be restricted to the enactment of general guiding principles, while enterprises should have exclusive disposition over the commodities entrusted to them. Real and property-like disposition rights were therefore promptly acknowledged, because the former was able to fall into the hands of collective enterprises which became the 'owner' of their resources, while the latter found its way to settle among state enterprises, which were enterprises of the whole people, and this exercise was then translated as the right of 'holder-ship' meaning the right to dispose of something that belonged to the whole people. This new development theory was eventually extended to intangible subject matters.[15] Thanks to this successful transformation of ideology, intellectual property, including patents, was integrated into the new socialist development model while the Chinese legislature managed to render protection to IPR in China. Subsequently, when the General Principle of Civil Law was promulgated in 1986, Arts.94–97 established civil and property ownership and protection, including IPR protection. Having said the above, the theoretical transformation came from academics and most likely stayed with academics. Whether the efforts succeeded in making an indelible imprint on Chinese society was doubtful. In any event, without constitutional support and with the deeply ingrained

13 For example, in 1983, China and Germany concluded an inter-governmental agreement on the Project of Promotion of the Patent System of the People's Republic of China. Based on the agreement, Germany assisted China in training examination personnel and in the construction of a patent documentation database. Ganea P., 'Patents, utility models and designs' in C. Heath C. (Ed.) *Intellectual Property Law in China* (New York: Kluwer Law International, 2005), p. 4.

14 China's current Constitution was adopted by the Fifth National People's Congress on 4 December 1982, with further revisions in 1988, 1993, 1999 and 2004. Article 13 of the Constitution 2004 stipulates that 'the state protects the right of citizens to own lawfully earned income, savings, houses and other lawful property. The state protects by law the right of citizens to inherit private property'.

15 Ganea P., 'Patents, utility models and designs' in C. Heath C. (Ed.) *Intellectual Property Law in China* (New York: Kluwer Law International, 2005), pp. 4–5.

ideology of collective property ownership embedded in society for almost four decades, the legal conception of IPR protection passed without being noticed amidst the many drastic societal changes that the nation overwhelmingly plunged into after the end of the Cultural Revolution.

Moreover, during the Cultural Revolution between 1966 and 1976, people lived with only the bare essentials, while private properties that were legacies acquired prior to 1949, such as factories and real properties, were either nationalised or confiscated. To some extent Chinese citizens feared owning any properties as that would invite the accusation of being a capitalist roader, in which case punishment was a likely event. Therefore, enforcing IPR protection in China has been a far more complicated endeavour than promulgating a piece of legislation. This provides an additional reason why weaker IPR enforcement in China is such a persistent ailment.

Unlike the previous patent regulations, the Patent Law 1984 was a complete piece of legislation of patent protection but the signature of absolute state control was nonetheless evident. For example, the legislation provided two scenarios upon which 'compulsory exploitation of patents' may be instructed. One of the scenarios was 'licencing according to the state plan'.[16] Under this scenario, a competent authority under the State Council or under a People's Government at provincial level had the authority to instruct a patent holder to transfer the patent rights to another entity if the state required this. At that time, China was transforming its economy and the private sector started to emerge and was permitted to join the state sector in economic activities, although the latter had much easier access to policies and facilities such as financial aid. 'Licence according to the state plan' reflected the beginning of the co-existence of both sectors in the same market, when the private sector was permitted to operate but under the government's keen supervision and property may be seized if the government deemed it necessary.

16 By virtue of Art.52 of the Patent Law 1984, the 'domestic working' requirement was the second scenario in which a compulsory licence may be issued. In this scenario, a compulsory licence may be issued if a patent holder, or an authorised person, failed to exploit the patent in question by manufacturing patented product or making use of the patented process in China within three years after the patent was granted.

The 'domestic working' requirement has existed since the 1800s. After the Paris Convention came into force in 1883, the 'domestic working' requirement continued to exist in many countries although it was against the principle of the national treatment enshrined in the Convention. In addition to the national treatment, Art.5A(4) of the Paris Convention states that, if a patent holder failed or insufficiently worked a patented invention without any legitimate reason, a compulsory licence would be issued within three years after the patent was first granted. The 'domestic working' requirement was abolished by many countries when the TRIPS Agreement came into force in 1995. Under Art.27 (1) of the TRIPS Agreement, patent rights shall be enjoyable without discrimination as to whether products are imported or locally produced. Nonetheless, some countries, such as India and Brazil, still retain the requirement in order to ensure that the domestic industries may continue to exploit foreign technologies.

The US brought Brazil to the WTO Dispute Settlement Body on 30 May 2000 because of Brazil's Industrial Property Law (Law No. 9,279 of 14 May 1996, effective May 1997) and other related measures that established the 'local working' requirement in order for the exchange of enjoyment of the exclusive patent rights. Under Brazil's patent laws, the 'local working' requirement could only be satisfied by the local production – and not the import – of the patented subject matter. More specifically, the 'local working' requirement stipulated that a patent should be subject to compulsory licensing if the subject matter of the patent was not 'worked' in the territory of Brazil. The US alleged that such requirements were in violation of Arts.27 and 28 of the TRIPS Agreement, as well as Art.III of the GATT 1994. However, the US dropped its complaint against Brazil on 5 July 2001. The answer as to whether 'local requirement' is consistent with Art.27 of the TRIPS Agreement is therefore left unanswered. See: Brazil – Measures Affecting Patent Protection. Available at: www.wto.org/english/tratop_e/dispu_e/cases_e/ds199_e.htm (last accessed 2 May 2016).

The Patent Law 1984 provided protection for inventions, utility models and designs. Conditions for granting a patent were novelty, inventiveness and usefulness.[17] The grace period was set for six months, during which time an invention would not be deemed as having lost its novelty although disclosure may have already taken place. The Patent Law provided three circumstances under which a grace period may be granted. The three circumstances were: disclosure at an exhibition sponsored or recognised by the Chinese government; disclosure in consequence of an abuse; and disclosure at a prescribed academic or technical conference. The first two kinds of disclosure are known as non-prejudicial disclosure while the last kind is known as lawful non-prejudicial disclosure other than at an exhibition, or general grace period. It is noticed that the six-month grace period, as well as the three circumstances under which a grace period may be granted in China, have been consistently upheld under each of the three patent law amendments that took place later. The same measures are maintained by the Draft Patent Law 2015.

The Patent Law 1984 adopted the first-to-file principle, stating that when two or more applications of the same invention-creation were filed by different applicants, the patent should be granted to the first applicant.[18] The Patent Law 1984 also asserted the 'work-for-hire' principle, for which an employee's patent application would automatically belong to the employer.[19] Under the Patent Law 1984, non-patentable subject matters were food, beverages and condiments, pharmaceutical products as well as substances obtained by means of a chemical process.[20] Invention patents were awarded a protection term of 15 years and patents for utility models and designs five years, counting from the date of filing in both cases.[21]

Statistics reveal that, during the seven and a half years between April 1985 and September 1992 when the Patent Law 1984 was in force, more than 284,000 patent applications were received, including 40,000 foreign applications representing 65 jurisdictions. Among the total applications, two-thirds were utility model and design patents.[22]

In the 1980s patent rights enforcement was weak. On the one hand, as mentioned before, the public awareness of IPR protection at large was seriously low and, on the other hand, at that time, a competent patent enforcement mechanism was not ready since, after all, China had just started its course of re-establishing a judicial system. Again, this was a legacy of the Cultural Revolution, when higher education was abandoned which resulted in the loss of a whole generation of legal professionals. In parallel, since being innocent or guilty was decided by the Communist Party, the legal profession became redundant in China and therefore legal professionals of the older generations were all compelled to change their job to become factory workers or peasants instead. For this reason, as a solution, when a series of elementary laws were enacted one after another in the wake of the Cultural Revolution, retired army officers joined the judiciary and were entrusted with the responsibility for enforcement. Another quick fix to remedy the lack of judicial capacity was to rely heavily upon administrative enforcement, when enforcement personnel required less legal competence and, in case there were miscarriages of 'justice', judicial enforcement could still be available for rectification, as is explained in the previous chapter.

17 Art.22, Patent Law 1984.
18 Art.9, Patent Law 1984.
19 Art.6(1), Patent Law 1984.
20 Art.25, Patent Law 1984.
21 Art.45, Patent Law 1984.
22 Zhou, Y., 'Foreign patent filings lag behind domestic increase'. *China Daily*, 12 April (1992).

Under the Patent Law 1984, enforcement measures also seemed hesitant since the scope for protection was narrow. For example, by virtue of Art.62(2) of the Patent Law 1984, if an infringement act took place 'without knowledge…', then no liability for infringement would be found. In a similar vein, by virtue of Art.62(3) of the same law, continuing to use or to manufacture a similar product after a patent application was submitted was not an infringement, as long as the use or the manufacturing of the similar product had already started before the application was submitted. As a result in the 1980s many ambiguous acts bordering on patent infringement were left without punishment in China.

IPR enforcement was undertaken by an administrative-judicial dual enforcement mechanism, as was stipulated by Art.60 of the Patent Law 1984. It is noted that the procedure of compulsory enforcement was a component of administrative enforcement, in order to safeguard the enforceability of administrative orders. As a result, if a party neither appealed against an administrative order nor complied with it, the administrative enforcement body could apply for compulsory enforcement of the order at a people's court.[23] Overall, the administrative enforcement measures provided by the Patent Law 1984 appeared inadequate, since the only available measures were ceasing the infringement act and awarding compensation for loss incurred as a result of an infringement act.[24]

2. *Patent Law 1992*

China's first patent law amendment took place in 1992 and is often seen as a result of the conclusion of the Sino-US Trade Negotiation and Memorandum of Undertaking (1992).

The progress that the Patent Law 1992 achieved included: 1) chemicals, pharmaceutical products, food, beverages and flavourings became patentable subject matters;[25] 2) using, selling and importing the products directly obtained from a patented process without authorisation of the patent holder became liable for infringement; 3) stricter conditions for granting compulsory licences; 4) an extended protection term for invention patents from 15 to 20 years and for utility model and design patents from five to ten years; and 5) established border measures for IPR enforcement.[26]

These improved patent protection measures led China, a developing country whose patent system was established less than a decade ago at that time, to become one of the global forerunners of patent protection in terms of patent legislation. Note that the US extended its patent protection term from 17 to 20 years in the same year, 1992, as China did, and Japan only started to provide invention patents with a 20-year protection term in 1995, one year after its WTO accession. When pharmaceutical products became a patentable subject matter in China as early as 1992, India, though equally a developing country

23 Art.60, Patent Law 1984.

24 Art.60, Patent Law 1984.

25 Exceptions to patentability included 'scientific discoveries, rules and methods of intellectual activities, diagnostic and therapeutic methods for the treatment of diseases, animals and plant varieties as well as materials obtained by means of nuclear transformation'. Art.25, Patent Law 1992.

26 Other measures that China undertook for better IPR protection included: 1) the Anti-unjust Competition Law was promulgated in 1993 to protect trade secrets; 2) granting administrative protection for chemicals and pharmaceuticals patented in the US from 1 January 1986 to 1 January 1993; and 3) other measures to protect copyright protection. See: Lin B. *et al.*, *Overview of Chinese Patent Law*, 35th International Congress of the PIPA, 19–22 October, Toyama, Japan (2004).

and a founding member of the WTO, did not provide the same protection until 2005, after the ten-year transitional arrangements prescribed by TRIPS duly expired.

Changes brought by the Patent Law 1992 with regard to the conditions for granting compulsory licence were significant. Compared with the Patent Law 1984, the Patent Law 1992 provided two more grounds for granting a compulsory licence. Under Art.51 of the Patent Law 1992, it became possible to grant a compulsory licence when 'any entity' failed to obtain an authorisation for exploitation from an invention or a utility model patent holder within a reasonable period of time. Since then, a national emergency or an extra-ordinary state of affairs may also warrant a compulsory licence.[27] In the meantime, the 'domestic working' requirement was abolished by the Patent Law 1992, while certain prerequisites *vis-à-vis* compulsory licences prescribed by the Patent Law 1984 were upheld by the Patent Law 1992. These prerequisites included: 'a compulsory licence applicant must prove that it has not been able to conclude a licencing contract with the patent holder on reasonable terms…' (Art.54); 'a granted compulsory licence must be registered and publically announced…' (Art.55); and 'any entity or individual granted a compulsory licence shall not have an exclusive right to exploit…' (Art.56). In retrospect, these provisions regarding compulsory licence brought about by China's Patent Law 1992 were very close to the requirements later set down by the TRIPS Agreement.

With regard to patent enforcement, unlike the Patent Law 1984 which failed to provide precise measures *vis-à-vis* infringement sanctions, Art.78 of the Implementing Rules of Patent Law 1992 made a slight improvement and stipulated that patent passing off would be fined between 1,000–50,000 RMB (135–6,726 EUR), or up to three times the illegal gains.

3. *Patent Law 2000*

China's second Patent Law amendment came into force in 2000, in the run up to the country's WTO accession that took place a year later.[28] The Patent Law 2000 was in full compliance with the TRIPS Agreement even ahead of China's acceding to the WTO Agreement and, in any event, China pledged to implement the TRIPS Agreement in full from the date of accession.[29] In this respect, the country decided to forego altogether the transitional arrangements that the TRIPS Agreement offers to developing countries and transitional economies.

As the patent protection measures provided by the first amendment in 1992 were nearing full compliance with the TRIPS Agreement, the developments made by the Patent Law 2000 were primarily to do with enforcement. For example, the Patent Law 2000 provided two new enforcement sanctions. First, the administrative enforcement authority was able to, from then on, confiscate illegal gains obtained as a result of patent infringement. Second, with respect to judicial enforcement, Art.60 stipulated that damages would be assessed on

27 Art.52, Patent Law 1992.

28 According to China's WTO Accession Protocol, China is obliged to administer its laws in a uniform, impartial and reasonable manner and to ensure transparency while legislating. China also pledged to amend its IP laws in order to bring full compliance with, and full application of, the TRIPS Agreement. In terms of IPR protection, China pledged to enhance IPR enforcement through the application of more effective administrative sanctions. See: Accession of the People's Republic of China, WT/L/432, 23 November 2001.

29 See: World Trade Organization, 'WTO successfully concludes negotiations on China's entry', Press Release, *WTO Press*/243, 17 September 2001. Available at: www.wto.org/english/news_e/pres01_e/pr243_e.htm (last accessed 20 December 2015).

the basis of the loss suffered by the patent holder or the profit gained by the infringer as a result of the infringement act. When it was difficult to determine the loss suffered or the profit gained, damages would be assessed 'by reference to the appropriate multiple of the amount of the exploitation fee of that patent under contractual licence'. The competence of the administrative authorities was defined for the first time by the Implementing Rules of the Patent Law 2010. Article 85 of the Implementing Rules provided that the administrative enforcement authorities were competent to mediate disputes in respect of rights to application and ownership, inventor or designer's eligibility, the rewards or the incentives concerning service invention, the remuneration for invention exploitation taking place after a patent application was published and before it was granted, etc.

The Patent Law 2000 introduced the procedure of consultation as far as dispute was concerned. By virtue of Art.57, when a dispute arose as a result of a patent infringement, the disputing parties should first try to settle it through consultation. In a case where the disputing parties were not willing to conduct a consultation or when consultation failed, the patent holder or any interested party could either institute legal proceedings or request that a patent administrative authority handle the dispute.

The Patent Law 2000 empowered the patent administrative authorities to mediate the compensation amount between the disputing parties. If mediation failed, the parties may resort to court proceedings.[30] In parallel, the new competence entrusted to judicial enforcement was that a people's court from then on has become competent to impose injunction measures and order property preservation.[31] Article 61 provided that a patent holder may apply for an injunction order and property preservation in court if the patent holder could prove that, without these measures, irreparable damages would take place as a result of the infringement act. In June 2001 the Supreme Court Interpretation clarified that, when applying for an injunction order, a bond must be provided and that, after the order is issued, a formal complaint must be filed in court within 15 days.

The Patent Law 2000 provided avenues for judicial review. The Patent Re-examination Board was established in order to handle re-examination and invalidation applications. From then on, a patent applicant was able to submit an appeal application at the Patent Re-examination Board should the patent application fail.[32] If ever a patent holder or any interested party is not satisfied with the Board's decision, they may institute legal proceedings at a people's court to challenge the decision.[33] The Patent Law 2000 also brought fairness to alleged infringers. Article 57 provided that, if not satisfied with the order to cease the infringement act issued by the administrative enforcement authority, the alleged infringer could institute legal proceedings in a people's court to challenge the desist order within 15 days of receiving the notification.

Equally ground-breaking in the evolution of China's patent legislation was that the Patent Law 2000 set down the precise amount of administrative fines that an administrative authority may impose against patent passing off. Article 58 of the Patent Law 2000 prescribed that a fine of no more than 50,000 RMB (6,809 EUR) may be imposed for the loss incurred as a result of a patent infringement. The previous two patent legislations were completely silent on the issue.

30 Art.57, Patent Law 2000.
31 Art.61, Patent Law 2000.
32 Art.41, Patent Law 2000.
33 Art.46, Patent Law 2000.

The Patent Law 2000 broadened the scope of protection for invention and utility model patents. For example, by virtue of Art.11, patent holders in China are provided with the right to prevent others from 'offering to sale' patented products or products obtained directly from a patented process.[34] This is fully in line with Art.28.1(a)(b) of the TRIPS Agreement. Likewise, thanks to Art.63 of the Patent Law 2000, the use or the sale of an infringed patented product has become an unequivocal infringement act irrespective of the knowledge of the user or the seller; the defence of 'good faith' was superseded from then on. As a result, since the Patent Law 2000 came into force, in order to overturn an infringement liability occurred when the use or the sale was unauthorised, the defendant must prove that the source of the product is legitimate. Notwithstanding this, despite the fact that Patent Law 2000 started to sanction the use and the sale of infringed patented products in 'good faith', it continued refraining from laying down any measure for punishment. Rule 84 of the Implementing Rules of the Patent Law 2001 stated that, if the source of the infringed patented products was proven lawful, the administrative enforcement authority should order the cessation of sales, but fines would not be imposed. This position remains the same under the Implementing Rules of the Patent Law 2010.

The Patent Law 2000 made two further improvements on compulsory licences. First, in line with Art.31 of the TRIPS Agreement with regard to dependent patent, 'important technological advance' and 'considerable economic significance' were laid down as the two prerequisites before a compulsory licence may be granted while, under the Patent Law 1992, being 'technologically more advanced' was sufficient under the same circumstances. Second, the lifespan of a compulsory licence was restricted. Article 52 of the Patent Law 2000 required that, while granting a compulsory licence, the scope and duration of exploitation must be specified on the basis of the reasons justifying the grant. Once such a justification ceased to exist and was unlikely to recur, the compulsory licence would be terminated.

Therefore, when reading Chapter VI of the Patent Law 2000 and Art.72 of the Implementing Rules of the Patent Law 2000 together, conditions for granting a compulsory licence prescribed by China's patent legislation were now in full compliance with the minimum standards set down by the TRIPS Agreement.

4. *Patent Law 2008*

The third amendment of China's Patent Law entered into force in December 2008 and it is still in force at the time of writing. It is noticed that, after China met its obligation of fully implementing the TRIPS Agreement, the country's third patent law amendment shifted its focus and started to emphasise the stimulation of domestic innovation by using patent protection as an engine.[35] The most noticeable change in this regard is that patent application is encouraged and facilitated while, on the other hand, the threshold test for novelty has become higher. Patent enforcement measures are also strengthened, with

34 Art.11, Patent Law 2000.

35 For example, the Seventeenth National Congress of the Communist Party issued the Outline of National Intellectual Property Strategy (2008) with the aim of 'improving China's capacity to create, utilise, protect and administer intellectual property making China an innovative country and attaining the goal of building a moderately prosperous society in all respects'. See: State Council of the People's Republic of China, *Outline of the National Intellectual Property Strategy*, issued by the State Council of the People's Republic of China, 5 June 2008.

increased administrative fines and higher compensation amounts for the loss incurred as a result of an infringement act. Changes are also made in relation to granting a compulsory licence for manufacturing patented drugs for export on the grounds of public health.[36] In addition, with regard to patentability, the Patent Law 2008 has made clear that inventions that violate social ethics and that are accomplished by relying on genetic resources obtained unlawfully will not be patentable.[37]

To facilitate patent application, the enabling measures are clear in the following aspects. By virtue of Art.19 of the Patent Law 2008, Chinese as well as foreign patent applicants who have no residential or business address in China can now appoint an eligible patent agent of their own choice to handle applications and other patent-related matters. Under the Patent Law 2000 only a patent agent designated by the patent administration authority under the State Council was qualified to act as patent agent. Second, when applying for a patent abroad for an invention or a utility model accomplished in China, the two requirements with regard to Chinese-patent-application-first and 'engaging a designated patent agent' were abolished, although such applications must still pass a confidentiality review first under Art.20 of the Patent Law 2008.[38] The procedural requirement of a confidentiality review is often misunderstood by some as China's protectionist move *vis-à-vis* home-created invention and utility model patent applications filed abroad. What is less known is that Art.73(b) of the TRIPS Agreement permits members to take necessary action in order to protect its essential security interests and this provision is incorporated in other patent jurisdiction as well. For example, the US conducts security reviews under the same circumstances. It is worth mentioning that, on the other hand, the requirement for a confidentiality review in Art.20 of the Patent Law 2008 is less cumbersome than that prescribed by Patent Law 2000 although, in the past, utility model patent applications filed abroad were not required to undergo a security scrutiny, this has now changed under the Patent Law 2008. Article 20 of China's Patent Law 2000 required that, if an invention-creation was made in China before the inventor filed a patent application in a foreign country, the inventor must first apply for a patent in China and engage a designated patent agent and, in the meantime, undergo a security check in accordance with Art.4 of the same law. Currently it takes six months to complete a confidentiality review before an invention or a utility model patent application may be filed abroad. The Draft Patent Law 2015 upholds the same position.

The Patent Law 2008 sets a higher threshold test for novelty. While previously 'relative novelty' sufficed to pass the test, by virtue of Art.22 of the Patent Law 2008 'absolute novelty' has now become the threshold. This means that any prior patent application filed for any identical invention or utility model, and any identical invention or utility model recorded or documented that is published or announced after the application date in China, will destroy the novelty of the invention or utility model and it will be disqualified from obtaining a patent grant. The Patent Law 2008 did not make any change in relation to the threshold test for 'non-obviousness' as well as for 'practical applicability'. This means that an invention must possess the qualities of 'prominent substantive features' and 'remarkable advancements', while a utility model must prove 'substantive features and progress', before the 'non-obviousness' test may be satisfied. To pass the test of 'practical

36 Art.50, Patent Law 2008.

37 Art.5, Patent Law 2008.

38 Art.71 of the Patent Law 2008 further sets down that if Art.20 is violated, and if state secrets are divulged, the violator will be subject to administrative sanction and criminal liability may become applicable.

applicability', an invention or a utility model must be able to be put into practical use and to produce effective results. Article 22 of the Patent Law 2008 has further clarified the term 'existing technology' as those technologies known to the general public both at home and abroad prior to the date of patent application.

The threshold test for patentability *vis-à-vis* design patents is further raised by the Patent Law 2008. With regard to 'novelty', Art.23 engages an approach similar to the 'absolute novelty' test that is applicable to invention and utility model patent applications. Article 23 prescribes that, to pass the 'novelty' test, a design must not be an 'existing design' but distinctly different from any existing applications filed for any identical designs prior to the application date of the design patent, and no identical design is recorded which may be announced after the date of application. As to a design patent application, the design must be 'distinctly different' from existing designs or the combinations of the features of existing designs which are 'designs that are known to the public both domestically and abroad before the date of application'. Under Art.23 of the Patent Law 2000, 'relative novelty', which suggests 'non-identical' or 'dissimilar', sufficed to pass the threshold test for patentability for a design patent application. However, the question of 'non-obviousness' is still left unanswered under the Patent Law 2008.

Compared with its previous amendment, patent infringement is more seriously punished under the Patent Law 2008. Article 63 of the Patent Law 2008 raised the level of administrative fines up to four times the illegal gains or 200,000 RMB (26,789 EUR) if there are no illegal gains. In relation to Art.58 of the Patent Law 2000, the maximum administrative fines against patent infringement were up to three times the illegal gains or 50,000 RMB (6,698 EUR) if there were no illegal gains. Under the Patent Law 2008, and as far as judicial enforcement is concerned, the compensation amount is increased and set between 10,000 and 1 million RMB (1,340–133,963 EUR). Note that this is the first time that a compensation amount under judicial enforcement is specified in patent law. Article 65 of the Patent Law 2008 also provides more comprehensive methods for calculating compensation. It stipulates that when the loss caused by an infringing act is hard to determine, the amount of compensation may be calculated according to the reasonably multiplied amount of the royalties of the patent in question and should include the reasonable expenses paid by the patent holder for stopping the infringement act. Article 60 of the Patent Law 2000 did not allow for the right for compensation for expenses, nor did it specify the compensation amount levels.

Furthermore, the administrative enforcement authority is entrusted with new enforcement powers of investigation to fight against acts of patent passing off. Article 64 of Patent Law 2008 provides that the patent administrative authority may inquire into the parties concerned and investigate the circumstances related to the alleged illegal act. In particular, the administrative enforcement authority may: 1) conduct on-the-spot inspection of the places where the infringement act is committed; 2) consult and make copies of relevant contracts, invoices, account books and other related materials; 3) check the products related to the alleged infringement act; and 4) seal or detain the products that are proved to be produced by the infringed patent.

5. *Draft Patent Law 2015*

China's fourth patent law amendment seems a natural consequence of the country's rapid progress achieved in patent protection, especially in the recent years after China has become one of the biggest patent offices in the world, both domestically and internationally, in terms of patent application numbers. Under the policy direction of transforming the country's development model from export-led to innovation-driven, which was announced by the National Patent Development Strategy (2011–2020), legislative measures on facilitating knowledge transfer, commercialising innovation as well as strengthened enforcement are the focus of the second draft of the Patent Law 2015, published in December 2015. The SIPO conducted two public consultation exercises in 2015 to prepare for the fourth patent law amendment.

To promote innovation, the newly added Art.14 of the Draft Patent Law 2015 sets down the principle and stresses that exercising patent rights shall not unfairly eliminate or restrict competition or hinder technological progress. Also, for the first time in China's history of patent legislation, the definition of 'service invention' is given, which is an invention accomplished in the cause of carrying out an employee's duty. On the other hand, if an invention or design is achieved using an employer's materials and technical facilities, and in case there is no prior agreement concerning the ownership, the employee concerned will be the owner of the invention or design.[39] To facilitate knowledge dissemination, according to Art.21 of the Draft Patent Law 2015, the patent administration department under the State Council will be obliged to provide basic patent information data.

In relation to enforcement, which has always been a weaker aspect in patent protection in China, the Draft Patent Law 2015 provides the patent administration department with increased competence, and this has been a continued effort seen in each patent law amendment. By virtue of Art.60 of the Draft Patent Law 2015, the patent administration department will be empowered to investigate and to deal with group infringement and repeated infringement aimed at disrupting the market order. In the event that an infringement and the facts of disturbing the market order are established, the patent administration department may order the infringer to cease the infringement act immediately and confiscate or destroy the infringing products, components and all tools used for the infringement act. Moreover, for repeated patent infringement, the patent administration department may impose a fine of up to five times the illegal gains should the illegal gains exceed 50,000 RMB (7,000 EUR), or a fine of not more than 250,000 RMB (35,000 EUR) may be imposed if there are no illegal gains or the illegal gains are less than 50,000 RMB (7,000 EUR). Criminal liability may be pursued at the same time.[40] Overall, the amount of administrative fines and judicial compensation against patent infringement have both gone up considerably. For increased administrative fines against patent passing off, the amount of fines is at the same level as that set against repeated infringement as mentioned above.[41] As to judicial compensation, by virtue of Art.68 of the Draft Patent Law 2015 the court may impose up to three times the actual loss suffered by the patent holder or impose a fine on the basis of the profit the infringer gained through infringement. If it is difficult to determine the amount of the loss or the profit, the court may impose between 100,000 and 5 million RMB (14,000–700,000 EUR) as a compensation award, which is a fivefold increase on what the Patent Law 2008 provided.

By virtue of Art.61 of the Draft Patent Law 2015, the patent administration department will be empowered to mediate the amount of compensation for the damages caused by patent infringement. Enforceability of such an agreement is guaranteed since the court may

39 Art.6, Draft Patent Law 2015.
40 Art.60, Draft Patent Law 2015.
41 Art.66, Draft Patent Law 2015.

intervene for compulsory execution. Moreover, the Draft Patent Law 2015 provides the patent administration department with absolute authority while discharging its duties. By virtue of Art.67, when the patent administration department is exercising its authority in enforcement, full cooperation from the parties concerned is obligatory, otherwise warnings may be issued and any violation to public security measures will be dealt with and criminal liability may be pursued.

A few new infringing acts will be dealt with by the Draft Patent Law 2015 and for which joint liability may be applied. Under the newly added Art.62 of the Draft Patent Law 2015, whoever knowingly provides raw materials, intermediate components, apparatus, etc. for patent infringement will bear joint liability with the infringer. Equally, whoever actively induces an infringer to infringe will also bear joint liability with the infringer. For a patent infringement committed via internet services, the internet service provider will bear joint liability with the internet user if the former fails to stop the infringement with necessary measures such as deleting, shielding or disconnecting the link to the infringing products.[42]

Other changes are also proposed by the Draft Patent Law 2015. For example, the scope for patentability has become narrower in the case of nuclear transformation methods, which now will fall under the exceptions to patentability.[43] Also, the protection term for design patents is extended from 10 to 15 years.[44] As to the 'right of priority', the draft amendment provides that design patent applications filed in a foreign country or at home will be from now on entitled to a six-month period during which time the right of priority may be claimed.[45] Previously, only invention or utility model patent applications enjoyed the right of priority of 12 months if prior and later patents are both filed in China, but the question of the 'right of priority' concerning design patent applications filed in China for the first time was not answered. Additionally, by virtue of Art.63 of the Draft Patent Law 2015, a patent infringement committed via the internet will be dealt with from now on. If the internet service provider knows or should have known that an internet user infringes upon patent rights by utilising the internet services that the provider provides, the internet service provider has the responsibility of taking swift measures by, for example, deleting, shielding or disconnecting the link to the infringing products, in order to stop the online patent infringement and to enforce patent rights within its online network. Otherwise, the internet service provider shall bear joint liability with the network user, who is the online infringer, for the infringement act.

The Draft Patent Law 2015 adds a whole new chapter on the exploitation and the utilisation of patent when, for example, the patent administration department at all levels is required to promote the exploitation and the utilisation of patent, to encourage and regulate the services of marketing patent information and the activities of patent operation.[46] Also, service patents may be 'liberated' from governmental research and higher learning institutes so that an invention or a design patent holder may exploit the patent on his own or licence others to exploit the patent and enjoy corresponding rights and benefits.[47]

42 Art.63, Draft Patent Law 2015.
43 Art.25, Draft Patent Law 2015.
44 Art.42, Draft Patent Law 2015.
45 Art.29, Draft Patent Law 2015.
46 Art.79, Draft Patent Law 2015.
47 Art.81, Draft Patent Law 2015.

A patent holder may equally declare that the patent is to be exploited by someone else with specified licencing fees and the patent administration department shall then make an announcement to this effect.[48]

III Conclusion

Reflecting on the evolution of China's patent law development, the following observations can be made.

During a short period of three decades only, China has situated itself in the forefront of patent rights protection worldwide in terms of legislation since 1992 when the country's first patent law amendment was published. After having gone through four amendments, patent enforcement measures have been much strengthened and, in particular, the administrative enforcement mechanism is provided with increased enforcement power, more predictability and enforceability. In each of the amendments, the levels of administrative fines and judicial compensation have been on the rise consistently over the decades.

From the very beginning of the law-making, China's patent legislation has shown high compatibility with international protection standards, which indeed appears unusual given the country's unfamiliarity with the patent system, its strict communist background in the early 1980s that disapproved of private property ownership, as well as other disadvantageous societal factors such as the legacy of the Cultural Revolution. The promulgation of each patent law amendment, with the fourth amendment still under draft at the time of writing, was motivated by the policy adjustments that took place alongside China's economic ambitions in different development stages: from attracting foreign investment to complying with the WTO accession obligations; from encouraging patent applications for nurturing an innovative economy to exploiting and commercialising patent to reap the economic gains accrued from the system, because China is now one of the world's biggest patent offices in terms of application numbers.

China is very determined, almost single-minded, in implementing an effective patent system. The country started to implement a patent system when the fundamentals were missing. China did not insist on enjoying the privileges that the TRIPS Agreement affords to developing countries or transitional economies, although certain sectors in China could have had a ten-year grace period before having to be exposed to the minimum patent protection standards imposed by the TRIPS Agreement. In these ways the course of the Chinese patent protection, which is itself a process of international patent rights harmonisation, marks a total contrast to the patent legislation development that took place in Japan and in India.

48 Art.82, Draft Patent Law 2015.

7 Patent policy and legislation

Japan v. China

The evolution of patent rights enforcement in Japan reflects a strong coordination between industrial policy and patent legislation in order to incentivise innovation for economic development. Patent is an effective driver in this process. From being technology-dependent, Japan has risen to become an innovation giant as well as one of the world's leading economies within a century. As Zenji Kumagai, former Commissioner of the Japan Patent Office (JPO), pointed out: 'the significance of the patent system for the development of the Japanese economy is obvious, when one considers that 60 per cent of Japan's economic growth after the end of World War II is considered to be attributable directly to technological progress, and that most of the technology that Japan introduced from abroad was patented'.[1]

Patent strategies implemented in Japan and China share certain similarities. Both countries embarked on patent protection when foreign advanced technology was much needed for economic development purposes. In the course of patent law development in both countries, amendments are generally motivated by economic development needs. For example, China's campaign for popularising innovation activities by facilitating utility model patent applications echo the Japanese tactics of encouraging incremental and sequential patents for the same policy objective. Obviously, in both countries, protecting inventors' limited monopoly rights in exchange for their disclosure of information on invention does not appear to be the sole objective for enforcing patent rights. Instead, the major objective looks to be fostering a knowledge-based economy in order to achieve sustainable growth for industrial progress. In this context, patent is a driver for economic development rather than a form of private property right. In Japan's case, especially in the early days of its patent law evolution, patent holders' rights were subservient to public good and collective interest. For example, based on the mechanism of patent certification trial, patent scope was determined by disclosure revealed at the time of application rather than by patent claim *per se*. As a result of the narrowly construed patent scope, minor technological modification would warrant a new patent grant while allegation of patent infringement would be difficult to sustain. Consequently, patent turnaround gained faster pace, innovative dynamics were achieved and innovative activities popularised, especially among small- and medium-sized enterprises because they were able to participate in innovation.

1 For detailed development of Japan's patent laws, see Rahn G., 'The role of industrial property in economic development: the Japanese experience'. 14 *International Review of Industrial Property and Copyright Law* 449 (1983).

In Japan, granting a patent is to confirm rights, which means an applicant makes a request for patent grant and the government confirms that the applicant has the limited exclusive rights of exploitation if all the requirements are met.[2]

I Introduction

Japan's patent law development, from the beginning until 1993, before the country became a member of the TRIPS Agreement, presents a unique perspective on how implementing an effective patent system has facilitated the take-off of an entire economy. However, in the same breath, the patent protection measures implemented to achieve the economic goals were not without controversy. For example, certain provisions were criticised for facilitating patent exploitation, including absorbing, transferring and diffusing foreign inventive achievements,[3] at the expense of patent protection.[4] Early disclosure of patent application and a lengthened application process were also tactics which contributed to the reasons for blame. The Japanese patent legislation was in the meantime branded protectionist against foreign patent applicants. However, these controversial provisions were abolished one after another because of the changing landscape of the country's industrial development. New patent protection measures were adopted progressively together with the country's rapid technological advancement until the Japanese patent legislation was in full compliance with the TRIPS Agreement in 1995.

The Japanese patent legislation consists of Patent Law and the Utility Model Law. Technological ideas of a higher level that utilise natural laws are protected under the Patent Law, while devices, which are also technological ideas utilising natural laws but that do not satisfy requirements as a patent, are protected under the Utility Model Law.[5]

II Pre-TRIPS era

The Story of the United States Patent Office (1972), a book published by the US Department of Commerce (Patent Office), noted that, while in Washington studying the American patent system, Korekiyo Takahashi, the founder of the Japanese patent system and the 20th Prime Minister in 1921, famously said that 'we have looked about us to see what nations are the greatest, so that we can be like them… We said, "what is it that makes the United States such a great nation?" and we investigated and found that it was patents, and we will have patents'.

2 Cohen M., 'Japanese patent law and the WIPO Patent Law Harmonisation Treaty: a comparative analysis'. 4 *Fordham Intellectual Property Media and Entertainment Law Journal* 847 (1994).

3 For example, industrial design patents were only required to demonstrate novelty but not inventiveness. As a result, utility model and industrial design patents allowed Japanese firms to receive protection on technologies which were 'only slightly modified from the original invention'. See: Maskus K. E. and McDaniel C., 'Impacts of the Japanese patent system on productivity growth'. 11 *Japan and the World Economy* 4 (1999), 557–574. Other patent policies in this regard were, for example: the pre-grant disclosure for patent examination; inspection or opposition and, until 1988, each patent application was only allowed one single narrow claim. See: Kumar N., *Intellectual Property Rights, Technology and Economic Development: Experiences of Asian Countries*, Study Paper 1b commissioned by the Commission on Intellectual Property Rights as a background paper (CIPR, 2002).

4 It was even alleged that the Paris Convention as well as the Berne Convention were negotiated in order to counter the rampant infringement seen in Japan (and also in the US) at the time. See Maskus K. E., 'Strengthening intellectual property rights in Asia: implications for Australia'. 37 *Australia Economic Papers* 3 (1998), 347.

5 Doi T., *The Intellectual Property Law of Japan*. (Leyden: Sijthoff and Noordhoff, 1980), p. 1.

A patent system was introduced in Japan in 1885, during the Meiji Restoration when the country abolished the feudal system and embraced sweeping reforms under the Emperor Meiji. Among the many reform measures, the new government annulled the bilateral treaties of peace and amity with various countries that were concluded in the 1850s and 1860s because these treaties recognised the extra-territorial jurisdiction and other unequal conditions to Japan's detriment. Alongside this exercise, the establishment of a modern legal system, including a patent system, was accelerated.[6] Prior to this, during the feudal era, the Tokugawa shogunate (1603–1868) discouraged inventions by prohibiting manufacturing and the sale of new products. For example, in 1721, *Shinki Gohatto*, or a 'ban on novelty', was issued in order to prohibit manufacturing and the sale of everything novel, especially clothing of rich design.[7] In keeping with the reforms, Japan acceded to the Paris Convention in 1899. At the time, Japan was greatly inspired to catch up with the world's leading countries and the strategy it adopted was to acquire technology.

The Meiji government promulgated the Summary Rules of Monopoly in 1871, which was Japan's first patent legislation.[8] The law set down the principle that granting a patent required examination and that priority would be given to the first inventor but not the first applicant. The legislation was nonetheless suspended in the following year because the government was ill equipped to administer patent applications.[9] There were actually no governmental departments that were competent to examine patent applications nor were there any officials who were able to handle patent affairs. Such unpreparedness was no doubt a consequence of the previous feudal government's long-standing Tokugawa seclusion policy, which meant that Japanese society hardly understood the patent system.[10]

The subsequent Patent Monopoly Ordinance, which was published on 18 April 1885, was effectively enforced and thus Japanese patent history was inaugurated. The 18 April, the date of publication, has since been pronounced as the Invention Day in Japan. Unlike China, which looked at the German patent law for inspiration at the beginning of the country's patent law development, the Ordinance incorporated some legal features from the French and the American patent laws. Administered by the Ministry of Agriculture and Commerce, all new and useful processes or products were eligible to apply for invention patents under the Ordinance. In the same year after the Patent Monopoly Ordinance came into force, 425 patent applications were submitted and 99 patents were awarded. Zuisho Hotta was awarded the first patent for his invention of a 'method for rust-stopping paint and painting method'.[11] Enforcing patent rights aside, the Japanese society experienced 'explosive advances' during the period between

6 Ichikawa K., *The Japanese Patent System* (Tokyo: Nihon Hatsumei Shinbunsha, 1965) and Yoshifuji K. and Kumagai K., *Outline of the Patent Law*. (Tokyo: Yuhikaku, 1998), pp. 35–43.

7 Japanese Government, *A 70-Year History of the Patent System*, Patent Office (Tokyo: Hatsumei Kyôkai, 1955), p. 36.

8 Some academics argue that the Japanese pre-modern patent system dated back to between the third and fifth centuries when craftsmen distinguished themselves from farmers as independent professionals. For a detailed discussion on the pre-modern intellectual property systems in Japan, see: Takenaka T., 'Does a cultural barrier to intellectual property trade exist? The Japanese example'. 29 NYU *Journal of International Law and Politics* 153 (1997), 76.

9 The absence of a patent law caused inventors to lose out to imitators or they resorted to trade secret protection of their inventions. See: Doi T., *The Intellectual Property Law of Japan*. (Leyden: Sijthoff and Noordhoff, 1980), p. 3.

10 Kamagai K., *History of Japanese Industrial Property System*, a joint production of the Japanese Patent Office and the Asia-Pacific Industrial Property Centre (Tokyo: JPO/APIPC, 1999), pp. 3–4.

11 Doi T., *The Intellectual Property Law of Japan*. (Leyden: Sijthoff and Noordhoff, 1980), p. 4.

1872 and 1885, a period when extensive measures for modernisation were implemented. At that time, young Japanese by the thousands were sent abroad to study American railways, British textiles and metallurgy, as well as French and German laws.[12] 'Foreign mania raged everywhere, and everything was manufactured in imitation of foreign articles'.[13]

Mirroring the American patent law at the time, the 1885 Ordinance adopted the first-to-invent rule. Patent markings were mandatory on patented products; if he failed to do so, the patent holder in an infringement action was not allowed to recover damages from the infringer.[14] The requirement that a description specifying the scope of the invention must be included in an application was also an American concept.[15] Also, as French patent law prescribed, the Ordinance stated that patent of addition was recognisable. It provided a maximum protection term of 15 years, although five or ten years were also possible depending on the choice of a patent holder. If a patent holder suspended the working of the patented invention for more than two years without justification, or imported the products covered by the patent from foreign countries, the patent could be cancelled.[16] Additionally, the 1885 Ordinance required that the principle of examination be adopted. It also set down the prerequisites of patentability, such as novelty and usefulness, in order to qualify a patent award and stated that there could be only one invention per application. Inventions contrary to public order or related to pharmaceuticals were not patentable.[17]

The Patent Monopoly Ordinance 1885 is a milestone in the history of Japanese patent legislation advancement. While the failure of its predecessor was largely due to the institutional and cultural unpreparedness in the wake of the feudal era, when the Ordinance was promulgated, Japan was already fast adapting to the changing world after the first Industrial Revolution when hand-production methods were replaced by machines and new chemical manufacturing and iron production processes. The awareness of innovation at all levels in the Japanese society was heightened. Looking at the list of the ten great Japanese inventors in history, from Sakichi Toyoda who invented a wooden weaving machine driven by human power to Kokichi Mikimoto who invented the methods of cultivating cultured pearls, from Kyota Sugimoto who invented a typewriter for the Japanese language to Yasujiro Niwa who invented the phototelegraphic method based on transmission through cables, it is noticeable that all of these inventors grew up at the end of the nineteenth century when some of them studied extensively in Europe and America.[18] The prevailing atmosphere of innovation at the

12 Rahn G., 'The role of industrial property in economic development: the Japanese experience'. 14 *International Review of Industrial Property and Copyright Law* 449 (1983), 458.

13 Lockwood W. W., *The Economic Development of Japan: Growth and Structural Change (1868-1938)*. (Princeton, NJ: Princeton University Press 1954), p. 326.

14 Arts.4(1), 10, 19, Patent Monopoly Ordinance 1885.

15 Notice No.5 of the Exclusive Selling Patent Procedure 1885 stated that the procedure for applying for a patent '[...] requires the inclusion in an application of a description specifying the scope of the invention. It is recommended that the phrase "the scope that is claimed for a grant of patent regarding this invention" be used'. See: Takenaka T., *Interpreting Patent Claims: The United States, Germany and Japan, Vol.17 Studies in Industrial Property and Copyright Law* (Munich: Max Planck Institute for Foreign and International Patent, Copyright and Competition Law, 1995), p. 40.

16 Arts.8, 3, 17, 15, Patent Monopoly Ordinance 1885.

17 Kumagai K., *History of Japanese Industrial Property System*, a joint production of the Japanese Patent Office and the Asia-Pacific Industrial Property Centre (Tokyo: JPO/APIPC, 1999), p. 6.

18 The list of Ten Great Japanese Inventors was compiled by Professor Seiji Kaya from the Tokyo University on the occasion of the 100th anniversary of the birth of industrial rights in Japan on 18 April 1985. Available at: www.jpo.go.jp/seido_e/rekishi_e/judaie.htm (last accessed 15 October 2015).

time must have considerably stimulated these inventors' creativity, which led towards the life-changing inventions that have continued to benefit future generations.

In 1888, under the new Japanese Patent Ordinance, the inventors' right to obtain patents was recognised. An examination procedure was installed so that the patentability of an invention patent application could be scrutinised before a patent award might be granted. Food, beverages and the methods of preparing medicines were excluded from the scope of patentable subject matters.[19] Note that all the afore-mentioned provisions were retained in the subsequent patent legislation. The Patent Ordinance 1888 continued to look to the American patent legislation for inspiration. For example, the first-to-invent principle persisted, and patent annulment would take place if the invention was proven not to be new or the specification was incomplete. The procedure for interference, which was an American practice at the time, was also introduced in the Patent Ordinance 1888. In line with the American patent law concept, the new Ordinance regarded patent right as a substantive right,[20] while previously it was recognised as a right to exclude others.[21] However, under the Patent Ordinance 1888, foreigners were not eligible to apply for patent at the Patent Office in Japan.

The Patent Law 1899 was enacted, together with the Design Law and the Trademark Law, in the run-up to Japan's accession to the Paris Convention, which took place in the same year. In order to comply with the Paris Convention, the Patent Law 1899 abolished the discriminatory measures against foreign patent applicants and recognised their right to application in Japan.[22] Compared with the previous patent laws, the Patent Law 1899 also provided the assignee or the successor of an inventor with the right to patent application. The Patent Law 1899 provided a 15-year protection term for all patents while the alternative five-year and ten-year terms were abolished. Additionally, the Patent Law 1899 provided patent applicants the recourse to appeal the decisions laid down by the Patent Office at the Great Court of Cassation if a grave error was committed by the Patent Office while enforcing the Patent Law.[23]

The Patent Law 1899 also updated the objective for patent protection. It recognised that patent right was to 'use exclusively and distribute the patented invention'.

One additional significant feature brought about by the Patent Law 1899 was the mechanism of certification trial in relation to patent scope, which was administered by the Patent Office. The implication of certification trial was that, although the scope for patent protection was defined by a patent claim, the explicit disclosure of invention specifications submitted upon a patent application became more crucial because it determined the scope

19 Arts.1, 4, 2, the Patent Ordinance 1888.

20 Under the German and French patent laws at the time, patent was respected not only as a means to exclude but also to exploit the patented invention. See: Fisher M., 'Growth of the Japanese patent system: a lesson for us all?' 22 *Intellectual Property Quarterly* 1 (2004), 85–113.

21 Takenaka T., *Interpreting Patent Claims: The United States, Germany and Japan*, *Vol.17 Studies in Industrial Property and Copyright Law* (Munich: Max Planck Institute for Foreign and International Patent, Copyright and Competition Law, 1995), p. 41.

22 The measure was three-fold. First, an applicant or a patent holder residing abroad was able to appoint an agent domiciled in Japan to handle patent related matters (Art.6). Second, a patent applicant from a Union member of the Paris Convention could claim a right of priority of seven months for filing a corresponding application in Japan (Art.4). Third, temporary protection was available for goods on display at exhibitions sponsored by the central and the prefectural Japanese governments and at international exhibitions in accordance with the Paris Convention (Arts. 14, 15).

23 Arts. 1, 39, 35, Patent Law 1899.

for patent protection. The mechanism not only enabled patent holders to seek redress at the Patent Office and to bypass the judiciary when a question of patent scope arose, but also served to orchestrate the separation of power between the administration and the judiciary as the Patent Office now replaced the judiciary where decisions on patent protection were concerned.[24] Consequently, the Patent Office stood in an advantageous position over courts since it held the authority to determine the scope of patent protection.

The mechanism of certification trial was a powerful driver that enabled Japan's rapid rise to catch up with the world's most innovative countries at the turn of the twentieth century. As a result of narrowed scope for patent protection, slight technological improvement would warrant a new patent resulting in faster-paced innovation as well as the development of patent 'clusters'. The phenomenon stimulated a boom in domestic enterprises and a lot of them later went on to become global industrial giants, such as the Sony Corporation. Although these enterprises initially survived on what might be seen as minor improvements on existing technologies, gradually they have achieved many breakthroughs thanks to their continued efforts in innovation. The success of the Sony Walkman, one of the Sony Corporation's signature products, is the epitome of this development path. The portable stereo was invented after the engineers at Sony looked into ways to improve on tape recording, for which the pioneer patent was not granted in Japan. After many painstaking improvements, the Sony Walkman was invented. When the product was launched it was an instant hit worldwide and it has been voted one of the hundred inventions in the past century that changed our lives. Although the Sony Walkman was an 'end invention' of a series of sequential technological improvements on a foreign patent, its significance to human life is acknowledged as being great as other revolutionary inventions such as the Epson HX-20, the world's first laptop, which came with a four-line by 20-character LCD screen, a cassette tape for data storage and a small printer.[25] To multiply the success of the Walkman, the Sony Corporation later invented the Watchman and the Discman, which both made it to the same list of the top 100 inventions that changed our lives in the past century.

Thanks to the huge success of the Walkman, Sony Corporation continued to introduce improvements so that it became smaller and had more extensive features. Therefore,

24 The certification trial mechanism was also considered as Japan's departure from American influence in patent legislation. In terms of interpreting patent claims, the Japanese courts were relegated to the second place, which was in line with Germany's practice. In countries such as the US and the UK, courts are competent in deciding both infringement as well as validity. Note, however, that the certification trial mechanism in Germany was restricted to determining the scope of granted patent, while in Japan the mechanism was extended to deny a patent protection. As a result, although with direct influence, the certification trial mechanism exercised in Japan was decisively different from the German system in practice. In Germany, a general inventive idea was utilised to expand the scope for protection to those devices that could have been conceived by the skilled workers based on the language and the disclosure of the specifications of a claim. In Japan, the scope for patent protection was limited to what the patent holder intended to disclose in the specifications upon an application. Therefore, the same mechanism in Germany was instrumental to expand the scope for patent protection for the first patent holder, while in Japan the effect was to narrow the scope for protection. See: Fisher M., 'Growth of the Japanese patent system: a lesson for us all?' 22 *Intellectual Property Quarterly* 1 (2004), 85–113.

25 The list of the Top 100 inventions in the past century was compiled following a survey of 3,900 gadget fans commissioned by *Gadget Show Live*, a British television series that previews and reviews the latest gadgets and broadcasts the latest technology news. The Epson HX-20 was also voted as one of the Top 100 inventions in the past century by the same survey. Available at: www.dailymail.co.uk/sciencetech/article-2449468/Sony-Walkman-zip-Past-centurys-100-inventions.html (last accessed 16 October 2015).

although in general each incremental technological improvement was not dramatic and the product of each generation performed basically the same functions, the product's utility expanded and was enhanced considerably. Such incremental technological improvements were encouraged and were made possible thanks to the mechanism of certification trial.

Reflecting on the impact of the Sony Walkman, similar examples are many in the history of Japan's industrial advancement.[26] This phenomenon mobilised the whole of Japanese society to participate in innovation, since invention became accessible to ordinary people and industrial application affordable to small- and medium-sized enterprises. An innovative society was therefore in the making.

One major reason that the mechanism of certification trial could achieve the intended policy objective was that the foundation of the measure corresponded with the Japanese cultural trait that collectivism and public interest prevail over personal gains and that public good should be shared by the public. Since incremental technological deviation could qualify as a new patent, the initial patent would be pushed out of context sooner and the patent holder's privilege of monopoly shortened while the benefits accrued from invention diminished faster. This consequence was positively welcomed by Japanese society because the value of collectivism was materialised, although, on the other hand, for mitigation, patent holders started to draw up cross-licensing agreements between each other so that relevant technology holders would be able to acquire the right to use all the relevant sequential patents. Despite being seriously criticised for the flood of minor and incremental patents, living standards were fast improving since new technologies were exploited steadily and resolutely. Also, the narrower scope of patent protection encouraged technology sharing and made it impossible for one individual or entity to control or hinder the pace of overall technological advancement. Inventive activities went beyond the hands of large corporations, although they remained the driving force for innovation. Thriving industrial progress took off in Japan.

Aside from the positive impact, drawbacks resulting from the certification trial were also obvious. For example, the scope of patent rights conferred appeared less important than the rights granted. Accordingly, form prevailed instead of content. Competitive technological advantage was not gained based on the quality of the progress made, but on the number of patents that could be thrown into the bargain.[27] The mechanism seemed to encourage assimilation and improvement on primarily foreign technologies. In any case, when technological progress in Japan reached an explosive rate, the mechanism of certification trial became an impediment to innovation and was abolished.

26 Another such example is the LCD calculator that was first invented by Sharp Corporation in the 1970s. Sharp Corporation subsequently exploited the use of LCD and invented wristwatches, video games, black-and-white video displays and, in 1987, a three-inch colour television was invented. By improving on the four-inch LCD video monitor, Sharp added the ViewCam and the wall-mounting TCVs to its list of inventions in 1993. Effectively, both inventions were developed because of the incremental technological advancement made on the basis of narrow patent protection defined by a series of previous inventions. Rosen D. and Usui C., 'The social structure of Japanese intellectual property law'. 13 *UCLA Pacific Basin Law Journal* 32 (1994), 33.

27 Fisher M., 'Growth of the Japanese patent system: a lesson for us all?' 22 *Intellectual Property Quarterly* 1 (2004), 85–113.

In 1909 an amended Patent Law came into force.[28] It introduced new provisions in respect of service invention, scope of prior art, rights of foreign patent applicants, scope for patent protection, licensing of basic patent against dependent patent, and patent protection term.[29] Later on, the first-to-file rule replaced the first-to-invent rule in the Patent Law 1921.[30]

The Patent Law 1959 was supplemented by a series of enforcement regulations[31] and codified a number of judicial principles such as, for example, inventive step, which has since been required by the substantive law in order for an invention to qualify for a patent grant.[32] In addition, the new law expanded the remit of restrictions on novelty claim and therefore, from then on, an overseas publication would destroy the novelty of an invention, thus disqualifying it from a patent grant. In the meantime, applying for a single patent that covered more than one invention became possible. By virtue of Art.70 of the Patent Law 1959, courts regained the absolute authority to determine the scope for patent protection on the basis of the claim submitted at the time of a patent application. The mechanism of certification trial was abolished.

A further amendment to Japan's patent law took place in 1970. It improved on patent examination by introducing the procedure of early disclosure and the principle of examination-on-demand. The Patent Law 1975 introduced a multiple claim scheme by increasing the number of claims admissible in a single patent application and,[33] additionally, pharmaceutical products and chemical compounds became patentable subject matters.

Pursuant to the two amendments taking place in 1978[34] and 1985 respectively, the Japanese Patent Law was amended again in 1987 and, from then on, multiple independent patent claims became possible.

Despite being a relative latecomer on the world stage in terms of patent enforcement, Japan's patent legislation has the longest history in East Asia. Although in the very beginning of the evolution the legislation suffered defeat due to institutional and cultural unpreparedness, the government subsequently adopted much more focused policies and enabling legislation to promote innovation. The tactics were practical and well received by society since they corresponded with the Japanese cultural traditions. Within a century, the Japanese patent

28 The Utility Model Law was enacted in 1905 and was modelled on the German *Gebrauchsmustergesetz*. The law protected new and useful devices with regard to configuration or structure, or the combination of both, of articles for manufacturing for three years. In terms of patent application, the priority was given to the first applicant but not the first inventor.

29 See: Doi T., *The Intellectual Property Law of Japan*. (Leyden: Sijthoff and Noordhoff, 1980), p. 7.

30 Art.8, Japanese Patent Law 1921.

31 The Patent Law was implemented by the Law for the Enforcement of the Patent Law (1959), the Patent Law Enforcement Order (1960), the Patent Law Enforcement Regulation (1960), the Patent Registration Order (1960) and the Patent Registration Order Enforcement Regulation (1960). See: Doi T., *The Intellectual Property Law of Japan*. (Leyden: Sijthoff and Noordhoff, 1980), p. 9.

32 Art.29(2) of the Patent Law 1959 stipulates that where an invention could easily be made prior to the filing date of the patent application by a person with ordinary skill in the art to which the invention pertains on the basis of an invention or inventions referred to in any of the paragraphs that provide the novelty requirements, a patent shall not be granted for such an invention.

33 Art.36, Japanese Patent Law 1975. Previously, it was possible to include only one independent and single claim in a patent application. Nonetheless, the number of patent claims was not reduced as a result of this new provision. Also see: Doi T., *The Intellectual Property Law of Japan*. (Leyden: Sijthoff and Noordhoff, 1980), p. 9.

34 The 1978 Patent Law amendment added a new chapter with regard to international patent applications submitted under the Patent Cooperation Treaty, which was ratified by Japan in 1978.

legislation succeeded in spearheading the nation's technological advance, transforming the country into an innovation giant in the world. Certainly, Japan's patent policies implemented in the pre-TRIPS era were not without controversy. Some of them appeared discriminatory in nature, such as the notoriously long patent application process for foreign applicants. In this regard, the Kilby patent is a case in point since it took approximately 17 years for the American patent to be granted after it was first submitted to the JPO.[35] Another conspicuous example, which denotes some discriminatory patent policies imposed in the pre-TRIPS era, concerns the role that the Japanese Ministry of International Trade and Industry (MITI) played in authorising licensing agreements. In the 1960s, in order to build up a favourable environment for accelerating technology transfer, the Japanese government insisted that all technology transfer agreements must be granted by the MITI, and American companies were the worst hit by this. This policy was motivated to redress Japanese companies' subservient position *vis-à-vis* their American counterparts in relation to technology transfer since, at the time, many technology transfer deals were effected from the US to Japan, and therefore American companies held the upper hand in the process. For example, there was often an 'exclusive grant back' provision in a licensing agreement indicating that if the Japanese company succeeded in their own innovation, pursuant to the licencing agreement, the American company should own the new technologies on an exclusive basis. However, this measure became less relevant after the innovative capacity of Japanese companies grew enough for them to become highly independent and competitive. In the 1980s, MITI relinquished its role of authorising licensing agreements.[36]

After ushering in the post-TRIPS era and standing as an innovation giant, Japanese patent policies were adapted so that they safeguarded the benefits accrued from innovation and for creating a harmonised international patent environment where Japanese patents could be best protected while venturing ***in tandem*** with Japanese companies' international undertakings.

III Post-TRIPS era

In the course of the late 1980s and the early 1990s, although Japan was already one of the most advanced economies in the world, its patent system was somehow lagging behind and did not correspond with the country's economic prowess. Measures such as the narrowly interpreted patent scope, the pre-grant patent publication mechanism as well as the pre-grant and the post-grant opposition procedures were perhaps held responsible for the controversies.

On 14 December 1994, the National Diet (Japan's bicameral legislature) approved the amended Patent Law that incorporated the TRIPS Agreement in the wake of Japan's WTO

35 In 1961 the electronic giant Texas Instruments obtained a basic patent in Japan covering the integrated circuit. Known as the 'Kilby patent', it was named after the Nobel laureate Jack St. Clair Kilby. Texas Instruments was required by the JPO to divide the application into 14 segments of which 12 were ultimately rejected. It took approximately 17 years for the first patent to be granted after it was submitted, during which time the basic patent was copied and huge quantities of chip products were exported by the Japanese semiconductor industry, earning enormous profit in return. Rohrabacher D. and Crilly P., 'The case for a strong patent system'. 8 *Harvard Journal of Law and Technology* 263 (1995), 265.

36 Wegner H. C., *Patent Harmonisation in the Pacific Rim.* in P. C. B. Liu and A. Y. Sun, 'Intellectual property protection in the Asia–Pacific region: a comparative study'. *Occasional Papers/Reprints Series in Contemporary Asian Studies*, No. 4 (135) (1996).

accession. Under the amended Patent Law, the term for patent protection was extended from 15 to 20 years. Other changes that came along with the amendment included simplified examination procedures for utility model patent applications, a streamlined patent appeal process and stricter requirements on the nature and the permissible extent of modifying a pending patent application (although such modification became admissible at any time since then).[37] In line with the then existing international standards, inventions concerning changes of molecular structures were not patentable. Transferring a compulsory licence without an associated business transfer was also prohibited.[38] The Amendment to Patent Law 1994 started to accept patent applications filed in English. Also, the requirements for specifications and the scope for a patent claim were extended. The mechanism of patent opposition after publication was replaced by post-grant opposition, which was to address the oft-heard criticism that it required an 'extraordinary long time' to grant a patent and the procedure of pre-grant opposition was made to encourage competitors to delay the grant of important patents, thereby shortening the effective term of patent.[39] Note that, for example, in the 1990s, the average pendency of a patent application in Japan was 30 months with a backlog of unexamined invention and utility model patent applications totalling 600,000, which was staggering compared with the situation in the US.[40]

The Patent Revision 1996 followed the American style of re-examination and adopted an *ex parte* procedure.[41] Subsequently, the Patent Law Revisions in 1998 and 1999 incorporated the American case law doctrine for assessing the amount of damages caused by patent infringement and adopted certain aspects of the American discovery procedures in order to assist patent holders to prove the causation between infringement and damages.[42] The Patent Law Revision 2003 merged the opposition and invalidation procedures into one single system.[43] Also, after the Japanese Cabinet approved the 'Japan Revitalisation Strategy' and the 'Basic Principles Concerning IP Policy' in 2013, the Act on the Partial Revision of the Patent Act and Other Acts came into force on 14 May 2014.

In the new Patent Act relief measures are enhanced so that patent applicants will be entitled to extend certain time limits required for filing, examination and other procedures when exceptional unavoidable circumstances, such as national disasters, take place. These measures are equally available in the Utility Model Act, Design Act, Trademark Act and Act

37 Richards J., 'Recent patent law developments in Asia'. 7 *Fordham Intellectual Property, Media and Entertainment Law Journal* 599 (1997).

38 Blakeney M., 'The impact of the TRIPS Agreement in the Asia Pacific Region'. 18 *European Intellectual Property Review* 10 (1996), 544–554.

39 Sagar R., 'India amends patent law to give effect to TRIPS'. 9 World IP Review 136 (1995).

40 Typically, at the time, the examination process would take three to four years to complete in Japan if an applicant requested an examination to be conducted immediately after application. In comparison, during the same period, the US had a patent pendency of 18.2 months and the backlog for utility model patent applications stood at 288,055. International Trade Administration, 'Japan Patent Procedures' in *Market Research Reports* IM1930125 2 (ITA, 1993).

41 Doi S., 'The patent opposition system in Japan following major changes'. 8 *CASRIP Newsletter* 1996 (Seattle: Center for Advanced Study and Research on Intellectual Property, Autumn 2001).

42 Act on the Partial Revision of the Patent Act and Other Acts (Japan) (Act No. 51 of 1998) and Act on the Partial Revision of the Patent Act and Other Acts (Japan) (Act No. 40 of 1999). See also: Takenaka T., 'International and comparative law issues: patent infringement damages in Japan and the United States: will increased patent infringement damage awards revive the Japanese economy?' 2 *Washington University Journal of Law and Policy* 52 (2000).

43 Act on the Partial Revision of the Patent Act and Other Acts (Japan) (Act No. 122 of 2003).

on International Applications under the Patent Cooperation Treaty, which were revised altogether after the above-mentioned strategy was announced in 2013. Second, in order to stabilise patent rights at an earlier stage, an opposition-invalidation combined procedure for granted patents was introduced. Under the new scheme, an opposition request may be submitted by any person either before or after legal revisions take place. But, if an application is filed after legal revisions take place and if it is within the first six months, the opposition request may only be conducted through documentary proceedings. After the six-month period expires, the invalidation proceedings will kick in and only interested parties may file an invalidation request through oral or momentary proceedings.

IV Characteristics of the Japanese patent legislation

After unveiling the evolution of the Japanese patent legislation, its characteristics are reflected in the following aspects.

I) Patent scope

Under the Japanese patent legislation, the scope for patent protection is determined by the disclosure sustained in the patent application at the time of filing.

Recall that, prior to the Patent Law 1959, the scope for patent protection was decided by the mechanism of certification trial, which was imposed by the Patent Law 1899. The purpose for imposing this mechanism was to establish general inventive ideas by relying on the specifications disclosed upon a patent application and then to extend the remit of protection from this point onwards.[44] As a change of course, the mechanism of certification trial was abolished and, by virtue of Art.70 of the Patent Law 1959, courts became competent to determine the scope for patent protection, and therefore the breadth of protection, by referring to the claim *per se*.

However, Japan's institutionalised perception remained unchanged and patent protection continued to be narrow in scope for which, as a tradition, the 'sub-literal' interpretation approach was usually employed in order to reach narrower understanding of a patent claim than what the actual wording implied. Under this approach public good seemed to be where the emphasis lay.[45] This practice was reinforced by the case law jurisdiction when the Japanese court ruled in *Denken KK* v. *Yuai Shoji*[46] that the scope for patent protection should be limited to what was indicated in the working sample. In other words, in Japan, the scope for patent protection is limited to what an inventor could actually realise, based on what was created and therefore what was fully disclosed to the public at the time of

44 Winkler H., 'The scope of patent protection: past, present and future'. 10 *International Review of Industrial Property* 3 (1979) 296.

45 In addition to the 'sub-literal' approach, there are two more approaches that are commonly undertaken in order to determine the scope for patent protection. The first is the 'literal' interpretation, which emphasises the importance of legal certainty and is usually the British approach. The second is the 'supra-literal' approach, which expands the scope for patent protection beyond the precise wording, thereby emphasising protection for the right holders, which is the traditional German process. Takura, a former High Court Judge, stated further that 'it is only a matter of course that an application should be given a high appreciation, if it is far from any prior art, by anyone's judgement … (However, if it is not then) the closer the invention is…, the more limited the protection ought to be'. See Takura O., 'Japanese claim interpretation'. 19 *AIPPI Journal* 5 (1994) 215.

46 Hanrei Jihou (Precedent Times) No.1390 (Tokyo: July 1999), p. 113. Available at: http://hanreijiho.co.jp/ (last accessed 3 January 2017).

application. Building on this premise, petty modification to an invention would not amount to infringement but, instead, it might qualify for a separate patent grant. As a result, incentives to innovation that an inventor ought to benefit from were curtailed. A further criticism of the 'sub-literal' interpretation approach to the scope for patent protection was that it appeared to promote the importation and assimilation of technology. The approach was even described as 'legalised piracy' for encouraging patent clusters, i.e., groups of patents that were narrow in scope and acquired only because of incremental advances over a prior art. The legacy of sub-literal interpretation persisted, although Art.70 of the Patent Law 1959 abolished the mechanism of certification trial. It is alleged that, as late as the 1990s, the sub-literal interpretation approach towards the scope for patent protection still stood as a guiding principle within the Japanese patent system.[47] Criticism aside, the practice of interpreting a narrower scope for patent protection did facilitate Japan's rapid technological progress, which is respected as an economic development miracle.

II) Pre-grant patent publication

The procedure of pre-grant patent publication is another characteristic of Japan's patent legislation that helped to expedite the process of popularising innovative activities among the country's general public. By virtue of Art.65(1)(2) of the Japanese Patent Law 1959, an application must be published twice before a patent was granted, regardless of the examination process and its result. The first publication took place 18 months after an application was submitted, while the second publication took place after the application was granted by patent examiners and the invention became patentable,[48] at which time the public could object to the patent award by launching the opposition proceedings.

The pre-grant publication procedure guaranteed competitors the convenience of continuously exploiting technologies made available in the public domain and applicants were prevented from obtaining patents that claimed broader scope for protection. As a consequence, for example, American companies complained about having difficulties in obtaining patents once Japanese companies began to compete in the same field as their inventions. There were also complaints about being unable to obtain patents for inventions that were already patented in other countries.[49] According to the respective statistics published by the EPO and the JPO in 1993, Japanese competitors filed objections against seven to eight per cent of all patent applications published by both offices. At the end of the opposition proceedings, more than 35 per cent of European and Japanese published patent applications were struck down by opposition, and another 35 per cent were amended for narrower patent scope in order to succeed in a novelty test.

Overall, although the intention of installing the pre-grant publication procedure was to avoid duplicated investment in the same technology and to facilitate knowledge dissemination, it provided the opportunity for competitors to monitor the R&D activities pursued by each other. It also served as an effective means by which competitors could improve on

47 Fisher M., 'Growth of the Japanese patent system: a lesson for us all?' 22 *Intellectual Property Quarterly* 1 (2004), 85–113.

48 Art.51, Japan's Patent Law 1959.

49 General Accounting Office (USA), *Intellectual Property: US Companies' Patent Experiences in Japan*. United States General Accounting Office (1993).

their own published invention or to 'invent around' the published inventions. Technology in the public domain was thus exploited very easily. The pre-grant publication procedure therefore unwittingly contributed to 'patent flooding', despite being recognised in the meantime as one of the reasons why the Japanese industries managed to progress so aggressively.

III) Pre-grant opposition, post-grant opposition and invalidation trial

As is briefly mentioned above, prior to the Patent Law amendment in 1995, Japan's patent system was criticised for taking an 'extraordinary long time' to grant a patent and the pre-grant opposition procedure was held responsible since competitors were able to rely on it to delay the process of patent grant, thereby shortening the effective term of protection.[50]

To address the delays caused by the pre-grant opposition procedure, coinciding with Japan's TRIPS accession, the Patent Law 1994 abolished the pre-grant opposition procedure and replaced it with the post-grant opposition procedure, which was again abolished pursuant to the Patent Law amendment in 2003. This left the invalidation trial procedure the only avenue for third parties to challenge a patent award.

Under the invalidation trial mechanism, any person, at any time, even without interest, could request an invalidation trial. Applicants for invalidation trial could also appeal against a trial decision affirming a patent grant at the Tokyo High Court, since legal revision was part of the overall invalidation trial procedure.

Nonetheless, leaving the invalidation trial mechanism alone to undertake the responsibility of opposition caused some side effects and one of them was that the number of requests for review was considerably reduced. Previously, several thousand opposition requests were filed annually and, after the post-grant opposition mechanism was replaced, only a few hundred were submitted. This phenomenon indicated that many patents remained unverified, which was an unwarranted outcome since Japanese companies that intended to exploit their patents globally required stronger, tested, patents granted at home. This being the case, the JPO introduced the simplified opposition-invalidation combined procedure for granted patents pursuant to the Act on the Partial Revision of the Patent Act and Other Acts which came into force on 14 May 2014. As has been mentioned previously, the new mechanism consists of two steps, of which one is opposition taking place in the first six months either before or during legal revisions, while another step is invalidation. Before legal revisions take place, any person may file an opposition application, through either oral or documentary proceedings, after legal revisions commence, and within the first six-month period any person may file an opposition application but through documentary proceedings only. After the six-month time limit expires, the invalidation trial proceedings will kick in, and by then only interested parties may file an invalidation request through oral or documentary proceedings in order to invalidate a granted patent.[51]

50 Sagar R., 'India amends patent law to give effect to TRIPS'. 9 World IP Review 136 (1995).
51 Available at: www.wipo.int/wipolex/en/text.jsp?file_id=370759 (last accessed 23 October 2015).

V Lessons for China

Reflecting on the success and controversies sustained by the Japanese patent legislation, and determined to catch up quickly with the world's most advanced countries, Japan has adapted some patent policies that fit best with the country's ideological foundations and industrial development aspirations. As a relative latecomer to patent rights enforcement on the world stage, the Japanese legislators initially looked at patent legislation from the US, France and Germany for reference. Later, the country took its own grip on providing patent protection and has been swiftly revising its patent legislation, including reinstating abolished protection measures, so that the patent protection measures remain relevant to innovation needs in the different stages of economic development. Patent legislation and government policies are closely coordinated in Japan. Legislation is motivated by policies in pursuit of the goal of building a technologically excellent nation. Patent is a driver for economic development, but less of a form of private property rights.

In recent years, as one of the world's most innovative nations, Japan is active in shaping the process of international patent rights harmonisation in order to safeguard the benefits accrued from innovation, including those of cross-border trade and investment. For example, as a member of the IP5 project, Japan works together with the world's four other biggest patent offices to harmonise the search and examination environment among the four offices and to standardise the information-sharing process as far as multiple patent applications are concerned.

I) Policy choice

Amendments to China's patent law have come so far in an eight-year cycle, during which time implementing rules are also updated, judicial interpretations issued, while new policies may be pronounced by governmental departments or by local governments. Though, in China's case, policy equally commands legislative changes, China's web of policies is much more complex than Japan's as China must accommodate two overwhelming needs – domestic as well as international. Both obligations are equally burdensome given the country's overall societal background. Domestically, economic reform is a constant and far-reaching process taking place in every corner of the society in the past decades in order to transform China's planned economy into a market-oriented economy. Following this course, after the policy of opening-up was implemented in the country in the late 1970s, China negotiated to accede to many trade-related international treaties that were subsequently incorporated in China's domestic legislation. In this process, the challenges for the Chinese legislators are, first, pursuing two imperatives, domestic and international, simultaneously and, second, striking a balance between the two imperatives if they do not work in tandem. It would be cordial, and indeed convenient, if the two imperatives are in agreement with each other. But this is usually not the case in China because of the many unique societal factors persisting in the country, as was mentioned in the previous chapter. Consequently, what has been witnessed in China's patent law-making is that domestic reforms were compelled to accelerate in order to keep up with the speedy process of internationalisation, especially in the beginning of the evolution when the prerequisites were conspicuously missing. Looking back at the Japanese patent law, although some of its patent protection provisions invited heavy criticism, such as the certification trial procedure, they conformed to the country's ideological traditions and were, therefore, positively embraced by society and duly delivered the policy objectives that such provisions were intended to achieve. As for China, on the other hand, the course of international patent rights harmonisation indeed requires an earth-shaking revision to China's ideological tradition, especially with regard to the conviction of unconditional sharing for the public good, which was upheld as one of the highest moral values for a few thousand years by Chinese society. However, this revision was omitted before the patent system, or the IPR system at large, was imposed. On the contrary, Chinese academics tried very hard to expedite the ideological transition by bringing about the concept of a 'socialist commodity economy'. A serious consequence of this omission was that Chinese society had no idea what patent right, or IPR in general, was, let alone protection and enforcement. This situation was further aggravated by the collective ownership of property rights, be it real or intellectual, which was in place after communism was established in the country in 1949. At the time, when accommodating contending ideologies proved to be difficult, China opted for the absolute course of international patent rights harmonisation and paid little attention to the domestic societal reality as they introduced the patent system in haste. A repercussion of this policy choice is that, to date, China's spectacular success in patent rights protection is still dented by its weakness in patent enforcement, or in IPR enforcement overall. In this respect, patent protection measures in Japan appeared more effective since the country's traditional ideological values are ingrained in the legislation.

Also, it is observed that in recent years China has aimed to popularise innovative activities by encouraging patent applications in order to nurture an innovative society. This policy was announced by the National Patent Development Strategy (2011–2020) in 2010 when it was declared that China aimed to achieve an annual patent filing of 'two million' by 2015. The policy objective echoes what Japan undertook in the past when it encouraged incremental and sequential patents to guarantee that innovation was accessible, especially among small- and medium-sized enterprises since their resources for investment in innovation were limited. Just like the controversies that Japan experienced, the Chinese patent policy of 'two million' has been criticised for pursuing patent quantity at the expense of quality, and for exchanging genuine motivation for technological advance for political ambitions.[52] Some pointed out that China's surging patent applications were fuelled by utility model patent applications,[53] which seem less valuable than invention patents since the thresholds for patentability are lower. Some also cast doubt on China's capacity for quality assurance in patent examination, and have cautioned that such a high number of patent grants may be used aggressively against foreign companies.[54]

52 For example, it is observed that, from 2001 to 2012, patent applications increased significantly in December of each year suggesting a quota may be imposed by the local governments. Zhen L., *Autumnal Hook 2012 Update* (16 February 2013). Guest post on China IPR blog. Available at: https://chinaipr.com/2013/02/16/autumnal-hook-2012-update/ (last accessed 13 August 2015).

53 China received by far the largest number of utility model patent applications in 2013, accounting for nearly nine-tenths of the world total. See: WIPO, *IP Facts and Figures (2014)*, p. 18. Available at: www.wipo.int/edocs/pubdocs/en/wipo_pub_943_2014.pdf (last accessed 13 August 2015).

54 Wild J., 'Chinese authorities plan to take action on bad faith utility model and design patent applications'. *Intellectual Asset Management*, 22 February (2013). Available at: www.iam-media.com/Blog/Detail.aspx?g=25712644-1578-46a0-9a8a-765632e9ec86 (last accessed 13 August 2015).

All these concerns are somehow justifiable. For example, although China has the world's biggest domestic patent application numbers, the country's innovation capacity is lagging behind[55] and, as a result, it is not yet considered as an innovative country.

In any case, the target application number of 'two million' was surpassed in 2014 when the country registered 2.361 million patent applications in total by the year end.[56] Against the controversies and the contrast between patent application numbers and innovative capacity, it is necessary to investigate the reality of China's soaring patent application numbers.

II) Patent quality

When examined in detail, the patent application number of 'two million' patents does not seem outrageous. At the outset, the two million applications cover all three types of patents: invention, utility model[57] and design. Second, it must be emphasised that the number of '2 million' refers merely to patent applications but not grants. Moreover, granting different types of patent requires different examination procedures in China, with invention patent applications requiring the most substantive check that consists of two steps: preliminary and substantive examination. An invention patent application may be published after a preliminary examination is completed within 18 full months counting from the date of application. An invention patent will not be granted at this stage, but only after a substantive examination that will be conducted within three years counting from the date of application and upon the applicant's request. However, utility model and design patents may be granted after a preliminary examination,[58] which means in less than a year. The latest statistics reveal that the pendency for patent examination in China is reduced to 3.5 months for utility model patent applications, compared with 21.8 months for invention

55 The Global Innovation Index 2015 positioned China as the 29th most innovative country in the world, behind Switzerland, the UK, Sweden, the Netherlands and the US, which obtained the top five rankings. China's ranking in 2015 remained the same compared with one year ago, although it has advanced six places on the chart since 2013. Co-published by Cornell University, INSEAD and WIPO, the Global Innovation Index is a leading reference on innovation and ranks countries' innovation capacity and results. Available at: www.globalinnovationindex.org/content/page/data-analysis/ (last accessed 26 October 2015).

56 Since 2006, China has seen a rapid surge of patent applications both domestically and internationally.

Domestically, according to the statistics revealed by SIPO, in 2014 patent applications totalled 2.361 million, equal to the figure reached in 2013. Among the applications there were 928,000 invention patent applications representing a year-on-year increase of 12.5 per cent, 868,000 utility model and 565,000 design patent applications, registering a year-on-year decrease of 2.7 per cent and 14.4 per cent, respectively. See: State Intellectual Property Office of the People's Republic of China (SIPO), *Intellectual Property Rights Protection in China*. (SIPO, 2014).

Internationally, based on the statistics provided by the WIPO, in 2014 China filed 25,539 patent applications under the PCT system registering an increase of 11.9 per cent compared with 2013, ranking the country the third largest patent applicant in the world under the system, after the US and Japan. See: www.wipo.int/export/sites/www/ipstats/en/docs/infographics_systems_2014.pdf (last accessed 13 August 2015).

57 On the other hand, one must note that not all countries grant utility model patents. For example, the US does not grant patent protection to utility models, while other countries, including some of the world's major industrial nations such as Australia, Germany, Japan and South Korea, do. There are currently approximately 75 countries that provide patent protection to utility models. Suthersanen U., *Utility Models and Innovation in Developing Countries, UNCTAD-ICTSD Project on IPR and Sustainable Development*, Working Paper No.13 (Geneva: International Centre for Trade and Sustainable Development, 2006). Available at: http://unctad.org/en/docs/iteipc20066_en.pdf (last accessed 8 May 2016).

58 Art.40, Patent Law (2008) China.

patent applications.[59] In case the question of its credibility is raised, one must take note of the fact that the simplified examination procedure for utility model patent applications is a global practice, seen in Australia for its innovation patents, in Germany for *Gebrauchsmuster*, in Hong Kong for short-term patents, in Japan and Korea for utility models and in Indonesia and Thailand for petty patents. In any event, none of the international or multilateral treaties that govern utility model patent protection, such as the Paris Convention, TRIPS and PCT, prescribe any substantive minimum standards for examination. Therefore, countries are indeed entitled to enjoy a great deal of flexibility when they determine their respective thresholds for patentability for utility models. At the same time, a swift examination procedure does not necessarily suggest that utility model patents are of inferior quality. Since there are no standardised objective ways to gauge the quality of utility model patents and to define what it is, one may look at their economic value for reference. It is recognised that petty patents, such as utility model patents, may be transformed into huge value and become a driver for economic development, and this may explain why there are many countries in the world, including industrialised countries such as Japan, that grant utility model patents. *Chint* v. *Schneider*[60] proves that this argument is true when, after Schneider China was sued for infringing a utility model patent owned by the Chint Group, Schneider China was ordered by the Intermediate Court in Wenzhou (China) to pay damages amounting to more than 44 million USD (39 million EUR), which is, so far, the largest compensation awarded in China's history of patent protection. The parties eventually reached a settlement on appeal. The *Chint* v. *Schneider* case reveals that a causal link between the swift examination procedure and the allegedly inferior quality of utility model patents granted in China does not exist. Besides, while invention patents are protected for 20 years, utility model patents are protected only for ten years in China,[61] which means a utility model patent will expire sooner. The Draft Patent Law 2015 proposes no changes in this respect.

From the point of view of policy, in addition to Japan, China is not alone in encouraging utility model patent applications in order to nurture an innovative society for economic growth. For the same purpose, some developing countries also introduced 'petty patents', or utility model patents, with varied thresholds for patentability and different protection terms. For example, Indonesia provides protection to 'simple patents', which is creation with small product improvements and a protection term of five years, Vietnam grants patent protection to 'utility solutions' for six years, and Malaysia grants 'utility innovation' patents a five-year protection term that is renewable for further five years.[62]

Coming back to China's policy of achieving 'two million' patent applications by 2015, although utility model patent applications are the main contributor to the surging patent application numbers witnessed in China domestically in recent years, statistics reveal that the Chinese patent applications filed under the PCT and the EPO have also been steadily increasing at the same time. Under the PCT system, with a growth of 1.7 per cent to 218,000 applications in 2015, it is acknowledged that the large increase in patent-filing activity conducted by China-based innovators accounted for much of the overall growth in

59 State Intellectual Property Office of the People's Republic of China (SIPO), *Intellectual Property Rights Protection in China*. (SIPO, 2014), p. 6.

60 Wenzhou Intermediate People's Court, Wenzhou, Zhejiang Province, PR China, 26 September 2007.

61 Art.42, Patent Law 2008.

62 Endeshaw A., *Intellectual Property in Asian Emerging Economies*. (London: Ashgate Publishing, 2010).

PCT patent applications worldwide. Compared with 2014, China registered a sizeable growth of 16.8 per cent in PCT patent applications. In 2015, among the world's top PCT applicants, Huawei Technologies, a Chinese home-grown company, took the lead for the second consecutive year with 3,898 published PCT applications – an additional 456 applications on 2014. The US-based Qualcomm Incorporated was the second largest applicant in 2015, with 2,442 published PCT patent applications, while China's ZTE Corporation ranked third with 2,155 PCT applications.[63] Statistics from SIPO also acknowledges that, in 2013, Chinese companies submitted 22,292 patent applications at the EPO where China is one of the top five applicants. Reflecting on Chinese applicants' success in the international patent filing systems as a yardstick, it is fair to conclude that China's overall patent quality is compatible with the international standards of patentability since international patents usually have a higher significance.

There is no doubt that achieving high patent application numbers is a means but not the end. Patience is also imperative since an innovative society can only be nurtured but not established, and this is a course that the contemporary technology-advanced countries have all undertaken, including Japan and the US[64]

Having presented the Japanese example of international patent rights harmonisation, the transformation of India's patent law depicts another picture of enforcing patent rights to advance national interest while complying with the TRIPS Agreement.

63 www.wipo.int/pressroom/en/articles/2016/article_0002.html (last accessed 30 June 2016).

64 For example, until a decade ago, the US was criticised for its low quality patents because of 'budgetary limitations, an exploding filing rate, and the increasing range of patentable subject matter'. See: Thomas J. R., 'The responsibility of the rule maker: comparative approaches to patent administration reform'. 17 *Berkeley Technology Law Journal* 727 (2002), 728.

One study equally noted that the US courts had found the patent invalid in 46 per cent of the 300 final validity decisions examined. See: Allison J. R. and Lemley M. A., 'Empirical evidence on the validity of litigated patents'. 26 *AIPLA Quarterly Journal* 185 (1998).

8 Patent policy and legislation

India v. China

Patent protection in India is governed by the Patents Act 1970, which was subsequently amended in 1999, 2002 and 2005. The present legislation, Patents (Amendment) Act 2005, was enacted in order to comply with the minimum protection standards prescribed by the TRIPS Agreement. Within the framework of the amendment in 2005, a big change in India's patent law history took place when pharmaceutical products, food products and chemicals became patentable as of 1 January 2005.

I Introduction

Since its independence in 1947, Indian citizens' constitutional right to health has been a permanent rival to patent protection and the former always gained the upper hand. The Indian legislature has resolutely facilitated the growth of the country's generic pharmaceutical industry, in the hope that citizens could afford generic medicine so that the government's constitutional obligation would be fulfilled. During the period between 1970 (when the Patents Act was enacted) and 2005 (when the amendment came into force), only pharmaceutical process was patentable in India, although pharmaceutical product was a patentable subject matter under the Patents Act 1856, which was India's first patent legislation. India's position against patenting pharmaceutical products is epitomised by the speech delivered by Indira Gandhi at the World Health Assembly in 1982, when the then-Prime Minister contended that '[t]he idea of a better-ordered world is one in which medical discoveries will be free of patents and there will be no profiteering for life and death'.[1]

India was compelled to amend its Patent Act in 2005 in order to incorporate the TRIPS Agreement into its domestic legislation, after the ten-year transitional period provided by TRIPS expired. However, by exploiting the principle of flexibility provided by the TRIPs Agreement, the newly amended patent law managed to assert a few crucial protection provisions in order for the privilege of right to health to maintain its dominance over patent protection when conflict between the two arises. As such, India has effectively entrenched domestic needs in its patent legislation which is, at the same time, in full compliance with the TRIPS Agreement. In effect, since independence, and thanks to the enabling patent legislation, India has established a thriving generic pharmaceutical industry whose products make up about 90 per cent of the domestic market.[2]

1 Geneva, May 1982.

2 Anon, 'Taking pains, Indian patent rules infuriate big pharma'. *The Economist* (8 September 2012), available at: www.economist.com/node/21562226 (last accessed 2 November 2015).

As could be expected, India's patent legislation has attracted many criticisms, especially from multinational pharmaceutical companies.

II Policy and legislation: an illustration by four cases

The characteristics of India's patent legislation can be best illustrated by the following four landmark cases, all of which took place after India acceded to the TRIPS Agreement in 1995.

The citizens' right to health is defended by the Indian patent legislation in three aspects, which are: the efficacy requirement, the pre-grant opposition mechanism, as well as the linkage between regulatory approval and patent protection provisions.

I) The mailbox case

India became a member of the TRIPS Agreement in 1995, when the country acceded to the WTO. Taking full advantage of the transitional arrangements granted by TRIPS, India did not provide patent protection to pharmaceutical, agricultural and chemical products until ten years later in 2005.[3] Before 2005 and during the ten-year transitional period, India was obliged, nonetheless, by virtue of Art.70(8)(a) of the TRIPS Agreement, to accept patent applications of all such products and to assign each application a filing date, but without the need to process these applications. This arrangement was commonly known as the 'mailbox' facility.[4] Moreover, in accordance with Art.70(9) of the TRIPS Agreement, during the transitional period when a patent application for a pharmaceutical, agricultural or chemical product was filed, India had to grant five-year exclusive marketing rights to the product concerned on the condition that it had already obtained a patent grant by another member of the TRIPS Agreement.[5]

In July 1996 the US filed a request for consultation with India at the WTO DSB alleging that the Indian government failed to incorporate the 'mailbox' facility into its legislation and did not provide legislative authorisation to grant the five-year exclusive marketing rights to patent applications of pharmaceutical, agricultural and chemical product inventions.[6] Subsequently, the DSB ruled in favour of the US but India appealed

3 Art.65, Transitional Arrangements, the TRIPS Agreement.

4 Thomas J. R., *Pharmaceutical Patent Law* (1st Ed.). (Edison, NJ: Bloomberg BNA Books, 2005), pp. 609–610.

5 Art.70(9) of the TRIPS Agreement stipulates that 'Where a product is the subject of a patent application in a Member in accordance with paragraph 8(a), exclusive marketing rights shall be granted, notwithstanding the provisions of Part VI, for a period of five years after obtaining marketing approval in that Member or until a product patent is granted or rejected in that Member, whichever period is shorter, provided that, subsequent to the entry into force of the WTO Agreement, a patent application has been filed and a patent granted for that product in another Member and marketing approval obtained in such other Member'.

6 To implement the overall 'mailbox facility', on 31 December 1994 an Ordinance was promulgated by India's President when the Parliament was not in session. The Ordinance came into effect on 1 January 1995, but then lapsed because the implementing legislation was not enacted within the requisite six-week time period following the Ordinance's introduction. The Lower House of India's Parliament subsequently passed a bill to implement the mailbox facility but the legislation was never enacted because the Upper House did not pass it before the Parliament was dissolved in May 1996. See: Mueller J. M., 'The tiger awakens: the tumultuous transformation of India's patent system and the rise of Indian pharmaceutical innovation'. 68 *University of Pittsburgh Law Review* 3 (2007), 491.

against the decision.[7] Later, the WTO Appellate Body decided in December 1997 that India failed in its obligation derived from the TRIPS on the above-mentioned two aspects. The Appellate Body ruled that the 'administrative practice', which was declared as a Presidential decree by the Indian Parliament, was insufficient for the purpose of implementing the 'mailbox' facility in the country, and was not an explicit 'means' within the meaning of Art.70.8(a) of the TRIPS Agreement by which applications of pharmaceutical, agricultural and chemical product inventions could be securely filed because such patent applications, filed under the administrative measures, could be rejected by courts as they were contradictory to the relevant provisions of the Patents Act 1970 that was still in force. As the provisions would not be overruled by an executive administrative order, Art.70.9 of the TRIPS Agreement was therefore violated as a consequence.[8] The Appellate Body further held that India failed to provide legislative authority for granting the exclusive marketing rights to such applications, although India argued that, since no party had yet qualified for the grant of such rights, there was therefore no such need for adopting a legislative change.

Later, to comply with the recommendations issued by the WTO DSB, India amended its Patents Act in 1999 and Section 11A was added in order to provide that patent applications for pharmaceutical, agricultural and chemical product inventions would be accepted and kept away in a 'mailbox', which would be examined in 2005. Nonetheless, there was a provision by which a compulsory licence would be automatically issued if a 'mailbox' application was granted patent protection, in the event that a generic pharmaceutical company made a significant investment and was producing and marketing the product covered by the 'mailbox' application prior to 1 January 2005.[9].

II) Novartis AG v. Union of India

The Novartis case provides a lucid picture of how India's judiciary defends the citizens' right to health by exploiting Section 3(d) of the Patents (Amendment) Act 2005 so that the effect of providing patent protection to pharmaceutical products, obliged by the minimum standards determined by the TRIPS Agreement, could be mitigated.

The contention in the Novartis case was in relation to Section 3(d) of the Patents (Amendment) Act 2005 that prescribes the threshold test for inventiveness of an invention patent application. Section 3(d) of the Patents Act 2005 states that 'the mere discovery of a new form of a known chemical compound which does not result in the enhancement of the known efficacy of that chemical compound or the mere

7 Lots of resistance was received in India after the WTO DSB's ruling was delivered. One lawmaker who opposed the ruling stated that 'we will see that pressure applied by external forces does not affect our independent decision'. See: Rao V., 'India plans committee on patent law reform'. *Journal of Commerce*, 21 August (1997) at A4.

8 India — Patent Protection for Pharmaceutical and Agricultural Chemical Products, WT/DS50/AB/R, 19 December 1997, available at: www.wto.org/english/tratop_e/dispu_e/cases_e/ds50_e.htm (last accessed 2 November 2015).

9 Also, it was provided that after a patent is granted for applications submitted by virtue of Section 5(2), the patent-holder would be entitled to receive reasonable royalty from such enterprises which have made significant investment and were producing and marketing the concerned product prior to 1 January 2005 and which continued to manufacture the product covered by the patent on the date of grant of the patent and no infringement proceedings should be instituted against such enterprises.

discovery of any new property or new use for a known chemical compound or of the mere use of a known process, machine or apparatus unless such known process results in a new product or employs at least one new reactant'. The Explanation of the Section further restricts that '... salts, esters, ethers, polymorphs, metabolites, pure form, particle size, isomers, mixtures of isomers, complexes, combinations and other derivatives of known chemical compound shall be considered to be the same chemical compound, unless they differ significantly in properties with regard to efficacy...'. In comparison, the provision has set a much higher threshold test for inventiveness than the TRIPS Agreement requires. Article 27(1) of the TRIPS Agreement only obliges members to guarantee that patent protection should be available for any invention as long as they are new, involve an inventive step and are capable of industrial application. Ingredients required by Section 3(d), such as 'enhancement of the known efficacy', although not obliged by TRIPS, are exceptionally powerful when containing the so-called 'evergreening' tactic practised by some global pharmaceutical companies. In this context, 'evergreening' refers to filing for sequential and overlapping patents on a single object through some trivial and secondary changes, such as size, colour, dosage, delivery mechanism and composition, etc., so that when the principle patent is about to expire its protection period may be nonetheless extended artificially because of the sequential patent.[10]

In 2005 the Novartis patent application for its cancer drug Gleevec was rejected by the Indian Patent Office on the grounds that the invention did not demonstrate 'enhanced efficacy', in accordance with Section 3(d) of the Patents (Amendment) Act 2005. Novartis challenged this decision and filed an appeal both at the Indian Patent Office and at the Madras High Court,[11] alleging that Section 3(d) was unconstitutional as the principle of 'equal protection'[12] was breached since the 'efficacy' requirement was vague and the provision was in violation of Art.27 of the TRIPS Agreement. In August 2007, the Indian High Court of Madras[13] laid down its decision and rejected the Novartis patent application for Gleevec. The High Court ruled that Section 3(d) was constitutional, although the Court in the meantime conceded that it had no jurisdiction to decide whether or not the provision was in violation of the TRIPS Agreement.[14]

Novartis first filed patent applications worldwide in 1993 for Imatinib, which is the underlying base compound for Gleevec. As India did not provide patent protection for pharmaceutical products before 2005, Novartis did not make a patent application for

10 Basheer S. and Prashant R., '"Ducking" TRIPS in India: A Saga Involving Novartis and the Legality of Section 3(D)'. 20 *National Law School of India Review* 131 (2008), 135–36.

11 Indian Patent Office, in the matter of application for Patent No.1602/MAS/98, 25 January 2006. See also: Sheehe J., 'Indian patent law: walking the line?' 29 *Northwest Journal of International Law and Business* 2 (2009), 577.

12 Entitled 'equality before law', Art.14 of the Constitution states that 'the State shall not deny to any person equality before the law or the equal protection of the laws within the territory of India prohibition of discrimination on grounds of religion, race, caste, sex or place of birth'.

13 In 1996, the state government of Tamil Nadu officially changed the name of the city of Madras to Chennai. However, the name Madras continues in occasional use for the city, as well as for places named after the city such as the University of Madras and the Indian Institute of Technology, Madras.

14 *Novartis AG* v. *Union of India*, 2007 A.I.R. 24759 (Madras HC).

Imatinib in India in 1993.[15] In fact, Imatinib was the first approved drug that was able to directly turn off the signal of a protein known to cause cancer. Clinical trials also revealed that Imatinib resulted in a significantly better response than conventional therapy in patients with previously untreated chronic myelogenous leukaemia (CML), it delayed the progression of the disease longer and produced milder side effects. Imatinib was subsequently further improved and became known as Gleevec. In 1997, relying on the 'mailbox' facility, Novartis filed a patent application for Gleevec before the Chennai Patent Controller. After 1 January 2005, when the 'mailbox' was opened, five pre-grant oppositions were submitted in order to oppose patenting Gleevec on the grounds of Section 3(d) of the Patents (Amendment) Act 2005. Novartis maintained that Gleevec was eligible for patent protection as it was novel, inventive and capable of industrial application. With regard to the additional requirement of 'efficacy', Novartis provided evidence that indicated that Gleevec was more effective than Imatinib because the former increased the active ingredient's absorption in the blood by 30 per cent.[16] Nonetheless, in the conclusion delivered by the Chennai Patent Controller, although the requirement of industrial applicability was deemed met, it was decided that Gleevec was neither novel nor inventive. Moreover, the Patent Controller did not consider the 30 per cent increase in the active ingredient's absorption in the blood had met the 'enhanced efficacy' requirement laid down by Section 3(d). Novartis' patent application for Gleevec was therefore rejected.

Subsequently, Novartis filed an appeal before the Madras High Court. The case was later transferred to the Intellectual Property Appellate Board (IPAB). However, Novartis lost its appeal. The Madras High Court affirmed the position that the constitutional 'right to health' should be given due consideration while approving patent applications *vis-à-vis* the right of 'equality before law' which is also constitutional. Regarding whether the decision laid down by the Chennai Patent Controller breached Art.14 of the Constitution, the Court stated that '... we have already found, analysing the alleged offending provision, that it is not in violation of Art.14 of the Constitution of India. We have borne in mind the object which the Amending Act wanted to achieve namely, to prevent "evergreening"; to provide easy access to the citizens of this country to life saving drugs and to discharge their Constitutional obligation of providing good health care to its citizens'.[17] This reasoning was applied by courts in later cases such as *F. Hoffmann-La Roche Ltd.* v. *Cipla Ltd.*, when the Delhi High Court was deliberating whether 'irreparable injury' to 'public interest' would occur if an injunction was granted. The Court then decided that if the defendant stopped producing the generic drug, it 'may lead to the shortening of lives of several unknown persons who are not parties to the suit'.[18]

Novartis did not further challenge the decision handed down by the Madras High Court. At the same time, the IPAB established that Gleevec was novel and inventive but

15 O'Brien S.G. *et al.*, 'Imatinib compared with interferon and low-dose cytarabine for newly diagnosed chronic phase chronic myeloid leukemia'. 348 *New England Journal of Medicine* 11 (2003), 994; also: Bazzle T., 'Pharmacy of the developing world: reconciling intellectual property rights in India with the right to health: TRIPS, India's patent system and essential medicines'. 42 *Georgetown Journal of International Law* 3 (2011), 785.

16 Basheer S. and Prashant R., '"Ducking" TRIPS in India: A Saga Involving Novartis and the Legality of Section 3(D)'. 20 *National Law School of India Review* 131 (2008), 137–38.

17 *Novartis AG* v. *Union of India*, 2007 AIR 24759 (Madras HC) 19.

18 Roche sought an injunction to stop the Indian manufacturer Cipla from producing Roche's patented anti-cancer drug erlotonib. See: *F. Hoffmann-La Roche Ltd.* v. *Cipla Ltd.*, I.A 642/2008 in CS (OS) 89/2008 (Delhi HC 19 March 2008), at 86.

failed to meet the requirement stipulated by Section 3(d) of the Patents (Amendment) Act 2005 on 'enhanced efficacy' and, as a result, Novartis' patent application was rejected. Later, it was against this specific part of the decision that Novartis filed a Special Leave Petition in the Supreme Court.[19] The question thus became whether Gleevec met the requirement of 'enhanced efficacy' set down by Section 3(d) in order to qualify for a patent grant.

In April 2013 the Supreme Court ruled that Gleevec should not be granted patent protection because the drug was too similar to Imatinib, its earlier version. The Court was convinced that Novartis made an older form of the drug but not the beta crystalline version, and that it appeared that Novartis may have been trying to use a patent in India to cover a drug that it was not actually selling.[20] The Supreme Court confirmed that the beta crystalline form of Imatinib failed the test of 'enhanced efficacy' laid down by Section 3(d) of the Patents (Amendment) Act 2005. The Court further emphasised that the quality of 'enhanced efficacy' should be understood as the ability to produce a desired, or intended, effect while, in the context of the drug, an efficacy claim must mean to cure disease and, therefore, the element of therapeutic efficacy must be proven. Reading together with the Explanation to Section 3(d), the Supreme Court continued to state that not all advantageous or beneficial properties would be considered 'efficacy' but only such properties that directly relate to efficacy that, in case of a drug, is the therapeutic efficacy. In line with the Explanation, the Supreme Court held that the physiochemical properties of the beta crystalline form of Imatinib mesylate cannot be taken into account to meet the requirement of Section 3(d) as these properties have nothing to do with therapeutic efficacy.

The Novartis decision clarified the meaning of 'efficacy' within the remit of Section 3(d) of the Patents (Amendment) Act 2005 and illustrated that mere advantages are not efficacy, for which the quality of being therapeutic must be proven. The decision of the Supreme Court in April 2013 also confirmed that the Patents (Amendment) Act 2005 reflected the Indian Parliament's aim to mitigate the impact of patenting pharmaceutical products that may substantially inhibit the availability of medicine for the population of India and the developing countries.[21] Thus, in effect, the decision of the Supreme Court provided a 'licence' to sell the generic version of Gleevec in India and in other countries where the product is not patented. In such countries, the generic version of Gleevec would cost less than one-twelfth of the roughly 70,000 USD (61,684 EUR)-a-year price that Gleevec costs in the US.[22]

On 15 May 2014, Novartis obtained a seven-month reprieve from Sun Pharmaceutical Industries, which had a tentative approval from the US Food and Drug Administration for producing a generic version of Gleevec. Under the terms of the settlement Sun could launch a generic version of Gleevec in the US on 1 February 2016. This arrangement

19 Grover A., 'Analysing the Supreme Court judgment'. *Economic and Political Weekly*, 10 August 10, Vol. XLVIII No. 32 (2013).

20 Abbott F. M., 'The judgment in *Novartis* v. *India*: what the Supreme Court of India said'. *Intellectual Property Watch*, 4 April (2013). Available at: www.ip-watch.org/2013/04/04/the-judgment-in-novartis-v-india-what-the-supreme-court-of-india-said/ (last accessed 18 November 2015).

21 Abbott F. M., 'The judgment in *Novartis* v. *India*: what the Supreme Court of India said'. *Intellectual Property Watch*, 4 April (2013), available at: http://www.ip-watch.org/2013/04/04/the-judgment-in-novartis-v-india-what-the-supreme-court-of-india-said/ (last accessed 18 November 2015).

22 India's Novartis Decision, available at: www.nytimes.com/2013/04/05/opinion/the-supreme-court-in-india-clarifies-law-in-novartis-decision.html?_r=1 (last accessed 18 November 2015).

granted Novartis seven extra months to monopolise the market of Gleevec, without facing the competition of its generic version coming from the Indian drug company. Novartis regarded this settlement as a validation of the Gleevec patent.

III) Tenofovir disoproxil fumarate

Similar to the effect of 'enhanced efficacy', the pre-grant opposition procedure provided by India's Patents (Amendment) Act 2005 may curtail the minimum patent protection standards set down by the TRIPS Agreement. Section 25(1) of the Patents (Amendment) Act 2005 states that 'any person may, in writing, represent by way of opposition to the Controller against the grant of patent on the ground... that the invention is not obvious and does not involve an inventive step'. Under the auspices of the provision, whoever, including advocacy groups,[23] wishes to oppose a pharmaceutical product patent application for their alleged potential undue burden on the affordability of an essential medicine is able to launch the pre-grant opposition proceedings. The controversy drawn to Section 25(1) is that the provision seems to have weakened the pre-grant opposition procedure by allowing 'any person' to object to a patent application, which is likely to open the floodgates of opposition requests even when a patent application is still under examination. The case of tenofovir disoproxil fumarate (TDF) epitomises this controversy.

Tenofovir disoproxil fumarate is an important antiretroviral drug, used as a first-line treatment for HIV/AIDS. Being highly recommended by the World Health Organisation, more than 80 per cent of the world's 33 million HIV-positive patients live within TDF-licensed countries and territories.[24] The drug manufacturer Gilead filed patent applications in India for TDF in 1998 and 2002 respectively. To oppose the application, the Delhi Network of Positive People, a network for people living with HIV/AIDS in India, and the Brazilian Interdisciplinary HIV/AIDS Association jointly filed a pre-grant opposition against Gilead's TDF patent application on 5 September 2006. The opposition was submitted on the grounds of: 1) the lack of novelty and inventive step, which were in violation of Section 2(1)(j) of the Patents (Amendment) Act 2005; 2) the lack of patentability, which was in violation of Section 3(d) of the same Act; 3) the patent application of the drug invention was a mere admixture of known chemical compounds, as was disclosed in the preceding and the following prior art, which only resulted in the aggregation of properties; and 4) the invention was publicly known and used in India and elsewhere before the priority date of the claim, which was in violation of Section 25 (1) (c) of the Patents (Amendment) Act 2005.[25]

The NGOs who opposed the TDF patent application further demanded that patents 'only be granted where they do not harm the public's needs'. They argued that the 'public interest' in 'good healthcare' was not just a supplementary factor since harm would flow

23 Such as I-MAK, a NGO consisting of lawyers and scientists who aim to increase the access to affordable medicines by making sure the patent system works, available at: www.i-mak.org/about-i-mak-mission/ (last accessed 3 November 2015).

24 Anon, 'US Gilead appeals against patent rejection of AIDS drug Viread'. *The Economic Times*, 8 December 2009. Available at: http://articles.economictimes.indiatimes.com/2009-12-08/news/28417227_1_aids-drug-viread-patent-claims-patent-rejection (last accessed 18 November 2015).

25 Representation of Opposition under Section 25(1) of the Patents Act 1970, available at: http://static1.1.sqspcdn.com/static/f/129694/5332169/1263217372017/3383-delnp-2005-+Gilead-+Cipla.pdf?token=5dPKRiqOVRvGHf70lhguQoo5iG0 per cent3D (last accessed 18 November 2015).

from patenting TDF in the foreseeable future (for example, the drying up of the generic drug production and the accompanying rise in the cost of antiretroviral drugs), and this should determine TDF's fate just as much as its efficacy and inventiveness.[26]

While the NGOs were pressing on with the pre-grant opposition procedures, Gilead offered to grant 'non-exclusive, voluntary licenses to generic manufacturers in India for the local Indian market as well as provision for manufacturers to export product to the 97 developing countries…', according to a press release issued by Gilead in May 2006. In the end, in India alone, Gilead had entered into licensing collaboration with 13 companies, allowing them to sell the generic versions of the drug in India and in 94 other countries by paying a five per cent royalty until TDF's global patent expires in 2018.[27] Note that a generic version of TDF would cost around one eighth of the Gilead-branded version, which would provide HIV/AIDS-positive patients, especially those in the developing countries, more affordable access to the life-extending medicine. However, Gilead's licensing model was criticised for 'renting out a house but without owning it' since, at the time, approval was pending in most of the countries where the TDF patent application was submitted.

Because Section 25(1) of the Patents (Amendment) Act 2005 provides 'any person' with the opportunity of challenging a patent application if it may be deemed potentially capable of undermining the principle of the right to health, the Brazilian Interdisciplinary HIV/AIDS Association was able to join the process of opposing patenting TDF in India. This was the first time that a foreign health advocacy group joined an Indian NGO to object to a patent application filed in India.[28] The Brazilian NGO declared that patenting TDF in India would have a direct adverse impact on Brazil's ability to produce affordable generic versions of the drug, and the result would be highly damaging since in Brazil there are 600,000 individuals who are affected by the disease.[29]

The pre-grant opposition procedure allows 'any person' from 'anywhere' to assert a 'right to health' claim in a patent application process, which indicates that the ingredient of public interest must be given due consideration while examining a patent application in India, especially when an application concerns a pharmaceutical product. In the case of TDF, in June 2009 the Brazilian Patent Office also issued a final refusal against Gilead's TDF patent application. In August of the same year, TDF was refused patent protection in India based on the overall argument regarding patentability and public interest.

IV) Bayer Corporation v. Union of India

The Bolar exemption, sanctioned by Art.30 of the TRIPS Agreement and Section 107A of India's Patents (Amendment) Act 2005, provides competitors with the opportunity to experiment on a patented drug in order to expedite the regulatory approval of the drug's generic version in order to enable its prompt entry into the market once the patent expires. The Bolar exemption ensures a quicker delivery of affordable generic medicines to the

26 Bazzle T., 'Pharmacy of the developing world: reconciling intellectual property rights in India with the right to health: TRIPS, India's patent system and essential medicines'. 42 *Georgetown Journal of International Law* 3 (2011), 785.

27 Anon, 'US Gilead appeals against patent rejection of AIDS drug Viread'. *The Economic Times*, 8 December 2009.

28 Available at: http://spicyip.com/2009/09/patent-office-rejected-tenofovir.html (last accessed 18 November 2015).

29 The Economist Intelligence Unit, 'India/Brazil Pharma: Of patents and prices'. *The Economist*, 2 July (2008).

market. The other side of the coin is that if the approval for the generic drug's market-entry is delayed, the patented drug would then enjoy a longer period of monopoly.

Within the context of Section 107A of the Patents (Amendment) Act 2005, contention brought along by the Bolar exemption centred on the issue of patent linkage. Patent linkage is a practice of linking regulatory approval of a generic drug to the patent status of the originating reference drug. Different patent jurisdictions uphold different opinions as to whether such practice is lawful. Opponents deny regulatory approval for any generic drug so long as the original drug's patent is still in force, while proponents argue that a robust patent system requires a patent linkage.[30] Patent linkage is unlawful under the EU patent law. According to the EPC, marketing authorisation bodies are not allowed to take the patent status of an original medicine into account when deciding whether to issue marketing authorisation of a generic medicine.[31] In India, the opposite position prevails. Under Art.30 of the TRIPS Agreement, with regard to the 'exceptions to rights conferred', the marketing regulatory authority and the Indian patent legislation are independent of each other by virtue of Section 107(A) of Patents (Amendment) Act 2015. This means that even when a patent is still in force, as long as the use is 'reasonable relating to the development and submission of information required under any law for the time being in force, in India, or in a country other than India', acts such as making, constructing, using, selling, etc., a patented invention are not an infringement of patent rights.[32] The case in point is *Bayer Corporation* v. *Union of India*, in which patent linkage was eventually established on the premise of 'right to health'.

The Bayer Corporation case concerns Section 2 of India's Drug and Cosmetic Act[33] and Section 48 of the Patents (Amendment) Act 2005.[34] When Cipla, Bayer's competitor, was seeking regulatory approval from the Drug Controller General of India (DCGI) for a generic version of Bayer's patented drug Nexavar, Bayer was against it and argued that patent linkage was necessary in order to effectuate the legislative intent of the Patents (Amendment) Act.[35] Nexavar is a drug for treating liver and kidney cancer and its patent was still in force when the Cipla-Bayer confrontation took place. Bayer contended that the DCGI would infringe its Nexaver patent if Cipla's generic version of the drug were to be approved, while Cipla replied that the (Indian) Parliament separated the marketing

30 't Hoen E. F. M., *The Global Politics of Pharmaceutical Monopoly Power* (Diemen, The Netherlands: AMB Publishers, 2009, pp. 70–72), cited in Bazzle T., 'Pharmacy of the developing world: reconciling intellectual property rights in India with the right to health: TRIPS, India's patent system and essential medicines'. 42 *Georgetown Journal of International Law* 3 (2011), 785.

31 Commission Executive Summary of the Pharmaceutical Sector Inquiry Report, at 23 (8 July 2009), available at: http://ec.europa.eu/competition/sectors/pharmaceuticals/inquiry/communication_en.pdf (last accessed 3 November 2015).

32 Section 107(A) of India's Patents (Amendment) Act 2005 provides that 'any act of making, constructing, using, selling or importing a patented invention solely for uses reasonably relating to the development and submission of information required under any law for the time being in force, in India, or in a country other than India, that regulates the manufacture, construction, use, sale or import of any products shall not be considered as an infringement of patent rights'.

33 Section 2 of India's Drug and Cosmetic Act provides that applications of other laws are not barred.

34 Section 48 of India's Patents (Amendment) Act provides that 'a patent granted [...] shall confer upon the patentee where the subject matter of the patent is a product, the exclusive right to prevent third parties, who do not have his consent, from the act of making, using, offering for sale, selling or importing for those purposes that product in India [...]'

35 *Bayer Corp.* v. *Union of India*, WP(C) No.7833/2008 (Delhi HC Aug. 18, 2009), at 5.

regulatory authority and the patent legislation as two regimes in order to allow each to fulfil their respective and distinct functions. If both regimes were to converge for the purpose of solving the present challenge, it would have amounted to impermissible 'legislating through interpretation'. Cipla further argued that enabling the DCGI to rule on patent validity through patent linkage would lead the DCGI to enforce both valid and invalid patents, and this would cause the adverse effect of 'creating additional and unnecessary hurdles for generic competition to the derogation of the public welfare and interest'.[36]

Bayer's argument for patent linkage was eventually dismissed by the Court on the grounds that linking marketing regulatory approval with patent legislation would undermine the Bolar exemption provided by the TRIPS Agreement and neglect the 'public health challenges'.[37] At the same time, the Court noted that granting marketing approval for developing a generic drug does not *ipso facto* amount to infringing a patent holder's rights to 'make, use, exercise, sell or distribute' the patented invention in India, so therefore the patent holder must formally allege and prove such an infringement before a court of law.[38]

In February 2010, Bayer's patent linkage claim was dismissed by the Delhi High Court which reaffirmed that the State must fulfil the 'essential elements' of the 'right to health'. The Delhi High Court noted the potentially disastrous effect that patent linkage could cause to the production of generic medicine. It acknowledged that many developing countries resist patent linkage in the interest of public healthcare, which should be affordable and accessible. Reaffirming the decision laid down by the Delhi High Court in February 2010, in December of the same year India's Supreme Court rejected the Special Leave Petition filed by Bayer Corporation in order to seek patent linkage for Nexavar in India.

Apart from the above-mentioned four cases, there are other controversial cases in the post-TRIPS era in India where pharmaceutical products failed to obtain patent protection, such as Roche's Pegasys case when the court decided to revoke the patent for the Hepatitis C drug, and the AstraZeneca appeal case when the court rejected patent protection for Iressa, a lung cancer drug.

In general, although patent protection is instrumental in promoting innovation in the pharmaceutical sector, at the same time it causes concerns about high drug prices because of which ordinary citizens may be deprived of access to drugs and their 'right to health' jeopardised. Reflecting on the decisions handed down by the Indian courts in the above-mentioned four cases, the judiciary was mainly against two adverse effects that a pharmaceutical product patent may potentially have. First, inventors may obtain patents for pharmaceutical products or research tools that stretch the statutory requirements for patenting. Second, patent holders in the market for pharmaceutical products may use legal loopholes or the patent registration system to extend the limited exclusive rights for inventions beyond what was anticipated by the Patents Act or the subsequent legislation.[39] At this juncture, it is necessary to provide a more complete picture of the evolution of India's patent legislation in order to illustrate how India defends national policy objectives

36 *Bayer Corp.* v. *Union of India*, WP(C) No.7833/2008 (Delhi HC Aug. 18, 2009), at 21.

37 *Bayer Corp.* v. *Union of India*, WP(C) No.7833/2008 (Delhi HC Aug. 18, 2009), at 44.

38 *Bayer Corp.* v. *Union of India*, WP(C) No.7833/2008 (Delhi HC Aug. 18, 2009), at 39.

39 Patil P. *et al.*, *Indian patent and Indian patient, friend or rival: a communication. Pharma Tutor Magazine*, ART-2057. Available at: www.pharmatutor.org/articles/indian-patent-patient-friend-rival-communication (last accessed 3 January 2017).

while, at the same time, complying with the minimum patent protection standards laid down by the TRIPS Agreement.

III A brief history of India's patent law development

I) Introduction

The above-mentioned four cases provide an accurate reflection of the key areas of debate revolving around India's patent legislation after 2005, when the provisions of the TRIPS Agreement were fully incorporated in the national patent legislation. After joining the TRIPS Agreement in 1994, India became a contracting party of the PCT in 1998. In the same year, India acceded to the Paris Convention.

II) Colonial era

Patent law was first imposed in India in 1856 during the colonial era by the British, based on its Patent Statute 1852.[40] It guaranteed the privileges of making, selling and using patented inventions for a term of 14 years in India from the date of filing a patent application.[41]

The Patent Act 1856 was modified in 1859 and renamed as the Act for Granting Exclusive Privileges to Inventors.[42] The Patents and Designs Protection Act was subsequently promulgated in 1872. In 1883 the Protection of Inventions Act came into force. Both acts were then consolidated as the Inventions and Designs Act 1888.

It was by the Patents and Designs Act 1911 that a patent system was created in India, administered by the Controller of Patents.[43] The Act also established a form of intra-British Empire priority system in which if an Indian patent applicant, within the previous 12 months, filed an application for the same invention in Britain, the applicant would be entitled to the benefit of an earlier British filing date.[44] As a result, during the intervening priority period, the publication or the use of the invention in India would not invalidate the Indian invention patent application.[45] Patents granted under the Act expired 16 years later counting from the date of filing, but an extension of up to seven additional years was possible. Despite the various subsequent revisions,[46] the Patents Act 1911 remained effective until 1970 when India enacted its own patent act. Note that before the Patents Act

40 Narayanan P., *Patent Law 7* (3rd Ed.). (Kolkata, India: Eastern Law House, 1998), p. 4.

41 Later, the statute was denominated Act VI of 1856. See Narayanan P., *Patent Law 7* (3rd Ed.). (Kolkata, India: Eastern Law House, 1998), p. 4.

42 Narayanan P., *Intellectual Property Law 1* (Hyderabad, India: Gogia Law Agency, 2005).

43 Narayanan P., *Patent Law 7* (3rd Ed.). (Kolkata, India: Eastern Law House, 1998), p. 4. From 1857 to 1888, the patent system in India was under the administration of the British Secretary to the Government in the Home Department. See: Mithal V. P., 'Patents in India'. 30 *Journal of the Patent Office Society (India)* 62, (1948), also: Mueller J. M., 'The tiger awakens: the tumultuous transformation of India's patent system and the rise of Indian pharmaceutical innovation'. 68 *University of Pittsburgh Law Review* 3 (2007), 491.

44 Section 78A(1), Patents Act 1911.

45 Section 78A(2)(a), Patents Act 1911.

46 Mithal V. P., 'Patents in India'. 30 *Journal of the Patent Office Society (India)* 62, (1948) at 65, also: Mueller J. M., 'The tiger awakens: the tumultuous transformation of India's patent system and the rise of Indian pharmaceutical innovation'. 68 *University of Pittsburgh Law Review* 3 (2007).

1970 came into force, all previous patent acts granted patent protection to pharmaceutical products.

Accompanying the evolution of patent legislation was the growth of India's domestic economy. By the time of World War I, India became the fourteenth most industrialised nation in the world,[47] although the industrialisation concentrated mostly in the sectors of textiles, food processing and metals.[48] Pharmaceutical manufacturing was very much lagging behind. For example, of all the Indian workers employed in factories in 1921, 41.62 per cent of them worked in textile production, followed by 7.2 per cent in food production and 4.6 per cent in metals and machinery. Only 2.6 per cent were employed in the chemicals industry. Although specific data on pharmaceutical manufacturing were not available,[49] before World War II there was 'virtually no basic drug manufacture in the country'.[50] Of course, one must also take note that, in the past, many Indians relied on herbs and plant extracts in traditional remedies such as Ayurveda to treat diseases, instead of visiting a pharmacist. Developing a pharmaceutical industry looked redundant in those days.

III) Independence and the Patents Act 1970

When India won its independence from the British in 1947 it became one of the poorest countries in the world, with a population of 400 million representing one-fifth of the world's population at that time. Providing affordable medicines to a huge impoverished population became urgent, especially because India's domestic pharmaceutical industry was so negligible that its limited capacity did not go beyond packaging and bottling. At the time, India largely depended on imports from Britain, France and Germany for medicine supply and was compelled to pay hefty prices.[51] For example, the tranquilliser meprobamate in India was 47 per cent more expensive than in the US in 1959, and it was sold for the highest price among all the countries included in the data set except Venezuela. The price for the tranquilliser Serpasil, although it was only 44 per cent of the US price, was higher than the price charged in France, Austria, Germany, England and several other developed countries. By the same token, India was completely reliant on critical but conventional drugs such as insulin and penicillin.[52] For overall medical provision, India's local pharmaceutical industry was only able to meet 13 per cent of the demand, which was far from being self-sufficient or self-sustainable.[53]

47 Judd D., *The Lion and the Tiger: The Rise and Fall of the British Raj, 1600–1947.* (Oxford: OUP, 2004), p. 53.

48 Kumar *et al.* (Eds), *The Cambridge Economic History of India, 1757–1970* (Cambridge: CUP Archive, 1982), p. 566, that 'large-scale private factory enterprise between 1850 and the First World War is associated almost entirely with developments in three industries – jute, cotton, and iron and steel'.

49 Roy T., *The Economic History of India 1857–1947* (Oxford: OUP, 2000), p. 158.

50 Hamied Y. K., 'Indian pharma industry, decades of struggle and achievements'. 19 *Chemical Business* 4; Apr., (2005), p. 2.

51 Chaudhuri S., *The WTO and India's Pharmaceuticals Industry: Patent Protection, TRIPS, and Developing Countries* (Oxford: OUP, 2005), p. 132.

52 Planning Commission, Government of India, 1st Five Year Plan, Chapter 32, pp. 96, 99 (Dec. 7, 1952).

53 In 1901, India established its domestic pharmaceutical industry with the creation of Bengal Chemical and Pharmaceutical Works. The two World Wars gave a boost to the development of the industry, although the development was still considered insignificant. See: Chaudhuri S., *The WTO and India's Pharmaceuticals Industry: Patent Protection, TRIPS, and Developing Countries* (Oxford: OUP, 2005), p. 22. See also: Sahu S. K., *Technology Transfer, Dependence, and Self-Reliant Development in the Third World: The Pharmaceutical and Machine Tool Industries in India.* (Santa Barbara, CA: Praeger, 1998), p. 55.

To increase the manufacturing capacity of the local pharmaceutical industry, the Indian government started to draft a new patent law in order to, among other objectives, empower lawful indigenous medicine manufacturing. In the process of legislation, a committee was established to 'review the patent laws in India with a view to ensure that the patent system was more conducive to national interests'.[54] Two reports on the patent system were then published by the committee. The first report, also known as *The Chand Report* and named after Bakshi Tek Chand who was then the Indian Supreme Court Justice, was published in 1950. *The Chand Report* noted that India's patent system failed to 'stimulate invention and encourage exploitation of new inventions for industrial purposes'. The report recommended that compulsory licenses ought to be issued and an 'efficient machinery should be evolved to tackle the issues of abuses' of the patent system.[55] Note that the compulsory licence provisions had been in place in India since the Patents Act 1911 came into force, and it remained in the patent legislation after the patent amendments took place in 1950 and 1952 respectively. The compulsory licence provisions appeared nonetheless redundant because patent owners were provided with the right to oppose and to appeal against compulsory licence applications.[56] Pursuant to *The Chand Report*, a patent bill was introduced in 1953 but nonetheless lapsed.[57]

The second report, *The Ayyangar Report*, was subsequently published in 1959. *The Ayyangar Report* analysed 'the adaptability of foreign patent regimes and policy options to address national issues' and 'highlighted the best practices in foreign patent regimes and examined their suitability to address public health and economic concerns of underdeveloped economies'.[58] The report recommended drafting a patent law in order to accommodate India's fledgling technological advances and industrialisation, to encourage and reward inventors, to increase the number of research institutes and to emphasise technical education. The report summarised the following strategies as a way forward to realise these goals, which were: 1) identifying the types of inventions for which patent protection should become available; 2) deciding either to prohibit granting Indian patents to foreign entities or to insist on 'working' such patents in India; 3) withstanding international pressures and not join international IPR conventions, such as the Paris Convention, which required national treatment.[59]

Despite the ambitions it professed, *The Ayyangar Report* was not able to deliver a new patent law until 1970 when the Patents Act 1970 was eventually enacted and the Patents and Designs Act 1911 was repealed. The objective of the Patents Act 1970 was to encourage innovation and to ensure that inventions were able to be commercialised and not granted merely to enable patent holders to enjoy a monopoly.[60] The most notable measure enacted to this effect was that pharmaceutical products were struck down as a patentable subject matter in India. Section 5 stipulated that 'substances intended for use, or capable of being used, as food or as medicine or drug, or … relating to substances prepared or

54 Ayyangar N. R., *Report on the Revision of the Patents Law*, Preface. (The Government of India, September 1959).

55 Narayanan P., *Intellectual Property Law 1* (Hyderabad, India: Gogia Law Agency, 2005), p. 1.

56 Chaudhuri S., *The WTO and India's Pharmaceuticals Industry: Patent Protection, TRIPS, and Developing Countries* (Oxford: OUP, 2005), pp. 93–94.

57 Narayanan P., *Patent Law 7* (3rd Ed.). (Kolkata, India: Eastern Law House, 1998), p. 5.

58 Ragavan S., 'Of the inequals of the Uruguay Round'. 10 *Marquette Intellectual Property Law Review* 273 (2006), 281, 282.

59 Narayanan P., *Intellectual Property Law 1* (Hyderabad, India: Gogia Law Agency, 2005), pp. 1–2.

60 Section 83 (a)(b), the Patents Act 1970.

produced by chemical processes (including alloys, optical glass, semi-conductors and intermetallic compounds)' were not patentable.[61] In the meantime, the Patents Act 1970 provided an easier route to granting compulsory licences. As a result, a patented process for manufacturing chemical compounds that were capable of being used as a medicine or food ingredient would be automatically subject to 'licensing of right'.[62]

Thanks to the legal safeguards provided by the Patents Act 1970, India's generic pharmaceutical industry welcomed the sharp boost it gave and a large generic pharmaceutical industry with over 16,000 companies was established.[63] Medicine prices decreased drastically in the meantime because India could, at its disposal, produce generic pharmaceutical products that were patented outside India, so long as the patent for the manufacturing process was not infringed, for which it was protected for only five to seven years.[64] In the mid-1970s India's drug manufacturers were able to start producing active pharmaceutical ingredients. Production steadily increased over the next three decades and India's generic pharmaceutical industry has since evolved to become highly competitive and diverse. From meeting just 13 per cent of the domestic needs in the 1940s, in 2000 70 per cent of the Indian domestic drug market was controlled by 20 local companies, although some are subsidiaries of multinationals such as Glaxo India. Large independent manufacturers, like Cipla, Ranbaxy, Dr Reddy's, Wockhardt and Sun Pharmaceutical Industries Ltd., produced many kinds of generic drugs for export, not only to the developing countries but also to industrialised countries such as America, Europe and Japan. By 1988 India had already transformed to become the 'pharmacy of the developing world' as a net exporter of high quality affordable drugs.[65] The country's generic drug manufacturers have significantly contributed to lower drug prices at the same time. For example, the 'cocktail' therapy for AIDS manufactured by Cipla, a pharmaceutical giant in India, cost as little as 83 USD (73.35 EUR) a month, while the same therapy will cost 1,000 USD (883.75 EUR) or more when it is manufactured in the West.[66] Cipla manufactures four out of the 14 drugs

61 Note, however, the same Section allowed for methods or processes of such chemical compounds to be patented, although the chemical compound itself was prohibited from patenting.

62 Section 87, the Patents Act 1970. In *Imperial Chem. Indus. Ltd.* v. *Controller Gen. of Patents*, 1987 AIR 77 (Calcutta), the Calcutta High Court affirmed the Controller of Patents' order that Imperial's patent, claiming a catalyst useful in hydrocarbon reforming as well as a process for making the catalyst, to be subject to licensing of right. Mueller J. M., 'The tiger awakens: the tumultuous transformation of India's patent system and the rise of Indian pharmaceutical innovation'. 68 *University of Pittsburgh Law Review* 3 (2007), 491.

63 Gupta R., 'TRIPS compliance: dealing with the consequences of drug patents in India'. 26 *Houston Journal of International Law* 599 (2005), 602.

64 Consequently, although India was criticised for being a 'pirate' nation, copying drugs patented in other countries, some argued that, until India has become member of the international patent treaties, such as the Paris Convention and the TRIPS Agreement, when it must comply with the treaty obligations, it was legitimate for India to 'copy' foreign-patented drugs as long as the copied drugs were manufactured in India and sold in India or other countries that did not recognise pharmaceutical products patents. In any case, patent rights are rights of territoriality. See: McNeil D. G. Jr., 'Selling cheap "generic" drugs: India's copycats irk industry'. *The New York Times*, 1 December 2000, available at: www.nytimes.com/2000/12/01/world/selling-cheap-generic-drugs-india-s-copycats-irk-industry.html?pagewanted=printandsrc=pm (last accessed 18 November 2015).

65 Grover A., 'Analysing the Supreme Court judgment'. *Economic and Political Weekly*, 10 August 10, Vol. XLVIII No. 32 (2013).

66 McNeil D. G. Jr., 'Selling cheap "generic" drugs: India's copycats irk industry'. *The New York Times*, 1 December 2000, available at: www.nytimes.com/2000/12/01/world/selling-cheap-generic-drugs-india-s-copycats-irk-industry.html?pagewanted=printandsrc=pm (last accessed 18 November 2015).

commonly used in the therapy[67] and India nowadays supplies a large percentage of the AIDS medicine used in developing countries.[68] For example, according to a survey conducted by Médicins Sans Frontières, 84 per cent of 60,000 patients living in nearly 30 countries received generic AIDS medicine made in India. In the meantime, building on the strengths gained from generic drug manufacturing, India's drug producers have become skilled in reverse engineering and in developing new processes for drug production, to the extent that some were able to launch foreign drugs locally even before the drug inventor companies did. Overall, the strategy of boosting generic drug manufacturing has benefited the Indian population considerably, with average life expectancy rising from 42 in 1960 to 65 in 2011. India became the biggest producer of generic drugs by volume and a leading exporter of medicine to developing countries

However, some caution must be taken when reflecting on the success of India's generic pharmaceutical industry since, after all, such success has little to do with innovation. India's patent strategy facilitated the thriving growth of the generic pharmaceutical industry but, to a certain extent, this is at the expense of some innovative pharmaceutical companies, which is unjustifiable and unfair. Due to the lack of patent protection, some global pharmaceutical companies left India and took with them R&D investment and scientists that were much needed for establishing the country's pharmaceutical industry. This cost India a huge brain drain. As a consequence, the downstream sectors within the pharmaceutical industry, such as the sectors of advanced clinical trials, genetic engineering, combinatorial chemistry, natural products, agro-chemicals and agricultural products, were left underdeveloped.

IV) Globalisation and the TRIPS Agreement

Against a backdrop of international patent rights harmonisation, India has been very assertive when upholding the principle of the 'right to health'. As one of the 140 founding members of the WTO, India was initially opposed to embedding provisions on IPR protection in the Agreement Establishing the WTO. Together with other developing countries,[69] India regarded IPR protection as an instrument used by wealthy Western countries in exchange for allowing developing countries access to their markets.[70] As to granting patent rights to pharmaceutical products, which was one of the most significant concessions that India had to make in order to accede to the WTO, India was convinced that the incentive was limited for developing countries and the most important potential gains, which were marginal for pharmaceutical innovation, would be provided by additional exclusivity in new countries.[71] Eventually, India conceded to the inclusion of the provisions on IPR protection

67 These four drugs are zidovudine, lamivudine, stavudine and nevirapine.

68 See: Press release, Médecins Sans Frontières, *Patent Application for AIDS Drug Opposed First Time in India*, 30 March 2006, available at: www.msf.org/article/patent-application-aids-drug-opposed-first-time-india (last accessed 18 November 2015).

69 There were at least 50 developing countries did not grant patent protection to pharmaceutical products at the time. See: Correa C. M. and Abdulqawi A. Y. (Eds), *Patent Rights in Intellectual Property and International Trade: The TRIPS Agreement* (2nd Ed.). (New York: Kluwer Law International, 2008), pp. 227, 229.

70 Seeratan N. N., 'The negative impact of intellectual property patent rights on developing countries: an examination of the Indian pharmaceutical industry'. 3 *Scholar* 339 (2001), 352–53.

71 Deardorff A.V., 'Should patent protection be extended to all developing countries?' 13 *World Economy* 497 (1990), 503.

in the WTO Agreement as it feared that, if it were to continue opposing the motion, restrictions would be imposed on its exports and those concessions on textile tariffs and economic aid coming from developed countries might be in jeopardy since they firmly advocated for stronger IPR protection. Nonetheless, while negotiating for certain provisions contained in the TRIPS Agreement where flexibility was permissible, India maintained that the extent of patent protection should vary based on an individual country's economic development capacity. Perhaps in order to offset the concession it made for pharmaceutical products patenting, India championed the transitional arrangements that TRIPS has offered to developing and transitional economies to a greater extent.[72] These arrangements were said to be initially strongly opposed by the multinational pharmaceutical industry.[73]

After becoming a member of the WTO as well as of the TRIPS Agreement in January 1995, India was obliged, among other obligations, to start offering patent protection to pharmaceutical products so as to fully comply with the TRIPS Agreement, especially with regard to the minimum patent protection standards set down by the agreement. Nonetheless, taking advantage of the transitional arrangements provided by the TRIPS Agreement, India took ten years to gradually adapt to those minimum protection standards in order to mitigate the impact that the TRIPS would have made on the domestic patent landscape and, particularly, on the local generic pharmaceutical industry. India's legislature launched a three-step process before amending the Patents Act 1970, which is referred to in India as the Principal Act.[74] The first step was to create a 'mailbox' facility as 'pipeline protection' for pharmaceutical, chemical and agricultural products patent applications. The 'mailbox' facility, together with the exclusive marketing rights, was incorporated in Patents (Amendment) Act 1999, after the WTO DSB ruled against India in the 'mailbox' case. The second step was to amend the Principal Act in order to provide: 1) a minimum 20-year patent protection term; 2) a reversal of the burden of proof for process patent infringement; and 3) modified compulsory licensing requirements. The Patents (Amendment) Act 2002 was thus promulgated to this effect. The third step was to start providing patent rights to pharmaceutical products on 1 January 2005, which resulted in the Patents (Amendment) Act 2005 and marked the beginning of India's full compliance with the TRIPS Agreement.

IV The process of international patent rights harmonisation in India

While amending the Patents Act in 2002, India's Parliament was mindful of the balance that it must strike between complying with the minimum patent protection standards set out in the TRIPS Agreement and defending its citizens' constitutional right to health by, for example, ensuring access to affordable generic medicine. Relying on the principle of

72 Foster G. K., 'Opposing forces in a revolution in international patent protection: the US and India in the Uruguay Round and its aftermath'. 3 *University of California Journal of International Law and Foreign Affairs* 283 (1998), 315–17, 311–12.

73 Weissman R., 'A long, strange TRIPS: the pharmaceutical industry drive to harmonize global intellectual property rules, and the remaining WTO legal alternatives available to third world countries'. 17 *University of Pennsylvania Journal of International Economic Law* 1069 (1996), 1084–85.

74 Chaudhuri S., *The WTO and India's Pharmaceuticals Industry: Patent Protection, TRIPS, and Developing Countries* (Oxford: OUP, 2005), pp. 65–70.

flexibility provided by the TRIPS Agreement, the Indian legislature set higher protection standards in relation to exceptions to patentable inventions, thresholds tests for patentability, as well as procedural requirements, patent misuse standards and injunctive remedies. Without doubt, the purpose for undertaking this legislative arrangement was to ensure that the right to health will always prevail over patent protection if conflict between the two arises. As a result, the legislative impact brought about by pharmaceutical product patenting on the generic pharmaceutical industry is mitigated.

The above-mentioned legislative arrangement was possible thanks to two provisions declared by the TRIPS Agreement. By virtue of Art.27 of the TRIPS Agreement, a patent application must satisfy the three-step test of novelty, inventiveness and industrial application before patent protection may be granted for 20 years. As Art.27 does not provide definitions for each step of the test, TRIPS members enjoy a good degree of liberty when deciding whether an application is patentable after Art.27 is duly interpreted and subsequently incorporated into their respective national patent law, although any interpretation must follow the relevant criteria set down by the Vienna Convention on the Law of the Treaties.[75] Additionally, Art.1.1 provides TRIPS members with the flexibility to impose stricter protection measures than those required under the Agreement and to determine the appropriate methods of incorporating the provisions prescribed by TRIPS pursuant to their respective legal system and practice.

I) Exceptions to patentable subject matters

In addition to subject matters that are contrary to *order public* and morality,[76] Art.27(3) of the TRIPS Agreement provides that 'diagnostic, therapeutic and surgical methods for the treatment of humans or animals' as well as 'plants and animals other than micro-organisms, and essentially biological processes for the production of plants or animals other than non-biological and microbiological processes' are not patentable subject matters. Despite being equipped with the principle of flexibility provided by TRIPS, exceptions to patentable subject matters prescribed by each member's patent legislation are not far from each other. For example, by virtue of Art.53 (b)(c) of the EPC, exceptions to patentable subject matters are: plant or animal varieties or biological processes for the production of plants or animals (except microbiological processes or the products thereof); and methods for treatment of the human or animal body by surgery or therapy and diagnostic methods practised on the human or animal body (except products, such as substances or compositions). In China's case, Art.25 of the Patent Law 2008 specifies that scientific discoveries, rules and methods for intellectual activities, methods for the diagnosis or treatment of diseases, animal or plant varieties (production methods of the products may be patentable), substances obtained by means of nuclear transformation and designs that are mainly used for making the pattern, colour or the combination of the two of prints are not patentable inventions. Article 25 of the Draft Patent Law 2015 adds that inventions of nuclear transformation method are not a patentable subject matter.

What is controversial in India's patent legislation is the much higher threshold prescribed by Section 3(d) of India's Patents (Amendment) Act 2005 and its Explanation, which

75 Correa C. M., 'Is Section 3(d) consistent with TRIPS?' *Economic and Political Weekly*, August 10, Vol. XLVIII No. 32 (2013).

76 Art.27(2), TRIPS Agreement.

allegedly draws a draconian demarcation between mere and patentable inventions concerning chemical compounds, as is discussed above in *Novartis AG* v. *Union of India*.

Entitled 'inventions not patentable' under Chapter II of India's Patents (Amendment) Act 2005, Section 3 stipulates a long list of non-patentable inventions, such as methods of agriculture or horticulture, and 'literary, dramatic, musical or artistic work or any other aesthetic creation whatsoever including cinematographic works and television productions'. Section 3(d) further emphasises that 'the mere discovery of a new form of a known substance which does not result in the enhancement of the known efficacy of that substance or the mere discovery of any new property or new use for a known substance or of the mere use of a known process, machine or apparatus unless such known process results in a new product or employs at least one new reactant' are not patentable subject matters. Moreover, Section 3(d) in its Explanation specifies a list of examples of non-patentable inventions such as, for instance, '... derivatives of known substance shall be considered to be the same substance, unless they differ significantly in properties with regard to efficacy'. Note that this restriction is said to be at the heart of the Patents Act 1970, and is simply reinforced by the amendment in 2005.[77] As such, although pharmaceutical product inventions have become patentable since 2005 in India, whether a particular invention is eligible for patenting is highly debatable – not to mention the public interest test that a pharmaceutical product patent application must still satisfy. The chances of granting patent protection to pharmaceutical products remains limited and uncertain, especially if pharmaceutical companies try to obtain successive patents as a means to extend their monopoly over a patented drug.[78]

As mentioned previously, while incorporating Art.27(1) of the TRIPS Agreement, Section 3(d) of the Patents (Amendment) Act 2005 sets a much higher threshold in order to curb the tactic of 'evergreening', which is allegedly often engaged in by some multinational pharmaceutical companies.[79] For this purpose, Section 3(d) rejects inventions of the new use, or the new forms, of known chemical compounds that do not enhance 'efficacy', which is a prerequisite for patenting pharmaceutical products. This being the case, in reality it means that, for example, the discovery that aspirin, which is a known analgesic, is equally useful in treating cardiovascular disease would not succeed in patent application in India, while a new and alternative method for preparing aspirin may be patentable because it is a new method of making a known chemical compound as opposed to a new method of using a known chemical compound. On the other hand, the test of efficacy is rather subjective when, for example, the Chennai Patent Controller in the case of *Novartis AG* v. *Union of India* did not consider the 30 per cent increase in the active ingredient's absorption in the blood achieved by Gleevec met the requirement of 'enhanced efficacy'.

Section 3(d) of the Patents (Amendment) Act 2005 has been a significant source of controversies. For example, in the Novartis case, as mentioned above, Novartis argued that the beta crystalline form had several qualities that made it more 'efficacious' than the base compound Imatinib, which was invented before 1995. Also, although beta crystalline was

77 *Novartis AG* v. *Union of India*, Supreme Court of India, para 102, 1 April 2013.

78 *Novartis AG* v. *Union of India*, Madras HC, 6 August 2007, at p. 10.

79 It is noted that over 75 per cent of the patented drugs were modifications of known chemical compounds, while only 15 per cent of the drugs approved by the US Food and Drug Authority between 1989 and 2000 were considered 'highly innovative'. Rangnekar D., 'The Supreme Court judgment, "law making" in the South'. *Economic and Political Weekly*, 10 August, Vol. XLVIII No. 32 (2013).

proven to be easier to store and to process, and 30 per cent more bio-available than Imatinib, the two lower courts in India both dismissed the Gleevec patenting request, and ruled that Gleevec did not meet the narrowly defined 'therapeutic efficacy' standard, which required the new form of chemical compound to show an improved healing effect in the body. This judicial interpretation has been since incorporated into India's Draft Patent Manual.[80] In April 2013, the Supreme Court of India confirmed that the beta crystalline form of Imatinib failed the test of Section 3(d), while 'efficacy', as contemplated under the provision, is meant to be therapeutic efficacy. Ultimately, Gleevec was denied patent protection because it was too similar to its earlier version, Imatinib.

Section 3(d) draws an equally sharp contrast to the threshold test enforced in the US and Europe in relation to patentability.[81] What is restricted by Section 3(d) as to the use of known chemical compounds is permissible under both patent regimes when, for example, the new use of a known chemical compound is recognised while a compound and its use in a particular way can be both protected.[82] Also, new forms of known chemical compounds that have 'pharmaceutical application' are also commonly patentable and structural forms of a compound with different properties may be claimed as long as the patenting requirements of novelty, inventive step and industrial application are met.[83] Essentially, by virtue of Art.53 of the EPC, an invention will be patentable as long as it does not fall under the list of exceptions to patentability. In the US pharmaceutical salts have been granted patents for decades if it can be proven that the salt differs from the previously disclosed compound in an unexpectedly beneficial way. While, in India, in accordance with Section 3(d) of the Patents (Amendment) Act 2005, salts and other derivatives of known chemical compounds are seen as the same chemical compound, unless they differ significantly in properties with regard to efficacy, which must be proven 'therapeutic'.

The higher threshold test for patentability set down by Section 3(d) is, nonetheless, legitimate under the terms of the TRIPS Agreement because, after all, the prerequisites prescribed by Art.27 of the TRIPS Agreement are entirely met.[84] On the other hand, since it is typical for legislation to serve policy needs, it is perhaps expected for Section 3(d) to be adopted in order to seriously narrow down the scope of patentable subject matters as

80 Patent Office (India), *Draft Manual of Patent Practice and Procedure 58* (2008). The draft manual is not the result of formal rule-making and does not have the force of law, but will play a substantial role in guiding examiners' decisions. Kapczynski A., 'Harmonisation and its discontents: a case study of TRIPS implementation in India's pharmaceutical sector'. 97 *California Law Review* 1571 (2009).

81 Note, however, countries, such as Argentina, Australia, Canada and Thailand, have adopted the same restrictions on patent applications for pharmaceutical products. Rangnekar D., 'The Supreme Court judgment, "law making" in the South'. *Economic and Political Weekly*, 10 August, Vol. XLVIII No. 32 (2013).

82 Thomas J. R., *Pharmaceutical Patent Law* (1st Ed.). (Edison, NJ: Bloomberg BNA Books, 2005), pp. 44–49. See also: International Centre for Trade and Sustainable Development and United Nations Conference on Trade and Development, *Resource Book on TRIPS and Development* (Cambridge: Cambridge University Press, 2005), 356–357.

83 Fanelli D. L., 'Claiming novel polymorphic forms of drug products'. 88 *Journal of the Patent and Trademark Office Society* 12 (2006), 1053–4.

84 Professor Correa illustrated the different standard of novelty established in different jurisdictions by using the US patent legislation as an example. The US maintained until recently that a novelty standard (35 USC. § 102(a)) must combine the local and the universal novelty depending on whether the disclosure of the invention had taken place within or outside US territory. The US argued that, in the TRIPS Agreement, there was 'no prescription as to how WTO members define what inventions are to be considered "new" within their domestic systems', and therefore the legislation was 'perfectly consistent with the provisions of the TRIPS Agreement'. Correa C. M., 'Is Section 3(d) consistent with TRIPS?' *Economic and Political Weekly*, August 10, Vol. XLVIII No. 32 (2013).

a precaution against the tactic of 'evergreening'. This being the case, Section 3(d) appears all the more necessary for India, especially in consideration of the policy objective of the 'right to health'. In any case, thanks to Art.1.1 of the TRIPS Agreement, TRIPS members are at liberty to set more or less rigorous criteria in terms of patentability as long as the minimum protection standards are met.

With regard to those non-patentable subject matters other than chemical compounds, in conformity with Art.27(3)(b) of the TRIPS Agreement, after the Indian patent legislation was amended in 2002 plants and animals (except micro-organisms) are no longer patentable. As to the patentability of micro-organisms, Section 3(j) of the Patents (Amendment) Act 2005 grants patents for micro-organisms and other living organisms other than plants or animals, provided the organism is novel, involves an inventive step and is industrially applicable.

II) Inventive step

Section 2(1)(ja) defines inventive step as 'a feature of an invention that involves technical advance as compared to the existing knowledge or having economic significance or both and that makes the invention not obvious to a person skilled in the art'. The provision established 'technical advance' and 'economic significance' as the two ingredients that must be present before a claim of 'inventive step', also known as 'non-obviousness', may be made. Much controversy has been drawn to these two ingredients for the following two reasons.

First, the 'economic significance' requirement is criticised for being exorbitant, vague and arbitrary. Second, and moreover, although 'technical advance' and 'economic significance' are commonly applied as prerequisites by TRIPS members, it is unusual that both ingredients are bound together and must both be satisfied before the threshold test of inventiveness may be passed.[85] For example, contrary to India's case, under both the Chinese patent law as well as the EPC, 'economic significance' is not a prerequisite before a 'novelty' test may be passed.[86] Having said that, the requirement of 'inventiveness' imposed by India has met the minimum standard of 'involving an inventive step' prescribed by Art.27.1 of the TRIPS Agreement, while the higher threshold test is legitimately set down on account of the principle of flexibility conferred by the same agreement. Besides, it is noticed that technologically less-advanced countries often erect a higher threshold test for inventiveness for the sake of public interest, so that domestic

85 In the US, 'commercial success' is a consideration under the 'secondary effects', see for example *Graham* v. *John Deere Co.*, 383 US 1, 17–18 (1966). In Europe, courts also consult such factors when assessing the quality of obviousness, see *Haberman* v. *Jackel Int'l, Ltd.*, [1999] FSR 683, 699–701 (Ch. (Pat. Ct.)) (UK). Kapczynski A., 'Harmonisation and its discontents: a case study of TRIPS implementation in India's pharmaceutical sector'. 97 *California Law Review* 1571 (2009).

86 It is also said that the prerequisite of 'economic significance' represents a departure from India's case law precedent, as India's Supreme Court previously simply equated 'inventive step' with 'non-obviousness' and acknowledged that the term has 'acquired special significance in the terminology of Patent Law'. In *Bishwanath Prasad* v. *Hindustan Metal Industry*, (1978) 254 SCR 757, 777, the Supreme Court upheld the trial court's decision to grant the defendant's petition to revoke the patented method of making utensils on the ground as that invention was 'neither a manner of new manufacture or novel improvement, nor did it involve any inventive step, having regard to what was publicly known or used at the date of the patent'. Mueller J. M., 'The tiger awakens: the tumultuous transformation of India's patent system and the rise of Indian pharmaceutical innovation'. 68 *University of Pittsburgh Law Review* 3 (2007), 491.

industries may be able to fend off the influx of foreign high technologies under certain circumstances.[87] But still, 'economic significance' is a requirement that is too subjective and marred by uncertainty.

When Section 2(1)(ja) is read together with Section 3(d), the chances of patenting a pharmaceutical product invention in India look doubtful. Indeed, even if a pharmaceutical product invention satisfies the test of 'patentable invention' prescribed by Section 3(d), it may very well fail the higher threshold set down by Section 2(l)(ja) concerning inventiveness for the lack of economic significance. India can thus effectively throw out an extensive number of pharmaceutical product patent applications. The consequence of this curtailment is that a substantial percentage of pharmaceutical products may remain open to generic manufacturing without the requirement of compulsory licence. In the end, the effect of patenting pharmaceutical products may be mitigated, while the generic pharmaceutical industry could maintain its access to products and the markets at home and abroad, and its opportunities for furthering continued growth are less affected.

III) Pre-grant and post-grant oppositions, revocation and disclosure

To challenge a patent grant, pre-grant and post-grant opposition are the two available procedures provided by India's patent legislation. While the pre-grant opposition procedure *vis-à-vis* pending patent applications has been in place since the Patents Act 1911 came into force, launching the post-grant opposition procedure became possible pursuant to the entry into force of the Patents (Amendment) Act 2005. Both opposition actions may be undertaken before the patent office, and the patent revocation procedure may also be instituted before the IPAB or by filing a counterclaim in an infringement lawsuit in court. Entitled 'opposition proceedings to grant of patents', Section 25 of India's Patents (Amendment) Act 2005 governs the procedures of opposition, revocation and disclosure.

India's pre-grant opposition is well-known for its expansive provision that 'any person', either competitors or NGOs from home and abroad, may oppose a patent application,[88] as is reflected in the above-mentioned TDF case. Section 25(1) of the Patents (Amendment) Act 2005 states that '[w]here an application for a patent has been published but a patent has not been granted, any person may, in writing, represent by way of opposition to the Controller against the grant of patent...'. In accordance with Section 25(1)(a)–(k) of the same Act, the grounds for pre-grant patent opposition are very broad, ranging from technical to scientific reasons, including the lack of inventive step, violation of Section 3 and particularly of Section 3(d), insufficient disclosure of invention in the patent application specifications, failure to disclose the source of biological material used for the invention, and inventions considered as traditional knowledge, etc.

The pre-grant opposition mechanism was first introduced by Section 9 of India's Patents Act 1911, when it was an oft-used legal procedure in patent examination employed by many countries, such as Germany, Britain and Japan, at the time. The mechanism started to be phased out in the 1980s because more and more countries began to favour the post-grant opposition procedure since the pre-grant opposition was blamed for having aggravated the

87 Correa C. M., 'Public health and patent legislation in developing countries'. 3 *Tulane Journal of Technology and Intellectual Property* 1 (2001), 49.

88 As to the post-grant opposition instrument, only 'any person interested' may file an opposition petition.

delays in patent application. Japan repealed its pre-grant opposition mechanism in January 1996, Germany switched from the pre-grant to post-grant opposition in 1981, and Britain abolished the pre-grant opposition mechanism by its Patents Act 1977. But the pre-grant opposition mechanism has remained in India's patent legislation as the legislature argues that the proceeding does not delay the patent application process and, instead, it is an effective way of discovering prior art in order to facilitate patent examination. According to India's Patents Rules 2013, after receiving a pre-grant opposition petition, the Patent Controller shall proceed to either reject the representation and grant the patent application in question or accept the representation and therefore reject the patent application. The whole proceeding should complete within one month.[89] Presently, Brazil[90], India and Jordan[91] are the only three countries in the world that still maintain the pre-grant opposition procedure in their patent legislation.[92]

Statistics reveal that generic pharmaceutical manufacturers, health NGOs and advocacy groups are frequent users of the pre-grant opposition proceedings as a potent weapon to use to challenge patents of essential medicine in India. The TDF case mentioned above is a case in point. Also, during the trial of the Novartis case, the Indian Cancer Patients' Aid Association, a patents' rights group, also challenged the patentability of Gleevec, as *amicus* of the seven respondents. Previously, a representation of a pre-grant opposition had to be submitted within three months counting from the date of publication or before the grant of the patent, based on the Patents Rules. However, at present, by virtue of Section 25(1) of the Patents (Amendment) Act 2005, pre-grant opposition proceedings may be launched at any time after a patent application is published but before a patent is granted.

As the pre-grant opposition procedure was phased out except in three countries, the post-grant opposition is the instrument adopted by most countries to safeguard patent quality. Under the America Invents Act 2011, the post-grant opposition proceedings may be initiated by anyone except the patent-holder within nine months after a patent is issued if a) non-patentability is 'more likely than not', or b) a question of novelty or (c) an unsettled legal question that is important to other patents or patent applications has been raised.[93] The grounds for opposition under the American patent law range from utility, eligibility, enablement, written description and definiteness, etc.[94] The America Invents Act 2011 also installed three post-grant procedures into the mechanism, including post-grant review, *inter partes* review and the transnational programme for covered business method patents. The overall post-grant opposition procedure is administered by the Board of Patent Appeals and Interference.

The post-grant opposition instrument was introduced into India's patent legislation by the Patents (Amendment) Act 2005. Section 25(2) prescribes that 'any person interested may give notice of opposition to the Controller' at any time within one year after a patent

89 Rule 55(6), Patents Rules 2013.

90 Art.158, Law No. 10.196 of February 14, 2001 (Amendments to the Law on Industrial Property).

91 Art.14, Amending the Patents Law 2007.

92 Having said that, it seems the pre-grant opposition procedure is admitted subtly under the EPC too. Article 115 of the EPC provides that, after a patent application is published, any third party may present observations concerning patentability of an invention described in the publication, although such third parties do not become a party to the proceedings. If the observations pose a real question on patentability, they must be admitted and considered in any ongoing proceedings before a department of the EPO.

93 35 USC. § 324(a)(b).

94 35 USC. § 282.

is granted. Grounds for initiating pre-grant and post-grant proceedings are the same, which are prescribed by Section 25(2)(a)–(k). Nonetheless, parties that wish to challenge a patent grant must be 'any person interested' rather than being 'any person', which is the case *vis-à-vis* the pre-grant opposition procedure. The definition of 'any person interested' is provided by Section 2(1)(t) of the Patents (Amendment) Act 2005, which means 'a person engaged in, or in promoting, research in the same field as that to which the invention relates'.

Section 8 of Patents (Amendments) Act 2005 requires an applicant to inform the patent office of an application that he (or with any other person) has filed for a patent in another country in respect of 'the same or substantially the same invention'. An applicant is also required, until the patent is granted, to keep the Controller up to date about the particulars of such an application in writing. In other words, patent applicants in India are expected to report any amendment made to the specific patent claims or any adverse office action that affects parallel applications. A patent will be revoked if the applicant fails to comply with the requirements of disclosure.[95]

Note that failing to sufficiently disclose the specifications of an invention patent also constitutes a ground for patent revocation. By virtue of Section 64(1)(h) of the Patents (Amendment) Act 2005, the specifications of an invention patent must be disclosed completely, sufficiently and fairly, or the best method of performing must be disclosed, so that the description can enable a person with 'average skill in, and average knowledge of, the art' to work the invention. The requirements of disclosure prescribed by India's patent legislation and Art.29.1 of the TRIPS Agreement[96] mirror each other, as the TRIPS Agreement also imposes conditions of disclosure on patent applicants so that their monopolies may be justified. Section 64(1)(h) is comparable with Art.26 of China's Patent Law 2008, which prescribes that 'a clear and comprehensive disclosure' is imperative so that 'a technician in the field of the relevant technology can carry it out', (although China forgoes the requirement of specifying the best mode of carrying out an invention). The same requirement is maintained by the Draft Patent Law 2015. Article 138(1)(b) of the EPC and China's patent law share similar requirements for disclosure as the former states that disclosure of an invention patent must be 'sufficiently clear and complete' so that a person skilled in the art can carry it out.

Other grounds for patent revocation under India's patent law range from technical non-compliance to patent rights infringement.[97] In any case, by virtue of Section 64 of Patents (Amendment) Act 2005, a patent may be revoked 'on a petition of any person interested or of the Central Government by the Appellate Board or on a counter-claim in a suit for infringement of the patent by the High Court'.

IV) Government authorisation and compulsory licence

So long as certain criteria are met by virtue of Art.31 of the TRIPS Agreement, members are offered the possibility of issuing compulsory licences and the flexibility to determine the

95 Section 64(1)(m), Patents (Amendment) Act 2005.

96 Article 29.1 of the TRIPS Agreement requires a patent applicant to disclose an invention 'in a manner sufficiently clear and complete' so that the invention can be carried out by a person skilled in the art and the applicant may be equally required to indicate the best mode for carrying out the invention.

97 Section 64(1)(a)–(q), Patents (Amendment) Act 2005.

circumstances under which a compulsory licence may be granted. As usual, India has fully exploited the principle of flexibility in this regard.

Governed by Sections 39 and 84(1) of the Patents (Amendments) Act 2005, compulsory licence may be applied for by any interested person at any time after the expiration of three years counting from the date when a patent is granted. There are three grounds upon which a compulsory licence may be applied for in India, namely: 1) the reasonable requirements of the public with respect to the patented invention have not been satisfied; or 2) the patented invention is not available to the public at a reasonable price; or 3) the patented invention is not worked in the territory of India.[98] Note that, in accordance with Section 84(2) of the Patents (Amendment) Act 2005, a compulsory licence holder must also exercise his licenced patent rights according to the aforementioned three conditions and, if he does not, any person may apply for a compulsory licence. In any event, an applicant must make out a *prima facie* case when applying for a compulsory licence.[99] For example, following the decision laid down by *Novartis AG* v. *Adarsh Pharma*,[100] if a company seeks to apply for a compulsory licence of an Indian pharmaceutical product patent, the company must provide evidence and compare the prices between the patented product and the available non-patented substitutes in India, and maybe also the prices charged by the patent holder outside of India.

Since coming into force in 1970, compulsory licence as a legal instrument has nonetheless rarely been used given the fact that, under the Patents Act 1970, pharmaceutical products were not patentable while patents for pharmaceutical production processes lasted only for five to seven years so, therefore, compulsory licence seemed a redundant instrument for patent exploitation. Statistics reveal that, until India fully complied with the TRIPS Agreement, the Indian Patent Office only granted between three and five compulsory licences.[101]

Among the three grounds upon which a compulsory licence may be granted in India, much controversy surrounds the 'domestic working' requirement. Pursuant to Art.27.1 of the TRIPS Agreement, due to the principle of non-discrimination in relation to the place of invention, the field of technology and whether products are imported or locally made, most countries removed the 'domestic working' requirement from their patent legislation. For example, China abolished the 'domestic working' requirement when its patent legislation was amended for the first time in 1992. Nonetheless, some countries, such as India and Brazil, have retained the 'domestic working' requirement in the hope that their domestic industries could continue to exploit patented foreign inventions by insisting on their working locally. For this reason, on 30 May 2000, the US brought Brazil to the WTO DSB because Art.68(1)(I) of the Brazilian Industrial Property Law 1996 (Law No. 9.279 of 14 May 1996)[102] has established that a compulsory licence may be issued if a patent holder fails 'to manufacture or incomplete manufacture of the product' or 'to make full use of the patented process' within the Brazilian territory, unless economically infeasible so that

98 Section 84(1), Patents (Amendment) Act 2005.

99 Section 87(1), Patents (Amendment) Act 2005.

100 2004 (3) CTC 95, 2004 (29) PTC 108 Mad, available at: http://indiankanoon.org/doc/1454766/ (last accessed 15 November 2015).

101 Mueller J. M., 'The tiger awakens: the tumultuous transformation of India's patent system and the rise of Indian pharmaceutical innovation'. 68 *University of Pittsburgh Law Review* 3 (2007), 491.

102 Brazil's Industrial Property Law 1996 was amended on 14 February 2001 (Law No.10.196). The same provision concerning the local-working requirement remains.

importation will be permitted. The US alleged that such requirements were in violation of Arts.27 and 28 of the TRIPS Agreement, as well as Art.III of the GATT 1994.[103] As the two countries reached a settlement between themselves on 5 July 2001, the question as to whether the 'domestic working' requirement is consistent with Art.27 of the TRIPS Agreement is, to date, left unanswered. On the other hand, echoing India's position, it is observed that Art.68(1)(II) of the Brazilian Industrial Property Law provides that if the commercialisation of a patent does not satisfy the needs of the market, which may include the scenario where a patented invention is not available to the public at a reasonable price, a compulsory licence may be issued.

In line with Art.31(b) of the TRIPS Agreement, when the Controller of the Patent Office decides whether a compulsory licence should be issued in India, a few factors must first be taken into consideration. One of them is whether the applicant has made efforts, but failed, to obtain a licence from the patent holder on reasonable terms and conditions within a reasonable period, which should not be more than six months.[104] Other factors that may be taken into account by the Controller while deciding on compulsory licence are, for example, the nature of the invention, the time which has elapsed after the patent was granted, the ability of the applicant to work the invention to the public advantage, or the applicant's capacity to undertake the risk of providing capital and working the invention, if the application were granted.[105]

In the same spirit of the Patents Act 1970, the Patents (Amendment) Act 2005 maintains that, upon obtaining a compulsory licence in accordance with the grounds set down by Section 84, a licensee may enforce the patent rights against an infringer if the patent holder fails to do so. Under Section 110, a compulsory licensee may 'call upon the patentee to take proceedings to prevent any infringement of the patent [...]'. In case the patent holder fails to do so within two months, the licensee 'may institute proceedings for the infringement in his own name as though he were the patentee, making the patentee a defendant [...]'. When such is the case, although the patent holder may be added as defendant, he 'shall not be liable for any costs unless he enters an appearance and takes part in the proceedings.'[106]

While determining the terms and conditions of a compulsory licence, the Controller shall 'endeavour to secure' for the 'predominant purpose of supply in the Indian market' as well as for the development of the Indian market, so as to meet the public interest requirement as is prescribed by Section 84(7)(a)(iii) of the Patents (Amendment) Act 2005.[107] Section 92(A)1 provides that compulsory licence may be granted for the manufacturing and exporting of patented pharmaceutical products to countries with insufficient or no manufacturing capacity for the concerned product if there are public health problems. Article 50 of the Chinese Patent Law 2008 provides the same condition for a compulsory licence to be issued.

Overall, thanks to the Patents (Amendment) Act 2005, India has modernised its patent system by gradually widening the scope for patent protection, while maintaining the

103 Available at: www.wto.org/english/tratop_e/dispu_e/cases_e/ds199_e.htm (last accessed 16 November 2015).

104 Section 84(6)(iv), Patents (Amendment) Act 2005.

105 Section 84(6)(i)–(iv), the Patents (Amendment) Act 2005.

106 Section 110, Patents (Amendment) Act 2005.

107 Section 90(1)(vii), Patents (Amendment) Act 2005.

supremacy of the public interest at the same time, in order to guarantee the enabling environment for the generic pharmaceutical industry to further progress.

V) Remedies

Under India's patent legislation, injunctive relief is engaged as a means to prevent exclusive access to medicine.[108] *F. Hoffmann-LA Roche Ltd. and Anr.* v. *Cipla Ltd.* can best illustrate India's position in this aspect.

1. Injunctive relief

In *F. Hoffmann-La Roche Ltd. and Anr.* v. *Cipla Ltd.*,[109] after Cipla manufactured and sold the generic version of Roche's drug Erlotnib under the name of Erlocip, Roche filed for permanent injunction before the High Court of Delhi on 19 January 2008 in the hope of restraining Cipla from manufacturing and selling a generic version of the Indian-patented drug, and from exporting the same drug to various countries. Cipla filed a counterclaim, pursuant to Section 3(d) of the Patents (Amendment) Act 2005. Cipla alleged that IN'774, the patent concerned, by which Roche had a licence to use, sell, offer for sale and was also licensed and authorised to enforce the rights,[110] should have been subject to revocation as it only sought to improve from existing prior art and was merely a derivative of a known compound and therefore not patentable. Cipla also counterclaimed that Roche's preliminary injunction application should not be granted, based on the 'overwhelming interest of society' and citizens' constitutional rights of access to affordable, life-saving medicine. The key issue before the court in the interim application was whether or not the patent holder, Roche, was entitled to a temporary injunction restraining Cipla from selling its version of 'Erlotnib' under the name 'Erlocip'.

While deciding whether an injunctive relief order should be issued, factors such as the likelihood of success on the merits, the irreparable injury and the balance of convenience had to be taken into account. On 19 March 2008 the High Court of Delhi refused to grant an interim injunction to restrain Cipla from manufacturing and selling the generic drug Erlocip. The court decided that Cipla had a credible case on the merits that the generic product Erlocip contained a polymorphic B variant of Erlotinib hydrochloride as the active ingredient and hence did not infringe the compound *per se* as Roche claimed in its patent claim. The court also compared the price differences between the drugs manufactured between Cipla and Roche and decided that it could not 'be unmindful of the right of the general public to access life-saving drugs which are available and for which such access would be denied if the injunction were granted'. The court further explained that 'the

108 Kapczynski A., 'Harmonisation and its discontents: a case study of TRIPS implementation in India's pharmaceutical sector'. 97 *California Law Review* 1571 (2009).

109 Roche filed a patent application in India on 13 March 1996, under the mailbox arrangement. Roche was given approval by the Drug Controller General of India for marketing 'Tarceva' in India on 13 July 2005 and the patent was granted to 'Tarceva' in India on 13 July 2007. The generic name of the drug, 'Erlotnib', which Roche markets under a patent of 'Tarceva' was launched by Cipla under the name of 'Erlocip' in January 2008. Available at: www.legal500.com/c/india/developments/3843 (last accessed 17 November 2015).

110 *F. Hoffmann-LA Roche Ltd. and Anr.* v. *Cipla Ltd.*, 10 August 2012, available at: http://indiancaselaws.wordpress.com/2013/08/10/f-hoffmann-la-roche-limited-switzerland-and-anr-v-cipla-ltd-mumbai/ (last accessed 17 November 2015).

degree of harm in such eventuality is absolute; the chances of improvement of life injuries to third party are un-compensable'. The cost of the once-a-day tablet manufactured by Roche was about 4,800 INR (64.75 EUR), while Cipla's generic version cost about 1,600 INR (21.58 EUR), which was one third of the price that Roche charged.[111] The court therefore concluded that Cipla could continue producing the generic version of 'Tarceva', Roche's patented anti-cancer drug, and ignore Roche's statutorily granted right.[112]

On 11 April 2008 Roche filed an appeal against the rejection order before the divisional bench at the High Court of Delhi. The decision laid down by the divisional bench of the High Court of Delhi delivered its decision on 7 September 2012 and upheld Cipla's position against Roche. It noted that, although the previous court decided that Roche held a valid patent for Tarceva, in view of the fact that the generic drug manufactured and sold by Cipla corresponded to a polymorph B form of Erlotinib hydrochloride, Cipla did not infringe the IN'774 patent *per se*[113] as Roche alleged. As a result, Roche failed to make a *prima facie* case for injunctive relief since Roche was deemed not to hold a patent for polymorph B form of Erlotinib hydrochloride in India.

The divisional bench at the High Court of Delhi further implied that a plaintiff must fulfil the requirement of 'must disclose' in order to make a *prima facie* case for an interim injunction as far as drug infringement cases are concerned. The 'must disclose' requirement insists that a plaintiff must, first of all, disclose the XRD data of the drug and make full disclosure of the complete specifications of the infringed patent. Second, the plaintiff must make an unequivocal disclosure of the patent that covers the drug and, third, must disclose any other pending applications and issued patents that are pertinent to derivatives, or forms, of the drug. It would amount to a case of suppression of material facts in a case where the 'must disclose' requirement is not fulfilled.

Concerning the validity of the IN'774 patent which was questioned by Cipla, and specifically in relation to the issues of 'public interest' and 'pricing' *vis-à-vis* the injunction order, it was held that, by virtue of Sections 83(e)(g) of the Patents (Amendment) Act 2005, gauging 'public interest' was not alien to the Indian patent law while the public's access to life-saving drugs was granted higher significance than an injunction. In the case *per se*, while comparing two public interests, which are the public interest of accessing a life-saving drug and the public interest of granting Roche an injunction order, the former outweighed the latter as Cipla demonstrated *prima facie* that Roche did not hold a patent for Tarceva and raised a credible challenge on the validity of the patent. Finally, the divisional bench of the High Court of Delhi decided that the IN'774 patent held by Roche required scrutiny based on Section 3(d) of the Patents (Amendments) Act 2005, and confirmed that Roche's injunction request against Cipla ought to be rejected.[114]

111 Available at: www.legal500.com/c/india/developments/3843 (last accessed 17 November 2015).

112 In-depth analysis of Tarceva patent litigation available at: http://patentcircle.blogspot.be/2012/11/in-depth-analysis-of-tarceva-patent_17.html (last accessed 17 November 2015).

113 After having survived the pre-grant opposition, the IN'774 patent for Erlotinib hydrochloride was granted to Roche by the Controller of Patents on 4 July 2007. The patent is jointly owned by OSI Pharmaceuticals and Pfizer for the anti-cancer drug compound Erlotinib hydrochloride.

114 In-depth analysis of Tarceva patent litigation available at: http://patentcircle.blogspot.be/2012/11/in-depth-analysis-of-tarceva-patent.html (last accessed 18 November 2015).

2. Discretion

The case of *F. Hoffmann-La Roche Ltd. and Anr.* v. *Cipla Ltd.* also raised the question of legitimacy when the Indian judicial authority exercised its discretion to refuse an injunction relief. The governing principle in this regard is underlined by Art.41.2 of the TRIPS Agreement that states that 'procedures concerning the enforcement of intellectual property rights shall be fair and equitable', while Art.41.1 of the Agreement also states that members are required to provide expeditious and effective remedies to prevent and deter infringement. Furthermore, and in relation to IPR border enforcement, Art.44.1 of the TRIPS Agreement provides that judicial authorities '... shall have the authority to order a party to desist from an infringement ...'. In the meantime, reflecting on the WTO case law jurisdiction, in the case of China – Measures Affecting the Protection and Enforcement of Intellectual Property Rights, the DSB Panel Report indicated that some degree of discretion may be required in order for a judicial authority to 'have the authority' to grant an injunction order,[115] for which the judicial authority's obligation to 'have the authority' is not the same obligation as to 'have the authority to order those remedies only', or to 'exercise that authority in a particular way, unless otherwise specified.'[116] Taking into consideration the above-mentioned rules, and especially by virtue of Arts.44.2 of the TRIPS Agreement concerning injunctions when 31(h) of the TRIPS Agreement shall be also taking into account, TRIPS does warrant members' discretion to award, or deny, injunction applications. This being the case, it was indeed legitimate for the divisional bench at the High Court of Delhi to exercise its discretion to deny the injunction application submitted by Roche.

Pursuant to the question of discretion, the case of *F. Hoffmann-La Roche Ltd. and Anr.* v. *Cipla Ltd.* also brings up the subject of awarding compensation for injuries sustained by a patent holder as a result of infringement. Under Art.45.1 of the TRIPS Agreement, 'adequate compensation' must be awarded, although the scale of the award may be defined by each member. As a result, members are granted a certain level of flexibility when determining the compensation amount in order to adequately award an aggrieved patent holder when infringement takes place.

Overall, to determine if the remedies provided by India's patent legislation are adequate, one must bear in mind the parameter between the right to health and patent rights protection, i.e., that the former shall always prevail should conflict between the two priorities arise. In essence, facilitated by the principle of flexibility provided by the TRIPS Agreement and empowered by the stricter patent protection measures such as Section 3(d) of the Patents (Amendments) Act 2005, the Indian legislature succeeded in upholding its national interest in the wake of pharmaceutical product patenting with absolute legitimacy.

V Lessons for China

India's patent legislation illustrates the following three characteristics in the process of international patent rights harmonisation. First, it took full advantage of the transitional arrangements afforded by the TRIPS Agreement including, in particular, the

115 China – Measures Affecting the Protection and Enforcement of Intellectual Property Rights, Para 7.252, WT/DS362/R, Dispute Settlement Body Panel Report, 26 January 2009.

116 Para 7.236, 238, 239, WT/DS362/R, 26 January 2009.

ten-year transitional period as far as product patent protection is concerned. Second, while incorporating the minimum protection standards prescribed by the TRIPS Agreement, India's legislature managed to mould the patent protection measures to the country's public interest of 'right to health'. Third, India's judiciary argues forcefully for and upholds Parliament's intention behind patent legislation, which is that the public interest of 'right to health' shall always prevail *vis-à-vis* patent protection when conflicts between the two priorities arise.

In comparison, China's patent legislation is one century younger than that of India. China harmonised its patent legislation with the TRIPS Agreement in full in the run-up to its WTO accession. In this context, China relinquished its privilege of transitional arrangements in total. Though the country's patent legislation was in its infancy at the time, China stood at the forefront of global patent protection by promulgating higher protection measures when, for example, it was one of the first countries in the world that provided a 20-year patent protection term in 1992. Pharmaceutical, agricultural and chemical products also became patentable subject matters in China ten years ahead of the country's accession to the WTO. The hurried patent legislative movement could perhaps be better understood against the backdrop of China's fierce ambition to catch up with the world's most advanced technologies. This objective seemed to be the sole aim behind the country's patent legislation, in order to facilitate technology transfer. In the process, societal factors were reduced to a secondary importance. Finally, China's judiciary was badly prepared for adjudicating, especially at the time when patent legislation was just imposed in the early 1980s. All in all, restrained by the communist ideology of collective property ownership and influenced by the Chinese traditional moral inclination of unconditional sharing, the Chinese judiciary was shy of enforcing patent rights since they are private property rights. There is no doubt that, in the eyes of the Chinese legislature, patent appeared to be a policy tool rather than a form of private property right. The mixture of these factors results in weaker patent enforcement in China, which is still the case to date.

Should China have gone Indian in its patent legislation? Perhaps not. India has chosen a patent legislation approach best suited to its national interest and that accommodates the country's development priority. China, through sheer determination, has attained high achievements in patent protection within three decades.

Despite all its unpreparedness, China has become one of the world's largest patent countries in terms of patent application numbers. Its capacity for innovation is also on the rise. In recent years the country has shown its confidence in enhancing patent protection, and reoriented its ambition in order to pursue an innovation-driven economy by engaging patent as one of the key drivers. Though weaker enforcement handicaps China's strengths in patent protection to date, the country's legislature has been consistently working towards installing stronger enforcement measures while the judiciary has focused on delivering more legal certainty. Citizens' awareness of IPR protection in general, and patent protection in particular, has likewise been increasing over the years.

9 International patent rights harmonisation – the case of China

Since China enacted its first modern-day patent law in 1984, the country has established a comprehensive framework of patent legislation that is in full compliance with the relevant international treaties such as the TRIPS Agreement. The SIPO is currently ranked the second biggest office in the world in terms of patent application numbers. Since 2011, China ranks fourth in the global PCT application system, behind the US, Japan and Germany. Huawei Technologies and ZTE Corporation, two Chinese home-grown companies, are among the top PCT applicants worldwide. As a member of the IP5 project, China joins the process of global substantive administrative harmonisation as far as multiple patent applications are concerned.

Aside from the spectacular achievements in patent legislation, weaker enforcement, especially at regional and local levels, continues to negate China's efforts in strengthening its IPR protection in general and patent protection in particular. This persists as a major challenge for its trading partners; China remains on the EU list of priority countries for IPR infringement.[1] On the other side of the Pacific, China consistently appears on the Priority Watch List of the US Special 301 Report. American businesses often blame China for their estimated huge losses in sales, royalties, or licence fees due to IPR infringement in the country.[2]

In view of the disproportionate success in China's patent protection efforts in legislation compared with enforcement, one may wish to enquire about the reasons behind such disparity. What are the modes and approaches undertaken by China to harmonise its patent

1 The European Chamber Business Confidence Survey 2013 shows that just 13 per cent of European companies surveyed regarded China's IPR enforcement as either excellent or adequate, whereas 69 per cent regarded it as either inadequate or very inadequate. In general, 1 per cent of the European companies surveyed regarded China's IPR enforcement as excellent, 12 per cent as adequate, 45 per cent as inadequate and 24 per cent as very inadequate (18 per cent replied n/a). See: European Business in China, *Business Confidence Survey 2013*, p. 21. (Beijing: The European Union Chamber of Commerce in China, 2013).

2 For example, the US International Trade Commission (ITC) estimated that 'firms in the US IP [intellectual property]-intensive economy that conducted business in China in 2009 reported losses of approximately $48.2 billion in sales, royalties, or license fees due to IPR [intellectual property rights] infringement in China'. See: US International Trade Commission Investigation NO. 332–519, USITC PUB. 4226, China: Effects of Intellectual Property Infringement and Indigenous Innovation Policies on the US. Economy xiv (2011).However, such estimated losses must be read with caution. According to Professor Abbott, such a calculation is almost certainly biased towards the magnifying of the extent of the problem because highly uncertain factors involving hypothesis and speculation are used. See: Abbott F. M., 'Protecting First World assets in the Third World: intellectual property negotiations in the GATT Multilateral Framework'. 22 *Vanderbilt Journal of Transnational Law* 4 (1989), 699–700 and Qian D. X., 'A survey of intellectual property issues in China-US trade negotiations under the Special 301 Provisions'. 2 *Pacific Rim Law and Policy Journal* 2 (1993), 259.

legislation with TRIPS? What kinds of higher level patent protection standards did China impose after having interpreted the minimum standards prescribed by the TRIPS Agreement and incorporated them into its national law? Are the patent protection measures imposed in China compatible with those in the US, one of the most innovative countries in the world? In the preceding chapters, our analysis focuses on the evolutionary characteristics of China's patent legislation, including the intrinsic limitations of its enforcement mechanism, and compares them with the same in the case of the Japanese and Indian patent legislations. In this chapter the process of international patent rights harmonisation taking place in China will be examined.

I Introduction

The TRIPS Agreement sets down the minimum standards for patent protection and provides the principle of flexibility so that the protection measures, including principles, can best be interpreted to fit each signatory country's domestic legislation based on their unique judicial practice, cultural background and economic development stage.

By virtue of Art.1 of the TRIPS Agreement, WTO members are entitled to employ their own means as they see appropriate while incorporating the Agreement in their respective legal framework. Subsequently, members will have to pass national legislation in order to implement the new law after incorporating the TRIPS Agreement. This is also the case for monist countries, where international law usually only needs to be incorporated into national legislation and its effects will take place automatically.[3] For the principles set out by TRIPS, such as judicial review with regard to revoking or forfeiting a patent,[4] members are obliged to substantiate them so that they may be constituted as legal provisions under national legislation. The Appellate Body in the mailbox case decided that the TRIPS Agreement should be interpreted within the meaning of Arts.31 and 32 of the Vienna Convention on the Law of Treaties (1969) and Arts.3.2 and 19.2 of the DSU, without adding to, or diminishing, the rights and obligations provided by the WTO Agreement. As a result, a particular term that is to be interpreted must be understood in accordance with the ordinary meaning in its context and in line with the jurisprudence decided by the WTO DSB. Equally, the principles laid down in prior GATT/WTO jurisprudence should be applicable to disputes that arise from the TRIPS Agreement.[5]

In terms of the time-frame for implementing the TRIPS Agreement, Arts.65 and 66 of the Agreement provide developing countries and transitional economies a grace period of five to ten years. Despite being a developing country and a transitional economy, China relinquished this privilege, as mentioned in the previous chapter. In fact, before China acceded to the WTO in 2001, the country's patent law was already in full compliance with the TRIPS Agreement.

By acceding to the Paris Convention in 1984, China embarked on the process of international patent rights harmonisation since the body of principles set down by the Convention, such as the national treatment, the most-favoured-nation treatment, the

3 Watal J., *Intellectual Property Rights in the WTO and Developing Countries.* (New York: Kluwer Law International, 2001), p. 49.

4 Art.32, TRIPS Agreement.

5 India — Patent Protection for Pharmaceutical and Agricultural Chemical Products - AB-1997-5 Report of the Appellate Body, WT/DS50/AB/R, 19 December 1997.

right of priority, and the conditions for compulsory licences and for forfeiture, etc.,[6] have all become components of the TRIPS Agreement by virtue of Art.2.1 of the Agreement.

Though, in principle, patent legislation enacted by any TRIPS member must have met the minimum protection standards set down by the TRIPS Agreement, differences lie in the details that reveal the higher level of protection measures that members may have adopted individually. Comparing members' patent legislations is therefore useful, especially in terms of enforcement measures, since the TRIPS Agreement merely sets down the principles for enforcement while members are not obliged to create an IPR-specific judicial system at all but to employ the existing legal enforcement instruments in general. In China's case, the enforcement obligations enshrined as principles in the TRIPS Agreement have been duly incorporated into China's patent legislation such as, for example, the provisional measures for evidence preservation, the border measures for preventing infringing goods from entering into the commercial channels, the judicial procedures that allow defendants to be heard, and the criminal penalties punishing infringers as well as the judicial review mechanism.

One enforcement aspect that some may allege as a discrepancy in China's compliance with the TRIPS Agreement is the lack of criminal procedures and penalties for commercial scale infringement, as was brought up by the case China – Measures Affecting the Protection and Enforcement of Intellectual Property Rights. Among others, an essential question raised by the US was that the numerical thresholds fixed by the Chinese criminal legislation, as 'commercial scale', effectively exempted some copyright and trademark infringements from criminal liability since the damages resulting from such infringements fell below the thresholds in terms of the amount of turnover, profit, sales or copies of infringing goods. Also, the US alleged that this was in violation of Arts.41.1 and 61 of the TRIPS Agreement. Ultimately, the DSB Panel avoided ruling on the question of the threshold of 'commercial scale', but pointed out that the factual evidence presented by the US was inadequate to establish the allegation that China failed the TRIPS standard of 'commercial scale' when it was applied to China's marketplace. As a result, the allegation that China's criminal enforcement measures failed to comply with the TRIPS Agreement is still a matter for debate.

As to the substantive subject matters upon which members' flexibility is admissible under the TRIPS Agreement, China's patent protection measures are in line with international norms, such as the rules concerning patent examination and the timeframe for granting a patent, as well as the six-month grace period that the EPC shares with China by virtue of Art.55 of the EPC. For patent publication of invention patents China provides a timeline of 18 months after an application is submitted and Art.93 (1) of the EPC offers the same.

II International patent rights harmonisation – the case of China

As is described in Chapter 3, China undertakes the process of international patent rights harmonisation by engaging the minimum and maximum harmonisation modes while

6 Arts.1–12 and Art.19 of the TRIPS Agreement.

taking advantage of the principle of flexibility. Certain patent protection measures imposed by the country stand higher than its counterparts, which will be further elaborated on below.

I) Minimum and maximum harmonisation

As is explained in Chapter 3, 'minimum harmonisation' means complying with the minimum patent protection standards set down by the TRIPS Agreement, while also exploiting the principle of flexibility in order to tailor the specific provisions in a member's national law based on the member's economic priorities, legal practices and economic development stage. As a result, provisions derived from the same international treaty may appear differently after being incorporated in national legislation, in terms of both scope and degree.

For example, in relation to 'grace period', when Art.2.1 of the TRIPS Agreement is read together with Art.11 of the Paris Convention, members of the TRIPS Agreement are required to grant temporary protection to inventions, utility models and industrial designs that are exhibited at official international exhibitions. When being incorporated in national patent legislation, the principle of 'grace period' is implemented with varied lengths and scopes. China provides a six-month grace period, so does the EPC, while the US grace period is 18 months. In terms of the scope of a 'grace period', China grants patent protection during the 'grace period' even when 'lawful non-prejudicial disclosure other than at an exhibition' takes place.[7] This is not the case under the EPC.

It was mentioned before that when incorporating a principle derived from an international treaty, different degrees of protection standard at the national level may also be observed. Using the minimum requirement of patentability as an example, Art.27 of the TRIPS Agreement provides that patents are available for all inventions, products or processes in all fields of technology as long as they are new, involve an inventive step and are capable of industrial application. When this was incorporated in national legislation, the Chinese Patent Law imposes a higher threshold test in which the requirement of 'absolute novelty' must be met as far as invention and utility model patent applications are concerned. Under the US patent law and the EPC, 'non-obviousness', which is of a lower threshold compared with the 'absolute novelty' test, will suffice to pass the 'novelty' threshold. Essentially, since the TRIPS Agreement does not require members to promulgate uniform provisions for patent protection, but to establish a level ground, Chinese legislators usually opt for a higher degree of patent protection, after meeting the 'minimum standard' set down by the TRIPS Agreement.

7 'Lawful non-prejudicial disclosure other than at an exhibition' is also known as the 'general grace period'. The principle of 'grace period' may be applied in three circumstances, i.e.: non-prejudicial disclosure at an exhibition; disclosure in consequence of an abuse; lawful non-prejudicial disclosure other than at an exhibition, which means an invention is disclosed by the inventor or lawfully disclosed by a third party in a way unrelated to the first two scenarios. For example, disclosure by publication in the form of a scientific article or a lecture or by public use (in particular, use made in order to test the invention).

II) The principle of flexibility

By virtue of Art.3.1 of the TRIPS Agreement concerning national treatment, members are provided with a degree of freedom to determine their respective standards of IPR protection based on national interest.[8] While applying the principle of flexibility, two rules must nonetheless be respected. First, the principle must be applied in consistency with the relevant obligations imposed by the TRIPS Agreement. Second, in conformity with Art.7 of the TRIPS Agreement regarding the objectives of IPR protection and enforcement, measures derived from the principle of flexibility must aim to mitigate the social costs that may result from IPR protection and to attain a balance of rights and obligations in order to achieve overall social and economic welfare. In essence, flexibility must not reduce the positive impact of IPR for promoting invention and enhancing a competitive business environment.[9] Based on this premise, there are four approaches that members may engage in order to apply the principle of flexibility while incorporating the TRIPS Agreement in national patent legislation.

1. Four approaches to apply the principle of flexibility

As explained in Chapter 3, thanks to Art.1.1 of the TRIPS Agreement the principle of flexibility is a powerful instrument when transferring principles set down by the TRIPS Agreement to national patent legislation. In practice, the principle of flexibility may be applied as: 1) a method of fulfilling the TRIPS obligations; 2) a substantive standard for protection; 3) a mechanism of enforcement, and; 4) areas of protection not covered by the TRIPS Agreement.[10]

Reflecting on how China applied the principle of flexibility while fulfilling the obligations set down by TRIPS and incorporating its principles of patent protection into its national patent law, one may focus on the provisions concerning the threshold test of 'inventive step' and the condition of 'predominantly for the supply of the domestic market' under which a compulsory licence may be issued. The former also exemplifies the so-called 'TRIPS-plus' flexibility while the latter 'TRIPS-minus'.

As far as the threshold test of 'inventive step' is concerned, unlike some patent jurisdictions or patent authorities such as the EPC[11] that apply only a non-obviousness test,

8 The principle of flexibility is derived from the principle of national treatment, which was first provided by the Paris Convention (1967). Article 2(1) of the Paris Convention provides that nationals of one Union country shall enjoy the same level of advantages, protection and legal remedy that nationals from all other Union countries may enjoy. At the same time, however, since the Paris Convention does not establish the minimum standards for protection for patents, but only for industrial designs, trade names, unfair competition and the direct or indirect use of a false indication of the source of goods, it has become legitimate for Union members not to grant patent protection to other Union nationals as long as the particular Union countries do not grant the same patent protection to their own nationals. Consequently, countries are at liberty to grant diverse standards of patent protection, or to grant no protection at all. This created barriers to the export of goods and services of which intellectual property is a component. Note that the Paris Convention provides minimum mandatory standards for the protection of industrial designs (Art.5-*quinquies*), trade names (Art.8), and unfair competition (Art.10-*bis*) and the direct or indirect use of a false indication of the source of goods (Art.10).

9 Carvalho N. P. *The TRIPS Regime of Patent Rights* (3rd Ed.). (New York: Kluwer Law International, 2010), p. 67.

10 Available at: www.wipo.int/ip-development/en/legislative_assistance/advice_trips.html (last accessed 22 May 2016). See also: Chapter 3 for detail.

11 Art.56, EPC.

Chinese Patent Law requires an absolute test by virtue of Art.22 of the Chinese Patent Law 2008. This means an invention must meet both the requirements of 'prominent substantive features' and 'remarkable advance' before an 'inventive step' may be considered accomplished. This position is upheld by China's Draft Patent Law 2015.

Article 31(f) of the TRIPS Agreement stipulates that a compulsory licence may be issued while the use shall be 'predominantly for the supply of the domestic market'. The provision was first fully incorporated into the Chinese patent legislation by Rule 72 of the Implementing Rules of the Patent Law of China 2000. Later, under Chapter VI of the Patent Law 2008, by exploiting the rule of flexibility, and more precisely the rule of 'TRIPS-minus' flexibility, all eligible compulsory licences will be issued for the supply of the domestic market in China, except for two types. The first type is those granted in order to eliminate or reduce the negative impact on competition as a result of a patent holder's monopolistic behaviour.[12] The second type concerns those granted on the grounds of public health for manufacture of patented pharmaceutical products and for their export to the countries and regions that conform to the relevant international treaties acceded to by China.[13] The Draft Patent Law 2015 continues this legal choice.

In general, when applying the principle of flexibility as a method of fulfilling the TRIPS obligations, the Chinese legislature usually sets higher protection standards and prescribes more restrictive conditions while incorporating the principles prescribed by TRIPS into its national patent legislation as substantive provisions.

Note that for 'TRIPS-minus' flexibility, also known as 'exceptions' and 'limitations', the above-mentioned example of 'predominantly for the supply of the domestic market' for the use of compulsory licence can best explain how China applied the principle of flexibility while granting 'exceptions'. As to 'limitations', reflecting on Art.33 of the TRIPS Agreement and Art.38(1) on design patents that prescribes a ten-year protection term, since 1992 the Chinese Patent Law provides a 20-year protection term for invention patents and a ten-year term for design patents, both counting from the date of filing. Article 42 of the Draft Patent Law 2015 increases the protection term for design patents from ten to 15 years.

Part III of the TRIPS Agreement grants members the right to exercise the principle of flexibility in enforcement. Primarily, for what is covered by the Agreement, members should ensure that IPR enforcement is carried out effectively by their judicial system, although members are not obliged to adopt a new judicial system distinctive from what exists for the enforcement of law in general in order to implement the TRIPS Agreement. By the same token, Art.41(5) assures members that TRIPS does not create any obligations concerning the distribution of resources between IPR protection and general enforcement in law.

Consistent with its legal enforcement instrument in general, IPR enforcement in China is undertaken by an administrative and judicial dual-track mechanism in which both tracks are of equal importance, as is mentioned in the previous chapters.

For administrative enforcement, infringement allegations are dealt with through mediation and the courts are not involved in the procedure. However, if ever a decision delivered

12 Art.48 (2), Patent Law 2008.

13 Art.50, Patent Law 2008.

by administrative enforcement is not executed or only partially executed, legal action may be taken at court for compulsory enforcement.

As the TRIPS Agreement does not provide protection to all and each single IPR subject matter, members therefore have the flexibility to base their legislation on their respective national interest or policy objectives. Under China's patent law, one good example in this regard concerns service invention.

Since 2010, China has been promoting innovation at all levels of society in order to nurture an innovative economy. The Draft Patent Law 2015 clearly bears this political imprint. For example, the Draft Law adds a whole new chapter on the exploitation and utilisation of patent and it also protects an inventor employee's right to apply for patent in order to encourage employment invention-creation, also known as service invention. Article 6 of the Draft Patent Law 2015 provides that, in the absence of an agreement concerning the ownership of a patent as well as its rights, the inventor or designer employee shall have the right to apply for patent grant. In addition, 'employment invention-creation' is defined for the first time by the Chinese patent legislation as 'an invention-creation that is accomplished in the course of performing the duties of an employee'. Moreover, Art.16 of the Draft Patent Law 2015 provides explicitly that an inventor or designer shall be rewarded with remuneration by the employer after an 'employment invention-creation' patent is granted and also when the patent is exploited. Under the Patent Law 2008, the inventor or designer may be rewarded only after the patent is exploited.[14]

2. *Summary*

Although not a TRIPS member until 2001, China amended its patent legislation based on the spirit of the TRIPS Agreement between 1992 and 2000. Later, while incorporating the TRIPS Agreement into its national patent law, the Chinese legislature often opted for the TRIPS-plus flexibility approach after complying with the minimum protection standards set down by the TRIPS Agreement for the purpose of international patent rights harmonisation. As far as patent enforcement is concerned, China engages the administrative-judicial dual-track enforcement instrument, which is an instrument used for general legal enforcement by the country. For those patent protection aspects not covered by the TRIPS Agreement, China's protection measures are motivated by its patent policy in which, for example, new provisions promulgated by the Draft Patent Law 2015 reinforce the country's efforts in promoting innovation at all levels in the society with the aim of nurturing an innovative economy.

After explaining the modes of international patent rights harmonisation taking place in China, this chapter will now proceed to compare in detail the patent legislation imposed in China, in the US, as well as by the EPC, in order to reveal the results of such harmonisation, and to discover the divergence between China's patent law and the other two patent jurisdictions using the minimum standards set down by the TRIPS Agreement as the benchmark.

14 Art.16, Patent Law 2008.

III Comparisons and analyses

I) China's patent law: a functional comparison with that of the US

The US plays the unique role of a promoter and, at the same time, a serious critic in the context of patent protection, or IPR protection at large, in China. As early as 1979, when China had just launched its economic reforms, the two countries concluded the Agreement on Trade Relations between the United States of America and the People's Republic of China (Beijing, 7 July 1979, entered into force on 1 February 1980), in which one of the articles dealt with IPR protection, for patent, trademarks, copyrights and unfair competition. Since IPR legislation did not exist in China at all at the time, both parties agreed to recognise the importance of IPR protection and pledged to provide IPR protection on a reciprocal basis based on laws and international practice.[15] In the same year, the China-US Agreement on Cooperation in Science and Technology was also concluded and it envisaged that 'treatment of IPR' would be a subject covered while implementing the Agreement.[16] The two agreements perhaps prompted China to accelerate the promulgation of its first Patent Law in 1984, and the Sino-US Trade Negotiation and Memorandum of Understanding (1992) resulted in China's first patent law amendment in 1992, which saw significant changes in China's patent legislation. The US has also been seriously critical of China's patent protection regime. To date, the US has brought China before the WTO DSB twice and alleged that China violated certain provisions of the TRIPS Agreement.[17] Obstacles to obtain and maintain patents for pharmaceutical inventions, unauthorised use of undisclosed data generated to obtain marketing approval for pharmaceutical products, etc. are said to be the serious concerns among US businesses in China. Despite the criticisms and disputes, on certain patent protection measures China nonetheless looks to the US legislation for reference concerning, for example, supplementary data to pharmaceutical product patent applications.[18] The US and China are also partners in a couple of global IPR cooperation projects – the IP5 project and the Five Trademark Offices.

As already mentioned, China's patent legislation was influenced by the German *Bürgerliches Gesetzbuch* but motivated by the government's prevailing policy priorities, while the American patent legislation is based on the English Statute of Monopolies 1624 and developed by the

15 US Government Printing Office, *US Treaties and Other International Agreements Vol. 31 Part 6, 1979* (Washington, US Government Printing Office, 1980). Article VI of the Agreement contains five paragraphs, three of which are on patents and trademarks, four on unfair competition and five on copyrights. Available at: http://tcc.export.gov/Trade_Agreements/All_Trade_Agreements/People_China.asp (last accessed 29 December 2015).

16 In 1979, the China-US Agreement on Cooperation in Science and Technology was concluded and signed by President Carter and Premier Deng Xiaoping. The diverse range of cooperative research fields includes fisheries, earth and atmospheric sciences, basic research in physics and chemistry, a variety of energy-related areas, agriculture, civil industrial technology, geology, health, and disaster research. Article 5 of the Agreement provides that 'treatment of IPR' may be a covered subject while implementing the Agreement. Available at: http://beijing.usembassy-china.org.cn/1979stagreement.html (last accessed 29 December 2015).

17 1) China — Measures Affecting the Protection and Enforcement of Intellectual Property Rights (DS362), 2) China – Measures Affecting Trading Rights and Distribution Services for Certain Publications and Audiovisual Entertainment Products (DS363).

18 2015 Special 301 Report, pp. 42–43. Available at: https://ustr.gov/sites/default/files/2015-Special-301-Report-FINAL.pdf (last accessed 30 December 2015).

ratio decidendi. It will therefore be interesting to compare and then to discover how divergent the patent legislation in the two countries is, pursuant to international patent rights harmonisation after the US first prompted China to protect IPR in 1979.

1. Introduction

The first patent was granted in the US in 1641[19] by the Massachusetts Colony, by virtue of the English Statute of Monopolies of 1624. The year 1789 marked the beginning of patent legislation in the US when the Constitution, based on which the US patent law was authorised, came into force at the height of the Industrial Revolution.[20] Article I, Section 8 of the Constitution stated that '[t]he Congress shall have power [...] to promote the progress of science and useful arts, by securing for limited times to authors and inventors the exclusive right to their respective writings and discoveries'.

The Chinese legislation is a combination of statutes, judicial interpretations, as well as governmental policies, regulations and rules. China's patent legislation is oriented towards governmental policies. In the US, patent is a fundamental form of private property rights. The US federal government, for example, does not issue policies in order to set changes to the patent legislation, although judges and the civil society may exert some influence.

Many similar provisions in terms of application and prosecution can be found in the American and Chinese patent legislation, and the divergence between both legislations is seen as follows.

2. Comparison

A. UTILITY MODEL PATENTS

The first divide between the patent legislation in China and the US is that utility models are patentable in China but not in the US. China's patent law grants utility model patents a protection period of ten years after a simplified examination upon application, in which, for example, a search for prior art will not be conducted.[21] Currently, examining a utility model patent application takes only 3.5 months in China. Utility model patent applications used to make up the lion's share of China's yearly total of patent applications. For example, in 2013, the SIPO received a total of 2,377,061 patent applications and, among these, invention patent applications amounted to 825,136, utility model applications to 892,362 and design applications to 659,563.[22] However, since 2014, invention patent applications have started to take the lead among the three kinds of patent applications. According to the SIPO, in 2014, inventions exceeded utility models in respect of patent

19 In the early colonial period there were no general laws to provide patent protection in America. If someone invented a new product he could appeal to the colonial governments that might grant him the exclusive commercial right to exploit the product. In 1641 the Massachusetts General Court gave Samuel Winslow the exclusive right to utilise a new process of making salt for ten years. The case is also known as the first 'patent' in America. Wegner H. C., *Patent Harmonisation* (London: Sweet and Maxwell, 1993), p. 8.

20 Machlup F. and Penrose E., 'The patent controversy in the nineteenth century'. 10 *Journal of Economic History* 1 (1950), 1.

21 R.44.1, Guidelines for Patent Examination (SIPO, 2010).

22 Available at: http://english.sipo.gov.cn/statistics/2013/12/201402/t20140217_905138.html (last accessed 31 December 2015).

application numbers, as invention patents hit 928,000 applications, utility models 868,000 and designs 565,000.[23]

B. EXCEPTIONS TO PATENTABILITY

Exceptions to patentable subject matters in China are listed under Art.25 of the Patent Law 2008 and these include: scientific discoveries; rules and methods for mental activities; methods for the diagnosis or for the treatment of diseases; animal and plant varieties. Article 25 of the Draft Patent Law 2015 also includes nuclear transformation methods as a non-patentable subject matter. To identify a patentable invention in the US, two criteria set out by 35 USC. § 101 must both be satisfied, which means that the claimed invention 1) must be directed to one of the four statutory categories, and 2) must not be wholly directed to a subject matter encompassing a judicially recognised exception. As is defined by the court, the four statutory categories of patentable invention are process, machine, manufacture and composition of matter. With regard to the judicially recognised exceptions to the four categories, they include laws of nature, natural phenomena and abstract ideas.[24] Therefore, when examining the patentability of an invention patent claim, the USPTO personnel must reach a conclusion as to whether it is more likely than not that the claimed invention as a whole, including, for example, the specifications, claims, relevant prior art, etc., either falls outside of one of the statutory classes or within one of the judicial exceptions to statutory subject matters. To compare non-patentable subject matters listed under the Chinese Patent Law 2008 and Sections 101 and 161 of the US Patent Act and the interim guidelines for patent examiners issued by the USPTO in 2015, methods for diagnosis or treatment of diseases, animal and plant varieties, and substances obtained by nuclear transformation are patentable subject matters in the US but not in China.

Additionally, in the US, business methods may be patentable as long as they represent 'real world' value, instead of being an idea or concept, and produce 'useful, concrete and tangible results', while the description of the patent application must clearly identify the invention. In China, business method inventions are generally not patentable unless a three-step test is satisfied. This means, to become patentable, the business method invention must 1) involve technology, 2) solve some technological problems and 3) achieve certain technological results, and such qualities must be all evidenced in the original disclosure. But, fundamentally, business methods are not patentable in China since they are considered as mental activities and are created in compliance with the 'law of society' instead of the 'law of nature', thus they are not a 'technical solution'.[25]

C. THRESHOLDS TEST

In both countries, invention patents must be novel, creative and of industrial applicability. In China's case, the same conditions are also applicable to utility model patent applications. Article 22 of China's Patent Law 2008[26] states that inventions (and utility models) must be

23 State Intellectual Property Office of the People's Republic of China (SIPO), *Intellectual Property Rights Protection in China*. (SIPO, 2014), at p. 5.
24 For details see: www.uspto.gov/web/offices/pac/mpep/s2106.html (last accessed 27 May 2016).
25 Available at: www.mondaq.com/x/320330/Patent/Business+Method+Application (last accessed 31 December 2015).
26 Art.22 of China's Draft Patent Law 2015 requires the same conditions for granting patent protection.

creative which means that, compared with the existing technologies, the invention must possess prominent substantive features and indicate remarkable advance. On the other hand, to qualify for novelty an 'absolute novelty' threshold test must be satisfied. This means the invention or the utility model patent application must not involve an existing technology, and no applications should have been filed for any identical invention or utility model before the date of patent application, and no publications of any identical invention are to be released after the application.

In the US, the subject matter of an invention patent application must be non-obvious, and this will be examined as a whole by looking at the prior art at the starting point against the final invention. In the meantime, patentability will not be negated by the manner in which the invention is made.

Like China, the US imposed the same 'absolute novelty' threshold test after the American Invents Act came into force. Prior to that, public use or sale was grounds for destroying novelty in the US, unless the public use or the sale took place in US territory. US 35 USC. § 102(b) prescribed that 'a person shall be entitled to a patent unless [...] the invention was patented or described in a printed publication in this or a foreign country or in public use or on sale in this country, more than one year prior to the date of application for patent in the United States'.

D. POST-DATA ADMISSIBILITY

Although both China and the US require that a patent application must be submitted with a complete description and a list of claims, the difference between the two legislations lies in post-data admissibility. With regard to invention description, it must enable a skilled person in the relevant technology field to carry out the invention, while each claim shall clearly and concisely state the requested patent protection scope in accordance with the specifications contained in the description.[27] If ever an application is rejected for the lack of obviousness or inventiveness, in China comparative data is usually not admitted in order to prove that, even though the two products may be similar, the claimed product will work differently and better than the prior art. In the US, however, it is a policy that primary examiners must review affidavit evidence traversing rejections or objections in order to decide if it is sufficient to overcome the rejection.[28] Admissibility of post data is of crucial importance to pharmaceutical patent applications because pharmaceutical companies tend to file a patent application for a promising composition early and then generate supplementary and comparative data later on. Therefore, in the US, the USPTO and courts routinely accept post-application data for chemical and pharmaceutical composition and for other products. As might be expected, post-data admissibility is a controversial area in Sino-American bilateral trade relations. In December 2013 the SIPO clarified that submitting post-filing experimental data would be only permissible in very limited instances, specifically only if those data are intended to confirm that the technical solution has the use or the effect asserted by the applicant in the specifications, such as to prove that the facts or the statements in the original specifications are

27 Art.26 of China's Patent Law and Section 112 of the US Patent Act.

28 Affidavits or Declarations Traversing Rejections, 37 CFR 1.132[R-11.2013]. Available at: www.uspto.gov/web/offices/pac/mpep/s716.html (last accessed 31 December 2015).

correct. Notwithstanding this, submitting post-filing experimental data will not rectify a disclosure that was insufficient at the time of filing.[29]

E. DISCLOSURE

The Chinese patent legislation does not require the description of a patent application to include 'the best mode' of carrying out an invention, as contemplated at the time of application, whereas, in the US, this is mandatory. In the past, in the case of non-compliance, a patent infringer could use it as a valid defence in infringement litigation but, after the America Invents Act came into force, this defence was scrapped.[30]

F. PRIORITY RIGHT

By virtue of Art.29 of the Chinese Patent Law 2008, while examining a priority right claim, the two scenarios must be scrutinised separately. First, filings take place between a foreign country and China and, second, within China. If the second and the first invention (and utility model) patent applications are filed for the same subject matter within 12 months in a foreign country and in China, a relevant bilateral agreement or international treaty shall determine if a priority right may be claimed. If a design patent applicant wishes to claim a priority right under this scenario, the timespan between the second and the first applications must not be greater than six months. If the second and the first invention (and utility model) patent applications are filed for the same subject matter within 12 months within China, the applicant may be entitled to claim a priority right.

In the US, by virtue of 35 USC. § 119, if the second and the first patent applications are filed for the same subject matter, and if the first application is filed in a foreign country and the foreign country affords the national treatment to US citizens or is a WTO member, a priority right may arise if the second application filed in the US is within 12 months of the first foreign application being filed. The 12-month time limit may be extended by an additional two months if there is an unforeseen delay in filing the application in the US. In the meantime, a US patent or patent application that claims priority in a foreign application may be applied as prior art as of the filing date (priority date) of the foreign application.[31]

G. EXAMINATION

By virtue of Art.708 of the *Manual of Examining Procedure* issued by the USPTO, a patent application will join the queue behind earlier-filed applications. As soon as it is its turn for applying for examination, substantive examination against prior art will take place. In China, however, it is the applicant's responsibility to request that SIPO conducts a

29 As to the relationship between the submission of post-filing experimental data and the sufficiency of disclosure during the examination of chemical and medical invention applications, the SIPO clarified that the sufficiency of disclosure involves determining the technical solution achieved by the claim and whether this solution is achieved as of the filing date of the application. See: 'Clarity regarding the use of post-filing data in China?' by Michael Best and Friedrich LLP. Available at: https://bricwallblog.wordpress.com/2014/02/26/clarity-regarding-the-use-of-post-filing-data-in-china/ (last accessed 11 January 2016).

30 Section 15 of the America Invents Act. Under Section 15, a patent may not be cancelled or invalidated based on an applicant's failure to disclose 'the best mode' of carrying out an invention.

31 35 US.C. § 102.

substantive examination within three years after an application is filed. If an examination request is not submitted, and unless there is valid justification for this, the patent application will be deemed withdrawn. On the other hand, although in both China and the US applicants are required to submit known prior art references when submitting a patent application, the difference is that Art.36 of China's Patent Law 2008 is silent as to any punishment that may be laid down in cases where applicants fail to comply with this requirement. In the US patent applicants have the moral obligation to submit known reference materials to the USPTO. Any failure in this regard will result in a defence against enforcement of a granted patent on the grounds of inequitable conduct or fraud inflicted on the patent office.[32] In addition, case law jurisdiction suggests that any patent attorney involved may be sanctioned or even barred from practice by the USPTO.[33]

In the event that a patent application is rejected after examination, in the US the applicant may file either a request for continued examination or a continuation application, which suggests that a patent application may be alive in the US for many years. However, in China, it is not possible to keep an application alive after rejection unless the examiner requests that the applicant divides the claimed subject matter into separate applications.[34] Otherwise, by virtue of Art.41 of the Patent Law 2008, the applicant may appeal to the Patent Re-examination Board for review. Article 41 of the Draft Patent Law 2015 adds that, while re-examining a patent application, the Parent Re-examination Board may conduct examination of other matters in order to determine if a patent may be granted. In the US, similarly, an applicant may appeal for re-examination to the USPTO Patent Trial and Appeal Board under the America Invents Act. If unsatisfied with the re-examination result, applicants may resort to judicial review in court in both countries.

H. INVALIDATION

A patent may be challenged for invalidity on the grounds of prior art or insufficient disclosure in both countries. Based on China's Implementing Regulations,[35] a challenge may be filed at any time after a patent is granted. Once a request for invalidation is accepted by the Patent Re-examination Board, supplementary grounds or evidence may be submitted within one month counting from the date when the request for invalidation is submitted. Additional information submitted after the one-month time limit may be ignored by the Patent Re-examination Board.[36] In the US, a re-examination may be conducted in order to reinforce patent validity. Or a third party may challenge the validity of a granted patent,

32 *Larson Manufacturing Company of South Dakota Inc.* v. *Aluminart Products Limited* (559 F.3d 1317, United States Court of Appeals, Federal Circuit 2009). The court concluded that the plaintiff engaged in inequitable conduct before the USPTO in the re-examination proceedings of United States Patent No. 6,616,998 conducted in 2004 to 2006, and, therefore, the patent in question was unenforceable. Available at: www.leagle.com/decision/20071615513FSupp2d1102_11535 (last accessed 11 January 2016).

33 *Weiffenbach* v. *Logan*, 27 USPQ2d 1870 (Comm'r Pat. 1993), aff'd subnom., *Logan* v. *Lehman*, 73 F.3d 379 (Fed Cir. 1994) (concealing date of Office action from client; concealing abandonment and true reason for abandonment). See: United States Patent and Trademark Office, *Practicing Before the USPTO in Today's Market: Conforming Your Conduct to the USPTO's Code of Professional Responsibility* (USPTO, 2008).

34 Rule 42, Implementing Regulations of the Patent Law of the People's Republic of China (January 2010).

35 Rule 65, the Transitional Measures of Implementing the Amended Implementing Regulations of the Patent Law, 21 January 2010.

36 Rule 67, Implementing Regulations of the Patent Law of the People's Republic of China (January 2010).

either *ex parte*[37] or *inter parte*,[38] and, in the latter case, a challenge may be filed only after a patent is granted, as a post-grant review.

With regard to third-party intervention, Rule 48 of the Implementing Regulations of the Patent Law of China 2010 provides that any person may submit to the patent administrative authority his observation if he finds the application does not conform to the provisions stipulated by the Patent Law. While, in the US, only interested third parties may submit relevant materials to intervene once an application is published.

The difference in the post-grant period in both countries is that procedures for correcting granted patents are not available in China. In the US correcting granted patents is possible since changes to patent claims are admissible and this will result in either re-issuing or re-examining a patent grant, or a post-grant re-examination. Nonetheless, the Patent Re-examination Board in China is authorised to initiate *ex officio* re-examination. This being the case, a patent re-examination may be conducted beyond the requested scope, grounds and evidence that are provided by the parties at the time of request. Eventually, re-examination may be pursued by the Board even if the request for re-examination is withdrawn or when the case is settled.[39]

I. COMPULSORY LICENCE

As far as a patent grant is concerned, in the US a patent holder is granted absolute rights to exclude others from using the patent during the full protection term while, in China, Arts.48–51 of the Patent Law 2008 provide grounds for issuing compulsory licences but, usually, exploitation can only be undertaken when it is for the supply to the domestic Chinese market unless otherwise specified.[40] Article 52 further requires that, if the invention involved in a compulsory licence is a semi-conduct technology, exploitation will only be admissible on the grounds of public interest.[41] Although, so far, no compulsory licence has ever been issued in China, global pharmaceutical and semi-conductor companies are known to be worried as, for example, their local businesses may one day be declared monopolistic by the Chinese authority and thus, by virtue of Art.48(2) of the Patent Law 2008, compulsory licences may be issued to enable exploitation,

J. ENFORCEMENT

When it comes to patent litigation, the US courts are competent to decide issues such as invalidation and infringement with a single judgment while, in China, invalidation may be decided by the SIPO, the courts, as well as by the patent administrative authority.[42] As mentioned earlier, since November 2014, with the status of intermediate court,

37 35 USC. § 302.

38 35 USC. § 311.

39 State Intellectual Property Office of the People's Republic of China (SIPO), *Guidelines for Patent Examination* (SIPO, 2010), at 590, 426.

40 Art.53, Patent Law 2008.

41 The Draft Patent Law 2015 made no changes concerning the grounds for issuing compulsory licences.

42 Arts.45, 61, Patent Law 2008. The Draft Patent Law 2015 made no changes in substance in this regard, although 'patent administrative authority' under the Patent Law 2008 has become 'Patent Administration Department' under the Draft Patent Law 2015. This suggests that a specific department for administrative enforcement on patent rights will be set up in China.

IP-specialised courts were established in Beijing, Shanghai and Guangzhou as a three-year experiment to adjudicate technologically complex cases of the first and the second instance for both civil and administrative disputes.

The procedures for instituting a patent lawsuit are very different in the two countries. In China, by virtue of Art.60 of the Patent Law 2008, parties are obliged to first go through consultation. If the parties are not willing to consult or if consultation fails, the patent holder or an interested party may bring a lawsuit against the alleged infringer in court or request the local patent administrative authority to settle the dispute. The patent administrative authority is granted the power to order an infringer to cease the infringement activities immediately and, upon the request of the parties, to conduct mediation in order to settle infringement compensation. If the parties are not happy with the outcome reached after mediation, they may go to court to settle the dispute. As mentioned previously, in recent years, as China's patent legislation has become better defined and more comprehensive, patent infringement cases are usually directly handled by the courts through judicial enforcement. On the other hand, although these days administrative enforcement is less used than before, the number of patent disputes dealt with by the mechanism is still high.

If infringement of a patented manufacturing process is alleged in China, the alleged infringer must prove that the manufacturing process of his own product is different from the patented process.[43] In the US the judicial authorities shall have the power to order the same, since patents enjoy a presumption of validity in courts and the burden of proof lies with the alleged infringer as a result.

In China, Art.64 of the Patent Law 2008 governs the procedures of investigating alleged patent counterfeit. Patent administrative authorities may, based on evidence, inquire into the parties concerned and investigate the circumstances related to the alleged counterfeiting act. It may: conduct inspection at the place where the suspected illegal act is committed; consult and make copies of the relevant contracts, invoices, account books and other related materials; and check the products related to the suspected illegal act and seal or detain the products that are proved to be produced by the counterfeited patent. By virtue of Art.67 of the Draft Patent Law 2015, when sealing or detaining products relating to the alleged illegal act, infringement or passing off, evidence must show that the product is a 'wilful infringement that disrupts the market order' or of patent passing off.

When submitting evidence only notarised documents are admissible as proof in the Chinese courts. In the US, however, evidence is simply provided through discovery, which constitutes a dominant part of litigation.[44] In court, statements under oath are equally admissible as evidence. Moreover, in the US, once a patent infringement allegation is filed in the Federal District Court in the locality concerned, the patent holder may request the alleged infringer to surrender all relevant information[45] and may depose witnesses who may include managers, financial, sales and technical employees of the defendant.[46] Products may be inspected and analytical information retrieved.[47] Rule 37(b) of the Federal Rules of Civil

43 Art.61, Patent Law 2008. Under the Draft Patent Law 2015, the requirement remains the same although Art.61 has become Art.64.

44 Jaeschke W. C. *et al.*, 'Comparison of Chinese and US patent reform legislation: which, if either, got it right?' 11 *John Marshall Review of Intellectual Property Law* 567 (2012).

45 Federal Rules of Civil Procedure Rule 34(a).

46 Federal Rules of Civil Procedure Rule 30(c).

47 Federal Rules of Civil Procedure Rule 34(a)(1).

Procedure imposes penalties if evidence is destroyed. Such penalties may include fines and even an adverse judgment.

The statute of limitations in the US is considerably longer than that in China, which allows only two years dating from the time the patent holder gains knowledge of or should have known about the infringement. It is six years in the US.

K. COMPENSATION

Compensation for infringement is much higher in the US than in China. In the US awards in billions of dollars and recoveries in millions are common.[48] In *Centocor Ortho Biotech* v. *Abbott Labs*, the plaintiff was awarded 1.6 billion USD (1.44 billion EUR) as compensation. In China damages awarded for losses incurred as a result of patent infringement are a lot lower. Article 63 of the Patent Law 2008 stipulates that an infringer for patent passing off will be fined no more than four times the illegal gains and, if there are no illegal gains, a fine of not more than 200,000 RMB (28,000 EUR) may be imposed, in addition to criminal liability if any. Note that the compensation amount in China has been raised by each patent law amendment, and the Draft Patent Law 2015 proves no exception. Compared with the afore-mentioned amount for patent passing off imposed by the Patent Law 2008, the Draft Patent Law 2015 has increased the fine to five times and to 250,000 RMB (34,900 EUR) if there are no illegal gains.[49] As for patent infringement, Art.65 of China's Patent Law 2008 sets the compensation amount between 10,000 to 1,000,000 RMB (1,400 to 140,000 EUR), in addition to expenses claims, while the Draft Patent Law 2015 increased the amount from 1 million to 5 million RMB (140,000 to 700,000 EUR).[50] However, though China has been consistently increasing the compensation/fine amount for patent infringement, the measures are still not seen as powerful enough in order to deter future infringers, rendering the whole patent system weaker.

L. SECURITY REVIEW

Both the US and China impose the requirement for a national security review before a patent application for a home-created invention may be filed abroad.[51] In China the patent administrative authority may spend up to six months in order to scrutinise and contemplate objections to a foreign patent filing.[52] In the US a security review may take a few days, especially if a request to expedite clearance for a licence is submitted.[53]

3. *Summary*

Given the principle of flexibility embedded in the TRIPS Agreement, varied patent protection levels in terms of procedure and substantive measures are seen in the patent

48 For example, in *Lucent Techs., Inc.* v. *Gateway, Inc.* (Fed. Cir. 2009), 357,693,056.18 USD (320,641,000.26 EUR) was awarded.

49 Art.66, Draft Patent Law 2015.

50 Art.68, Draft Patent Law 2015.

51 Art.20, Patent Law 2008, as well as 35 USC. § 184 (2006), which sets down that any application is subject to a national security review under section 181.

52 General Introduction to the Third Revision of the Patent Law of the People's Republic of China and Its Implementing Regulations 3 (Dec. 2010).

53 35 USC. § 184 (2006).

legislation in the US and in China. However, the primary difference between the two patent legislations lies in government intervention, in which regard patent in the US is a form of private property rights while, in China, it is considered as more of a policy driver. As a result, the US patent legislation inherits the common law tradition so that, in addition to the statute, patent protection is influenced by judicial precedence. In China's case, certain patent protection areas, such as service patent as reflected in the Draft Patent Law 2015, follow policies pronounced by the government depending on economic motivations.

On the premise of this argument, it looks like a natural consequence that utility models are not patentable in the US because, typically, utility models are employed by government as a policy instrument to encourage innovation as is revealed earlier. Second, China demarcates wider boundaries on exceptions to patentable subject matters while the restrictions in the US are only a fraction of what is non-patentable in China. If it were not for the purpose of complying with the minimum patent protection standards set down by the TRIPS, exceptions to patentable subject matters would have been even more limited in the US legislation.

II) China's patent law: a substantive comparison with the European Patent Convention

1. Introduction

As mentioned in Chapter 3, while substantive maximum harmonisation has achieved little progress at the international level in recent years, regional patent harmonisation continues to develop. At the same time, more and more patent regimes, albeit 'latecomers', started to enact internationally compatible legislation, mainly as a result of their respective WTO accessions. The former is epitomised by the EPC, the latter by the Chinese patent regime.

The EPO and China stand as the world's forerunners of patent protection in terms of legislation. The EPC and the Chinese patent law are, of course, both compatible with the TRIPS Agreement, but divergence between the two regimes exists too, for example concerning the degree of protection. China's Patent Law is a complete piece of legislation on patent application, examination, protection and enforcement. The EPC does not legislate on matters that fall under the competence of the national patent office, such as infringement, enforcement and compulsory licencing. Second, the Chinese Patent Law provides protection for invention, utility model and design patents, while the EPC deals with invention patent protection only.

2. Similarities

It is observed that the identical patent protection measures shared by the EPC and the Chinese Patent Law are those explicitly prescribed by the TRIPS Agreement.

Both patent laws provide a 20-year protection term to invention patents and require that disclosure in a patent application must be sufficiently clear so that the invention may be carried out by a person skilled in the art. Foreign applicants enjoy the national treatment under EPC as well as under Chinese patent law. For the former, application is simply open to any individual or entity in the world. For the latter, foreign applicants, with or without a residence address, may apply for patent or undertake patent-related activities in China by engaging an authorised patent agent.

Under the auspices of Art.73 of the TRIPS Agreement, both Chinese Patent Law and the EPC require a confidentiality review before an application for a home-created patent may be filed abroad. However, while Chinese Patent Law since 2008 quashed the 'China-application-first' requirement,[54] the EPC leaves the national patent office to decide on detail and Art.75 of the EPC stipulates that a patent application may be required to be first submitted to the national authority or to another authority subject to prior authorisation.

3. *Divergence*

Although the EPC and Chinese Patent Law share some similarities in patent protection measures, the divergence between the two appears substantial, as outlined below (See below Table 9.1, page 206).

A. PATENTABILITY

To qualify as a patentable invention in China and among the EPC countries, the invention must involve a new technical solution relating to a product, a process or an improvement thereof, and it must be novel, creative and of practical use. Restrictions on patentability imposed by the EPC mirror those stipulated by Art.27 of the TRIPS Agreement. To examine whether an invention is patentable under China's Patent Law 2008, Arts.2[55] and 22 must read together.

It is noticed that, under the EPC, 'patentability' and 'exceptions to patentability' are two separate subjects that oblige a two-stage test. In order to be eligible for a patent grant, a subject matter must first qualify as an invention. Only then will the subject matter be examined to see if it falls under the exceptions to patentability. Under the Chinese Patent Law, the first test is omitted. It is, perhaps, assumed that a subject matter will automatically qualify as an invention – as long as it is a new technological solution '... relating to a product, a process or an improvement thereof'. It seems that no requirements need to be met before the thresholds test of novelty, inventive step and industrial application is applied. Therefore, within the context of patentability, the Chinese Patent Law and the EPC do not seem to be discussing the same subject. The Chinese Patent Law discusses 'patentability' and 'exceptions to patentability' together.

B. EXCEPTIONS TO PATENTABILITY

In accordance with Art.27 of the TRIPS Agreement, patent protection will not be granted to an invention if it contravenes *ordre public* or morality, although the Chinese Patent Law goes a step further by stipulating that if an invention is a detriment to public interest it will be excluded from becoming patentable. Inventions accomplished by relying on illegally

54 Art.20, Patent Law 2008.

55 In terms of the definition for 'design', Art.2 of the Draft Patent Law 2015 confines design to 'the overall or part of' a product, which is a new element compared with the Patent Law 2008.

obtained genetic resources will not be eligible for patentability either.[56] The Draft Patent Law 2015 holds the same position. Additionally, when Art.5 is read together with Art.26 of the Patent Law 2008,[57] if the direct sources of an invention are based on genetic resources then the sources must be explained in the application document. If the genetic resources are obtained or used in violation of the relevant laws, patent rights will not be granted to such inventions.

Both the EPC and Chinese patent law set down restrictions on patentability in relation to 'animal or plant varieties', although the measures imposed by the EPC are stricter. By virtue of Art.25 of the Chinese Patent Law 2008, production methods of animal and plant varieties are patentable but the EPC does not sanction this. The EPC specifies that biological processes for the production of plants or animals are not patentable, unless they are microbiological processes or products. Under the EPC, methods for treatment of the human or animal body by surgery or therapy and diagnostic methods practised on the human or animal body fall under the exceptions to patentability, although 'products, in particular substances or compositions for use in any of these methods' may be patentable.[58] China does not offer patentability in this respect.

Scientific theories and mathematical methods or mental and intellectual activities are not patentable inventions under both laws.

On the other hand, the EPC is silent on the patentability of substances obtained by nuclear transformation while, by virtue of Art.25, the Chinese Patent Law 2008 rejects their patentability. China's Draft Patent Law 2015 further excludes 'nuclear transformation methods' from being patentable.[59]

When the issues of 'patentability' and 'exceptions to patentability' are examined together, it is clear that the Chinese patent law is less restrictive than the EPC because, in any case, the former does not strictly differentiate between patentable and non-patentable inventions. The Chinese patent law does not exclude 'scientific theories and mathematical methods; aesthetic creations; playing games or doing business, and computer programmes; presentations of information' from being patentable, while the EPC does. It shows therefore that the EPC has a more unambiguous stand when it specifies that patentable inventions do not include non-technological subject matters.

C. CREATIVITY

In relation to 'creativity', or the 'inventive step' as the EPC calls it, China prescribes a higher threshold test than its EPO counterpart. By virtue of Art.22 of Chinese Patent Law, an invention must demonstrate the quality of 'absolute novelty', and must meet the requirements of 'prominent substantive features' and 'remarkable advancements', before

56 Art.5, Patent Law 2008.

57 The fifth paragraph of Art.26 of the Chinese Patent Law reads that, when an invention is accomplished by relying on genetic resources, 'the applicant shall, in the patent application documents, indicate the direct and original source of the genetic resources. If the applicant cannot indicate the original source, he shall state the reasons'.

58 Art.53 Exceptions to Patentability, EPC.

59 Art.25, Draft Patent Law 2015.

the threshold test of creativity may be passed.[60] For the EPC, the quality of 'non-obviousness' will suffice.[61]

D. GRACE PERIOD

The EPC and Chinese patent law both grant a six-month grace period and, during this time if certain conditions are met, an invention will not be considered as having lost its novelty although disclosure may have already taken place. Consequently, a prior date will not be established and an invention may still be granted patent protection if the thresholds test is passed.

As was mentioned previously, in general a 'grace period' may be applicable under three circumstances: non-prejudicial disclosure at an exhibition; disclosure in consequence of an abuse; and lawful non-prejudicial disclosure other than at an exhibition, also known as 'general grace period'. Article 24 of the Chinese Patent Law grants a six-month grace period in all the circumstances mentioned above although, for non-prejudicial disclosure at an exhibition, the location of the exhibition must be in China. As for the EPC, though Art.55 also offers a six-month grace period, the 'general grace period' is not available to European patent applicants.[62]

E. PRIORITY RIGHT

Priority right is granted under different scenarios under EPC and Chinese patent law. Under Art.87 of the EPC priority right may be granted for a 12-month period from the date of the first filing to all European patent applications of the same invention, if the first filing takes place in another EPC member or in a third country where a bilateral or multilateral agreement may give rise to a priority right claim. Equally, while every patent application may be granted a 'priority right' regardless of examination outcome, a subsequent filing on the same subject matter may be considered as the first filing as far as priority right is concerned if it is filed in, or for, the same EPO Member State, in cases where certain conditions are met. These conditions include that the previous filing has been withdrawn, abandoned or refused and without disclosure to the public, etc.[63]

As was mentioned earlier in this chapter, by virtue of Art.29 of the Chinese Patent Law 2008, before granting a priority right in China two scenarios must be examined. First, filings taking place between a foreign country and China, and, second, within China. Under the first scenario, a relevant bilateral agreement or international treaty shall determine if a priority right may arise while, for a design patent applicant, the timespan between the second and the first applications must not be greater than six months. Under the second scenario, as long as the second and the first applications are filed within 12 months, the applicant may claim a priority right.

60 China's Draft Patent Law 2015 made no changes in this regard.

61 Art.56, EPC.

62 Except in Spain where patent applicants may enjoy a six-month grace period for tests carried out, by virtue of Art.7(c) of the Spanish Patent Law 1998.

63 Art.87, EPC.

Under the EPC a 'bilateral agreement' or 'international treaty' is equally a prerequisite *vis-à-vis* third countries before a priority right may be claimed, unless the first and the second filings both take place within the jurisdiction.

F. TRANSPARENCY AND CONFIDENTIALITY

Both the Chinese Patent Law and the EPC specify an 18-month timeline after which a patent application must be published, counting from the date of submission. The EPC is, nonetheless, more precise as to the content of the publication. Article 93 of the EPC stipulates that specifications of a European patent must be published together with the application when a decision to grant patent protection becomes effective.

By virtue of Art.21 of the Patent Law 2008, the patent administration authority must release 'patent-related information in a complete, accurate and timely manner'. But it is not clear how detailed patent specifications must be published. The Implementing Regulations of the Patent Law of China 2010 is also silent on this. Article 21 of the Draft Patent Law 2015 continues to oblige the patent administration department to release patent-related information in the same manner, and requests the department to publish 'the basic patent information data'.

G. EXAMINATION AND TIMEFRAME OF GRANTING A PATENT

In relation to invention patent applications, the Chinese Patent Law differentiates between preliminary and substantive examination. Preliminary examination must be conducted within 18 months after an application is submitted. As to substantive examination, it may be conducted within three years counting from the filing date and after the invention patent applicant submits a request for substantive examination. Only after a substantive examination is completed, and if all requirements are met, a patent may be granted.[64] Note that, by virtue of Art.34 of the Patent Law 2008, the 18-month timeframe applies only to 'preliminary examination', which includes formality and substance check.[65] If all requirements are met after preliminary examination, a patent application must be published.

Under the EPC, a patent application should be published as soon as possible. The time limit for granting a patent is not specified. But, judging by Art.93 of the EPC regarding publication, a patent may be granted any time after the 18-month period expires.

H. APPEAL

Both the Chinese Patent Law and the EPC provide applicants with chances to appeal, but the difference between the two patent legislations lies in procedures. By virtue of Art.41

64 Arts.34 and 35, Patent Law 2008. The provisions remain unchanged in the Draft Patent Law 2015.

65 By virtue of Rule 44, the Implementation Regulations of the Patent Law of China 2010, 'preliminary examination' means to check a patent application to ensure it contains all the required documents following the required form, as prescribed by Arts.26 and 27 of the Patent Law 2008. In the meantime, patentability, exceptions to patentability and confidentiality, etc. will also be examined.

of China's Patent Law 2008, if a patent application is rejected the applicant may ask the Patent Re-examination Board for a decision review within three months. Note that under the Draft Patent Law 2015, while re-examining a patent application the Patent Re-examination Board may examine other related matters in order to decide whether the application should be granted a patent after all. Nonetheless, before a rejection is announced, and if an application is found not qualifying for a patent grant, the applicant will be notified and can explain and amend the application in question within a time limit that is not specified by the law.[66]

The EPC does not provide applicants with chances to explain and to amend an application before issuing a rejection.

I. OPPOSITION

An opposition mechanism is embedded in both patent laws, and the EPC lays down more specific requirements. Under the EPC, after a patent grant is published an opposition must be submitted within nine months and the ramifications of the opposition will apply to all the EPC Contracting States in which the patent concerned has effect.[67] Article 100 of the EPC further provides grounds upon which an opposition may be submitted. Under China's patent law, grounds for opposition are provided by Rule 65 of the Implementation Regulations of the Patent Law of China 2010, including violation of the security check, non-patentability, application submission irregularity, etc. Chinese Patent Law does not specify the time limit within which a party may object to a patent grant. Article 45 of the Patent Law 2008 only stipulates that, from the date when a patent grant is announced, 'a unit or an individual' may request the Patent Review Board to declare the patent invalid. The same provision is maintained by Draft Patent Law 2015.

4. Summary

While the EPC and Chinese patent law both abide by the minimum standards of patent protection set down by TRIPS, the differences in substantive protection measures between the two patent systems appear absolute in detail, although they do share certain positions at the same time. Among the prevailing differences, some look to be technical, such as under Chinese Patent Law 'patentable invention' and 'exceptions to patentability' are examined together, while others appear to be more ideological in nature such as, for example, concerning the general grace period, the non-obviousness test, priority right claim, etc. It may be equally true that the technical differences are also influenced by the ideological discrepancies between the two.

66 Art.37, Patent Law 2008. The same provision is maintained by Draft Patent Law 2015.
67 Art.99, EPC.

Table 9.1 A substantive comparison between China's Patent Law and the European Patent Convention

	China's Patent Law (2008)	*European Patent Convention*[1]
Patentability	**Art.2**[2] 'Invention-creations': inventions, utility models and designs. Invention: any new technological solution relating to a product, a process or an improvement thereof. Utility model: any new technological solution relating to a product's shape, structure, or a combination thereof, fit for practical use. Design: any new design of a product's shape, pattern or a combination thereof, as well as the combination of the colour and the shape or pattern of a product, which creates an aesthetic feeling and is fit for industrial application. **Art.22** For inventions and utility models: novel, creative and of practical use.	**Art.52 Patentable inventions** Invention: technology in all fields, provided that they are new, involve an inventive step and are susceptible of industrial application. The following are not inventions: Discoveries, scientific theories and mathematical methods; aesthetic creations; schemes, rules and methods for performing mental acts, playing games or doing business, and programmes for computers; presentations of information.
Exceptions to patentability	**Art.5** No patent shall be granted to: • inventions against any law or social moral or that is detrimental to public interests; • inventions accomplished by relying on genetic resources which are obtained or used illegally. **Art.25**[3] Patent rights will not be granted to the following: Scientific discoveries; rules and methods for intellectual activities; methods for the diagnosis or treatment of diseases; animal or plant varieties (except: production methods); substances obtained by means of nuclear transformation; designs that are mainly used for marking the pattern, colour or the combination of the two of prints.	**Art.53 Exceptions to patentability** No patent shall be granted to: Inventions contrary to '*ordre public*' or morality; Plant or animal varieties or essentially biological processes for the production of plants or animals (not applicable to microbiological processes or products); Methods for treatment of the human or animal body by surgery or therapy and diagnostic methods practised on the human or animal body; this provision shall not apply to products, in particular substances or compositions, for use in any of these methods.
Patentability thresholds test	**Art.22** Novelty: not an existing technology; no prior patent application is filed; no identical record is found after the application date. Existing technologies: the technologies known to the public both domestically and abroad before the date of application.	**Art.54 Novelty** Invention must not form part of the state of the art – which should comprise everything made available to the public either written or by oral description, by use or in any other way, including the European patent applications filed previously, substance or composition – before the European patent filing date.

	Creativity: compared with the existing technologies, the invention possesses prominent substantive features and indicates remarkable advance, and the utility model possesses substantive features and indicates advancements. Practical use: invention or utility model can be used for production or be utilised, and may produce positive results.	**Art.56 Inventive step** If, having regard to the state of the art, it is not obvious to a person skilled in the art.
	Art. 23 Design 1) No attributes from existing design, no prior applications; 2) distinctive features. Existing design: design known to the general public both at home and abroad prior to the date of application.	**Art.57 Industrial application** If it can be made or used in any kind of industry, including agriculture.
Grace period	**Art.24** Six-month grace period before application if an invention is disclosed: 1) at an international exhibition sponsored or recognised by the Chinese Government; 2) at a prescribed academic or technological meeting; 3) by any person without authorisation.	**Art.55 Non-prejudicial disclosure** No earlier than six months preceding the filing date and if it was because of: 1) an evident abuse; 2) at an official international exhibition based on the Convention on international exhibitions signed at Paris on 22 November 1928 and last revised on 30 November 1972.
Disclosure	**Art.26** Invention or utility model: Description of an application should enable a person skilled in the relevant field of technology to carry it out; where necessary, drawings are required. Scope for patent protection in accordance with the specifications should be specified in patent claim. For an invention based on genetic resources, the applicant shall state the direct source and the original source of the genetic resources in the application documents, or explain why he could not. **Art.27** Design: Pictures or photos of the design, a brief introduction to the design, and other documents. Pictures or photos must clearly show the product's design for which the patent protection is requested.	**Art.83 Disclosure of the invention** Disclosure must be made in a manner sufficiently clear and complete for it to be carried out by a person skilled in the art.

(Continued)

Table 9.1 (Continued)

	China's Patent Law (2008)	*European Patent Convention*[1]
Priority right	**Article 29**[4] A priority right may arise, if • between a foreign country and China, if the first application is filed in a foreign country, then… within twelve months from the date of the first application for an invention or utility model patent; or within six months from the date of the first application for a design patent, filing an application in China for the same subject matter, a priority right may arise based on the relevant bilateral agreements concluded. • Within China, within 12 months from the date the first application for an invention or utility model patent is filed, when a second application is filed for the same subject matter.	**Art.87 Priority right** A priority right may be granted for a 12-month period from the date of the first filing to all European patent applications of the same invention: • if the first filing takes place in another EPC member; or • in a third country where a bilateral or multilateral agreement may give rise to a priority right claim. A subsequent filing on the same subject matter may be considered as the first filing as far as priority right is concerned if it is filed in, or for, the same EPO Member State, in case certain conditions are met. These conditions include that the previous filing has been withdrawn, abandoned or refused and without disclosure to the public, etc.
Infringement	**Art.11** For invention or utility model, without permission of the patent holder, entity or individual make, use, promise the sale of, sell or import the patented product, or use the patented process and use, promise the sale of, sell or import the product directly obtained from the patented process, for production or business purposes constitutes infringement. For design, without permission of the patent holder, entity or individual make, promise to sell, sell, or import the product incorporating its or his patented design, for production and business purposes constitutes infringement.	**Art.64 Rights conferred by a European patent** Any infringement of a European patent shall be dealt with by national law.

Exceptions to unauthorised use	**Art.69(4)** Using relevant patents solely for scientific research and experiment is not infringement. **Art.69(5)** Producing, using or importing patented medicine or patented medicinal equipment for providing information required for administrative examination and approval; and producing and importing the patented medicine or patented medical equipment for administrative examination and approval are not infringement.	Nil. *Nota bene*: a subject matter falls under each member's national patent legislation.
Foreign patent applicants	**Arts. 18, 19**[5] Foreign applicants, including foreign enterprises or organisations, without a residence address or business site in China may apply for a patent in China based on relevant agreement concluded, or engage an authorised patent agent to apply for a patent, or to manage other patent-related matters, in China.	**Art.58 Entitlement to file a European patent application** Any natural or legal person, or any entity equivalent to a legal person, is entitled to apply for a European patent.
Confidentiality review	**Art.20**[6] Chinese inventors should report in advance to the patent administrative department of the State Council for a confidentiality review, before filing an application of the same made-in-China invention or utility model in a foreign country, or for an international patent. **Art.71**[7] If Art.20 is violated, and if a state secret divulged, the violator will be subject to an administrative sanction. Criminal liability may apply.	**Art.75 Filing of a European patent application** When a European patent is filed in a contracting state, an application may not be communicated abroad without the prior authorisation of the relevant competent government body. Or, an application may be requested to file initially with the national authority, or make direct filing with another authority subject to prior authorisation.
Transparency and confidentiality and publication	**Art.21**[8] Before a patent application is published or announced, the invention contents will be kept confidential. **Art.34** Preliminary examination upon application. If all requirements are met, within 18 months the application should be published, or earlier upon applicant's request.	**Art.93 Publication of the European patent application** An application will be published as soon as possible after the expiry of 18 months after the date of filing or, if priority has been claimed, from the date of priority. Or, earlier, at the applicant's request. An application will be published at the same time as the specifications when the decision to grant the patent becomes effective.

(Continued)

Table 9.1 (Continued)

	China's Patent Law (2008)	*European Patent Convention*[1]
Examination and timeframe of granting a patent	**Art.34** Preliminary examination upon application. If all requirements are met, within 18 months the application should be published or earlier, upon applicant's request. **Art.35** Invention patent applicant must apply, within three years after the application, for substantive examination on the application. Patent administrative authority may, on its own initiative, conduct substantive examination on the invention patent application. **Art.39** If all the requirements are satisfied after the substantive examination, patent will be granted. **Art.40** For utility model or design, patent will be granted upon preliminary examination, and announcement will be made.	**Art.93 Publication of the European patent application** The application will be published as soon as possible after the expiry of 18 months after the date of filing, or at the same time when a patent is granted. If priority has been claimed, from the date of priority; or at the request of the applicant.
Review and appeal	**Art.37** If, after substantive examination, the application is found not qualifying for a patent grant, the applicant will be notified and given the chance to explain and amend the application, within a specified time limit. **Art.41**[9] Within three months of rejection, an applicant may ask the Patent Re-examination Board to review the decision. The applicant may bring a lawsuit to the court within three months, if is dissatisfied with the review decision.	**Art.106 Decisions subject to appeal** An appeal shall lie from decisions of the Receiving Section, Examining Divisions, Opposition Divisions and the Legal Division. An appeal shall have suspensive effect.
Term of protection	**Art.42**[10] Invention: 20 years from the date of application. Utility model or design: 10 years, from the date of application.	**Art.63 Term of the European patent** Twenty years from the date of application (invention patent only).

Opposition	**Art.45** Any entity or individual, starting from the date when the patent is announced, may launch the opposition procedure. **Art.46**[11] The patent review board should examine the declaration of invalidity in a timely manner. If a patent is ruled invalid upon challenge, within three months the patent holder may bring a law suit to the court if is dissatisfied with the decision.	**Art.99 Opposition** Any person within nine months after a patent grant is published may object to the decision. An opposition will have the effect in all the EPC contracting states in which the patent in question has effect. **Art.100 Grounds for opposition** Subject matter; insufficient disclosure; subject matter beyond the application content; the patent was granted on a divisional application or on a new application filed under Art.61 beyond the content of the earlier application.

[1]The latest version of the EPC contains the revised texts of the Convention and its protocols which entered into force on 13 December 2007, and the Implementing Regulations as in force since 1 April 2014. Available at: www.epo.org/law-practice/legal-texts/html/epc/2013/e/ma0.html (last accessed 1 June 2016).

[2]Art.2 of the Draft Patent Law 2015 specifies that design refers to 'the overall part of' a product.

[3]Art.25 of the Draft Patent Law 2015 adds that nuclear transformation method is not a patentable subject matter.

[4]Art.29 of the Draft Patent Law 2015 adds that, for a design patent application to enjoy the right of priority, the applicant must file an application within six months from the date of the first submission in China.

[5]Art.19 of the Draft Patent Law 2015 adds that a patent attorney may handle patent applications or patent-related matters for a foreigner, foreign enterprise or other foreign organisation without a regular residence or business site in China.

[6]Art.20 of the Draft Patent Law 2015 guarantees that a Chinese unit or individual may file international applications and 'obtain the relevant protection' in accordance with the relevant international treaties to which China has acceded. It also adds that the patent administration department under the State Council shall handle such international patent applications.

[7]Art.71 of the Patent Law 2008 has shifted to become Art.76 under the Draft Patent Law 2015.

[8]Art.21 of the Draft Patent Law 2015 adds that the patent administration department under the State Council shall provide the basic patent information data.

[9]Art.41 of the Draft Patent Law 2015 adds that, while re-examining a patent application, the Patent Re-examination Board may conduct examination on other matters as to whether or not a patent application may be qualified for a patent grant.

[10]Art.42 of the Draft Patent Law 2015 increases the protection term for design patents from 10 to 15 years.

[11]Art.46 of the Draft Patent Law 2015 adds that, upon receiving the request for patent invalidation, the Patent Re-examination Board may conduct examination of other matters in order to determine the patent rights.

IV Conclusion

After comparing patent legislations imposed by China, the US and the EPO, it is evident that, once the minimum protection standards laid down by the TRIPS Agreement are met, higher or lower levels of protection measures are set out by individual countries and regional patent offices in different patent protection areas based on policy needs and societal factors, thanks to the principle of flexibility guaranteed by TRIPS. As is further revealed by the comparisons, for certain patent protection areas China imposes higher standards than its counterparts, be it the US or the EPO while, in other areas, the opposite is true.

Despite its weaknesses in patent enforcement, it is worth noting that after China acceded to the WTO there have been, so far, no complaints brought to the DSB against China's patent protection regime.[68] Until now, out of the total of 34 disputes[69] with China, there is only one case that concerns IPR infringement with regard to copyright and trademark infringements, as was discussed in the previous chapter. Another case that involved some elements of IPR is the case China – Measures Affecting Financial Information Services and Foreign Financial Information Suppliers, which was brought up by the European Communities for undisclosed information. The dispute was solved at the consultation stage.[70]

Having established a comprehensive patent protection regime three decades ago, in recent years China has appeared ready to embark on innovation on the world stage and the country's strength in innovation is emerging. According to the World IP Report 2015 published by the WIPO, China is the world's only emerging middle-income country moving closer to a group of advanced industrialised nations, such as Japan, the US, Germany, France, the United Kingdom and the Republic of Korea, which are leaders in breakthrough innovations in the areas of 3D printing, nanotechnology and robotics, the three frontier technologies that hold the potential to boost future economic growth.[71]

68 See: the list of 11 patent disputes filed so far under the WTO Dispute Settlement mechanism. Available at: https://www.wto.org/english/tratop_e/dispu_e/dispu_subjects_index_e.htm#selected_subject (last accessed 14 January 2016).

69 See: www.wto.org/english/tratop_e/dispu_e/dispu_by_country_e.htm for details. (last accessed 26 May 2016).

70 DS372, China – Measures Affecting Financial Information Services and Foreign Financial Information Suppliers. On 3 March 2008, the European Communities (EC) requested consultations with China. The EC claims that a number of Chinese measures were adversely affecting financial information services and foreign financial services suppliers in China. Such measures included no fewer than a dozen legal and administrative instruments that empowered the Xinhua News Agency, the State news agency in China, to act as the regulatory authority for foreign news agencies and for foreign financial information providers. As a result, these foreign suppliers could only operate in China through an agent designated by Xinhua. As such, they were not allowed to directly solicit subscriptions for their services in China. The EC considered that the measures at issue were inconsistent with China's obligations under various provisions of the GATS, the TRIPS Agreement and China's Protocol of Accession. On 4 December 2008, China and the EC informed the DSB that they had reached an agreement in relation to the dispute in the form of a MoU.

71 For patents filed since 2005 Chinese applicants account for more than a quarter of patents worldwide in the area of 3D printing and robotics – the highest share among all countries. In the case of nanotechnology, Chinese applicants make up close to 15 per cent of filings worldwide – the third largest origin of patents. World Intellectual Property Organization, 'Small group of countries drives innovation in breakthrough technologies', press release, 11 November, on the occasion of launching the *World Intellectual Property Report 2015* (Geneva: WIPO, 2015).

In relation to international patent rights harmonisation, since China acceded to its first international IP treaty, the Paris Convention, in 1984, the country is now a signatory of 19 treaties administered by WIPO,[72] in addition to the TRIPS Agreement. From a passive 'norm taker' to an active 'norm shaker',[73] China's tortuous patent protection development is, nonetheless, not new. Japan and the US, the world's two most innovative countries, shared the same experience.

History has witnessed that Japan was widely criticised in the past for, among other things, encouraging sequential/incremental and cumulative patents that were regarded as 'low value' innovation. In the 1980s the country was even placed on the US priority watch list for not providing sufficient IPR protection under the Special 301 provisions.[74] But nowadays, as an innovation giant, Japan is an advocate for stronger global patent rights protection[75] and cooperation. According to the *World Intellectual Property Report 2015*, eight out of the top ten patent applicants in the technology field of robotics are from Japan – namely, Toyota, Honda, Nissan, Denso, Hitachi, Panasonic, Yaskawa and Sony. For nanotechnology patents, six Japanese companies have reached the top ten ranking worldwide – Nippon Steel, Toshiba, Canon, Hitachi, Panasonic and TDK. Among the 3D printing patent applications, three Japanese companies – Mitsubishi, Hitachi, and Toshiba – are included in the list of the top ten.[76] As just mentioned, these three frontier technologies hold the potential to boost future economic growth.

Look at the evolution of patent legislation in the US, perhaps Japan's closest rival in innovation nowadays, for further illustration. When the first patent law in the US was adopted by Congress in 1790,[77] the US legislature's aim was to encourage and facilitate the migration of valuable inventions to its territory. Although the US government appeared most zealous when President Lincoln affirmed that 'the patent system added the fuel of interest to the fire of genius', protection measures were, overall, weak in the country and especially biased against foreigners. In order to entice technology transfer so that the expenses incurred on inventors' exclusive rights would be kept to a minimum, foreigners and foreign inventions were not eligible to claim US patents until 1836 and were burdened thereafter by higher costs.[78] Also, for the purpose of promoting technology transfer and diffusing innovation, the 'domestic working' requirement was in force in the US (until 1908) and therefore patent holders were compelled to work invention and process patents

72 For details of the WIPO-administered IP treaties to which China has acceded see: www.wipo.int/treaties/en/ShowResults.jsp?country_id=38Candstart_year=ANYandend_year=ANYandsearch_what=Candtreaty_all=ALL (last accessed 3 June 2016).

73 Yu P. Y., 'The middle kingdom and the intellectual property world', paper given at Symposium: China's Role in Regulating the Global Information Economy. 13 *Oregon Review of International Law* 26 (2011), 209.

74 Bloomberg BNA, 'China, India and Thailand Named in First Priority Foreign Country List'. 42 BNA's *Patent, Trademark and Copyright Journal* 8 (1991).

75 During the Uruguay Round, Japan, together with the US and the EC, pushed for the establishment of the TRIPS Agreement. See: Gervais D., *The TRIPS Agreement: Drafting History and Analysis* (3rd Ed.). (London: Sweet and Maxwell, 2008).

76 World Intellectual Property Organization, 'Small group of countries drives innovation in breakthrough technologies', press release, 11 November, on the occasion of launching the *World Intellectual Property Report 2015* (Geneva: WIPO, 2015).

77 *A Brief History of the Patent Law of the United States* by Ladas and Perry LLP. Available at: http://ladas.com/education-center/a-brief-history-of-the-patent-law-of-the-united-states-2/ (last accessed 15 January 2015).

78 Beatty E., 'Patents and technological change in late industrialisation: nineteenth-century Mexico in comparative context'. 24 *History of Technology* 121 (2002) 127, 123–32.

within American territory.[79] At the time using the patent system also remained inexpensive, so much so that the US had convenient access to the world's leading technologies at a cost lower than for other nations.[80] It was not until the late 1880s that a stronger patent protection system in the US came into being, when the country had its highest economic growth rate in the last two decades of the Second Industrial Revolution.[81] Nonetheless, at the turn of the twentieth century, patenting became a business strategy and was driven by the business model of monopolistic control and erecting barriers to market entry, while innovation was reduced to secondary importance. After a period of scepticism towards the patent system finally, at the beginning of 1980s, stimulating innovation for competitiveness gained prominence while patent protection and competition achieved an equal footing in the US national policy debate. Since then, legislation has weighed more and more towards stronger patent protection because innovation is recognised increasingly as a driver to bring about competitiveness for economic growth.[82] As the world's largest economy, in 2015 innovators based in the US filed the largest annual number of international patent applications for 38 years.[83]

The highlights of the progress and hindrance that the respective patent systems in Japan and in the US experienced unveil the fact that, in the course of patent law development, governments incline towards a more tolerant judicial approach with lesser protective measures at the outset since, after all, legislation follows policies that are formulated in conformity with a country's level of social and economic development. But, once a nation adapts to the patent system and starts to get to grips with the notion of innovation, the legislature will engage stronger patent protection measures in order to further pursue innovation and, in the meantime, to protect economic competitiveness that has been amassed – very much in the way that Mark Twain summarised: 'a country without a patent office and good patent laws was just a crab and couldn't travel anyway but sideway or backwards'.

The evolution of patent protection in China does not appear that different from the Japanese and the American experience – from facilitating technology transfer to encouraging overall domestic innovation – except that China has progressed faster in the last three decades.

79 Dhar B., 'The convention on biological diversity and the TRIPS Agreement: compatibility or conflict?' in C. Bellmann *et al.* (Eds) *Trading in Knowledge: Development Perspectives on TRIPS, Trade and Sustainability* (Abingdon: Routledge, 2003) pp. 77, 84.

80 Jeremy D., 'Patents and technology transfer between nations: 1790-1851: help, hindrance, or irrelevance: lessons from history'. ESRC Research Seminar Series: Intellectual Property Rights, Economic Development and Social Welfare: What Does History Tell Us? 38 *Loyola of Los Angeles Law Review* 1 (2004), 267.

81 Vatter H. *et al.*, 'The onset and persistence of secular stagnation in the US economy: 1910–1990'. 29 *Journal of Economic Issues* 2, 591–600 (1995), pp. 591–600.

82 After having engaged patent as a tool for monopoly, there came a movement against patent protection and, therefore, lax patent policies were implemented towards the end of the Second World War. The 1940s to the 1970s were marked by aggressive anti-trust enforcement and judicial attacks on patent protection as the system was regarded inconsistent with the public policy of free competition. For details about how patenting became a business strategy employed by, for example, Thomas Edison, see: Sell S., 'Intellectual property and public policy in historical perspective: contestation and settlement', paper given at Symposium: Intellectual Property at a Crossroads: The Use of The Past in Intellectual Property Jurisprudence. 38 *Loyola of Los Angeles Law Review* 1 (2004), 267.

83 World Intellectual Property Organization, 'US extends lead in international patent and trademark filings', press release, 16 March, PR/2016/788 (Geneva, WIPO, 2016).

10 Conclusion

The increasing volume of international trade has brought greater opportunities for patents to be exploited beyond national borders. Alongside this phenomenon, risks of patent infringement become greater if heightened measures for cross-border protection are not delivered, since patent protection is initially only valid within the territory where rights are conferred. Conversely, the remit of patent rights may be forced to stay within the locality concerned if the conflict between territoriality, an intrinsic characteristic of patent rights, and de-territoriality, the nature of international trade, is left unsettled. Should this happen, the growth of international trade will be hindered because patents that are derived from advanced technology are a key component thereof.

I Constraints and solutions

In past decades, although cross-border trade has been increasing drastically, patent rights protection has not been able to extend beyond borders with the same vigour due to the fragmented global patent system. This paradox suggests that more international trade may be achieved for greater economic growth if patent rights could be recognised and protected beyond borders under harmonised terms among trading partners. This has not happened, although such demands were recognised as early as the end of the Industrial Revolution when international trade volume surged.

As a facilitator for procedural compatibility the Paris Convention, concluded in 1883, made the first step towards achieving international patent rights harmonisation among its Union members when it set down principles such as the national treatment and the most-favoured-nation treatment. The deliberation on international patent rights harmonisation has been continuing ever since. A series of international treaties, such as the PCT and the TRIPS Agreement, were concluded subsequently.

The PCT, as an example of procedural patent rights harmonisation, standardises rules and forms with respect to filing, prior art search, examination and publication as far as multiple patent applications are concerned. Thanks to the PCT, applying an international patent in multiple countries with a single domestic filing has become a reality. The harmonised procedures reduce costs for multiple patent applications, expedite the application process and enable fast dissemination of technological information, so that industrial application and technology transfer, including buying, selling and licensing, would be realised sooner for economic gains.

Juxtaposed with the PCT, the TRIPS Agreement harmonises the substantive patent protection standards among the WTO members. This objective is achieved by requiring members to incorporate into their respective national legislation the minimum patent protection standards laid down by the TRIPS Agreement, and members may enact 'TRIPS-plus' or 'TRIPS-minus' provisions on specific substantive protection subject matters thanks to the principle of flexibility. Consequently, to determine if a patent holder's rights suffer derogation when the principle of flexibility is applied in the course of legal incorporation, the three-step test must be brought in for verification.

Nonetheless, after TRIPS has achieved substantive legal harmonisation at the minimum level, attempts for further harmonisation at the maximum level on substantive patent protection measures have not come to fruition since the SPLT negotiations were suspended in 2006.

Unlike TRIPS, SPLT was expected to resolve the maximum patent protection standards on subjects such as the exceptions to patentability, the grace period and disclosure. The negotiations fell through as a result of the divergent positions sustained by the negotiating countries. Without substantive legal harmonisation on specific patent issues the aim of a global patent system will not be achieved, which means the world's fragmented patent protection system will continue to impede the further growth of international trade. Global technological advance will also be delayed.

As Professor Ladas pointed out, in relation to patent harmonisation the question that one should always ask is on what level and in which order should harmonisation take place, and how should it be implemented? Aside from substantive legal harmonisation, the process of international patent rights harmonisation has been pursuing the course of substantive administrative harmonisation following the success of the PCT. To this end, the work-sharing mechanism has emerged as a viable, swift and economical means for achieving patent rights harmonisation at the working-level, restricted to examination procedures as far as multiple patent applications are concerned.

Depending on the circumstances and the objectives, three different work-sharing modalities may be identified. For example, when the patent legislation among a few offices is similar, sharing decisions or opinions on search results would be more productive than action-sharing, which is sharing information on search results and office actions in order to synchronise examination results. Nonetheless, action-sharing can be a useful instrument if examination speeds among the offices are very different so that exploiting information in a timely manner will be difficult and sharing workload becomes impossible. Apart from decision-sharing and action-sharing, in the case where countries' patent laws are substantially different, and if there are serious discrepancies in work-speed and legal cultures, then search-sharing, which is sharing the same prior art search strategy and search result, may be more practical for the purposes of cooperation. On the other hand, the three work-sharing modalities can be implemented by way of 'mix and match' in order to maximise the benefits of work-sharing as a whole. For example, the benefits accrued from PCT procedural harmonisation may be further optimised by combining the PCT with the decision-sharing procedure, as the PPH project has proven. In the case where cooperating countries share the same legal backgrounds and practices, then search-sharing or action-sharing may be implemented together with decision-sharing so that the whole process of patent examination can be streamlined and expedited as far as multiple patent applications are concerned.

Additionally, since the certainty for cooperation is guaranteed by bilateral or multilateral agreements, substantive administrative harmonisation has the advantage of not requiring treaty ratification, so therefore cooperating countries' sovereign power of legislation remains intact. The possibility of relinquishing legislative power, however partially, is often an impediment to international cooperation on whichever subject it may be, and substantive legal patent harmonisation is no exception. ARIPO, ASPEC, EPC, and IP5 are examples of the work-sharing mechanism, which are established either at the regional level or among a few patent offices.

II International patent rights harmonisation

Once procedural examination rules are harmonised among a group of patent offices, such rules may be promoted to other countries by way of, for example, capacity-building, whereby these rules would be extended to, and adopted by, a wider range of national patent offices. The EPO conducted many such capacity-building projects worldwide in order to provide technical assistance to countries in need, which often included assistance in drafting patent examination manuals. Aid-receiving countries' patent examination procedures and principles are therefore naturally influenced by those adopted by the EPO to a great extent, while the purpose of harmonisation may well be delicately achieved.

History has also proven that the process of international patent rights harmonisation has been making great strides in the last centuries by way of knowledge-diffusion. For example, China's patent law was influenced by the German *Bürgerliches Gesetzbuch*, Japan's initial patent law was based on a mixture of provisions seen in the American and French legislation, and the English patent law was transplanted into India, the US and into other countries in the Commonwealth due to colonisation.

In parallel, as a result of subtle self-adaptation, international patent rights harmonisation has been progressing through gradual assimilation of procedural rules in recent years. In March 2013, when the Invents Act came into force in the US, the first-to-file procedure, which has been applied worldwide for a long time, was finally admitted by the American patent filing system. The rule of first-to-invent, once the hallmark of the American patent legislation, was superseded. The American Invents Act also abolished the 'pre-grant opposition' mechanism that was practised in the US and, in the past, by a handful of other countries such as Germany, Japan and the UK. In fact, in the 1930s, there existed globally no less than five different procedural models, ranging from the pure registration model (France), to the models of novelty examination without opposition (the US) and with pre-grant opposition (Germany, the UK and Japan). Little by little, harmonisation took hold and the stark divisions between the different procedural rules were diminished. These days, the post-grant opposition procedure has become an international norm and the pre-grant opposition is in practice only in Brazil, India and Jordan. All EPC members have adopted the mechanism of post-grant opposition, including Germany and the UK. As for Japan, it scrapped both the pre-grant and the post-grant opposition mechanisms. In 2014, the JPO introduced an opposition-invalidation combined procedure in order to challenge a patent grant. Under the new procedure, in the first six months, and after the legal revisions take place, any person may file an opposition request through documentary proceedings. Once the six-month period expires, the invalidation proceedings kick in and only interested parties may file an invalidation request through either oral or documentary proceedings. At the opposition stage, and before legal revisions take place, any person may file an opposition request through either oral or documentary proceedings.

China started to embark on the process of international patent rights harmonisation in 1985 when it became a Union member of the Paris Convention. The process has been heightened since 2005 when the SIPO became one of the world's leading patent offices as far as patent application numbers are concerned. Since some of the Chinese high-tech companies, such as ZTE Corporation and Huawei Technologies, are now the world's top PCT applicants and have also established R&D centres in a network of foreign countries, it is naturally in China's best interests to encourage the creation of a favourable international patent protection environment to facilitate the country's economic expansion, for inbound as well as for outbound investment. For inbound investment, a stricter patent protection regime will encourage foreign investment in R&D and safeguard technology transfer, which will enhance the country's ability to access the world's advanced technologies, leading towards expedited national technological progression. For outbound investment, a harmonised international patent protection system will further promote China's position in international trade because, once patent rights protection of high technologies, a key component of international trade, are guaranteed, trade expansion will follow with fewer constraints. On the other hand, commercialising and utilising patents, which is now China's aspiration, also requires a favourable international patent protection environment in order to maximise the potential of this endeavour worldwide.

In recent years, although a newcomer to the global patent system, China has been actively participating in international patent cooperation projects, such as the IP5 project, thanks to its increasing influence as a top world patent office. Cooperating with patent practitioners and policy makers from other major patent offices around the world provide valuable opportunities for China to learn good practices from others and vice versa, thus pushing forward the process of international patent rights harmonisation.

III International patent rights harmonisation – the case of China

Patent was first granted as a form of privilege to reward loyalty for a limited period in England in 1449. Venice aspired to encourage innovation so, therefore, a patent system was introduced in the city state in 1474. From then on, the notion of patent protection spread over the world, although each country's motivation varied when adopting the system.

I) International patent rights harmonisation in China

China promulgated its first modern-day patent law in 1984 in the wake of the government's Four Modernisations Campaign, including modernisation in science and technology, agriculture, industry and national defence. At the time, China was in serious need of foreign technology and investment in order to succeed in a fast recovery from the social/economic turmoil caused by the Cultural Revolution. As early as in 1979, without a single piece of IPR legislation, China committed to IPR protection when it concluded the Agreement on Trade Relations between the United States of America and the People's Republic of China, which prescribed the rules governing bilateral trade, including those rules concerning patents, trademarks, copyrights and unfair competition.

China certainly endured a testing time when its patent legislation was just starting to evolve, and the conflict between private property rights (for example, IPR) and collective property ownership, that China imposed as a communist country, was the main reason for this. The conflict was not resolved until 2004, after the third amendment of the Constitution came into force when private property rights became recognised and their protection guaranteed. This delay meant that, for 20 years between 1984 and 2004, patent protection did not have the Constitutional blessing that it ought to have had. The consequence of this absence was that Chinese society was unaware of, and therefore had little regard for, patent rights or IPR at large, especially when the legislation was first enforced. This constitutional absence can also help to explain why, in the past, the legislature was not able to award adequate remedies for loss incurred as a result of patent infringement.

Having said that, the ill-prepared start did not deter China from formulating, in the following decades, a comprehensive patent legislation system that consists of patent law, implementing rules, judicial interpretations and other related laws such as, for example, the Law Applicable to Foreign-related Civil Relations.

China's first patent law amendment was made in 1992, pursuant to the conclusion of the China–US Memorandum of Understanding on Protection of Intellectual Property Rights in the same year. Thanks to the amendment, China became one of the world's forerunners of patent protection because the country started to impose higher protection measures ahead of the majority of the countries in the world at the time. After the Patent Law 1992 came into force, China started to offer patent protection to pharmaceutical, agricultural and chemical products and to enforce a 20-year protection term to invention patents. With hindsight, these measures were fully in compliance with the TRIPS Agreement, although China only acceded to this Agreement in 2001, which was 10 years later.

In 2000, in anticipation of the WTO accession, China conducted its second patent law amendment by fully incorporating the minimum protection standards laid down by the TRIPS Agreement into its Patent Law, without taking advantage of the transitional arrangements provided by Art. 65 of the TRIPS Agreement. The Patent Law 2008 saw China setting out the 'TRIPS plus' protection standards with, for example, regard to the thresholds test for patentability. The third amendment took place after China began to experience, after 2006, a surge of patent applications domestically as well as internationally via the PCT system, and increased enforcement standards and higher protection thresholds became indispensable in order to safeguard patent quality and to further encourage innovation. One of these enhanced enforcement measures concerns judicial compensation for loss incurred as a result of infringement under judicial enforcement. Fixed between 10,000 and 1 million RMB (1,340– 133,963 EUR), this is the first time that a compensation amount under judicial enforcement is specified by the Chinese patent legislation.

As to the Draft Patent Law 2015, reflecting on the second draft text that was published by the SIPO in December 2015, the new patent legislation focuses on promoting innovation, further enhancing enforcement measures and encouraging the commercialisation and the utilisation of patent. These new focuses correspond with China's accelerated innovation capacity when, for example, the WIPO acknowledged that the patent-filing activity undertaken by China-based innovators accounted for much of the overall global growth in PCT applications in 2015. The draft law deals with new forms of infringement, such as group infringement as well as online infringement when the internet service provider may bear joint liability with the infringer. China's fourth patent law amendment continues to put into place strengthened enforcement measures, following the trend established by the previous three amendments that took place in past decades. Moreover, the Draft Patent Law 2015 provides the patent administration department with increased authority for patent rights enforcement by, among other things, considerably raising the amount of administrative fines against patent infringement. In addition, the Draft Patent Law 2015 adds a whole new chapter on the commercialisation and the utilisation of patent. Of course, such objective may only be achieved if patent rights protection is guaranteed and infringement dealt with forcefully and effectively.

In parallel with its fast development in patent legislation, China in recent years has become one of the world's top patent applicants. After the US and Japan, China was the world's third largest PCT applicant in 2015 and submitted 29,846 applications – an increase of 16.8 per cent compared with the year before. In the same year, China's homegrown company ZTE Corporation ranked third on the PCT top applicant chart with 2,155 published applications, while Huawei Technologies led for the second consecutive year with 3,898 published PCT applications. US-based Qualcomm Incorporated was the second largest PCT applicant in 2015, with 2,442 published applications.

Despite China's spectacular success in establishing a comprehensive and internationally leading patent protection system within three decades, enforcement remains the country's Achilles heel. However, before identifying the Chinese case for international patent rights harmonisation, it is important to first present an evaluation of patent legislation development in Japan and in India, respectively, in order to set the scene. This is because the Chinese case shares a degree of similarity with these two countries, while their success will help to reveal the characteristics of the harmonisation process that China has undertaken.

IV International patent rights harmonisation in Japan and India

Japan and China launched patent protection for the same reason, which was to enable technology transfer. Both countries' patent law evolution is a journey of international patent rights harmonisation. India gives priority to citizens' rights to health over patent protection, should conflict between the two objectives arise, with a view to empowering its generic pharmaceutical industry for fast development. Probably less seen as a form of private property, patent legislation has been adjusting its course pursuant to governments' patent policy changes in all three countries. These changes are commonly determined by domestic needs and external challenges, arising either from international treaty obligations or from requests submitted by foreign trading partners. In the case of China, it is evident that external challenges have played a more prominent role in prompting the country's progress in international patent rights harmonisation.

I) Japan

Japan, once a technology-deprived country, promulgated its first patent law, Summary Rules of Monopoly, in 1871. In the era of the Meiji Restoration, encouraging innovation was identified as a means to catch up with the almighty American technology and science. Prior to that, a patent system was unknown to Japanese society. Since the government was totally unequipped for patent administration with regard to, for example, conducting patent examination and handling patent applications, the first patent legislation fell into suspension. Despite the unfortunate start, in order to press on with patent protection the Japanese legislature subsequently reintroduced patent legislation and a series of amendments followed in the next century. In 2015, standing as the second largest PCT applicant in the world, Japan submitted 44,235 applications to the PCT system and registered a 20.3 per cent share of the world total. Today, Japan is one of the most innovative countries in the world.

Notwithstanding this, it is observed that, although effective and moulded to the Japanese ideological foundation and the industrial development aspirations, some patent protection measures appear controversial in nature, especially concerning those enforced in the beginning of the country's patent history. Certification trial, narrowly interpreted patent claim, MITI's pre-approval for licensing agreement and pre-grant patent publication were just a few such examples. On the other hand, Japanese patent legislation has been swiftly revised in the course of the last century based on the prevailing development priorities and, as a result, patent protection measures remain relevant throughout the country's economic expansion. For example, although the mechanism of patent certification trial adopted by the Patent Law 1899 was a major contributor to Japan's industrialisation through innovation, it was abolished in 1959 when the country's technological progress reached an explosive rate and when it was feared that the same mechanism was no longer relevant and an impediment to further innovation capacity.

China and Japan started to institute patent protection when both countries were unequipped, ideologically and institutionally. As the patent system also shouldered the responsibility of stimulating domestic economic reforms, such as to facilitate technology transfer for modernisation, the legislature in both countries was obliged to seek legislative balance among the international patent treaty obligations, trading partners' requests and the domestic development agenda. In the Japanese case, the domestic development agenda gained supremacy in the early stage of the country's patent law development. Although such a policy choice brought about some controversial patent protection measures, because they conformed to the country's ideological tradition, they were positively embraced by the society and duly delivered the objectives that were meant to achieve.

II) India

Japan's swift adjustment on patent policy offers a serious contrast to India's consistent policy objective, which is to defend citizens' constitutional right to health by protecting an enabling environment for the growth of the generic pharmaceutical industry. Imposing a higher and narrowly defined thresholds test on patentability is a powerful example in this respect, as illustrated in Chapter 8.

In order to uphold citizens' right to health, the Indian legislature first revoked patent protection for pharmaceutical products after independence, when the Patents Act 1970 came into force. In the wake of the WTO accession, while complying with the TRIPS Agreement, a balance between furthering the growth of the generic pharmaceutical industry and providing patent protection to pharmaceutical products – an obligation imposed by TRIPS – is skilfully reached by means of, for example, Section 3(d) of the Patents (Amendment) Law 2005. The implication of this policy choice is that if conflict between public interest and patent protection arises, such as when citizens' access to affordable medicine would likely be in jeopardy if patent protection is granted to a particular pharmaceutical product invention, public interest shall always prevail. Indeed, thanks to the enabling patent legislation, since the 1970s India's generic pharmaceutical industry has experienced gigantic growth in terms of size and capacity. In less than half a century, from being unable to meet the country's own needs, the generic pharmaceutical industry has been transformed to become one of the world's biggest generic medicine suppliers as well as manufacturers. Indian citizens' access to medicine is assured; their right to health is guaranteed. The life expectancy of the country was extended from 42 in 1960 to 65 in 2011.

The Indian experience in international patent rights harmonisation highlights the following characteristics. India took full advantage of the enabling provisions offered by the TRIPS Agreement, such as the transitional arrangements afforded to the developing and the transitional economies. Secondly, while incorporating the minimum protection standards stipulated by TRIPS in its national patent law, the national provisions were moulded to India's development needs, especially with regard to its generic pharmaceutical industry. This characteristic is depicted in Section 3(d) and Section 2(1)(ja) of the Patents (Amendment) Act 2005. Thirdly, India's judiciary steadfastly upholds the policy objective of citizens' right to health, which it has championed ever since independence, and the public interest always prevails *vis-à-vis* patent protection in case of conflict.

Nonetheless, India's unique success in international patent rights harmonisation must be viewed with reservations. Certainly there are other policy tools that the Indian government could engage in order to uphold citizens' rights to health by, improving sanitary conditions, investing in affordable public housing, increasing spending on healthcare and implementing effective health insurance etc. On the other hand, the highly successful generic pharmaceutical industry has brought adverse consequences reflected in, for example, poor foreign pharmaceutical R&D investment, although the country has a strong scientific tradition and a competent work force with proficiency in the English language. Until 1993, only 16 of the world's 30 largest pharmaceutical manufacturers had direct investment in India. Although the R&D investment level increased more than before after 2005 when pharmaceutical products began to receive patent protection, investors tend to be sceptical due to the fact that patent protection often concedes to public interest, as is revealed by the cases presented in Chapter 8. After all, once the generic pharmaceutical industry decides to focus on innovation instead of reverse engineering, imposing higher patent protection measures will become imperative. Otherwise, an innovation strategy would backfire since the present thresholds test for patentability set down by the Patents (Amendment) Act 2005 is draconian, so patent protection is doomed to fail *vis-à-vis* public interest if conflict between the two arises.

The process of international patent rights harmonisation undertaken by China brings a contrast to India's process. With hardly any experience in providing patent protection, and hindered by all the unpreparedness, China rose to become a forerunner of patent protection in the world in 1992 when the country's patent legislation was still in its infancy. Its patent legislation was amended for the second time in order to conform to the TRIPS Agreement in 2000, a year before its WTO accession. In this respect, enabling technology transfer was of paramount importance to China and seemed the only policy objective when the patent system was newly introduced in the country. Policy adjustment did not take place until the Patent Law 2008 entered into force, when nurturing an innovative society by encouraging patent application was elevated to become the policy objective. To further pursue this ambition, a whole new chapter on the commercialisation and the utilisation of patent was added to the Draft Patent Law 2015. The new patent policy no doubt stands as a cornerstone following the launch of the National Patent Development Strategy in 2010, whereby encouraging IPR commercialisation and utilisation was identified as a strategy in order to transform China's economy from being manufacturing-based to innovation-driven. Of course, a prerequisite for implementing such strategy is high innovation capacity as well as a patent pool that is large enough for the purpose of commercialisation and utilisation. This prerequisite obviously materialised when the number of China's domestic patent applications amounted to 2.361 million in 2014.

Should China have followed India in its patent legislation? I think not. Without the willpower, China would not have attained such high achievements in patent protection within three decades; neither would China have been ready to nurture an innovative society and to transform to become an innovative economy for sustainable development.

V Lessons for China

I) Policy, law and cultural tradition

When the policy of opening-up was first implemented in the late 1970s, one of the most popular expressions in Chinese society was 'internationalisation'. In earnest, China was hoping to catch up with the rest of the world and, as a result, the Four Modernisation campaign was launched in order to 'recapture' the time lost as a result of the devastating

Cultural Revolution. Most fundamentally, at the outset, when patent legislation was imposed in haste, perhaps due to the pressure from trading partners such as the US, patent protection was probably seen by the society as just one of the many governmental policies announced at the time. Many might not have realised that it was a legal instrument to protect and enforce private property. Therefore, the legitimacy for patent protection was a dubious question among the people.

The Patent Law 1984 was silent about any tangible protection measures. The strongest measure against patent infringement was an order to cease the infringement act and to compensate for the losses incurred, but without any specifics about compensation. It is without any doubt that China spared no efforts in order to promulgate its first patent law. It deployed many scholars to learn patent protection practices from technologically advanced countries such as Germany, and translated dozens of foreign patent laws for reference purposes. However, in comparison, drafting laws is relatively easier than implementing and enforcing legislation. Furthermore, it's obvious that patent rights enforcement in China was constrained by the absence of constitutional justification. This attribute can be best illustrated by the fairly timid protection measures contained in the Patent Law 1984, although other provisions were in conformity with the prevailing patent legislations existing at the time. Certainly, without forceful enforcement measures, patent protection was nothing but a facade.

Thanks to the General Principles of Civil Law 1986, civil and property rights, including IPR, were recognised (through the back door) and, as a result, patent rights protection found justification, however limited, in legislation. However, the Patent Law 1992 offered little change in enforcement. It was not until the second Patent Law amendment entered into force in 2000 that China started to impose specific protection measures whereby illegal earnings gained from infringement may be confiscated and a fine imposed. But, the amount of the fine looked negligible, as is highlighted in Chapter 6, and it was unfit to serve as a deterrent to future infringers. Enforcement measures were further enhanced under the Patent Law 2008 when, among others, the compensation amount resulting from an infringement act was raised. The Draft Patent Law 2015 continues to raise the compensation amount to up to five million RMB (677,117 EUR). Though the higher compensation level reached may still be seen as inadequate before some jurisdictions, it is no doubt a substantive increase if only one would take into account the overall evolution of China's patent legislation.

On the other hand, unlike Japan, whose patent protection measures were laid down upon the country's cultural tradition, which stood as the ideological backbone of the legislation, China did not look back at its cultural traits while embracing 'internationalisation'. It adopted foreign patent law models and principles with little reservation. Fulfilling international obligations and satisfying trading partners' requests gained an absolute upper hand in the course of international patent rights harmonisation in China. The domestic development agenda as well as the Chinese ideological tradition of unconditional sharing, which was held as one of the highest moral values for a few thousand years by Chinese society, were not given due consideration when China started to institute a patent system. In practice, the legislature did not offer any transitional measures, such as the 'mailbox facility' introduced by India, in order to help mitigate the impact of the patent legislation; in fact the very nature of patent protection was perceived by the society as a gain-seeking behaviour actuated by selfish human motives. Patent protection therefore earned little acceptance from Chinese society. Likewise, copyrights and trademark protection suffered the same fate in China as far as enforcement was concerned. Consequently, while implementing the substantive patent protection measures prescribed by the TRIPS Agreement, China did not choose a phase-in approach. Among other things, it did not take into account the extra time required before rendering 'product patent protection to areas of technology not so protectable'. Neither was the social unpreparedness, such as the lack of legal professionals, given due consideration by the legislature. China went all out to embrace 'internationalisation'. This being the case, China restricted itself with a straightjacket when implementing those patent protection provisions that, in fact, did not correspond to its societal background and economic development stages, especially when patent legislation was first imposed in the country.

Overall, Chinese legislature's attempt to conciliate the two contending ideologies – limited monopoly for exploiting patent rights and unconditional sharing for altruism – was insufficient. Actually, such conciliation would only be possible if either one of the ideologies submitted to another. Japan did just that when traditional ideology prevailed and patent protection came the second. China opted for the opposite. In China's case, international patent rights harmonisation was granted absolute supremacy while domestic social reality was reduced to a negligible position. One serious consequence of this policy option has been the weaker enforcement that still remains to be addressed, which negates China's overall achievements in patent protection. Without effective patent enforcement, the policy objective of commercialising and utilising patent will be difficult to attain, while the country's substantial pool of patents accumulated in recent years risks becoming just a number.

II) Rights and obligations before international patent rights harmonisation

Despite all the missing prerequisites, China successfully promulgated its first patent law. But, as mentioned just now, it was much more difficult to implement the legislation and to enforce patent rights protection. During the process of international patent rights harmonisation, China did not attempt to pace its progress in patent protection with the country's economic development reality; 'internationalisation' was championed and proceeded far ahead of the necessary social change. One result of this mismatch is the striking disproportionate development witnessed in the comprehensive patent legislation, the world's leading position in PCT application and the overall weak patent enforcement. The failure of bringing about any strengthened enforcement measures while, on the other hand, elevating China to be a world's forerunner of patent protection, seen by the Patent Law 1992, is a perfect example in this respect.

Regarding the relationship between public interest and patent protection, although in some countries patent protection stands absolutely paramount since it is a form of property rights and these are sacred, in India public interest is granted supremacy over patent protection during the process of international patent rights harmonisation. To realise this policy objective while conforming to the minimum protection standards prescribed by the TRIPS Agreement, India's legislature exploited the principle of flexibility offered by the Agreement to its fullest extent, and the judiciary defended the domestic generic pharmaceutical industry on each occasion when its sustainable development was in conflict with patent rights protection.

Compared with the Indian example, it seems China had lesser pressing domestic interests to address while pursuing international patent rights harmonisation. In fact, all along, the country has been faithfully following a 'TRIPS-plus' protection standard as Chapter 6 illustrates, with encouraging technology transfer as seemingly the sole purpose. From 1976, when China purchased a series of foreign technologies amid the worst political and natural disasters in its history as well as acute financial difficulties, to 1979 when the Sino-US trade agreement entered into force, and from the Sino-US MOU concluded in 1992 to the WTO accession in 2001, much progress in patent protection was brought forward after each of these landmark events. But, looking deeper, every 'great leap forward' was really at odds with the prevailing societal reality that China experienced during the same period when the cultural tradition and economic growth level were overlooked. China was audacious. In 1976, China even chose to take the risk of departing from the Communism dogma that was in strict practice in the country. At the time, contacting the West could be condemned as 'Capitalist roader' for treason. In any case, such policy choice seems to be the direct opposite of the Indian example of international patent rights harmonisation where public interest should always prevail. With a top-down approach, China established a comprehensive patent legislation framework and increased its innovation capacity to a globally commendable level within three decades. However, with regard to enforcement, it still requires urgent improvement despite the legislature's efforts made in recent years. China's success in international patent rights harmonisation is indeed mixed.

Moreover, in the process of international patent rights harmonisation, India did not forego any of its rights and privileges, such as the ten-year transitional arrangements provided by TRIPS, which China relinquished in total. Likewise, India took advantage of the principle of flexibility in full while incorporating the TRIPS Agreement in Patents (Amendment) Act 2005 for its domestic needs. As a result, the impact of the drastic legislative change in offering patent protection to pharmaceutical products was limited while the growth of the domestic generic pharmaceutical industry remains unfettered.

VI Further challenges in enforcing patent rights in China

As the cardinal reason blamed for weak enforcement in China is the 20-year-delay in constitutional acknowledgement of private property rights, one consequence of this delay is that grievances about private property rights violation were handled with hesitation and inadequacy. And infringers were probably not deterred from committing future infringement acts since enforcement measures were weak. Though it's undeniable that in the last decades Chinese legislature has made much effort in strengthening patent rights enforcement, further challenges are reflected in the following aspects that require more improvement.

I) Administrative enforcement: a quasi-judicial power, less powerful to deter future patent infringement

As is explained earlier, administrative enforcement is a cultural choice based on Chinese traditional values and it was also a quick solution in order to find sufficient enforcement personnel since, after the Cultural Revolution, the country was left with fewer legal professionals, too meagre a number for adjudication purposes. Staff were recruited and conveniently filled in the vacuum with (or without) initial training and the administrative enforcement track came into operation. In parallel, looking at the judicial enforcement personnel, they were mostly retired army officers. Their competences in adjudication were perhaps just as doubtful as those that the administrative enforcement personnel possessed at the time. As a consequence, the complete patent enforcement system was simply not equipped for the purpose of enforcing patent rights protection.

Administrative enforcement continues its function these days with strength and the number of infringement cases dealt with by the mechanism is on the rise on a yearly basis. After all, the administrative enforcement mechanism holds an equal importance with judicial enforcement. However, despite all the advantages mentioned before, the deficiency of the system is also fairly obvious, mainly due to its intrinsic characteristics of unpredictability and unenforceability. No doubt, the Chinese legislature attempted to improve the administrative enforcement mechanism by granting it judicial powers at each amendment in order to inject certainty as well as authority. The Draft Patent Law 2015 continues this effort in that, for example, the patent administration department will have the authority to mediate in the amount of the fine for the damage caused to the patent right holder as a result of infringement, which is a newly entrusted power. Nonetheless, being administrative in nature, the enforcement mechanism remains 'administrative' and the essential ingredient of enforcement, which is enforceability, will always be in doubt.

Another flaw of the mechanism is that a mediation agreement reached under administrative enforcement does not include compensation for loss incurred as a result of infringement. The patent administration department is only competent to issue administrative fines, confiscate illicit income and to order the infringement act to be ceased if infringement is established. Restricted by its 'administrative' nature, it is perhaps justified in not imposing compensation because, otherwise, the administrative enforcement procedure would trespass on the competence of judicial enforcement. But, without the power to impose compensation, justice is unlikely to be delivered in full, and it will also be doubtful whether future infringers will be deterred. The meaning of enforcement may thus be lost. Anyhow, the feature of 'fine without compensation' persists, which is also seen in the Draft Patent Law 2015, although the amendment is more precise on the amount of the fine that the patent administration department may issue in relation to patent passing off.

As to judicial enforcement, after three patent law amendments (with the fourth in the making), it managed to claim back much adjudicating power from administrative enforcement. However, the patent administrative authority still retains the quasi-judicial competence to collect evidence, decide on an infringement act and impose administrative fines on infringers. Note that China has become the world's most IP litigious country since 2005 and the judiciary is certainly a lot better qualified than 30 years ago. But the tradition of administrative enforcement has survived since the procedure has the advantage of being convenient, fast and cheap, and therefore it is still as frequently used as judicial enforcement nowadays. Notwithstanding this, aggrieved patent holders are caught in dilemma because, on the one hand, the administrative enforcement procedure has the advantages that they hope to benefit from but, on the other hand, should they succeed in enforcement they will be left without compensation by the same procedure.

Similarly, these days, although more and more eligible personnel have joined the administrative enforcement body, one should not overlook the fact that they remain legally unqualified for undertaking enforcement work. This being the case, no matter how powerful the patent administrative enforcement measures may become, their effective implementation may still be in question.

Having said the above, it is observed that the Chinese legislature has been consistently promoting judicial enforcement in recent years, including issuing a series of judicial interpretations in order to facilitate case transfer from the administrative to the judicial enforcement route for adjudication. In general, the number of patent cases dealt with by people's courts has been on the rise on a yearly basis.

II) Judicial enforcement: inadequate compensation and less efficient case-handling capacity

Criticisms of the judicial enforcement mechanism focus on inadequate compensation and the less-than-desirable efficiency in case-handling. Inadequate judicial compensation defeats the purpose of patent protection, which is provided in exchange for disclosure of an invention that results from hard intellectual work and heavy investment. If the limited exclusive rights for exploitation are not guaranteed, and when loss incurred as a result of infringement is not compensated for adequately, skilled people will be discouraged from inventing and inventors will not be motivated to disclose their inventions to the public. Low compensation equally undermines the aims of the patent grants that are protecting patent holders' rights, encouraging innovation, promoting industrial application, enhancing innovation capacity and facilitating the advance of science and technology. All these aims are particularly important to China's sustainable economic development goal whereby the country is most ambitious to establish an innovative economy.

The Chinese legislature is certainly aware of the problems engendered by inadequate compensation since the compensation amount has been steadily increasing after each patent law amendment. For example, by virtue of Art.68 of the Draft Patent Law 2015, the judicial compensation amount is drastically increased to the range of 100,000 to 5,000,000 RMB (14,000–700,000 EUR), which is a ten-fold increase compared with what is prescribed by the Patent Law 2008. Equally, the Draft Patent Law 2015 stipulates that, in the case of a wilful act of infringement being established, the damages may be increased to more than one times but less than three times the usual amount of damages that are awarded for patent infringement 'based on the circumstances, the scale of the infringement and the damaged result caused by the infringement'. However, it is noticed at the same time that the Draft Patent Law 2015, as it was published in December 2015, did not propose any increased enforcement measures with regard to criminal liabilities as far as infringement is concerned.

On the other hand, an oft-heard complaint about the judiciary's less-than-desirable case-handling capacity is that decisions laid down by the IP chambers sometimes appear inconsistent, with some judges lacking expertise, especially if a case is technologically challenging. The situation is no doubt improving, all the more so because IP-specialised courts were established in Beijing, Shanghai and Guangzhou in November 2014 to adjudicate technologically complex cases of the first and the second instance comprising both civil and administrative cases. Under the specialised IP courts, which have the status of an intermediate court, technology experts will serve as assistants to judges.

Also, as a major move to increase case-handling capacity, China's People's Procuratorate finally established the website of Case Information Disclosure of the People's Procuratorate of the People's Republic of China in October 2014, which is a great leap forward in China's legal history. In the past, case information was held as a privilege and disclosing case information to ordinary citizens was considered unnecessary, if not unthinkable, due to the feudal mentality of Chinese society, which was divided into those who ruled and those who were ruled for four thousand years. Nowadays, though only selected cases are published, the case-reporting system will undoubtedly help to increase judicial transparency and instil a much stronger sense of checks and balances among the citizens and the judiciary, so as to facilitate the judiciary in enhancing its case-handling capacity. At the moment, case procedural progress and defence documents, major cases, submitted case documents, appeals as well as final decisions, etc., are posted on the website.

III) Local interest

Equally, another bequest of China's extremely long history of feudalism, although China is not run as a federal state, local administration is empowered to legislate based on local circumstances. This being the case, local interest may easily interfere with judicial impartiality. Additionally, since local judges are appointed and removed by local governments, judicial independence is thus in doubt and local interest may be engendered too, which may even interfere with adjudication, especially when cross-jurisdiction is involved. By the same token, decisions laid down by the central government may not be implemented faithfully at the local government level simply because local administration swears its loyalty only to the territorial chief, such as the governor of a province, but not to the central government. The old Chinese saying of 'the sky is high while the emperor is far away' is an illustration of this situation which seems still valid to date.

Moreover, China's complex and opaque legislative framework and the overlapping institutional structures adversely contribute to weak patent, or overall IPR, enforcement. Tracking laws, regulations and administrative rules promulgated by the central and the local governments and by the departments is a difficult undertaking, which causes concerns about 'non-transparency' in addition to the already complex IPR legislation framework. One should not forget that these days the boundaries between policy and law are also blurred; policies may be interpreted as law thereby aggravating the already complex and opaque legislative framework.

VII Finally…

Despite all the criticisms, it is evident that in recent years China has implemented a series of legal measures to strengthen patent enforcement, which is in the country's best interest. Overall, with more and more competent IPR judges ready to adjudicate, transparency, enforceability and judicial predictability are expected to be further improved. All these qualities were in effect commitments that China pledged to establish in its administration and the judiciary in the run up to the WTO accession. As is often the case, internationally compatible legislation is relatively easy to promulgate in comparison with changing legal habitual behaviour which is more difficult, although this is exactly where effective judicial implementation and enforcement stem from. Given the Chinese traditional value of altruism, and with the heavy burden of feudalism mixed with communism, it is indeed a huge undertaking for China to depart from its ideological origin in order to enforce patent rights protection, a branch of private property law that is unheard of in Chinese society.

As one of the world's biggest patent offices nowadays, China has been actively participating in the process of international patent rights harmonisation ever since the country became a member of the Paris Convention in 1984. China has achieved a remarkable amount in patent legislation and in raising the country's innovation capacity within three decades. This is unprecedented in the world's patent history.

Bibliography

Abbott F. M., 'Protecting First World assets in the Third World: intellectual property negotiations in the GATT Multilateral Framework'. 22 *Vanderbilt Journal of Transnational Law* 4 (1989)

Abbott F. M., 'The judgment in *Novartis* v. *India*: what the Supreme Court of India said'. *Intellectual Property Watch*, 4 April (2013)

Abramowicz M. and Duffy J. F., 'Ending the patenting monopoly'. 157 *University of Pennsylvania Law Review* 1570 (2009m

Alfred, W. P., *To Steal a Book is an Elegant Offense: Intellectual Property Law in Chinese Civilisation.* (Palo Alto, CA: Stanford University Press, 1995)

Allison J. R. and Lemley M. A., 'Empirical evidence on the validity of litigated patents'. 26 *AIPLA Quarterly Journal* 185 (1998) 205

Anderson M. *et al* (Eds), *The Modern Law of Patents.* (London: Butterworths, 2005)

Anon, 'Taking pains, Indian patent rules infuriate big pharma'. *The Economist* (8 September 2012), available at: www.economist.com/node/21562226 (last accessed 2 November 2015)

Arai H., *WIPO Intellectual Property Handbook: Policy, Law and Use* (Geneva: WIPO Publication No.489(E), 2004)

Ayyangar N. R., *Report on the Revision of the Patents Law*, Preface. (The Government of India, September 1959)

Baechtold P. and Miyamoto T., 'International patent law harmonisation – a search for the right balance'. 10 *Journal of Intellectual Property Rights* 177 (2005)

Barton, J. H., 'Non-obviousness'. 43 *The Intellectual Property Law Review* 3 (2003)

Basheer S. and Prashant R., '"Ducking" TRIPS in India: a saga involving Novartis and the legality of Section 3(D)'. 20 *National Law School of India Review* 131 (2008)

Bazzle T., 'Pharmacy of the developing world: reconciling intellectual property rights in India with the right to health: TRIPS, India's patent system and essential medicines'. 42 *Georgetown Journal of International Law* 3 (2011)

Beatty E., 'Patents and technological change in late industrialisation: nineteenth-century Mexico in comparative context'. 24 *History of Technology* 121 (2002) 127, 123–32

Bender G. A., 'Clash of the Titans: the territoriality of patent law v. the European Union'. 40 *The Journal of Law and Technology* 1 (2000)

Benson R. B., 'The impact of the Patent Cooperation Treaty (PCT) and the European Patent Convention (EPC) on US practitioners'. 60 *Journal of the Patent and Trademark Office Society* 118 (1978)

Berrier E. F. Jr., 'Global patent costs must be reduced'. 36 *The Journal of Law and Technology* 473 (1996)

Blakeney M., 'The impact of the TRIPS Agreement in the Asia Pacific Region'. 18 *European Intellectual Property Review* 10 (1996)

Bloomberg BNA, 'China, India and Thailand Named in First Priority Foreign Country List'. 42 BNA's *Patent, Trademark and Copyright Journal* 8 (1991)

Bodenhausen G., *Guide to the Application of the Paris Convention for the Protection of Industrial Property as Revised at Stockholm in 1967* (WIPO, 1968)

Bouazzaoui A., *The Impact of the International Patent System on Developing Countries* (WIPO, 2003).

Cao J., 'Speech: the WTO and the Rule of Law in China'. 16 *Temple International and Comparative Law Journal* 379 (2002)

Carvalho N. P. *The TRIPS Regime of Patent Rights* (3rd Ed.). (New York: Kluwer Law International, 2010)

Chaudhuri S., *The WTO and India's Pharmaceuticals Industry: Patent Protection, TRIPS, and Developing Countries* (Oxford: OUP, 2005)

Chisum D. S. and Farmer S. J., '"Lost in translation": the legal impact of patent translation errors on claim scope' in T. Takenaka (Ed.), *Patent Law and Theory: A Handbook of Contemporary Research* (Cheltenham: Edward Elgar, 2008)

Chun D., 'Patent law harmonisation in the age of globalisation: the necessity and strategy for a pragmatic outcome'. 93 *Journal of the Patent and Trademark Office Society* 2 (2011)

CIPR, *Integrating Intellectual Property Rights and Development Policy*. (London: Commission on Intellectual Property Rights, September 2002), pp. 159–62

Cohen M., 'Japanese patent law and the WIPO Patent Law Harmonisation Treaty: a comparative analysis'. 4 *Fordham Intellectual Property Media and Entertainment Law Journal* 847 (1994)

Cornell University, INSEAD, and WIPO, *The Global Innovation Index 2015: Effective Innovation Policies for Development*. (Fontainebleau, Ithaca, and Geneva: Cornell University, INSEAD and WIPO, 2015)

Correa C., *An Agenda for Patent Reform and Harmonisation for Developing Countries*, a paper prepared for the Bellagio Dialogue on Intellectual Property and Sustainable Development: Revising the Agenda in a New Context, organised by International Centre for Trade and Sustainable Development, September 24–28, Bellagio, Italy (ICTSD, 2005)

Correa C. M., Intellectual Property Rights, The WTO and Developing Countries: the TRIPS Agreement and Policy Options (London: Zed Books, 2000)

Correa C. M., 'Public health and patent legislation in developing countries'. 3 *Tulane Journal of Technology and Intellectual Property* 1 (2001)

Correa C. M., 'Is Section 3(d) consistent with TRIPS?' *Economic and Political Weekly*, August 10, Vol. XLVIII No. 32 (2013)

Correa C. M. and Abdulqawi A. Y. (Eds), *Patent Rights in Intellectual Property and International Trade: The TRIPS Agreement* (2nd Ed.). (New York: Kluwer Law International, 2008)

Deardorff A.V., 'Should patent protection be extended to all developing countries?' 13 *World Economy* 497 (1990)

Dhar B., 'The convention on biological diversity and the TRIPS Agreement: compatibility or conflict?' in C. Bellmann *et al.* (Eds) *Trading in Knowledge: Development Perspectives on TRIPS, Trade and Sustainability* (Abingdon: Routledge, 2003)

Dinwoodie G. B., 'Developing private international intellectual property law: the demise of territoriality?' 51 *William and Mary Law Review* 713 (2009)

Dinwoodie G.B., 'International intellectual property litigation: a vehicle for resurgent comparativist thought'. 49 *American Journal of Comparative Law* 429 (2001)

Doi S., 'The patent opposition system in Japan following major changes'. 8 *CASRIP Newsletter* 1996 (Seattle: Center for Advanced Study and Research on Intellectual Property, Autumn 2001)

Doi T., *The Intellectual Property Law of Japan*. (Leyden: Sijthoff and Noordhoff, 1980)

Drahos P., 'book review on Evans G.E., *The Global Governance of Knowledge: Patent Offices and Their Clients*'. 33 *European Intellectual Property Review* 1 (2011)

Endeshaw A., *Intellectual Property in Asian Emerging Economies*. (London: Ashgate Publishing, 2010)

European Business in China, *Business Confidence Survey 2013*. (Beijing: The European Union Chamber of Commerce in China, 2013)

Evans G. E., *The Global Governance of Knowledge: Patent Offices and Their Clients*. (Cambridge: Cambridge University Press, 2010)

Everson R. E., 'Intellectual property rights, R&D, inventions, technology purchase and piracy in economic development: an international comparative study' in R. E. Everson and G. Ranis (Eds) *Science and Technology: Lessons for Policy*. (Boulder, Co: Westview Press, 1990)

Fanelli D. L., 'Claiming novel polymorphic forms of drug products'. 88 *Journal of the Patent and Trademark Office Society* 12 (2006)

Fentiman R., 'Choice of law and intellectual property' in J. Drexl and A. Kur (Eds) *24 Studies in Industrial Property and Copy-right Law, Intellectual Property and Private International Law – Heading for the Future*. (Oxford: Hart Publishing, 2005)

Ficsor M., *The Law of Copyright and the Internet* (Oxford: OUP, 2002)

Fisher M., *Fundamentals of Patent Law: Interpretation and Scope of Protection* (Oxford: Hart Publishing, 2007)

Fisher M., 'Growth of the Japanese patent system: a lesson for us all?' 22 *Intellectual Property Quarterly* 1 (2004)

Foster G. K., 'Opposing forces in a revolution in international patent protection: the US and India in the Uruguay Round and its aftermath'. 3 *University of California Journal of International Law and Foreign Affairs* 283 (1998)

Fowler P. N., *International Policies and Norms to Address Emerging IP Challenges*, at WIPO High Level Forum on the Global Intellectual Property Infrastructure for Promotion of Innovation, 1–2 March. (WIPO, 2010)

Ganea P., 'Patents, utility models and designs' in C. Heath C. (Ed.) *Intellectual Property Law in China* (New York: Kluwer Law International, 2005)

Ganea P. and Pattloch T., *Intellectual Property Law in China* (New York: Kluwer Law International, 2005)

General Accounting Office (USA), *Intellectual Property: US Companies' Patent Experiences in Japan*. United States General Accounting Office (1993)

General Patent Corporation, 'First-to-file *vs.* first-to-invent: who really benefits from changing the US patent system?' *Wealth of Ideas* Newsletter (October 2007). Available at: www.generalpatent.com/first-file-vs-first-invent-who-really-benefits-changing-u-s-patent-system (last accessed 23 February 2016).

Gervais D., 'Intellectual property and human rights: learning to live together' in P. Torremans (Ed.) *Intellectual Property and Human Rights – Enhanced Edition of Copyright and Human Rights* (New York: Kluwer Law International BV, 2008)

Gervais D., *The TRIPS Agreement: Drafting History and Analysis* (3rd Ed.). (London: Sweet and Maxwell, 2008)

Gervais D., 'Towards a new core international copyright norm: the reverse Three-Step Test'. 9 *Marquette Intellectual Property Law Review* 1 (2005)

Ginsburg J. C., 'Toward supranational copyright law? The WTO Panel decision and the "Three-Step Test" for copyright exceptions'. *Revue Internationale du Droit d'Auteurs*, January 2001

Gluck C., *Japan's Modern Myths, Ideology in the Late Meiji Period*. (Princeton, NJ: Princeton University Press, 1985)

Goldstein P., *International Intellectual Property Law: Cases and Materials*. (St Paul, MN: Foundation Press, 2008)

Grover A., 'Analysing the Supreme Court judgment'. *Economic and Political Weekly*, 10 August 10, Vol. XLVIII No. 32 (2013)

Guiso L. *et al.*, 'Does culture affect economic outcomes?' 20 *Journal of Economic Perspectives* 2 (2006)

Gupta R., 'TRIPS compliance: dealing with the consequences of drug patents in India'. 26 *Houston Journal of International Law* 599 (2005)

Halydier G., 'A hybrid legal and economic development model that balances intellectual property protection and economic growth: a case study of India, Brazil, Indonesia, and Vietnam'. 14 *Asian-Pacific Law and Policy Journal* 1 (2012)

Hamied Y. K., 'Indian pharma industry, decades of struggle and achievements'. 19 *Chemical Business* 4; Apr., (2005) p. 1

Hanrei Jiho (Precedent Times) No.1390 (Tokyo: July 1999). Available at: http://hanreijiho.co.jp/ (last accessed 3 January 2017)

Harhoff D., *Final Report on Economic Cost-Benefit Analysis of a Unified and Integrated European Patent Litigation System* (Institute for Innovation Research, Technology Management and Entrepreneurship, 26 February 2009).

Hari H., 'Changing Japan's patent law'. *World Intellectual Property Review*, 1 February 2014

Harmon S., 'The rules of re-engagement: the use of patent proceedings to influence the regulation of science (what the science does when the salmon comes back downstream)'. 4 *Intellectual Property Quarterly* (2006)

Hauda K. M., 'The role of the United States in world-wide protection of industrial property' in F. Gotzen (Ed.) *The Future of Intellectual Property in the Global Market of the Informational Society: Who Is Going to Shape the IPR System in the New Millennium* (Brussels: Les Éditions Bruylant, 2003)

Helfgott S., 'Cultural differences between the US and Japanese patent law'. 72 *Journal of Patent and Trademark Office Society* 231 (1990)

Ho C. M., 'Biopiracy and beyond: a consideration of socio-cultural conflicts with global patent policies'. 39 *University of Michigan Journal of Law Reform* 3 (2006)

Hoekman, B., 'Services and intellectual property rights' in S. M. Collins and B. P. Bosworth (Eds) *The New GATT: Implications for the United States* (Washington, DC: The Brookings Institution, 1994)

Huang J., *Private International Law* (Beijing: Law Press, 1999)

Hudec R., *Enforcing International Trade Law: The Evolution of the Modern GATT Legal System* (London: Butterworth, 1993)

ICC Commission on Intellectual Property, *Cooperation Between Patent Offices: Prior Art Searching of Patent Applications*, prepared by the ICC Commission on Intellectual Property, document no. 450/ 1056 – 28 June (2010)

Ichikawa K., *The Japanese Patent System* (Tokyo: Nihon Hatsumei Shinbunsha, 1965)

Intellectual Property Basic Act (Japan) (Act No. 122 of 4 December 2002, as last amended by Act No.119 of 16 July 2003)

International Trade Administration, 'Japan Patent Procedures' in *Market Research Reports* IM1930125 2 (ITA, 1993)

Jackson J. H. and Sykes A. (Ed.), *Implementing the Uruguay Round* (Oxford: Clarendon Press, 1997)

Jackson J. H., 'The WTO Dispute Settlement Understanding – misunderstandings on the nature of legal obligation'. 91 *American Journal of International Law* 60 (1997)

Jaeschke W. C. *et al.*, 'Comparison of Chinese and US patent reform legislation: which, if either, got it right?' 11 *John Marshall Review of Intellectual Property Law* 567 (2012)

Janis M. D., 'Rethinking reexamination: toward a viable administrative revocation system for US Patent Law'. 11 *Harvard Journal of Law and Technology* 69 (1997)

Japanese Government, *A 70-Year History of the Patent System*, Patent Office (Tokyo: Hatsumei Kyôkai, 1955)

Jenei S., 'Patent reform: what does first-to-file mean to me?' (*Patent Baristas*, 17 January, 2008). Available at: www.patentbaristas.com/archives/2008/01/17/patent-reform-what-does-first-to-file-mean-to-me/

Jeremy D., 'Patents and technology transfer between nations: 1790-1851: help, hindrance, or irrelevance: lessons from history'. ESRC Research Seminar Series: Intellectual Property Rights, Economic Development and Social Welfare: What Does History Tell Us? 38 *Loyola of Los Angeles Law Review* 1 (2004)

Judd D., *The Lion and the Tiger: The Rise and Fall of the British Raj, 1600-1947.* (Oxford: OUP, 2004)

Kamagai K., *History of Japanese Industrial Property System*, a joint study by the Japanese Patent Office and the Asia-Pacific Industrial Property Centre (2005)

Kapczynski A., 'Harmonisation and its discontents: a case study of TRIPS implementation in India's pharmaceutical sector'. 97 *California Law Review* 1571 (2009)

Kay H. H., 'A defence of Currie's Governmental Interest Analysis'. 215 Recueil Des Cours 19 [Hague Academy of International Law], 1989–III (1989)

Kazenske E. R., *Patent Offices: Strategies for Work Sharing 'Need for a Pragmatic Outcome'*, Microsoft Corporation, Fordham IP Conference, 15–16 April (Microsoft Corporation, 2009)

Keating R. J., *Patent Reform: Protecting IP, Enabling Innovation and Bolstering Entrepreneurship* (Oakton, VA: Small Business & Entrepreneurship Council, p. 18)

Korea Intellectual Property Office (KIPO), *A Study on Mutual Recognition of Patent Examination* (Korea: KIPO, 2008)

Kotabe M., 'A Comparative study of US and Japanese patent systems', 23 *Journal of International Business Studies* 1 (1992)

Kumagai K., *History of Japanese Industrial Property System*, a joint production of the Japanese Patent Office and the Asia-Pacific Industrial Property Centre (Tokyo: JPO/APIPC, 1999)

Kumar *et al.* (Eds), *The Cambridge Economic History of India, 1757–1970* (Cambridge: CUP Archive, 1982)

Kumar N., *Intellectual Property Rights, Technology and Economic Development: Experiences of Asian Countries*, Study Paper 1b commissioned by the Commission on Intellectual Property Rights as a background paper (CIPR, 2002)

Ladas S., *Patents, Trademarks, and Related Rights, National and International Protection*, Vol.1. (Cambridge, MA: Harvard University Press, 1975)

Leith P., *Harmonisation of Intellectual Property in Europe: A Case Study of Patent Procedure*. (London: Sweet and Maxwell, 1998)

Lin B. *et al.*, *Overview of Chinese Patent Law*, 35th International Congress of the PIPA, 19–22 October, Toyama, Japan (2004)

Lindgren J. C. and Yudell C. J., 'Protecting American intellectual property in Japan'. 10 *Santa Clara High Technology Law Journal* 1 (1994)

Liu D., 'Now the wolf has indeed come! Perspective on the patent protection of biotechnology invention in China'. 53 Winter, *American Journal of Comparative Law* 207 (2005)

Lockwood W. W., *The Economic Development of Japan: Growth and Structural Change (1868-1938)*. (Princeton, NJ: Princeton University Press 1954)

London Economics, *Economic Study on Patent Backlogs and a System of Mutual Recognition – Final Report to the Intellectual Property Office*. (London: London Economics, 2010)

Longacre J., '35 USC. § 102 and the First to File System'. (*LexisNexis® Legal Newsroom: Intellectual Property*, 31 October 2011)

MacDougall C., 'The Chinese economy in 1976'. No. 77, June, The China Quarterly (1977)

Machlup F. and Penrose E., 'The patent controversy in the nineteenth century'. 10 *Journal of Economic History* 1 (1950)

MacQueen H. *et al.*, *Contemporary Intellectual Property: Law and Policy* (1st Ed.). (Oxford: OUP, 2007)

Mansfield E., 'Patents and innovation: an empirical study'. 32 *Management Science* 173 (1986)

Markus K. E., 'The role of intellectual property rights in encouraging foreign direct investment and technology transfer'. 9 *Duke Journal of Comparative and International Law* 109 (1998)

Maskus K. E., 'Strengthening intellectual property rights in Asia: implications for Australia'. 37 *Australia Economic Papers* 3 (1998)

Maskus K. E. and McDaniel C., 'Impacts of the Japanese patent system on productivity growth'. 11 *Japan and the World Economy* 4 (1999)

Mazzoleni R. and Nelson R., 'Economic theories about the benefits and costs of patents'. 32 *Journal of Economic Issues* 4 (1998)

McNeil D. G. Jr., 'Selling cheap "generic" drugs: India's copycats irk industry'. *The New York Times*, 1 December 2000

Menell P. S., 'Intellectual property and the property rights movement'. 30 *Regulation* 3 (2007)

Menell P. S., 'The property rights movement's embrace of intellectual property: true love or doomed relationship'. 34 *Ecology Law Quarterly* 713 (2007)

Mengistie G., *The Impact of the International Patent System on Developing Countries: a Study by Getachew Mengistie*, 16, A/39/13 Add.1, 15 August (Geneva: WIPO, 2003)

Mithal V. P., 'Patents in India'. 30 *Journal of the Patent Office Society (India)* 62, (1948)

Mohanty N. K., *The Advantage/Disadvantage of the Harmonisation of the Patent System*. (Japan Patent Office, October 2007–March 2008)

Mossinghoff G. J. and Kuo V. S., 'Post-grant review of patents: enhancing the quality of the fuel of interest'. 43 *Idea* 83 (2002)

Mossinghoff G. J., and Kuo V. S., 'World patent system circa 20xx, AD'. 80 *Journal of the Patent and Trademark Office Society* 523 (1998)

Mueller J. M., 'The tiger awakens: the tumultuous transformation of India's patent system and the rise of Indian pharmaceutical innovation'. 68 *University of Pittsburgh Law Review* 3 (2007)

Mühlendahl A. and Stauder D., 'Territorial Intellectual Property Rights in a Global Economy - Transit and Other "Free Zones"' in M. J. Adelmann, *et al.* (Eds) *Patents and Technological Progress in a Globalised World* (London: Springer, 2009)

Muttart D. M., *Legal Reasoning in the Supreme Court of Canada: An Empirical Study* (doctoral dissertation for Osgoode Hall Law School), 2004

Narayanan P., *Intellectual Property Law 1* (Hyderabad, India: Gogia Law Agency, 2005)

Narayanan P., *Patent Law 7* (3rd Ed.). (Kolkata, India: Eastern Law House, 1998)

O'Brien S.G. *et al.*, 'Imatinib compared with interferon and low-dose cytarabine for newly diagnosed chronic phase chronic myeloid leukemia'. 348 *New England Journal of Medicine* 11 (2003)

Patil P. *et al.*, 'Indian patent and Indian patient, friend or rival: a communication'. *PharmaTutor Magazine*, ART-2057. Available at: http://www.pharmatutor.org/articles/indian-patent-patient-friend-rival-communication (last accessed 3 January 2017)

Pattloch T., 'Enforcement' in C. Heath (Ed.) *Intellectual Property Law in China* (New York: Kluwer Law International, 2005)

Pechman, R. J., 'Seeking multilateral protection for intellectual property: the United States 'TRIPS' over Special 301'. 7 *Minnesota Journal of Global Trade* 179 (1998)

Pelkmans J. and Hu W. *et al.*, *Tomorrow's Silk Road, Assessing an EU-China Free Trade Agreement* (Brussels: Centre for European Policy Studies, 2016)

Pitts A. and Kim J., 'The patent prosecution highway: is life in the "fast lane" worth the cost?' 1 *Hastings Science and Technology Law Journal* 127 (2009)

Pottelsberghe B. V. and Danguy J., *Economic Cost-Benefits Analysis of the Community Patent*, Working Paper 336 (Brussels: Bruegel.org, 2009)

Qian D. X., 'A survey of intellectual property issues in China-US trade negotiations under the Special 301 Provisions'. 2 *Pacific Rim Law and Policy Journal* 2 (1993)

Quinn G., 'Kappos talks patent reform and gene patents at BIO Convention', 4 May (*IPWatchdog*, 2010). Available at: www.ipwatchdog.com/2010/05/04/kappos-talks-patent-reform-and-gene-patents-at-bio-convention/id=10382/

Ragavan S., 'Of the inequals of the Uruguay Round'. 10 *Marquette Intellectual Property Law Review* 273 (2006)

Rahn G., 'The role of industrial property in economic development: the Japanese experience'. 14 *International Review of Industrial Property and Copyright Law* 449 (1983)

Rai A. *et al.*, *Patent Reform: Unleashing Innovation, Promoting Economic Growth and Producing High-paying Jobs*, A White Paper from the US Department of Commerce (13 April 2010).

Rangnekar D., 'The Supreme Court judgment, "law making" in the South'. *Economic and Political Weekly*, 10 August, Vol. XLVIII No. 32 (2013)

Rao V., 'India plans committee on patent law reform'. *Journal of Commerce*, 21 August (1997)

Raskind L., 'Licensing under United States antitrust law'. 20 (1) *Brooklyn Journal of International Law* 49 (1994)

Redwood H., *New Horizons in India: the Consequences of Pharmaceutical Patent Protection*. (Felixstowe, UK: Oldwicks Press, 1994)

Reichman J. H., 'The TRIPS Agreement comes of age: conflict of cooperation with the developing countries'. 32 *Case Western Reserve Journal of International Law* 2 (2000)

Reichman J., 'Universal minimum standards of intellectual property protection under the TRIPS component of the WTO Agreement' in C. Correa and A. Yusuf (Eds) *Intellectual Property and International Trade: The TRIPS Agreement* (2nd Ed.). (New York: Kluwer Law International, 2008)

Reichman J. H. and Dreyfuss R. C., 'Harmonisation without consensus: critical reflections on drafting a substantive patent law treaty'. 57 *Duke Law Journal* 85 (2007)

Reimann M., 'Savigny's triumph? Choice of law in contract cases at the close of the twentieth century'. 39 *Virginia Journal of International Law* 571 (1999)

Richards J., 'Recent patent law developments in Asia'. 7 *Fordham Intellectual Property, Media and Entertainment Law Journal* 599 (1997)

Rohrabacher D. and Crilly P., 'The case for a strong patent system'. 8 *Harvard Journal of Law and Technology* 263 (1995)

Romano F., 'Global trademark and copyright 1998: protecting intellectual property rights in the international marketplace' in *International Conventions and Treaties.* (New York: Practising Law Institute, 1998)

Rosen D. and Usui C., 'The social structure of Japanese intellectual property law'. 13 UCLA *Pacific Basin Law Journal* 32 (1994)

Rotstein F., 'Is there an international intellectual property system? Is there an agreement between states as to what the objectives of intellectual property should be?' 33 *European Intellectual Property Review* 1 (2011)

Roucounas E., 'The debate regarding the grace period in international patent law: a reminder' in *All European Academies Biennial Yearbook: New Perspectives in Academia* (Amsterdam: ALLEA, 2006)

Roy T., *The Economic History of India 1857–1947* (Oxford: OUP, 2000)

Ruse-Khan H. G., 'The international legal framework for the protection of utility models: unmatched flexibility for domestic experimentation?' 4 *The WIPO Journal* 2 (2013)

Sabakibara M. and Branstetter L., *Do Stronger Patents Induce Innovation? Evidence from the 1988 Japanese Patent Law Reforms.* NBER Working Paper No. 7066, April. (Cambridge, MA: The National Bureau of Economic Research, 1999)

Sagar R., 'India amends patent law to give effect to TRIPS'. 9 *World IP Review* 136 (1995)

Sahu S. K., *Technology Transfer, Dependence, and Self-Reliant Development in the Third World: The Pharmaceutical and Machine Tool Industries in India.* (Santa Barbara, CA: Praeger, 1998)

Seeratan N. N., 'The negative impact of intellectual property patent rights on developing countries: an examination of the Indian pharmaceutical industry'. 3 *Scholar* 339 (2001)

Sell S., 'Intellectual property and public policy in historical perspective: contestation and settlement', paper given at Symposium: Intellectual Property at a Crossroads: The Use of The Past in Intellectual Property Jurisprudence. 38 *Loyola of Los Angeles Law Review* 1 (2004)

Shanghai Higher People's Court, The 2003 Selected Cases Tried by People's Courts in Shanghai (Shanghai: Shanghai People's Publishing House, 2004)

Sheehe J., 'Indian patent law: walking the line?' 29 *Northwest Journal of International Law and Business* 2 (2009)

Shi W., 'Globalization and indigenization: legal transplant of a universal TRIPS regime in a multilateral world'. 47 *American Business Law Journal* 3 (2010)

State Council of the People's Republic of China, *Outline of the National Intellectual Property Strategy*, issued by the State Council of the People's Republic of China, 5 June 2008. Available at: www.gov.cn/english/2008-06/21/content_1023471.htm

State Intellectual Property Office of the People's Republic of China (SIPO), *Intellectual Property Rights Protection in China.* (SIPO, 2014)

Stenger W. 'Cohen M.: global intellectual property ambassador'. 15 *SMU Science and Technology Law Review* 41 (2011)

Straus J., 'Implications of the TRIPS Agreement in the field of patent law' in F.-K. Beier and G. Schricker (Eds) *From GATT to TRIPS: the Agreement on Trade-Related Aspects of Intellectual Property Rights* (Munich: Max Planck Institute for Foreign and International Patent, Copyright and Competition Law, 1996)

Straus J. and Galama J., *Introduction of a Grace Period into European Patent Law- Submission of Expert Opinions, European Patent Office, Doc. CA/41/00* (Munich: Max Planck Institute for Foreign and International Patent, Copyright and Competition Law 2000)

Strauss J. and Klunker N-S., 'Harmonisation of international patent law'. 38 *International Review of Intellectual Property and Competition Law* 907 (2007)

Su E., 'The winners and the losers: the agreement on trade-related aspects of intellectual property rights and its effects on developing countries'. 23 *Houston Journal of International Law* 169 (2000)

Suthersanen U., *Utility Models and Innovation in Developing Countries, UNCTAD-ICTSD Project on IPR and Sustainable Development*, Working Paper No.13 (Geneva: International Centre for Trade and Sustainable Development, 2006)

Svantesson D. J., *Private International Law and Internet* (New York: Kluwer Law International, 2007)

Takenaka T., 'Does a cultural barrier to intellectual property trade exist? The Japanese example'. 29 *NYU Journal of International Law and Politics* 153 (1997) 165–66

Takenaka T., 'International and comparative law issues: patent infringement damages in Japan and the United States: will increased patent infringement damage awards revive the Japanese economy?' 2 *Washington University Journal of Law and Policy* 52 (2000)

Takenaka T., *Interpreting Patent Claims: The United States, Germany and Japan, Vol.17 Studies in Industrial Property and Copyright Law* (Munich: Max Planck Institute for Foreign and International Patent, Copyright and Competition Law, 1995)

Takenaka T., 'The Role of the Japanese patent system in Japanese industry'. 13 *UCLA Pacific Basin Law Journal* 1 (1994)

Takura O., 'Japanese claim interpretation'. 19 *AIPPI Journal* 5 (1994)

Tang Z., 'International treaties in Chinese private international law'. 42 *Hong Kong Law Journal* 597 (2012)

't Hoen E. F. M., *The Global Politics of Pharmaceutical Monopoly Power* (Diemen, The Netherlands: AMB Publishers, 2009, pp. 70–72)

The Economist Intelligence Unit, 'India/Brazil Pharma: Of patents and prices'. *The Economist*, 2 July (2008)

Thomas J. R., *Pharmaceutical Patent Law* (1st Ed.). (Edison, NJ: Bloomberg BNA Books, 2005)

Thomas J. R., 'The responsibility of the rulemaker: comparative approaches to patent administration reform'. 17 *Berkeley Technology Law Journal* 727 (2002)

Torremans P., *Intellectual Property Law* (5th Ed.). (Oxford: OUP, 2008)

United Kingdom Intellectual Property Office, *The Patent Office Cooperation Plan 2005.* (UKIPO, 2005)

United Kingdom Intellectual Property Office (UKIPO), *Informal Consultation on Reform of the Patent Cooperation Treaty (PCT).* (UKIPO, November 2009) Available at: www.ipo.gov.uk/consult-pct.pdf (last accessed 1 January 2013)

United States Patent and Trademark Office, *Practicing Before the USPTO in Today's Market: Conforming Your Conduct to the USPTO's Code of Professional Responsibility* (USPTO, 2008)

US Government Printing Office, *US Treaties and Other International Agreements Vol. 31 Part 6, 1979* (Washington, US Government Printing Office, 1980)

Van den Broek N., 'Legal persuasion, political realism and legitimacy: the European Court's recent treatment of the effect of WTO agreements in the EC Legal Order'. 4 *Journal of International Economic Law* 2, 411–440 (2001)

Vatter H. *et al.*, 'The onset and persistence of secular stagnation in the US economy: 1910–1990'. 29 *Journal of Economic Issues* 2, 591–600 (1995)

Watal J., *Intellectual Property Rights in the WTO and Developing Countries.* (New York: Kluwer Law International, 2001)

Wegner H. C., *Making Patent Work-sharing Work: Need Complementary Reforms*, paper prepared for the 18th Annual Conference Intellectual Property Law and Policy, 8–9 April. (New York: Fordham Intellectual Property Law Institute, Fordham University School of Law, 2010)

Wegner H. C., *Patent Harmonisation* (London: Sweet and Maxwell, 1993)

Wegner, H. C., 'Patent harmonisation in the Pacific Rim' in P. C. B. Liu and A. Y. Sun, 'Intellectual property protection in the Asia–Pacific region: a comparative study'. *Occasional Papers/Reprints Series in Contemporary Asian Studies*, No. 4 (135) (1996)

Weiler J. and Kocjan C., *Intellectual Property in The Law of European Union*, NYU School of Law Teaching Material (Academy of European Law at the EUI in Florence and the Jean Monnet Center at NYU School of Law, 2004/05)

Weissman R., 'A long, strange TRIPS: the pharmaceutical industry drive to harmonize global intellectual property rules, and the remaining WTO legal alternatives available to third world countries'. 17 *University of Pennsylvania Journal of International Economic Law* 1069 (1996)

Wild J., 'Chinese authorities plan to take action on bad faith utility model and design patent applications, *Intellectual Asset Management*, 22 February (2013). Available at: http://www.iam-media.com/Blog/Detail.aspx?g=25712644-1578-46a0-9a8a-765632e9ec86

Winkler H., 'The scope of patent protection: past, present and future'. 10 *International Review of Industrial Property* 3 (1979)

World Intellectual Property Organization, *World Patent Report: A Statistical Review*. (WIPO, 2008)

World Intellectual Property Organization, *Implementation of Recommendations to Improve the Functioning of the PCT*, by Patent Cooperation Treaty (PCT) Working Group, Fifth Session, 29 May to 1 June, 2012, PCT/WG/5/3, (Geneva: WIPO, 8 May, 2012)

World Intellectual Property Organization, *World Intellectual Property Indicators 2015*. (Geneva: WIPO, 2015)

World Intellectual Property Organization, 'Small group of countries drives innovation in breakthrough technologies', press release, 11 November, on the occasion of launching the *World Intellectual Property Report 2015* (Geneva: WIPO, 2015)

World Intellectual Property Organization, 'US extends lead in international patent and trademark filings', press release, 16 March, PR/2016/788 (Geneva, WIPO, 2016)

World Trade Organization, *Report of the Working Party on the Accession of China*, WT/ACC/CHN/49, 1 October. (WTO, 2001)

World Trade Organization, *Accession of the People's Republic of China*, WT/L/432, 23 November. (WTO, 2001)

Xue H. Q. and Qian J., 'International treaties in the Chinese domestic legal system'. 8 *Chinese Journal of International Law* 299 (2009)

Yoshifuji K. and Kumagai K., *Outline of the Patent Law* (Tokyo: Yuhikaku, 1998)

Yu P.Y., 'The harmonisation game: what basketball can teach about intellectual property and international trade'. 26 *Fordham International Law Journal* 218 (2003)

Yu P. Y., 'The middle kingdom and the intellectual property world', paper given at Symposium: China's Role in Regulating the Global Information Economy. 13 *Oregon Review of International Law* 26 (2011)

Zhang M., 'Codified choice of law in China: rules, processes and theoretic underpinnings'. 37 *North Carolina Journal of International Law and Commercial Regulations* 1 (2011)

Zhen L., *Autumnal Hook 2012 Update* (16 February 2013). Guest post on China IPR blog. Available at: https://chinaipr.com/2013/02/16/autumnal-hook-2012-update/ (last accessed 13 August 2015).

Zheng H.R., 'The patent system of the People's Republic of China'. 21 *University of San Francisco Law Review* (1987)

Zhou, Y., 'Foreign patent filings lag behind domestic increase'. *China Daily*, 12 April (1992)

Index